Rich DeVos has had a tremendous impact on Georgia Lee's and my direction and purpose in our life. At the ages of 31 and 27, before we were introduced to the "Amway Sales and Marketing Plan" 21 years ago, our life was what I would call a "wandering generality." Like a river we were wandering aimlessly through life as an accountant and a waitress, with no goals, dreams, or direction. We had become victims of the "rut system." A system that promised us, through the education process, that all we had to do was get "good education," "good jobs," work hard and be loyal to our companies, and we would be successful and happy for the rest of our lives. We followed that counsel and ended up broke, in debt, working long and hard hours, headed for a divorce with two sons, aged five and three, and terribly frustrated and disillusioned with the "American Dream." If the Amway opportunity had not come our way, we would have ended up like that river, following the path of least resistance and getting dumped at the lowest point in its environment.

Rich's dream in 1959 to make the free enterprise system (owning your own business) available and affordable to anyone that had a dream for a better way of life, gave us the second chance in life that we needed. We will be forever grateful to Rich DeVos and Jay Van Andel, his partner, for that second chance. We are grateful that their dream for a better way of life was big enough to include our dreams and goals as well as those of millions of others around the world.

Rich DeVos is truly a great American. Never in the history of this country has one man been more responsible for allowing so many to enjoy the fruits of their own labor by opening the door to a business of their own. He has given Georgia Lee and myself the opportunity to live a meaningful and rewarding life—to once again become goal-oriented people with a vision for the future, hope in our hearts and a positive outlook on today and tomorrow.

I urge you to read this book. It is my prayer that this book become required reading in the school systems of this country, so that others will not have to come as perilously close to meeting the final destiny of that river as Georgia Lee and myself.

Ron Puryear

Rich DeVos is an extraordinary businessman. But he is more than just a successful entrepreneur; he is a visionary leader. What Rich believes in his heart he puts to work in his business.

I have been a friend of Rich DeVos for twenty years and know firsthand that there is no division between his public and private selves. Rich has always been a people person. He has put into practice the principals of compassion in the conduct of his own business. Amway is a model of what capitalism can be: free enterprise with a human face.

Rich is one of my heroes. He has been one of America's champions of free enterprise and, of course, one of mine as well. His personal life, more than his great speaking ability, convinces those who know him that his Christian values are real. He and his partner, Jay Van Andel, have charted a course through many rough seas so that those of us who follow will have smooth sailing. In the years to come, we all have much more to learn from Rich DeVos.

It is my hope that you will read this book with care and openness. Rich DeVos is truly a master mentor. *Compassionate Capitalism* will teach you valuable lessons. The pages of this text will challenge you to rethink some of your assumptions about free enterprise. Rich's words will inspire you to dream dreams and renew your vision of capitalism rooted in compassionate values. And the stories of success against the odds will stimulate you to imagine again what it is possible for you to achieve.

When Rich leads, follow, if you can keep up!

Bill Britt

Praise for *Compassionate Capitalism*

"Rich DeVos is uniquely qualified to explain why *Compassionate Capitalism* can lead to financial success for the individual, the community and the nation. By his own lifetime achievements, Rich has proven why compassion for all of one's fellow citizens is a mandatory key to success."

—Gerald R. Ford, Honorary Co-Chairman,
The Compassionate Capitalism Foundation

"This credo for compassionate capitalism springs up directly from the heart of my partner and friend for half a century. Whatever you may need to succeed in business, above all learn compassion. This book is a giant step in that direction. I am confident that Rich's words will inspire and inform millions of others as they have touched me."

—Jay Van Andel, Honorary Co-Chairman,
The Compassionate Capitalism Foundation

"Rich DeVos is the thinker of the hour. In a world disillusioned by Marxism, people are turning to capitalism. If they find a hard-boiled capitalism where many are crushed in a cold 'devil take the hindmost' attitude, it may cause another disillusionment. So this book presents the answers for the future—'a compassionate capitalism.' The book is well-written, consistently interesting, logical, and persuasive."

—Norman Vincent Peale

"Rich DeVos has now given an entirely appropriate name to the business philosophy which he has demonstrated. While many authors have tried over the years to define 'the American dream' and how to share it, Rich has been making us all richer by showing us the way and calling out 'Follow me!' Lead on, dear friend."

—Paul Harvey

"Having known many successful individuals who are practitioners of free enterprise, there are few as successful, as committed to the basic tenets of capitalism and especially 'compassionate capitalism,' as Rich DeVos. It is a mark of Rich's commitment that he shares his 'personal credo' with us and with generations yet to come. *Compassionate Capitalism* is a must read for the aspiring entrepreneur as well as for those who have realized the personal successes of our free market system."

—Alexander Haig, Jr.

"In *Compassionate Capitalism,* Rich DeVos tells you how you can make your dreams come true by centering your life in love of God and country and an authentic desire to help other people. Read this helpful and practical book by one of the world's greatest and most positive compassionate capitalists. I loved it!"

—Robert Schuller

"I have personally known Rich DeVos for many years. He is a unique combination of a great success as a capitalist and a tremendous example of compassion . . . Rich is an example to me, whose words off the playing field are always backed up by his all-pro performances in the heat of battle. Anyone who reads this book will have his or her outlook on time, energy, and money permanently changed."

—Tom Landry

"My friendship with Rich DeVos over the past twenty years has indeed been a fruitful one. His love for people and his vision to help them to be the best that they can be has deeply affected me and my personal outlook. *Compassionate Capitalism* captures the essence of his own successful life as a compassionate capitalist and passes it on to us. What a gift!"

—C. Everett Koop

"This is the perfect book not just for the successful entrepreneur or the person who punches a clock and dreams of owning his or her own business. It is also for the athlete or the artist, the writer or the wrangler. Rich makes it clear. We are all in business and compassion is the key to our success. Over the past thirty years he's taught me that lesson through his own example. I'm glad at last I can share his wisdom with my friends."

—Bobby Richardson

COMPASSIONATE CAPITALISM

People Helping People
Help Themselves

RICH DEVOS

A DUTTON BOOK

DUTTON
Published by the Penguin Group
Penguin Books USA Inc., 375 Hudson Street,
New York, New York 10014, U.S.A.
Penguin Books Ltd, 27 Wrights Lane,
London W8 5TZ, England
Penguin Books Australia Ltd, Ringwood,
Victoria, Australia
Penguin Books Canada Ltd, 10 Alcorn Avenue,
Toronto, Ontario, Canada M4V 3B2
Penguin Books (N.Z.) Ltd, 182–190 Wairau Road,
Auckland 10, New Zealand

Penguin Books Ltd, Registered Offices:
Harmondsworth, Middlesex, England

First published by Dutton, an imprint of New American Library,
a division of Penguin Books USA Inc.
Distributed in Canada by McClelland & Stewart Inc.

First Printing, April, 1993
10 9 8

Excerpt from "The Creation" from GOD'S TROMBONES by James Weldon Johnson. Copyright
1927 The Viking Press, Inc., renewed © 1955 by Grace Nail Johnson. Used by permission of
Viking Penguin, a division of Penguin Books USA Inc.

REGISTERED TRADEMARK—MARCA REGISTRADA

LIBRARY OF CONGRESS CATALOGING-IN-PUBLICATION DATA:
DeVos, Richard M.
  Compassionate capitalism : people helping people help themselves / by Rich DeVos.
    p.   cm.
  ISBN 0-525-93567-3
  1. Captialism. 2. Capitalism—Moral and ethical aspects.
I. Title.
HB501.D44   1993
330.12′2—dc20   92–40323
                                                                          CIP

Printed in the United States of America
Set in Times Roman
Designed by Leonard Telesca

To Helen
My best friend, supporter, mentor.
Loving wife, mother, grandmother.
Always faithful, gracious, and understanding.
She didn't have to write a book or make speeches about compassion.
She taught us daily about being compassionate by her life.

Contents

Part IV. Reaching Our Goals:
Helping Ourselves and Helping Others

COMPASSIONATE CAPITALISM

INTRODUCTION
Compassionate Capitalism—
The Best Way of Caring for People and the Planet

Compassionate capitalism?" a university student exclaimed with a cynical grin. "Isn't that a contradiction in terms, like 'cruel kindness' or 'living death'? Those two words just don't go together!"

For the past four or five years people have been kidding me about my obsession with compassionate capitalism. I had no idea that capitalism was such a dangerous and divisive word, evoking memories of robber barons and cruel child labor, poisoned rivers, and smokestacks belching pollution into powder blue skies.

"Capitalists succeed because they aren't compassionate," a college professor argued angrily after my presentation to his class.

"Without capitalism there could be no compassion," I replied, and the students stared at me in disbelief, as if I had just claimed the world was flat or the sea filled with dragons.

In that moment of silence I realized again how important this compassionate capitalism project has become to me. While much of the world is rushing to embrace capitalism, we who have enjoyed its benefits most are still embarrassed by its weaknesses and focused on its failures. Worse yet, millions of our own people don't know how compassionate capitalism works or how the system can help them make a better living and a better life.

Why do so many college professors and newspaper columnists forget or refuse to acknowledge capitalism's incredible strengths and successes? Why do they cling to outdated notions about socialism and even communism when the promises made by those economic systems have been tried and found wanting?

Certainly, capitalism has its faults. Past failures are clear and we all must seek to avoid repeating them in the future. But in spite of those faults, capitalism has become the world's economic system of choice, and it is easy to understand why. And although this book is not just about the Amway Corporation, the story of Amway's success in the past thirty years is a good example of the power of compassionate capitalism at work.

Fidel Castro and his communist revolutionary allies took over Cuba on January 16, 1959, promising to restore the economy of that once rich island nation. That same week, Jay Van Andel and I founded the Amway Corporation in the basements of our homes in Ada, Michigan. In those days socialism was regarded as the "world's great economic hope." Free enterprise was dead. At least that's what Jay and I were told. American capitalism was "on its way out," while the Marxist communism that Russia and China were exporting was "bound to triumph."

"This is no time to go into business for yourself," some people warned us. "Those days have passed forever." Then, with frowns and angry gestures, they would add: "Capitalism has failed us and it will fail again. Socialism is our only hope."

We listened to the critics of free enterprise. We thanked them for their advice and then ignored it altogether.

"We call our company Amway," I said in those early "Selling America" speeches, "because the American way of private ownership and free enterprise is the best way."

I made that speech thousands of times during the next few years, not just at Amway meetings but in high schools, churches, and civic clubs. Americans were losing faith in the economic system that had brought us the highest standard of living in history.

"We built this nation on private ownership and free enterprise," I said to anyone who would listen. "Capitalism is not perfect, but it is the only way to keep this nation strong."

Our critics pointed to the socialist economic policies of Chairman Mao, Premier Khrushchev, and Comrade Castro as the wave of the future. Now our critics are no longer laughing.

The communist dream is dead. How quickly that dream became a nightmare. The Marxist–socialist economies are in shambles. It has been just thirty-four years since Castro took over Cuba promising prosperity and reform. Today most Cubans live in poverty and despair.

During those same few years Amway, on the other hand, became a four-billion-dollar corporation with more than two million independent distributors who own their own businesses in fifty-four nations and territories around the globe.

The Rush to Make a Better Living

I love the Amway Corporation and her independent distributors around the world. I will be telling the stories of compassionate individuals and compassionate corporations wherever I find them, but Amway and Amway's worldwide network of independent distributors are what I know best. When Lee Iacocca writes, he writes about Ford and Chrysler. General H. Norman Schwarzkopf filled his autobiography with stories of his army career and of Desert Storm. My friend Max DePree illustrated both of his thoughtful and moving works on leadership at least partially from his experiences as chairman of the board of the Herman Miller Corporation. So, being true to my own experiences, there will be illustrations throughout this manuscript from Amway.

For example, its growth in the countries that once made up the Soviet bloc is one proof that compassionate capitalism really works when given a chance. People want to live in a nation where they are free to try new solutions, to trade without restrictions, to compete in a free marketplace, to choose careers, and to own their own businesses. They are tired of empty shelves and broken promises. They want the things we have, things we take for granted.

When the walls came down between East and West Germany, not only did the East Germans flock across the border, but West German Amway distributors rushed into the eastern zone to offer their fellow Germans a chance to own their own Amway direct-sales businesses. And East German entrepreneurs jumped at the chance. Today we have more than a hundred thousand Amway distributors in what was East

Germany experiencing for the first time in their lives the joys of free enterprise.

Jay Leno, the *Tonight Show* host, read about Amway's rush to bring free enterprise to Eastern Europe and said with tongue in cheek, "If you think they had trouble getting rid of the communists . . ." I take that as a compliment, a tribute to the tenacity of Amway people worldwide. Peter Mueller-Meerkatz, one of our company's leaders in Europe, says it this way, "We believe in capitalism. We are convinced that democracy and free enterprise are the world's only economic hope. Why wouldn't we want to share it?"

Besides the hundred thousand Amway distributors in East Germany, already forty thousand Hungarians are involved in our business and thousands of Poles are preparing for our opening in that nation this year. And this rush to participate in a free-market economy, to liberate a whole new generation of entrepreneurs, is happening not just in former communist countries but in every place where economic barriers are coming down.

In 1990, when Mexico's President Salinas had the courage to bulldoze the trade walls between our two countries, Amway entered Mexico. Now more than a hundred thousand excited, determined, committed Mexican men and women have their own Amway businesses. They, too, are discovering how free enterprise in action can help overcome years of poverty and despair.

In Indonesia, there are almost fifty thousand independent Amway distributors. Even in Japan, when workers saw the chance to own their own businesses and advance into the exclusive ranks of the shoguns (owners) and samurai (upper-level management), they gave up their cradle-to-grave security and started direct-sales businesses of their own. Today Japan boasts a million independent Amway distributors, and Amway Japan has become that nation's third largest foreign corporation.

Kaoru Nakajima, one of our major distributors headquartered in Japan, says it simply: "I was a salaried man working in a company for eight years. Now I am my own boss. Now I am free. Now I am selling products that make me proud. Now I am helping people in five different countries to own their own businesses. When I see so many people getting more abundant lives, I feel really excited. This is no job to me. It is more like play."

The Rush to Make a Better Life

Don't misunderstand. This rush to free enterprise is not just about making money. Of course people want financial security for themselves and their families. Why shouldn't they? But they want more, much more.

People in East Germany, Hungary, Poland, Czechoslovakia, and China, like people everywhere, want deeper satisfaction as well. Not just material freedom, but freedom of the spirit. The freedom to become complete and whole persons. The freedom to become what God intends all of us to be. The freedom of mind and imagination that can only exist in a truly democratic society. The freedom not just to scrape by, but to find genuine satisfaction in life.

At the heart of the deep desire for change being experienced in Marxist–socialist countries is one simple fact: communism experienced a profound crisis of the spirit. It was not just communist economics that were bankrupt. The poverty of communism's values brought about its collapse. The founder of the modern communist movement, Karl Marx, had an impoverished view of the human spirit. This view has not proven to be an adequate foundation on which to build either nations or individual lives.

On July 18, 1969, Jay Van Andel, my lifelong friend and partner in this business, demonstrated the compassionate capitalist's view of people when an explosion and fire in our plant in Ada, Michigan, almost destroyed our dream. The deadly blast occurred just before midnight. A large building that housed both offices and assembly lines was almost engulfed in flames when Jay arrived on the scene. Employees had already risked their lives to climb aboard tractors to pull semitrailers and a tanker from the blazing warehouse. Others were about to enter the 14,000-foot burning building to rescue files loaded with important documents. Jay stopped them with these unforgettable words: "Forget the papers! Get the people out!"

What we think about people matters a great deal. If we think of them as children of God, possessing a divine spark and having God-given worth, it follows that we ought to treat all people with respect and dignity. But if we think of people in a strictly material sense, devoid of any spirituality and gaining worth only through the state, then what happens? We need only to look at communist history to answer that question.

What we think about the nature of planet Earth is also crucial to the decisions we make about our use of her bountiful resources. If we think of this amazing globe and all her treasures as God's gifts to us, of ourselves as God's appointed caretakers of these priceless gifts, then it follows that we will love and care for the planet.

Capitalism: A Simple Formula to Get Us Started

During the month of May 1986, more than eight thousand American eleventh- and twelfth-graders in forty-two states were tested to find out what they knew (or didn't know) about capitalism. When the results were tallied, it was discovered that 66 percent of those quizzed—5,415 young Americans—didn't even know enough about capitalism to define the word *profit*.

Headlines all across the country read: "U.S. Students Score Low on Economic Tests." Comparisons were made to Japanese and German students, who are required to master basic economic principles in their high school curricula. The "disastrous" results of the test were announced at a national press conference by the distinguished American economist Paul A. Volcker, a former Federal Reserve Board chairman. When a young reporter asked Dr. Volcker if he had studied economics in high school, the poor man had to confess before the world that he had not.

I hate tests. I remember flunking my own share of them. And I feel sorry for the students who took that pop quiz in economics, but I also understand why business and labor leaders commissioned the study. This nation cannot afford another generation of Americans who don't understand capitalism or how it works.

Let's start where the students failed. What is profit? The correct multiple-choice answer is: "revenue minus costs." Oliver Wendell Holmes answered the question in this very short poem:

> I only ask that Fortune send
> A little more than I shall spend.

If you want to know one important way that a capitalist measures success, memorize this verse. Profit is making more money than you spend. With profit, your business will succeed and you will have the power to accumulate capital. With that capital you can build your own business, create new businesses, and improve the quality of your life and of the lives of others. Without profit, your business will fail and your dreams of accumulating capital will go with them down the drain.

I have a simple formula to help you understand how the process of making profit, capitalism, really works. The formula looks like this:

$$MW = NR + HE \times T$$

No, this is not a solution to some problem in quantum physics. It is simpler than it looks. In fact you may agree with those who think my theory is too simple. Never mind. It gets the discussion going and sometimes being too simple helps us understand things that are too complicated.

Spelled out, the formula reads like this: Our *material welfare* (MW) comes from *natural resources* (NR) that are transformed by *human energy* (HE) that has been made more effective through the use of *tools* (T). Let's look at the formula one part at a time.

Material Welfare. Capitalism is the process of producing and/or distributing capital, another word for material. The reason you are seriously considering becoming a capitalist is this: you want to provide material welfare for yourself and for those who are (or who will be) dependent on your support. Don't let the word *material* (or even materialism) throw you or make you defensive. Our homes, schools, and churches are made of material. Material feeds and clothes the people of the earth. Material is the stuff of life, and there is absolutely nothing wrong with wanting to have a decent share of material to make life easier, fuller, richer.

Natural Resources. Most material comes from the earth, the sea, or the sky. Directly or indirectly every capitalist is dependent on the supply of natural resources. Look around the room. Do you see anything that doesn't have its origins, no matter how distant, in natural resources? The fiber in the slacks I am wearing comes from a sheep who eats grass from the earth and drinks water from a flowing stream. The threads in my tie were produced by tiny silkworms eating the leaves of a mulberry tree and drinking drops of rain that fall from the sky. My desk is made from trees that plant their roots in the earth above and take nourishment from the water below. The computer I am using is made of plastic, which comes from petroleum, aluminum, which comes from bauxite, and steel, which comes from iron ore, all minerals buried deep in the earth. But each of these natural resources was transformed by human energy, the other primary source of material.

Human Energy. Natural resources lying in their habitat don't do anything. The sheep won't give you wool and the silkworm's fragile threads can't be woven into fabric or cut and sewn into ties without the aid of human brains and fingers. You can't process words on petroleum, bauxite, or iron ore lying deep in the earth. A mountain of coal won't heat your living room. You have to find the resources, harvest them, prepare them, and transform them into more usable forms through human genius and hard work.

Tools. In Peru I saw a man walk by with at least a hundred pounds of timber on his back. The only tools he had to move that load of tent poles were his gnarled, leathery hands and his bent but muscular back. Today I watched an Amway driver get into his big-wheel rig, fire it up, and carry forty thousand pounds of material at fifty-five miles an hour while listening to a stereo recording in his soundproof cab. It is so much easier, safer, simpler, cost-effective, and productive to develop and use tools in the process of creating material welfare.

The tool most responsible for Amway's success is not something you can touch like a machine or turn on like a motor. The primary tool behind this corporation's phenomenal growth is our unique sales and marketing plan. Marxist socialists had natural resources and human energy, but the workers weren't motivated to work. Our multilevel marketing plan, with its independent ownership and its many-leveled, life-long, built-in bonuses, fires enthusiasm, loyalty, and commitment in the hearts of our two million independent distributors around the world.

Marxist socialism failed for many reasons, but at the heart of that economic system's collapse was this: people were not motivated to get the job done. They couldn't own their own piece of the world's natural resources. They couldn't even own the tools with which they worked. As a result, they didn't even own their own human energy. Like natural resources and tools, the worker was owned by the state.

That's why I have traveled across this country for the past twenty-five years speaking out for free enterprise and its four pillars: freedom, reward, recognition and hope. The capitalist is free to own the natural resources and the tools necessary to his trade. And in so doing, the capitalist herself is free. And what a difference freedom makes.

Look at Marxist history. Every time a government took over another natural resource or another tool of production, productivity decreased. And every time the government gave back to the people the rights of ownership, productivity increased. The reason is clear.

When my son, Dick, was sixteen, I gave him an automobile. It was my car. I bought the gas. I bought the tires. I repaired the brakes. Is it any wonder that Dick left black rubber marks on the driveway, returned from carting his buddies about town with the car a mess and the gas gauge on empty, and when something went wrong he left the car in the garage until I had it repaired?

When he was eighteen, I turned the ownership of the car over to Dick. Suddenly there were no more skid marks. Dick had to buy the tires. The long rides got shorter. Dick had to buy the gas. And he quit hauling his buddies and their gear all over town. The maintenance on the car was Dick's responsibility. My son went on to become the president of his own investment company, the Windquest Group. Now he is President of the Amway Corporation and a responsible leader in our community. Somewhere along the way he learned the freedom and the responsibility of ownership.

Two things always happen when natural resources and tools are owned by the people: they last longer and they are used more effectively. That's why the American farmer who owns the land and the tractor on it keeps the land groomed and the tractor in condition. When it is time to harvest, he puts lights on his tractor and works through the night. And as a result, that farmer receives greater and greater rewards for a job efficiently done.

Let's look at the formula one more time:

$$MW = NR + HE \times T$$

For years I traveled about the country using these letters to help explain how capitalism works. I still believe it. But there is still one missing ingredient in the formula.

The secret to real, lasting success in business is compassion. Now when I present the formula, I add compassion to every stage of the process. The formula for compassionate capitalism looks like this:

$$MW = (NR + HE \times T) \times C$$

When we multiply the strength of each item times compassion, amazing things happen. We must let compassion guide us at every stage on our road to material welfare and eventually in the use of that wealth. Compassion must also guide us in our use of natural resources, human energy, and tools.

There are those who laugh when I say compassion, not profit, is the ultimate goal of capitalism. Say it any way you want, but know this. When compassion inspires and informs free enterprise, profits follow, the quality of human life is advanced, and the earth is restored and renewed. When compassion is not an active ingredient in the process, profits may follow temporarily, but the long-term cost in human suffering and in the depletion of the earth is far more than we dare to pay.

In the following credo or statement of my beliefs, I will try to explain this vision of compassionate capitalism, which has captured my entrepreneurial spirit and which directs and confronts me every business day. And I want you to meet a company of my friends whose ideas about compassionate capitalism will inform and inspire you as they have me.

Right now I think it is enough to say that capitalism has become the world's economic system of choice because it grants people everywhere the freedom to dream about making a profit (the money we have left after the bills are paid) and the means to see those dreams come true. Capitalism isn't great because it allows a handful of people to make millions. It is great because it allows millions of people to become what they want to be.

Regrettably, there have always been (and will always be) greedy, ruthless, uncaring capitalists who think it's all right to make a profit even if that process leads to the suffering of people and to the destruction of our planet. Compassionate capitalists still want to make a profit, but they are determined that real profits come when the good of people and the planet comes first.

"Profit" made at the expense of human or planetary suffering is not profit at all. The real costs are not being figured in. Those bottom lines should be written not in black, but in blood red. "Profit" that demeans and dehumanizes our brothers and sisters or depletes and destroys the earth will lead eventually to the death of us all as surely as the wish of King Midas to turn everything he touched to gold led to the destruction of his dreams and to the death of those he loved most.

Compassionate capitalism distinguishes real profit from fool's gold. It cares about setting people free to dream great dreams for themselves and for the planet, and then gives them the means to see that their dreams come true.

In the pages that follow, I will use stories from inside and outside our business to illustrate and inform the principles of compassionate capitalism as I understand them. To tell these stories, I am taking something of a risk. First, because you who lived the stories and told them to me can tell them so much better. And second, because there are so many of you whose stories are equally moving, but I just didn't have the space to include all of them. Remember, even if your story is not told in the following pages, I will always include you in my company of friends!

The Compassionate Capitalism Foundation

The world is changing at a dizzying pace. People everywhere are sensing the difficulties our planet is facing. I feel the weight of it every time I pick up a newspaper or scan the shelves of our local bookstore. And the issue that is unsettling us most is our economic malaise. People can ignore or deny a great deal, but they cannot ignore their pocketbooks, at least not for long.

Massive structural changes are shaking our society. Social historians have been calling our time the "post-modern era." Futurists have been saying that we are suffering from "future shock." Social historians have suggested that we are undergoing a "paradigm shift." Scientists have described Western assumptions as being at a "turning point." Demographers report "massive changes" in the shapes of families. Economists warn that "fundamental alterations" in the national economy are taking place.

All of this makes us feel unsettled. Even under the best of circumstances, change is difficult. People don't like it. They tend to cling to old solutions. Tensions run high. Thomas Kuhn invented the popular buzz phrase *paradigm shift.* In his book *The Structure of Scientific Revolutions,* he describes the reactions of scientists to new discoveries and how hard it has been for them to make changes in their basic beliefs.

Kuhn noticed that scientists would go to any length to deny the validity of new theories or the need to change their minds. He describes the symptoms associated with fundamental change: persistent denial, refusal to consider evidence, reluctance to criticize old ideas, slander of new-thinking colleagues, and anger at having to give up cherished dogmas.

We aren't much different from those scientists. We feel uncomfortable with the changes in our lives: the social restructuring, the economic uncertainties. The world seems a little bit too unpredictable and we don't like it. We all rejoiced at the fall of communism, but now we worry about what will replace it. We feel that capitalism has been vindicated, but we harbor concerns about its flaws.

With this book, its upcoming four-part video series, and its various user's guides and support materials, I am launching the Compassionate Capitalism Foundation. My wife, Helen, and I and a company of our friends who are underwriting this new foundation with us have these simple goals: we want to help renew your faith in free enterprise, to build your hope that it is possible to cope with the change and uncertainty we are facing, and to point to compassion as our guiding light for every step on the journey.

We are also underwriting an annual Compassionate Capitalism Prize. Beginning in 1994, we will be awarding prizes, large and small, to individuals and institutions in this country and around the world who are models of compassionate capitalism for the rest of us. I realize that I have not spent enough of my life focused on compassion. I am determined to give a great deal more of my time, money, and energy to helping people and the planet. In fact, Helen and I have decided to give away everything in our foundation while we are still alive. If you wait until you're dead to be generous, somebody else has all the joy of giving in your name. For many decades I have enjoyed wading at the shores of compassionate capitalism; now, in these last years of my life, I want to explore its depths as never before.

When vintners make new wine, they put it into barrels and allow it to ferment. In modern wineries the new barrels have large bottles for stoppers instead of corks. As it ages, new wine gives off carbon dioxide. If a barrel is tightly corked, it will explode. The bottles give the wine "room to breathe." In biblical times, Jesus said it was the reason that new wine was never put into old wineskins. They were inflexible and would break. "No," said Jesus, "you put new wine into fresh wine-skins; then both will be preserved."

It seems to me that our task is to help people grow a new capitalism from an old vine stock—the best wines come from old roots—and put the new wine into "new skins." I think the new wineskin is *compassion.*

"Now We Are Free! We Can Do Anything!"

Andrej Zubail is a twenty-three-year-old former East German who lives in the suburbs of Leipzig with his wife, Maria, and their twin boys, Rolf and Heinz. When I first met Andrej, he was carrying those two beautiful babies in his arms and at the same time was steering his wife across a crowded hotel ballroom in my direction. I had just finished a speech on compassionate capitalism to a convention of new distributors in Berlin. Slowly, Andrej and his little family made their way to the platform.

"Mr. DeVos," he said softly in heavily accented English, "I am Andrej Zubail. This is my wife and these are my sons."

For a moment the young man smiled down at his family. Then suddenly he looked up at me. I could tell that he was struggling to find the right words. When he finally spoke, his lips were trembling and a single tear trickled down his cheek. I could see that even as he held his infant sons, his hands were shaking with excitement.

"When freedom came to East Germany," he said, "I didn't know what to do first. I wanted everything for Maria and the children, everything we have not these many years. But knowing where to start . . . not easy. We had no money—no, is it said, equity?—to get a loan, nothing to sell or trade. We wanted to start a business of our own, but how?"

He paused and looked at his wife for moral support. She smiled at him and put her arm around his waist.

"So I say to Maria, 'What shall we do?' And she answer, 'Now we are free. We can do anything.' "

Andrej went on to thank all of us for the opportunity our company had given him. In just six months he and Maria had created an impressive small business. But Andrej's story is not about Amway. It is about compassionate capitalism and the remarkable difference it can make in our lives even in small doses.

"Now we are free," Maria said. "We can do anything." She and her husband believed those simple words, and together they went on to prove them right.

I will never forget Maria's words or the look in Andrej's eyes as he quoted them to me. What a moment in history this is. All across the world, walls are crumbling. Prison doors are being flung open. Men, women, and children are stepping stunned and blinking into freedom's bright new day.

It won't be easy to jump-start these ruined economies. It isn't going to be easy for us to turn our own economy around. But as long as we are free, the problems can be solved.

We must resist anyone or anything that threatens our freedom no matter what "solutions" they offer us. Let these long years of communist tyranny remind us that without freedom, all is lost. And let Maria Zubail's words stay always in our minds: "Now we are free. We can do anything."

PART I

Get Ready!

1

Who Are We?

CREDO I

We believe that every man, woman, and child is created in God's image, and because of that each has worth, dignity, and unique potential.

Therefore, we can dream great dreams for ourselves and for others!

Nas Imran sat on the edge of an iron bunk in his small cell in a Washington state prison. He couldn't sleep. And when he did doze off, his dreams were haunted by dark, threatening shadows and angry, garbled voices.

"In 1969, I was just nineteen," Nas remembers, "a black kid trying to escape the sadness and the terror of the inner city by enrolling in the University of Washington to play football. In those days," he adds, "my dreams included a Heisman Trophy, a championship season, a starting position at the Rose Bowl, and eventually a contract with the pros."

Through his bars Nas could see an overweight white guard, feet propped against his metal desk, drinking coffee and watching a late-night movie on television while the mostly black prisoners in his charge slept restlessly or paced their cells.

"I listened to the wrong crowd," Nas continues. "I got into trouble with the law and suddenly found myself in a courtroom standing before a judge. I ended up spending two years in a state prison. And believe me," he remembers, "it is difficult to keep your dreams alive behind bars." For a moment he pauses. Then quietly he adds, "Of course, keeping dreams alive has never been easy for my family."

Nas Imran's great-grandfather was a slave, and both of his mother's parents died before she was five years old. Even after Abraham Lincoln signed the Emancipation Proclamation, Americans with African ancestry were still denied the basic human rights the rest of us take for granted. They could not vote, speak out, write, or assemble freely. The law prohibited them from the benefits of free enterprise, of property ownership, or credit. It was even illegal for them to learn to read or write, let alone to own a home or business.

The forebears of today's African Americans had little incentive to foster self-confidence or independence, let alone any inclination to become capitalists. The slave owners and sharecrop bosses kept slaves and former slaves dependent and in debt. The majority of black Americans lived in bondage to their employers and in fear of the lynch mob or the Klan.

Those tangled roots left generations of our fellow Americans feeling hopeless and helpless. They went on dreaming, but they could not exercise their power to realize their dreams. During those long months in prison, Nas was surrounded by men who were produced by this tragic legacy.

"I saw the stooped, gray-haired lifers shuffling through another hopeless day," he remembers. "I saw young ones, eyes downcast, dutifully hammering out license plates and leather purses. There were Black Panthers fresh from guerrilla warfare in the urban ghettos and Black Muslims praising Elijah Muhammad and plotting the 'revolution.' But most of the prisoners just went on blaming others for their circumstances. They blazed with silent anger, eating, sleeping, and pumping revenge."

"Hey, Nas," the guard growled as he made his midnight rounds. "Quit pacing your cage. It's making me nervous."

At first Nas didn't move. Then, slowly, he lowered himself onto the hard, dirty mattress and lay there staring at the ceiling.

Now, for a moment I want you to stretch your imagination to the limits. How do you think Nas Imran might have reacted that night if the guard had left his little booth, walked down the long corridor to Nas Imran's cell, and spoken quietly those words at the beginning of this chapter from Credo 1?

Picture it. "Hey, Nas," the guard might have called out, "get this. Rich DeVos thinks you ought to know that 'every man, woman, and child is created in God's image, and because of that each has worth, dignity, and unique potential.' Got that?"

After Nas's grim laughter or angry retort, the guard would never have dared to share the action premise that follows: "Therefore, you can dream great dreams for yourself and for others!" For sure, that young black American would have struck back angrily or laughed the guard into an embarrassed silence.

Yet there it is at the very beginning of this book, ready for you to consider, to ridicule, or to ignore altogether. And I put it there because I am convinced with all my heart that believing and practicing Credo 1 will make an incredible difference in your life as it has in mine and in the lives of a great number of my friends.

How Do You See Yourself?

Don't worry. I'm not out to proselytize you to my own Judaeo-Christian tradition. You can be a successful capitalist and care less about God. And you certainly can believe in evolution, with or without God's power and presence, and still make a go of it in the business world. In our business, as in yours, there are distributors and employees at every point of the theological and philosophical spectrum.

The real question is this: Who do you think you are? To what end do you think you were born? Where do your dreams come from? What hope do *you* have for seeing those dreams come true? Is it all a great coincidence, a genetic joke, an unknowable mystery, or was there a purpose to your creation?

A biochemist friend of mine answers the question "How do you see yourself?" with this tongue-in-cheek reply: "I am sixty percent water," she begins, "enough to fill a very small bathtub. Most of the rest is fat, enough to make at least four to five bars of soap, and a variety of common chemicals. I am enough calcium to make a large piece of chalk, enough phosphorus to light a small pack of matches, enough sodium to season a bag of microwave popcorn, enough magnesium to set off a flashbulb, enough copper to make a widow's mite, enough iodine to make a child jump up and down in pain, enough iron to make a ten-penny nail, and enough sulfur to rid a dog of fleas. All in all," she concludes, "figuring in the current recession, I am about $1.78 worth of water, fat, and chemicals."

Buckminster Fuller, the philosopher, architect, and city planner, also answered the question "How do you see yourself?" I've paraphrased below his much longer reply.

I am a self-balancing, twenty-eight-jointed adapter-base biped, an electrochemical processing plant with integrated and separate facilities for maintaining energy in storage batteries for the subsequent powering of thousands of hydraulic and pneumatic pumps, each with their own motors attached; sixty-two thousand miles of small blood vessels, millions of warning-signal devices, railroads, and conveyor systems; plus crushers and cranes, a widely distributed telephone system needing no service for seventy years if well maintained; all guided from a turret in which are located telescopes, microscopic, self-registering range finders, a spectroscope, et cetera.

B. F. Skinner, psychologist and father of behaviorism, answered the question this way: I am a series of learned responses to my environment. Like Pavlov's dogs, I am trained by forces beyond my control to salivate on cue. I can neither "initiate action nor make spontaneous or capricious changes." Everything is conditioned. Choice is an illusion. Dreams are self-deceit.

How do those answers make you feel? Stand in front of a mirror somewhere, look yourself directly in the eye, and ask yourself the question: "How do I see myself?"

Do you think of yourself as a pile of chemicals or an elaborate machine set on automatic pilot or an organism trained to salivate on cue? If you do—and I don't believe it for a moment—there isn't much future for $1.78 worth of water, fat, and magnesium. A machine doesn't have a heart, a mind, or a conscience. Pavlov's dogs may dream, but they have no way of seeing that their dreams come true. Don't you believe in your heart that you are more than all these answers put together?

That's why I love the richness and beauty of the Bible. In Genesis, Moses gives *his* answer to the question. In his poetic and deeply moving account of creation, the old prophet shares his views on who we are and why we dare to dream.

He begins this most famous literary passage in history with these simple words: "In the beginning God created the heavens and the earth" (Genesis 1:1). On the sixth day of creation, Moses writes, "God created man in his own image. In the image of God he created him; male and female he created them" (Genesis 1:27). "The Lord God formed the man from the dust of the ground and breathed into his nostrils the breath [spirit] of life, and the man became a living being" (Genesis 2:7).

Moses did not believe that we are an accident of evolution, but someone that God carefully and lovingly created (Genesis 1–2). We are not just another plant or animal, for we have received the "divine breath" of God and thus share our Creator's very nature and purpose (Genesis 2:7).

And Earth is not just another planet whirling around the sun on its endless journey through infinite space. It is our God-given home. We are meant to find sustenance and joy from this planet. In return we share the privilege and responsibility of caring for the Earth and for each other as God cares for us (Genesis 1:28). We are God's special creation, made to enjoy fellowship with our Creator and with our fellow creatures (Genesis 1:31).

In "God's Trombone," James Weldon Johnson's inspiring and whimsical account of creation, the African American poet brings Moses' story to life in his own unique way. On the sixth day of creation, God pauses to reflect.

> Then God walked around,
> And God looked around
> On all that he had made.
> He looked at his sun,
> And he looked at his moon,
> And he looked at his little stars;
> He looked on his world
> With all its living things
> And God said: I'm lonely still.
>
> Then God sat down—
> On the side of a hill where he could think;
> By a deep, wide river he sat down;
> With his head in his hands,
> God thought and thought,
> Till he thought: I'll make me a man!
>
> Up from the bed of the river
> God scooped the clay;
> And by the bank of the river
> He kneeled him down;
> And there the great God Almighty
> Who lit the sun and fixed it in the sky,
> Who flung the stars to the most far corner of the night,
> Who rounded the earth in the middle of his hand;
> This Great God,
> Like a mammy bending over her baby,
> Kneeled down in the dust

Toiling over a lump of clay
Till he shaped it in his own image;

Then into it he blew the breath of life,
And man became a living soul.
Amen. Amen.

Who am I? Who are you? Our tradition replies in a deeply personal way. We are children of a loving Creator who bent down in the dust and placed His dreams in our heart like "a mammy bending over her baby." The implications of that creation account have staggering consequences for Nas Imran and for us all.

We are created. We are not just an assemblage of chemicals or a mindless machine. We are human beings made in the very image of our Creator. When we were born, God held each of us in His arms and whispered, "I created you and what I have created is good!"

Remember the bumper sticker "God don't make no junk!" It's true. Life may have been tough on you. You may feel angry or deprived. You may see yourself as a dropout or a failure. You may think that you've blown your chance, that there is no way to begin again.

For a change, try to see yourself as your Creator sees you. Whatever you have or have not done, God sees you as His own son or daughter. And whatever may have happened along the way, like the father of the prodigal son, God is waiting patiently for you to come home, to receive His gifts, and to take your place at your Creator's bountiful table.

We are created to dream. Our dreams, too, are created in the image of God's dreams. Imagine what it will mean for you to begin to have the same kinds of dreams that your Creator dreams for you and for the planet. Henry David Thoreau said, "Dreams are the touchstones of our character." Your dreams determine who you are and what you care about. The size of them determines the size of your soul.

I understand how difficult it may be for you to dare to dream. Like Nas Imran, maybe you've inherited a bitter legacy. You may have been abused or molested as a child. You may have grown up in poverty or fear or neglect. You may be hauling around a terrible load of guilt or debt, pain or disability. You may be carrying the scars of lost battles and broken dreams.

Nevertheless, as the old saying goes, it's never too late to dream. If you're too afraid or too wounded to have big dreams right now, dream little ones. "I have learned," Thoreau also said, "that if one advances confidently in the direction of his dreams, and endeavors to live the life which he has imagined, he will meet with a success unexpected in common hours."

Most people begin their own businesses just to make a few extra dollars a month. Few start out to become independently wealthy. Then, little by little, step by step, their dreams grow with the size of their business. Small dreams are a good place to start. What small dream could you dare to have today?

We are loved by God and empowered by our Creator to see our dreams come true. God didn't create and run. The Creator is as active and interested in your life now as He was the day He created you. You may feel that nobody loves you, that you are alone and struggling in this world. But it isn't true. God is with you and has planted dreams in your heart to guide you on your journey. Your dreams are not just giant impossibilities rumbling around in your head to mock or ridicule you. They are real and should be carefully considered.

Of course, there is a danger here. Along the way we may envision scenarios that are not realistic. I would love to sing like Pavarotti or pass like Joe Montana or shoot like Shaquille O'Neal or write like Toni Morrison. It is really important to get regular reality checks from those we love and trust. On occasion unrealistic dreams become obsessive and need a counselor's help. But often the most "unrealistic" dreams are the most important ones to keep on dreaming. Sometimes, even dreams that are not sound or sane will lead you back to the dreams God planted in your heart.

Sitting in that lonely prison cell in the ruins of his Rose Bowl dreams, Nas Imran, a child of slavery and injustice, went on dreaming. At first they were angry. Upon his release from prison, Nas joined the Black Muslim nation. He helped in the transition of leadership in Chicago when Elijah Muhammad died. Eventually he was appointed minister to Seattle's large Black Muslim population.

"Then I learned," Nas explains, "that what has happened to my people in this country could not be avenged. It had to be healed. The Black Muslim dream was built on hatred and on blaming others. There could be no healing with hatred and blame in my heart. Then somebody told me that the Christian dream is built on love. Love heals. With Jesus as my example, I learned to forgive the past and dream great dreams, in black and white, for the future."

Today, Nas and Vicki Imran own a very successful Amway distribution business. And he has passed on his free-enterprise dream to his wife, their eight children and to hundreds of people who now own their own successful businesses. With his new financial security Nas is free to use his time, money, and creativity to serve others in his community.

In fact, because of Nas Imran and hundreds like him in the Amway family with their own deep roots in Africa, Asia, and Latin America, the company is being transformed. We are developing and marketing products for peoples once slighted or ignored. We are opening doors to people once left out. And we are using corporate funds to support scholarships with such worthy organizations as the United Negro College Fund because Nas Imran and people like him dared to dream big dreams for themselves and for us.

How Do You See Others?

Credo 1 has inspiring personal implications for each of us. Once we really grasp its idea, then we are ready to begin our journey. But Credo 1 also has important ethical and moral considerations. How you see yourself is just the beginning. Over the long haul, how you see others may be even more important in helping your dreams come true. If you and I are truly created in God's image to dream great dreams for ourselves, then everybody else is also created in God's image and our dreaming must reach out to help their dreams come true.

Take Credo 1 a step further. It isn't enough to believe that I am created by a loving Creator to dream great dreams. I must also believe that you are created in the very same way to the very same end.

Throughout history terrible things have happened when one man or group believed themselves superior to the rest of us. Tragedy often occurs when we regard ourselves as priceless creations but see others as little piles of chemicals worth $1.78.

In my own lifetime, not much more than fifty years ago, on Hitler's command, the Nazis gassed and burned six million European Jews. At least another six million religious, military, and political prisoners were tortured and killed during Hitler's reign of terror.

These victims of his lie were men, women, and children created by God to dream, but to Hitler they were chaff. It is easy to burn $1.78 worth of chemicals. No one's conscience hurts when a noisy, troublesome machine is trashed. Few people get upset when a stray dog is put to sleep.

And so they died. Millions of them. People created just like you and me, their dreams cut short by a terrible, untimely death. Never forget those pictures taken at Auschwitz and Buchenwald. Mothers, fathers, and little children clutching one another in terror as storm troopers and police dogs herded them toward concentration camps. Whole families crowded into gas chambers, their clothing, gold fillings, and eyeglasses more valued than their lives. Lamp shades made of human skin. Children's skulls used for target practice or for ashtrays. Twisted, starved, naked bodies stacked up like cordwood or tossed into great open pits.

Read the *Gulag Archipelago,* Alexander Solzhenitsyn's moving eyewitness account of the Soviet communist butchers. Stalin and his henchmen sent an estimated ten million men, women, and children to prison, where they were tortured and murdered. During the last decade the Khmer Rouge butchered a million of their gentle compatriots in Cambodia. In Iraq, even as I write, Saddam Hussein is still murdering his nation's minorities: Kurds in the north and Shiite Muslims in the south; Yugoslavian Serbs are slaughtering Bosnians; Irish Catholics and Protestants are still bombing, kidnapping, and shooting one another; while in the Holy Land, the innocent children of Jews, Christians, and Muslims are still being killed and maimed in endless, bloody rounds of revenge.

But we don't have to cross the seas to find examples. America, too, has a tragic history of undervaluing our brothers and sisters. The Native Americans were betrayed and eventually almost eliminated because our ancestors didn't believe that red men, women, and children, too, are created by God to dream. And though our new nation was built on the truth that "all men are created equal and that they are endowed by their Creator with certain unalienable rights," even our founding fathers didn't grasp the idea that those same rights belonged to women and children, let alone to slaves and their American progeny.

In 1681 there were only two thousand slaves in this country, mainly in Virginia. But by the mid-nineteenth century more than four million Africans had been kidnapped from their villages and shipped like cattle across the Atlantic. In this strange new land slaves were often separated from their families, auctioned as property to the highest bidder, carried off in chains, forced to spend their lives at hard labor, starved and whipped, compelled to live in poverty and discomfort, stripped of dignity and self-worth and buried in unmarked graves.

Once again this low view of humankind led to tragedy. In Hitler's words, black-skinned people were not part of "the good race." So they were seen as machines to pick cotton and plow fields.

We still haven't really dealt with slavery and its long-term consequences for this nation. We still don't seem to really believe that all men (women and children) are created equal.

Seeing others as we see ourselves is more than the first step to owning your own successful business. It is the beginning of the answer to all the problems that plague our nation and the world. Just before his crucifixion, Jesus summarized his life and teachings in these simple, eloquent words: "This is my commandment, that you love one another."

How do you see your neighbor, your customer, your boss, the stranger in need who wanders in, the person who nearly drives you mad? If you want to be a success, you must see these others as you see yourself. For they, too, are created to dream and they, too, are loved by God, who wants them to see their dreams come true.

Old prejudices die hard. We seem able to hate far longer than we love. Nevertheless, seeing our neighbors as the Creator sees them can be done. We all need to try. Even our smallest attempts can make a difference.

Thomas Jefferson said, "One man with courage is a majority." I wonder if Lincoln had read those words when he presented the Emancipation Proclamation to his cabinet. After they had voted a resounding no to his plan to free the slaves, the president raised his hand and said, "The ayes have it!"

My friends in Amway have taught me so much. David and Jan Severn shared this saying with me: "You can have anything in life you want if you are willing to help enough other people get what they want first." What better summary could be made of Credo 1?

Because we have been created by a loving God, we can dream great dreams for ourselves and for others. Living out that ideal has been the key to the Severns' success as independent owners of their own business.

Dave Severn grew up in Boise, Idaho. Before enlisting in the United States Army, he graduated from the University of Idaho, where he was a member of the R.O.T.C. After graduation, Dave went to work for Ernst and Ernst, the international accounting firm. Jan Severn was raised in Twin Falls, Idaho, population roughly twenty thousand. In 1969, Jan and Dave were married. About the same time Dave was called to active duty in the U.S. Army, and the newlyweds spent their first three years of marriage serving their country in Europe. They had their first child in Germany and upon Dave's discharge returned to the U.S.

"Those were tough times financially," Dave told me. "Even though Jan wanted to stay home with our new baby, she had to find a job as a receptionist for an independent insurance agent to help us make ends meet. It's funny," he adds quietly, "how quickly reality began to put a damper on our dreams."

"We needed more income," Jan says, continuing the story. "So, to make a few extra dollars, we tried to renovate old houses." She laughed ruefully at the memory. "That idea, like many others we tried, only drove us further into debt."

"I was doing taxes for people who owned their own businesses," Dave explains. "I was stunned to learn how much more they could make than the rest of us, and immediately I began to dream of opening a private CPA practice. But start-up costs were outrageous, and that dream, too, went by the wayside."

"Then we discovered this business," Jan said, grinning, "and the rest is history."

When asked to share the key to their success, Dave answered without a moment's hesitation.

"We started out with one goal," he remembers, "to get rich. We needed money to see our dreams come true, and we began with a 'go-go-go' attitude. I told everybody, 'You're going to make money. You're going to get rich.'

"Then we began to watch the people who had really succeeded in this business," Jan continues. "They taught us that the difference between really having a big business and just having a little business is the number of people you are willing to serve."

"I'll never forget what Ron Puryear told us," Dave explains. " 'As you show the plan and sponsor people,' he said, 'don't look at people as a body with a mind, but rather see each of them as a beautiful mind with a body.' "

"I think," Jan adds, "it was at that rally that it dawned on us for the first time: You can have everything in life that you want if you are willing to help enough other people get what they want first. And when we put that ideal into practice, when we began to see other people as created by God with dreams of their own, dreams that we could help come true, our business began to boom."

Ken Stewart was twenty-seven when he first heard about our business. He was a successful contractor in Springfield, Missouri, building and selling fifty or more homes a year in that prospering Midwestern region. Ken and his wife, Donna, were on the fast track to success.

"We were young and we were ambitious," Ken remembers. "But we were also $300,000 in debt and running kind of scared about ever catching up with the cash that was flowing out."

"Owning our own distribution business seemed the answer," Donna says, "and we jumped in with both feet, trying to find and sponsor a group made up of ambitious couples like ourselves. Then we began to listen to the leaders whom we respected most in this business," she adds. "It didn't take us long to realize that they saw people in a unique and wonderful way."

"After our first conversation," Ken continues, "Dexter Yager, one of our mentors, nicknamed me 'The Kid.' I was young, ambitious, energetic. I saw myself as a winner and I wanted winners on my team. I didn't see people as God sees them. I didn't understand that those winner–loser categories are dangerous and misleading, because over the long haul you're going to be surprised who really succeeds and who fails."

"It took us a while," Donna explains, "but over the years we've really learned to be less judgmental. We had no right to type a couple as sharp because they came on strong with grins and glitter or to type another couple as dull because they seemed rather weak or shy."

"Like a lot of people," Ken continues, "we can be driven too hard and too fast to notice people's undeveloped or partially developed gifts and talents. We can lose sight of people's potential."

"We began to succeed in this business," Donna adds, "when we quit evaluating people by first impressions and began to really believe in their God-given gifts."

Then Ken sums it up: "We had to learn to accept people where they really are, to find out where they want to be and then to do our best to help them get there. Understanding that process and giving our lives to it brought a new kind of joy to our lives and real success to our business."

"If a man wants his dreams to come true," says the old proverb, "he must first wake up!"

I'm not sure I've said it well or clearly enough, but at the heart of Credo 1 is a kind of wake-up call for all of us. If you want to succeed as a compassionate capitalist, what you think of yourself (and therefore of others) will make all the difference.

Can you see yourself as a child of a loving Creator? Can you picture your own birth as James Weldon Johnson pictures it?

> This Great God,
> Like a mammy bending over her baby,
> Kneeled down in the dust
> Toiling over a lump of clay
> Till he shaped *you* in his own image.
> Then into *you* he blew the breath of life,
> And *you* became a living soul. [italics added]

Can you see your fellow creatures—white, black, red, yellow—all of them everywhere as children of a loving God created to dream as you dream, with worth, dignity, and potential?

If you can, you are already well on your way to dreaming for yourself and for others the kinds of dreams that can turn the world right side up!

2

Where Are We Going?

CREDO 2

We believe that most people feel that they are not living up to their potential and are grateful for any practical, realistic help they can get to change for the better.

Therefore, we all need to take an honest look at where we are, where we want to be, and what we may need to change to get there.

Joe Foglio walked angrily through the kitchen of his large oceanfront home on a marina in Coronado, California. He slammed open the back door, charged out into the desert sunshine, and growled his way across the steaming asphalt driveway.

"Joe? Don't go. Please. Not now."

For a moment he turned to look at his wife, Norma, standing in the open doorway. Her hands were trembling. Her eyes glistened with tears.

"I'm out of here!" he answered, opening the car door, afraid and embarrassed to look his wife in the eye, both wishing she would stop him and afraid that she might try.

"When are you coming home?" she said, moving across the driveway in his direction, wanting him to hold her, for everything to be right between them, the way it had once been.

"None of your damn business," he shouted, angrily slamming the door. Then, without looking back, he gunned the engine and screeched down the driveway in reverse.

For a moment Norma stood rock still, choking back her tears. She carefully kept her back to the house, knowing that Nicky and Joey, their nineteen- and sixteen-year-old sons, and Charrie, their seventeen-year-old daughter, were watching from the windows, feeling frustrated and frightened by this latest battle in the ongoing war between their parents. Then Norma took a deep breath and turned to face them.

"I knew why Joe slammed the door and screeched away," she recalls quietly. "He was miserable. We both were. No matter how hard we worked, we could never get ahead, and almost every day something else would go wrong. The worst part was the helplessness. Everything we loved was going down the drain, and we didn't know how to stop it."

Joe crossed the Coronado Bay bridge and raced down Highway 5 toward the Mexican border. He was building a tract of houses in Rosarita Beach, Mexico, and his workers were waiting. He ached with anger at himself for losing his temper once again. He imagined his life spiraling downward into a black hole, and he felt old, familiar terrors begin to rise.

"I had been on cortisone for ten years," Joe remembers, "fighting multiple sclerosis. I had ballooned in weight. After going through two bankruptcies already, my international high-rise business was running out of funds. Days earlier, Mexico had devalued its currency. The country was plunged into economic chaos. My net worth dropped to zero. Once again I was perched on the edge of bankruptcy."

Norma sat silently in the kitchen of their home, drinking coffee and trying to calm her nerves. Charrie sat nearby, not knowing how to comfort her mother. Joey had retreated to his room, headsets firmly in place, music blaring. Their elder son, Nicky, had disappeared on his motorcycle in a cloud of dust and anger.

Joe steered his silver Jaguar down a narrow dirt road that ended on an isolated Mexican beach. The sun made a shining pathway across the Pacific. He remembers wondering where that path led. Then, his head in his hands, he slumped over the wheel and began to cry.

"I was a wreck," Joe recalls, "physically, emotionally, spiritually, and financially. I was afraid that I was about to lose my wife and family, and depression was growing like a great, dark cloud inside my head."

Does any of this sound familiar? I hope your dreams are not being frustrated to the extent that Joe and Norma were experiencing that day. I hope depression isn't haunting your life as it haunted theirs. But everyone has a time when his dreams falter or end up on the rocks. Maxwell Anderson, the American playwright, said it perfectly, "If at first you don't succeed, you're running about average." After every failure there is a good chance that depression will set in. After all, it's been that way since the beginning of time. Almost three thousand years ago, the psalmist David confessed his own depression:

> How long, O Lord?
> Will you forget me forever?
> How long will you hide your face from me?
> How long must I wrestle with my thoughts
> and every day have sorrow in my heart?
> How long will my enemy triumph over me?
>
> (PSALM 13:1–2 N.I.V.)

Writing in 1854, Thoreau said it all in nine short words: "The mass of men lead lives of quiet desperation."

Throughout time, people have turned their anger and frustration inward. In our own era, depression has become a plague. According to the National Institute of Mental Health, a growing number are "struggling with persistent feelings of sadness or emptiness, loss of interest in sex and other pleasurable activities, fatigue, insomnia, irritability, excessive crying and thoughts of death or suicide."

Westinghouse Electric researchers say, "About twenty cents of every dollar spent by U.S. businesses on health care goes for mental health and chemical-dependency treatment." And they add this fascinating note: "One of the most cost-effective areas for preventive medicine programs, it seems, is mental health."

In other words, if we could get our lives together, our bodies might heal themselves. This idea gives an entirely new meaning to the Old Testament wisdom of Solomon, who wrote almost a thousand years before Christ: "As a man thinketh in his heart, so is he." Depression and depression-related illnesses cost U.S. employers $17 billion annually. As depression spreads downward to younger and younger persons, the cost in wasted time and money, chronic illness and ruined lives, is incalculable.

A recent *Time* magazine cover story described the current mode as "a national sense of uncertainty and malaise." In October 1991, *Money* magazine's Consumer Comfort poll said simply, "Gloom reigns." Their editors described the current depression-index rating as minus 24, lower than the minus 19 of April that year when the headline had been "Americans sink into a deep funk."

Alexis de Toqueville, the great French observer of life in America in the 1830s, sounds like he's writing about us in the 1990s when he describes our great-grandfathers and -mothers more than 160 years ago: "A cloud habitually hung on their brow, and they seemed serious and almost sad even in their pleasure . . . they never stop thinking of the good things they have not got."

Dr. Gerald Klerman of New York Hospital–Cornell University Medical College said it this way, "In general, people are more pessimistic now. People get depressed when there's a gap between expectation and fulfillment."

There it is: Credo 2. Too often reality doesn't measure up to our dreams, and so we get depressed. Then, to cope with our depression, we begin to think and act destructively. As a result, our lives spiral ever downward until there seems no way to pull ourselves back up again.

What happens when dreams die and depression sets in? Some people respond to the cycle of failure and depression in fairly predictable ways. At first they are tempted to deny or ignore it. Then they try to fix blame on themselves or blame on others. Invariably they try to escape it. Some become immobilized by depression. Others do desperate, destructive things to end it. Some go on living with depression forever. Others just sit down and die, but they don't have to.

Option: Deny Depression or Ignore It

Joe Foglio drove home from Rosarita Beach late for dinner again. Norma greeted him at the door as though nothing had happened. Joe made small talk with his wife and children as they sat around the dinner table, pretending that everything was all right. Norma darted back and forth between the oven and the table, a smile planted firmly on her face. Everyone was polite, cordial, and nearly doubled up with pain. Why do you think Thoreau said lives of quiet desperation? Even from Walden Pond the early-American poet could see that people put on masks with painted smiles to pretend they are okay when down inside they are miserable.

There is a tremendous temptation to suffer silently. Our pride keeps us from admitting the truth. We don't want people to know we've failed. In the Orient, for example, "keeping face" is everything. The British say, "Keep a stiff upper lip." It is a macho American myth that real men don't cry. I don't know anyone who likes to deal with conflict. It's so much easier, at least at first, to pretend that all is well. Our misery becomes a terrible secret. We build walls around ourselves and cut ourselves off from those who would empathize with and even help us. Like a sick animal, we slink away and wait to heal.

Are you that way? When your dreams are threatened and you are lost in a fog of depression, do you become silent and wander away? Or do you hang in there, smiling bravely, pretending that nothing is wrong when in fact your whole world is collapsing around your head?

"We had been living the financial good life when Joe went bankrupt," Norma recalls. "We owned a beautiful home, a boat, and fancy cars. And when it all went belly-up, we didn't want people to know. So we tried to go on living the good life even if we couldn't afford it."

"A rich friend sold me his silver XJS Jaguar for nothing down and whatever I could pay per month," Joe says, smiling to himself and shaking his head. "And we signed a lease on a large California waterfront house in the exclusive island Cays across Coronado Bay from San Diego."

"It isn't hard to maintain the illusion of success," Norma admits sheepishly, "for a while at least. So, even when we were broke and feeling desperate and depressed, we wore our masks and went on pretending."

At church, at parent–teacher conferences, at the office, the bank, the grocery store, everything was smiles and good cheer. Joe and Norma Foglio were leading double lives and feeling more and more depressed by it. To the outside world they wore masks to hide their deteriorating relationship; yet few who knew them ever suspected that anything was wrong.

Sound familiar? We can't even help ourselves when we pretend to be okay. And no one else can help us when we don't admit that we're in need. "Life is perfect. Please pass the Rolaids!" It seems especially sad that in our churches and synagogues—where love should prevail—so many people put on that heavenly face while in reality they are living in hell. Depression can't be treated until we quit denying or ignoring it. The beginning of the end of that struggle is to admit that you are struggling, first to yourself and then little by little to people you can trust to walk with on the road to recovery.

Option: Find Someone to Blame!

By the time the dishes were washed and Joe and Norma had retired to their bedroom, they were at it again. "If you hadn't ..." "If you wouldn't always ..." Their voices rose. Their anger pierced the thin walls and ricocheted around their children's rooms.

"We were yelling at each other at such high decibels," Norma confesses, "that it drowned out our kids' rock music. When we weren't blaming each other for our troubles, we were blaming someone else."

"We blamed parents or teachers. We blamed friends or co-workers. We even blamed the American government," Joe says quietly. "As a businessman, I was tired of taxes and the endless forms. I hated all the regulations and the regulatory agencies that dogged my every step. Finally I got so fed up I decided to leave my country. When the Rosarita project began to fail, I was already five years into a seven-year requirement to drop my American citizenship and become a Mexican citizen."

"Then Mexico devalued her currency," Norma remembers. "Our net worth plummeted. We were sure that the president of Mexico was out to destroy us. Actually, it was rather nice to have someone new to blame."

Blaming often leads to complete breakdown in family communications. Yelling and calling each other names can quickly become physical violence. In fact, violence in the family constitutes a major health crisis in this country.

"I even tried to shoot Joe once," Norma admits sheepishly. "Thank God I never could hit the broad side of a barn with a shotgun. The pellets hit the car and broke the bedroom window but missed Joe completely. If I'd had better aim, I might have killed him." Then after a long, thoughtful pause she adds, "And just think of all the good years we would have missed together if I had killed him during the bad."

Physical abuse at home, especially wife beating, claims a victim every fifteen seconds. Personal injury, much of it caused by family fighting, annually accounts for an estimated $180 billion in medical care.

During such desperate times people do a lot of crazy, dangerous things. Norma Foglio still remembers one special long-distance phone call from her husband in the middle of the night. Joe was calling collect from a Mexican jail. She listened with growing disbelief.

"I'm in trouble," he said, his voice weak and quavering.

Norma strained to hear her husband explain what had happened. Apparently, feeling desperate to produce some much needed cash, he had volunteered to help some acquaintances smuggle drugs across the U.S. border.

"We didn't do it," Joe said, "but the Mexican authorities found out about our plan. They've arrested me. They've questioned me for four miserable days and nights. Now they want money—lots of money—to pay my fine or they're going to throw away the key."

Somehow Norma found the necessary funds to secure her husband's release. It was a painful and terrifying time for them both. But now, looking back, the Foglios see the dangerous, embarrassing episode as a perfect example of the crazy, irresponsible things people are prone to do when they are feeling desperate and depressed.

Sometimes we blame ourselves and feel guilty. Sometimes we blame others to relieve our guilt. Blaming quickly becomes a dangerous and endless cycle that may escalate into acts of violence and crime. Burton Hillis once said, "There's a mighty big difference between good, sound reasons and reasons that sound good." When our dreams die and depression sets in, it's time to quit blaming and set out to find the good, sound reasons that got us into this mess and to create a good, sound plan to get us out.

Option: Escape Depression

During those years of conflict and depression, Joe and Norma Foglio used alcohol to escape their stressful lives.

"We depended on alcohol to deaden our pain," Joe admits, "and to bring a temporary calm between us."

"When we went out to dinner, just the two of us," Norma adds, "we had to drink fairly heavily just to stand being together."

"I never got into hard drugs, thank God," Joe continues. "But I was smoking a lot of marijuana just to sleep at night. Now, looking back, I realize that our drinking and my smoking pot left a tragic example for our son Nicky, and may even have led to his death a few years later."

Escaping depression is the number one growth industry in this nation and around the world. The facts are chilling. Nobody knows for certain how many trillions of dollars are spent every year by people attempting to divert or entertain away pain.

For example, in California, the fruit and salad bowl of this nation, the leading cash crop is not oranges or grapes, lettuce or tomatoes. It's marijuana. For escape, or as users aptly say, for "getting wasted," marijuana is America's number one drug. Approximately twenty-two and a half million men, women, and young people, almost ten percent of the nation's population, admit to "occasional to regular" use.

Currently, a typical user pays from $100 to $500 an ounce, depending on the quality, for those thin green leaves to roll into joints or bake into brownies. If a "recreational user" goes through six ounces a year (at the approximate cost of $600 to $3,000) it means that in the U.S. alone, as much as $70 billion dollars a year is going up in marijuana smoke to help people "get high" when in fact they're feeling low.

Cocaine and heroin abuse is also epidemic in this country. We don't know how many millions escape into the dangerous and deadly euphoria that these drugs produce, but we do know that almost five hundred thousand Americans are addicted to heroin, currently the escape drug of choice in the U.S. and in Europe. In Milan, Italy, for example, the city picks up three to four thousand used syringes every day off the streets.

Who counts the used needles found in ghetto Dumpsters or exclusive high-rise trash compactors from New York to San Francisco? Who adds up the empty plastic vials found on beaches, in national parks, behind high school and junior high school bleachers or even in corporate boardrooms and five-star hotels across our land? The 202,000 people under treatment for drug abuse in our country are more than the entire work force of the nation of Luxembourg.

Richard Asher wrote in *Lancet,* the British medical journal, "Despair is best treated with hope, not dope." I like his aphorism because I believe it's true. But it's also the kind of bumper sticker we use to warn our children against drugs while forgetting that alcohol abuse has become an even more costly and deadly escape than heroin, cocaine, or marijuana.

One of the really dangerous myths making the rounds these days is that Americans have cut down on their drinking habits. Supposedly we know that alcoholic drinks are loaded with calories and grams of fat, and we have learned that booze is a depressant with a short high and a longer low. We have seen how much beer, wine, and liquor costs a personal or a family budget in dollars and cents. So we thought the nation had "gone on the wagon." No way.

Alcohol abuse has reached epidemic proportions in this country, Europe, and Japan. In the U.S., for example, over the past thirty years alcohol use has increased by more than half; in Germany alcohol consumption is up by 64 percent; and in Japan drinking has increased by an unbelievable 73.5 percent.

During recent years I've learned to love and respect the people of Japan. It makes me nervous to see how large a problem alcohol abuse has become in their country. And worse, they don't know it or won't admit it publicly. In a recent worldwide study, Japan reported the lowest level of concern, with only 17 percent surveyed believing that alcohol was a serious problem. On the other hand, 74 percent of Americans surveyed reported "very serious concern" over alcohol abuse and alcoholism.

On an average in the U.S., for example, there are 1,844,000 alcohol-related traffic accidents a year. In 1989, 20,208 Americans, many of them teenagers, were killed by drunk drivers. More than 100,000 additional victims were permanently maimed or injured. I share the anger and grief of the Mothers Against Drunk Driving (MADD), who have seen their own children killed and permanently disabled by drunk drivers.

Don't worry. I'm not a crusader about to splinter the bar in your local saloon. But we need to support the people in Alcoholics Anonymous and other treatment programs for whom abstinence seems to be the only way. We also need to be aware that under pressure, all of us are vulnerable to alcohol misuse and even addiction.

Seneca, the Roman philosopher and writer of tragedies during the time of Christ, said, "Drunkenness is simply voluntary insanity." Almost two thousand years later, Bertrand Russell added: "Drunkenness is temporary suicide . . . the happiness that it brings is merely negative, a momentary cessation of unhappiness." Alcohol abuse has become a national tragedy, but for me it is a symptom of an even larger malaise. We are using booze to escape depression when we need instead to find a way to deal with our depression head-on with courage and creativity.

During the past few decades, prescription drugs have also been widely used to control the symptoms of depression. When prescribed by reputable physicians and psychiatrists, drugs like Valium, Xanax, and Prozac can be safe and helpful in treating anxiety. But the rapid rise of the popularity of these drugs must give us pause. To escape depression people are popping tranquilizers, mood elevators, and antidepressants as if they were M&Ms.

Take Valium, for example. In the 1970s, when the Swiss-based pharmaceutical company Hoffman-LaRoche introduced Valium and its sister tranquilizer, Librium, to the North American market, the company's stock climbed like a rocket. Halfway through 1989, it was the most expensive stock on Wall Street, selling at $160,000 a share. That year Hoffman-LaRoche declared a fifty-for-one stock split. The reason for this incredible success? One doctor told me that there were more Valium pills being sold in America during the late 1970s and early 1980s than all the other pills of any kind put together.

But we must not forget that these prescription drugs can also have wide-ranging adverse effects, especially when they are combined with other drugs such as alcohol. If the celebrities pouring in and out of the Betty Ford Clinic in Palm Springs, California, for treatment of prescription-drug dependence is any indicator, we need to be very careful about the use of such drugs in our struggle to overcome depression.

"What is dangerous about the tranquilizers," writes one observer, "is that whatever peace of mind they bring is a packaged peace of mind. When you buy a pill and buy peace with it, you get conditioned to cheap solutions instead of deep ones."

A cheaper form of escape from depression, but one that equally numbs the mind, is television. If statistics can be trusted at all, the whole world is becoming addicted to the tube.

I don't know how it is possible, but one reputable source claims that people in Japan spend an average of 9.12 hours per day with their televisions playing. Americans win second prize in the couch potato Olympics with a staggering 7 hours spent daily before the tube. I believe in television. It is a wonderful source of information and entertainment. But these data show us that something has gotten out of hand. And I believe this television addiction results directly from humankind's incredible need to escape depression and to put off dealing directly with its causes.

I hope you've not become numb from all these numbers. I'm overemphasizing to make a point. The whole world seems to be depressed, and in our need to escape, we are wasting our lives away. However, what's happening out there is not nearly as important as what is happening in your life and in mine. How are you handling your own failed dreams and the depression that almost certainly follows?

Option: Give In to Depression

Frank and Barbara Morales, friends in our business from San Juan Capistrano, California, told us of a moving experience that Barbara had when she was just seventeen years old and a brand-new teller in a bank in Kansas City. "In the coupon department of that bank," she remembers, "there was an older woman who had spent her lifetime in loyal service to her employers and their customers. When she reached mandatory retirement age, the bank honored her with a surprise party, a cake, and gifts of appreciation. I still remember the woman standing in the center of her own party with tears streaming down her face and a kind of haunted, desperate look in her eyes.

"The very next morning," Barbara says sadly, "just one day after her retirement party, the woman appeared at the bank and stood looking in the window. Finally she came in, walked up to her old desk, and stood over the young woman who had replaced her, trying to tell her how to do the job that she had been doing for all those years.

"I found out later," she adds, "that the older woman had never taken a vacation or even a day off for sickness or personal business. Her whole life was that bank, and when her job ended, her life ended. Day after day she came back to her old desk and stood there looking more and more helpless, more and more desperate. Finally the manager told the bank guard to escort that poor woman from the building. We never saw her again. I've often wondered how long it took after the death of her dreams before she, too, ended up in the grave."

How many people die simultaneously with their dreams or go on existing in a kind of living death brought on by their sense of failure and depression? Bertrand Russell expresses the terrible agony of dreamers who are convinced that they are powerless to see their dreams come true. "Brief and powerless is Man's life," he writes. "On him and all his race the slow, sure doom falls pitiless and dark." Upon seeing his dreams die for his children and his kingdom, Shakespeare's King Lear cries out, "When we are born, we cry that we are come to this great stage of fools."

Joe and Norma Foglio know well such agony. Like King David, whose sins led to the death of his own son, Absalom, the Foglios have cried, "O my son, my dear son, would to God I had died for thee." On

February 11, 1988, their eldest child, Nicky, died in a motorcycle accident. He had struggled with alcohol and drug abuse from early adolescence. Late that winter night his struggle ended. High on some drug or other, feeling young and invincible, Nicky Foglio pressed down the accelerator pedal on his Yamaha motorcycle and roared around a corner and off the coast highway to his death.

I know our lives have moments of great tragedy and terrible suffering. I don't believe in "putting on a happy face" when it is time to mourn. To deny our depression, to mask it, or to try to escape it forever leads to misery. There are certain dreams that once they are dead can never be dreamed again. When they die, the only thing we can do is weep and wait until the tears pass and somehow God gives us the courage to dream once more.

But we must not give in to grief or let our failures and disappointments turn us into victims. Pessimism is a dangerous disease that can stifle or kill our human potential. I believe in passing on hope, not despair. Let us share our joy, not just our sorrow. I believe in telling and retelling the stories of God at work in men and women I know who rose from deep depressions to love and to dream again.

If our dreams are not coming true, if depression plagues our steps, we should remember that there is always hope. The true story of Joe and Norma Foglio and other stories told me by friends do not imply that getting into our business (or into any other business, religion, or care group, for that matter) is a guaranteed cure for depression. There is no guaranteed way for you or me to see reality measure up to our dreams.

But I do know for certain that a large percentage of our friends and co-workers joined with Jay and me for the very reason that they weren't seeing their dreams come true and they were depressed about it. However, instead of spiraling downward, these people saw their negative feelings as a beginning, not the end. Now they look back at those "down times" with gratitude. The "up times" couldn't have come without them.

What a waste it is to drug or even kill ourselves during the dark night of depression when sunrise may be just a few hours away. I hope these next words don't sound too Pollyannaish because in my lifetime I have learned that there really is light at the end of most tunnels. Rainbows really do come out after almost every storm. Crying will probably give way to laughter. Mourning will one day succumb to joy. So far in my sixty-three years on this planet, after every long, dark night the sun has risen to warm the earth again.

After crucifixion comes resurrection. After death comes life. After hopelessness comes hope. Depression deceives us when we think it will never end. In fact, the end of your depression may be just around the corner.

I am not minimizing in any way depression or its terrors. I have great sympathy for people who are suffering through private nightmares of hopelessness and loss. I've had my own bitter, battering bouts with the blues. Sometimes we need Valium or Prozac to see us through lonely nights. Professional counselors, psychiatrists, and psychiatric hospitals have great gifts to offer. Concerned family or friends can be godsends along the way. But if we succumb to depression, if we kill ourselves or settle into a kind of miserable living death, we will miss the opportunity that depression presents.

Joe and Norma Foglio didn't succumb to depression. Instead they saw it as a warning signal, a great "Stop! Danger Ahead!" sign. They interpreted their depression as a sign that serious change was needed, and somehow through the love and presence of God and their friends, they came out of their depression with a new understanding of the past, new zest for the present, and a wholly new dream for the future.

Joe and Norma are just one of hundreds of stories that illustrate that your dissatisfaction may be a hopeful sign. Rather than an ending, depression might be a beginning. Feeling down may lead you to a brand-new height.

Janet Evans, the twenty-year-old freestyle swimmer who won three gold medals in Seoul during the 1988 Olympics and a gold and silver in 1992, put it this way: "There's been hard times and good times. But the bad times make the good times feel so good!"

Ask Joe and Norma Foglio. For a while they thought that they would never dream again.

"When Nicky died," Joe remembers, "the grief and guilt I felt almost overwhelmed me. I stood by my son's casket in that funeral home in San Diego wondering why Nicky had died instead of his father. Norma, Charrie, and Joey were there. Our grieving family was surrounded by our friends who had flown or driven from across the state and around the country to stand with us in our pain.

"In the awful silence of that moment," he admits, "I prayed a desperate prayer. 'God, give me another chance,' I whispered quietly. I had failed with Nicky. I wanted to make up for the terrible mistakes I had made during his childhood and youth. And though Joey and Charrie had grown into young adults who made us proud and grateful, I wanted another son to take Nicky's place.

"Just a few weeks later," Joe says with excitement flashing in his eyes, "I presented the Amway plan to a young sailor who was a member of the tough and courageous Navy Seals. These skilled divers are flown across the world to do everything from rescuing hostages from their terrorist kidnappers to saving submariners from their sunken ships. That first young Seal spread the word about our business to his fellow Seals, their wives, and friends. Before long I was godfather to a whole squadron of Seals who were as tall, strong, and handsome as my son Nicky had been."

When they were bankrupt financially and spiritually, Joe and Norma Foglio had the courage and the wisdom to begin again. Today the Foglios have a successful business with an impressive income. Not only have they recovered all they lost in bankruptcy, they have gained so much more. Their bills are paid. They own their beautiful home in the Coronado Cays, and they are donating their time and money to support such important causes as their church and the March of Dimes. Best of all, they have a company of new friends. As Joe says, "If my car won't start, I know that with one phone call, five hundred friends that I've made in this business will show up to carry the car with me in it anywhere I need to go."

Even more important, Joe realized his dream of having another son to replace his beloved Nicky—and not just one son, but hundreds of young Navy Seals and other young men and women whom he loves as his own. When your dreams die, when depression threatens your future, remember Joe and Norma Foglio.

"A few weeks ago," Norma told me sadly, "we got a phone call from Bill and Annie Symington, two of our friends in this business. Their young son had been injured seriously in a terrible traffic accident. He was dying in a Phoenix hospital.

"Joe rushed to the San Diego airport," she recalls. "He flew to Phoenix to be with our friends in their time of suffering. When the Symingtons' son died, Bill called Joe on the car phone and asked him simply, 'How did you handle it, Joe?' For a moment my husband paused, swallowing hard, remembering his own time of grief and suffering. Then he said simply, 'It's going to be okay, Bill. You and Annie will be fine.' "

Tears still fill Joe Foglio's eyes when he remembers that call.

"Suddenly I realized how it all works," he says. "In our own times of suffering, God is preparing us to help others who we will meet along the way. When our own dreams die, God is strengthening us to be there for our brothers and sisters when they lose dreams of their own. These are tough times. Our dreams are threatened by forces beyond our control. Sometimes we lose the battle. But together we will win the war. With each other's help, we learn to dream again and then, one day, when we least expect it, we are surprised to see those dreams come true!"

3

Where Would We Like to Go?

CREDO 3

We believe that change for the better begins when we order our lives around those individuals and institutions that we value most, for example: God, country, family, friendship, school, and work.

Therefore, we need to decide what we want to be and do, and we need to arrange our goals accordingly.

Late in the spring of 1955, growers in the state of Washington's Yakima Valley issued an urgent call. Workers were needed to harvest the year's bountiful crop of Bing and Queen Anne cherries. The Daughery family made their meager yearly income following the harvest. So they packed their few belongings and rushed to southeast Washington. In the spring, the rolling hills around Yakima Valley turn snow white with cherry and apple blossoms. When the wind is blowing, you can smell those fragile, fragrant flowers all across Benton and Yakima counties.

Jack Daughery was just ten years old, but already he had worked five hot summers in those sweet-smelling orchards near the Snake River. At dawn that first morning of the cherry harvest, Jack finished the pancake breakfast his mother had prepared for their family over a camp cook stove. Sitting on the steps of their migrant shack, the bright-eyed child watched his father wipe streaks of white grease from an empty can of lard. With a sharp knife held in his leathery red hands, Jack's father poked two holes in the side of the can, threaded a piece of rusty wire through the holes, and tied off the loop long enough so that the can would hang from Jack's neck to just below his waistline.

"Perfect fit," his father said as he stood back to admire his handiwork.

The loud honking of a grower's truck broke the early morning silence.

Jack's mother took her son's hand and led him down the gravel road toward the nearby orchards. Jack still remembers walking beneath those cherry branches bending under their load of deep purple fruit:

"I was no taller than a yardstick, but I could stand on my tiptoes and pick handfuls of cherries to fill my little lard bucket. The first few days, half the berries would go into the bucket and the other half would disappear into me. Bright red cherry juice would run down my chin and stain my face and fingers.

" 'We can't put you on the scales, son,' my father warned good-naturedly as we stood in line to dump the fruit we had picked into the large boxes where they were weighed and sorted.

"We were migrant workers," Jack explains. "And we were totally dependent on the money we made harvesting fruit or working in the fields from Coalinga, California, to the Canadian border. Because we were paid by the pound, every cherry I ate affected the family's income.

"More often than not," he says, "we lived in shacks, tents, or hot, airless trailers with hose showers and portable toilets. Mom kept us clean and patched, but we dressed in tattered jeans, old cotton work shirts, and shoes that were scuffed and worn. We ate in the fields or on the open road. We traveled in caravans of used cars and old trucks loaded down with all our worldly possessions, rushing from farm to farm, looking for 'pickers wanted' signs, feeling dusty, poor, and exhausted most of the time."

Jack doesn't remember exactly when he began to dream of a better life. He does remember, even as a child, hating the field bosses and the "fat-cat" owners.

"I remember one time in California," he says with a touch of melancholy. "My folks and I were picking cherries in a hundred and ten-degree heat while the owner's kids swam in an Olympic-size pool behind their mansion. I was twelve or thirteen at the time. I remember standing in the fields, angry and jealous, watching the maid serve lunch to the owner's children.

"Even as a teenager, I decided that *my* family would not have to pick cherries or apples in the blazing sun. Somewhere out there was a better life and I would find it. My migrant-worker parents were good people who lived honorable, hardworking lives, but I wanted something more. Watching those owners and their families made me angry at first; then, slowly, I began to realize that I wanted the same opportunities for my family. That's when I began to dream of owning my own business."

"I want something more!" "Dreaming of owning my own business." Sound familiar? You don't have to be the child of migrant workers to know that feeling. For some of us, wanting something more was a dream passed on to us in earliest childhood. My own father said over and over to me, "Rich, one day you will own your own business."

Did your father say things like: "Daughter, one day you'll be the first woman president of the United States"? Or did you hear your mother say, "Son, I expect one day to be sitting in the front row when you win your Oscar, your Emmy, your Pulitzer, or even your Nobel prize"?

Some children never hear such hopeful words from parents, teachers, pastors, or friends. And so they never dream that they, too, could be a world traveler or a Catholic priest or a movie star or the CEO of a Fortune 500 company. Still, they dream: to make a few hundred dollars extra every month, to buy a car or house of their own, to get a high school diploma or a real estate license, to have a vacation in a two-star hotel or a savings account in the bank for the rainy days ahead.

Whether you want to be the first woman president or just have an evening by yourself now and then, the goals you set will make or break your future.

Remember, it's only the beginning to say, "I want to be something more" or "I want to do something better!" The American author Ben Sweetland wrote, "Success is a journey, not a destination." Dreaming is the first step of a lifelong trek away from mediocrity and failure, toward accomplishment and a sense of fulfillment and self-worth. And it's compassionate capitalism that helps make that journey possible.

Capitalism is not great because it makes millions for a handful of people. It's because it helps millions of people to be what they want to be. That's the issue behind Credo 3. What do you want to be?

If Credo 1 proclaims that we are created to dream great dreams, and if Credo 2 acknowledges that too many of us are not seeing those dreams come true, then Credo 3 raises the important question: "How?" If our dreams have been derailed, how do we get them back on the right track again?

Norman Vincent Peale once said, "Change your thoughts and you change your world." If we don't find ourselves doing or becoming all we dream, then what changes should we make in our thinking to see those dreams come true?

Too many of us have fuzzy dreams. We don't know where we are going, so why should we be surprised when we don't get there? Alfred North Whitehead wrote, "We think in generalities, but we live in detail." It isn't enough to have pie-in-the-sky dreams. We have to get specific. How can you make your dreams more specific?

Other people have no dreams at all. When I was in high school, I went to an assembly that featured a slide presentation by a young man who had set twenty "almost impossible" goals for his life. At just eighteen years of age, he had set a goal to travel all the way around the world like his hero, Phineas Fogg. Somehow he had accomplished that goal and was in my high school auditorium showing us slides of his journey, "Around the World in Eighty Days."

I sat in that hard auditorium seat wondering what my goals would be and why I hadn't made them. I was barely getting through school. My grades were mediocre, my attendance record average. My teachers and principal were not impressed. In fact, I wasn't impressed. The night after that assembly I began to write down goals for myself.

Most of us live defensively. Every morning we get up without a goal and wonder why we go to bed that night with nothing accomplished. Life becomes a kind of obedient drudgery. We do what our parents demand, what our teachers assign, what our boss orders, what our family or friends expect of us, and what the church or government requires. We let law determine our morality and tax credits limit our charitable giving.

Writer, actor, producer, philanthropist Bill Cosby said it this way: "I don't know the key to success, but I know the key to failure is trying to please everybody."

Do you remember that *Saturday Night Live* expression: "Get a life!" It isn't a bad idea. And it starts with those two simple but devastating questions at the heart of Credo 3. What do you want to be? And what do you want to do?

It's your life. The clock is ticking. The seconds are disappearing even as you read. Stop. Grab some paper and a pen. Write at the top of the page: What are my life goals? What kind of person do I want to be? What exciting, fulfilling, profitable things do I want to do during my short span on planet Earth? What am I doing to accomplish those goals today, in the next week, the next month or year?

Do it! Really. Stop right now and spend a few minutes thinking about the goals that direct your life. Write them down. But don't put away that pen or pencil. Indulge me one more time. Look over your list and circle the most important goal on the page. Read it to yourself out loud. Then ask yourself this question: What am I doing to reach that goal today? If you aren't sure, make it up! Now, don't rest until you have taken at least one short step today in the direction of reaching this most important goal in your life.

By the way, if you said your first goal is to make more money and your second, third, and fourth goals are to do the same and ditto to the last six goals on your list, you may be in trouble from the start. In my experience, people who set out just to make more money seldom succeed at it, whereas people who know why they need more money and what they want to do with it are more likely to reach their goals.

Dr. Stuart Menn is a case in point. In 1968 he finished his medical-school residency. After two years of active service in the Air Force, he began his practice in internal medicine and pulmonary diseases. In a very short time he discovered that owning a medical practice, paying the monthly costs of overhead and the malpractice-insurance premiums, caused him to see his patients as customers, not people in need.

"I needed a second source of income," Dr. Menn admits, "to set me free to make decisions for my patients that were not so economically driven." In five years of working part-time in his own distribution business, Dr. Menn doubled an income that had required several hundred thousand dollars, four long, hard years of medical school, a year of internship, a year of residency, and several years of on-the-job training. At last he was doing what he wanted. Because he had taken the time to create a second income, he could treat his patients without worrying about who could pay. He could see patients in a more leisurely way, and he could take time off from his practice to pursue his special interest in sleep-disorders medicine.

"When people take their energy," Dr. Menn told us, "and channel it into meeting their own life goals, amazing things happen."

Margaret Hardy migrated to America from Kingston, Jamaica. She met and married her husband, Terral Hardy, and worked as a legal secretary to help Terral finish his studies in construction technology at New York University.

Terral was born outside Spartanburg, South Carolina. He had experienced his share of prejudice and bigotry, but with his impressive, hard-earned engineering degree and his beautiful and intelligent bride,

Terral knew in his heart that one day soon he, too, would experience a part of the American dream.

After working for sixteen months in a prestigious New York engineering firm, Terral should have been promoted along with his white co-workers. "There was no question about it," he remembers. "I earned that new position. I shouldn't have been surprised or disappointed," he adds, "when my supervisor called me into his office to explain that I would not be promoted.

" 'You've gone as far as you can go in this office,' my boss said without shame. 'I don't like it any more than you do, Terral,' he said earnestly, 'but we just can't have black people supervising white people, can we?' It wasn't just my hopes that took a tumble that day," Terral says. "At that moment the whole American dream died for me."

Terral and Margaret Hardy needed income, but they needed much more. They needed a business where the rules would be fair, where they would be judged on the basis of productivity alone, and where they would be rewarded fairly for their efforts. Today the Hardys have their own successful Amway business, earning and giving away more money than they ever dreamed.

Leif Johnson was an optometrist when he began his own distribution business. He had earned the required eight-year medical degree to help guarantee a quality of life for his six growing sons, and he hoped to raise extra income along the way to assist others in need. But higher insurance rates, increased government intervention, and rising overhead were forcing Dr. Johnson to work longer and harder with even less time and money to use for his family, let alone to give away.

Leif's wife, Beverly, a gifted musician, had been working as a music professor at Azusa Pacific University when she experienced a difficult divorce. She continued to build the Amway business she had started with her former husband. "Teaching in a Christian school doesn't pay much," she remembers. "I needed to supplement my income to help support my two children, and I wanted to help the talented music students that I taught with financial aid as well."

Beverly Johnson feels strongly that direct sales businesses such as Amway offer the best possible opportunity for the single mother to make the extra income she desperately needs while still working out of her own home, where she feels safe and comfortable and available for her children.

Merging their busy lives, their growing families, and their successful businesses has not been easy, but even in the hardest times, Beverly and Leif Johnson have found an amazing amount of extra time and money to use on behalf of people in great need. Leif and Bev have underwritten scholarships for music students and athletes, founded a discount athletic-equipment store in Watts, sponsored young conductors from Eastern Bloc countries to study in the West, helped subsidize the appearances of European musicians at the Bach Festival at the University of Oregon, and have been involved in raising hundreds of thousands of dollars for Easter Seals and other causes to which they are committed.

The stories of Dr. Stuart Menn, Terral and Margaret Hardy, and Leif and Beverly Johnson are not about making money. As I said, compassionate capitalism is not great because it makes a few people millionaires. It is great because it helps millions of people to become what they want to be.

Dr. Menn didn't simply want to make more money. He wanted to be the kind of doctor who treated his patients with compassion and to do the kind of clinical research that would help people with a rare disease. Likewise, Margaret and Terral Hardy wanted to be free from injustice and intolerance, and to do something that made them proud, happy, and secure. Beverly and Leif Johnson didn't begin their businesses just to make more money. They had children to care for and causes to support across Oregon and around the world. Compassionate capitalism is not about making money, but about being free to be and to do what we dream.

These short testimonials are not meant to promote our company. There are countless opportunities outside the Amway Corporation for compassionate capitalists to succeed in this country and around the globe. "The opportunity is always there," Terral Hardy reminds us. "Don't give up. Your time is coming, but you have to be ready for it," he adds with a grin. "And when it comes, don't let it get away. We just grabbed something that we believed in, and we hung on to it and made it give us what it promised it would give. That's all."

Dr. Menn and the Hardys wanted to make extra money in order to reach deeply personal goals. Why do you want to make more money? What do you want to be and do with your life? Great goals come out of great beliefs. What do you believe in? What are the values that motivate and guide your life?

A generation ago, if you had asked a stranger on the street what were the institutions that she valued most, she would probably have answered something like this: "God, country, family, friends, education, and work!" and probably in that order. In the more recent tumultuous and cynical days following Vietnam, Watergate, the Wall Street and television evangelist scandals, things have changed. Although pollsters disagree, there seems to be more and more evidence that people are losing confidence in the institutions that once enjoyed our greatest trust.

Although ninety-eight percent of all Americans still believe in God, our mainline denominations are in rapid decline. The "Episcopal News Service," for example, reports, "A financial crisis is sending a shudder through all levels of the Episcopal Church and forcing some serious rethinking of the church's mission in today's world." The Episcopal Church recently cut its national budget by five percent and has frozen hiring and salaries.

The Presbyterian (U.S.A.) denomination is also operating under a hiring freeze and dipping into reserve funds to pay bills. Officials admit that by 1994 those reserves will be exhausted, and with offerings falling and congregations also under a cash crunch to meet their local obligations, the national cash flow could dry up.

Even the Southern Baptist Convention, with 14.9 million members, has seen its income levels drop from a growth of about eight to thirteen percent a year to current levels which don't even equal the nation's rate of inflation.

If the churches are losing membership and income offerings, political institutions have suffered an even greater loss of confidence. In a recent Gallup study only 35 percent of those polled said they had a "great deal" of confidence in Congress. When subjects were asked to score their individual senators and congressmen on honesty and their ethical standards, 76 percent ranked senators and 79 percent ranked their congressmen, "average to low."

Americans are first among the world's democracies who say they are actively interested in politics, but last in actual voter turnout. We are lucky to get fifty percent of registered voters to a voter's booth, whereas in Switzerland, for example, nearly eighty percent on average turn out to vote.

The traditional American family is also in decline. What we once regarded as the mainstay of our society has become the exception and not the rule. Between 1960 and 1980, the number of divorces in this country shot up by a hundred percent. If the numbers hold, an alarming fifty percent of all first marriages will end in divorce. That means that fifty percent of America's children will live at least part of their lives in a single-parent household.

Marriage is no longer sacrosanct. In fact, it isn't even seen as necessary. In 1970, 5 percent of American babies were born out of wedlock. By 1988 that number had increased to 26 percent. In 1970, 12 percent of America's children lived in a single-mother household, but in 1992 that number had doubled to 25 percent.

My point is not to raise moral judgments or to criticize or condemn. Although I am committed to traditional family values, sometimes divorce is the best way to protect a spouse or a child from constant conflict, violence, or sexual abuse. I wish every child had the opportunity to grow up in a home with strong and loving parents, but I have seen courageous and committed single parents raising their children well. I know divorced parents who have worked out loving, effective arrangements to share the parenting of their children to greatly limit the suffering their divorce might have caused.

Beyond marriage, even friendship is losing its place in American society. Phillipe Aries, in his classic book *Centuries of Childhood: A Social History of Family Life,* declares that "professional and family life have stifled the other activity [friendship] which once pervaded the whole of life." Apparently, we believe in friendship, but here again we just don't have enough time or energy to practice our beliefs.

As Americans seem to be losing confidence in God and the church, in their country and those who govern it, in their parents and the traditional American family, so we are losing confidence, it seems, in the other two great institutions that remain: our schools and our work.

"We have three kinds of deficits in this country," says a former secretary of education, "a trade deficit, a budget deficit, and an educational deficit." Twenty-seven million Americans are functionally illiterate, and sadly, many of them "earned" a high school diploma on their way to functional illiteracy.

"If an unfriendly foreign power had attempted to impose on America the mediocre educational performance that exists today," writes one educator, "we might well have viewed it as an act of war." Not only are schools failing, but the national dropout rate is now over twenty percent and rising. And those students who remain show signs of mediocrity in the education they receive. Most high school seniors, for example, perform below eighth-grade levels in math, and the SAT scores of current students rank well below those of twenty-five years ago.

Work, while traditionally marked last in the list of institutions we value, hardly even appears on the list anymore. Thirty-three percent of the workers surveyed recently answered simply, "I hate what I do and I can't wait to stop doing it." While even the most "trusted" institutions in America (churches and the military) enjoy the confidence of only slightly more than half the population, big business enjoys the trust of only one of four Americans.

When all added up, if the traditional institutions once basic to the lives of our parents and grandparents—God, country, family, friends, education, and work—are losing the confidence of the general population, we have at least two major problems.

First, throughout history these major institutions were the primary sources of human values. Where will we go for guidance without them? Second, they have always been the primary sources of strength and support in times of trouble. Where will we go now for help when we need it?

"Where would you like to go with your life?" is the question behind Credo 3. Before you can truly succeed as a compassionate capitalist, you need to answer that question honestly. Maybe you haven't thought much about the question of values. Maybe you've just gone on assuming that what was important to your parents or grandparents is still important to you. Maybe you still value these venerable institutions, and although you see weaknesses in them you are working to see them changed. Maybe you've given up on the old institutions and have found some new credo to guide you. Maybe you're just confused and turned off by the whole discussion, and you want simply to be left alone to make a few bucks to pay your bills and to afford a vacation now and then.

I'm not writing this book to proselytize you to my values or to convince you of my goals. That's your business ultimately. It's a very personal matter. There are successful compassionate capitalists who have come out of very different ideologies. But unless you have a set of positive values at the very core of your life, your goals will be inadequate and untrustworthy. In fact, rather than helping you succeed in life, your goals may lead you down a dangerous, destructive path.

When I was a child growing up in Grand Rapids, Michigan, every Sunday my mother would cook the family breakfast and head us toward the door. "Sunday is God's day," she would remind anyone not in the mood for Sunday school or church. "And like it or not, we're going to be there in the front row together."

I didn't have any idea what was happening to me during those early childhood years, and there were times I resisted that Sunday morning tradition with all my young heart and soul. But although I won an occasional battle, Mom won the war. Rain or shine, snow or hail, the DeVos family went to church. And during those Sunday school lessons, hymns, and sermons that seemed to go on forever, a seed was being planted in me that would permanently change my life. My parents and that long list of pastors, teachers, deacons, and lay volunteers whose names I can't even remember were passing on to me life's greatest gift: a road map to follow on my journey and a source of strength and comfort on the way.

Thanks to my mother, my value system is based on the Christian tradition. "What is the great commandment," a young lawyer once asked Jesus. What was he asking? The question behind Credo 3. What must I do to find meaning in my life? On what one commandment or value should I build my goals?

Jesus' answer was simple, but it wasn't easy. "Love God," he said, "and love your neighbor as yourself." Out of that commandment all my values come. And in the hot, bright light of his answer, all my goals should be examined. Following Christian tradition, I am on this earth to love God, to love myself, and to love my neighbor. I know I'm oversimplifying, but these are the values on which I try to base my decisions. Sometimes I succeed. Sometimes I fail. But always the success of what I do or say should be evaluated on this simple question: How well have I loved?

Robert Frost, the American poet laureate, in his wonderful work *The Black Cottage,* writes these important words: "Most of the change we think we see in life is due to truths being in and out of favor." Right now love is out of favor. If our institutions have failed or are failing, it is because they have forgotten that love comes first.

If the church needs reform, that reform begins when we rediscover what it means to love God, to love ourselves, and to love our neighbors. If the government is not doing its job, it's because those who govern have forgotten that every budget and every law should be based on love. Families and friendships that fail are those that no longer have love at their center. If you want your grades to go up and your productivity to increase, give love a chance in our schools and in the marketplace. The great renewal we need as a people and as a nation will begin when individuals in this nation's great institutions begin again to love one another.

W. H. Auden said, "We must love one another or die." I don't know exactly what it means to love one another. Do you? Almost two thousand years ago the apostle Paul came close to describing it in one of the most beautiful and instructive passages ever written.

> I may speak in tongues of men or angels,
> but if I am without love, I am a sounding gong
> or a clanging cymbal. I may have the gift of
> prophecy, and know every hidden truth; I may
> have faith strong enough to move mountains;
> but if I have no love, I am nothing. I may dole
> out everything I possess, or even give my body
> to be burned, but if I have no love, I am none
> the better.
> Love is patient; love is kind and envies
> no one. Love is never boastful, or conceited,
> or rude; never selfish, not quick to take offense.
> Love keeps no score of wrongs; does not gloat
> over other men's sins, but delights in the truth.
> There is nothing love cannot face; there is no
> limit to its faith, its hope, and its endurance.
> Love will never come to an end. Are there
> prophets? their work will be over. Are there
> tongues or ecstasy? they will cease. Is there
> knowledge? it will vanish away; for our knowledge
> and our prophecy alike are partial, and the partial
> vanishes when wholeness comes.
> When I was a child, my speech, my outlook,
> and my thoughts were all with childish things. Now
> we see only puzzling reflections in a mirror, but
> then we shall see face to face. My knowledge now
> is partial; then it will be whole, like God's knowledge
> of me. In a word, there are three things that last for
> ever: faith, hope, and love; but the greatest of them
> is love.
>
> (I CORINTHIANS 13:1–13 *New English Bible*)

Learning about love takes a lifetime. How we stumble and fail along the way. But what an incredible gift it is to have love as the great value upon which all our goals are based, all our actions measured. Now, here's where compassionate capitalism comes in. It is capitalism based on love. Compassionate capitalists do their best to love God, to love themselves, and to love each other. Love is the foundation value upon which all the rest is built.

Do you remember this old proverb: "When poverty comes in the door, love flies out the window"? Compassionate capitalists know that all this talk of love is humbug and poppycock when people are hungry, homeless, and unhappy. Compassionate capitalism reaches out in love to those in need for whatever reason and says, "Come on in. There's plenty for everyone!"

"When I was a child," Jack Daughery recalls, "picking cherries ten hours a day in the hot summer sun, I remember hating those fat-cat owners and their field bosses. And when I saw their pretty children riding ponies through the fields, I hated myself for my torn clothes and my dirty face. And if I'd thought much about God back then, I'd have probably hated Him, too, for the injustice and the inequality my parents and I suffered all through my childhood years."

At age fourteen, Jack went to work with his parents in a huge potato-processing plant in Grandview, Washington. "My first job was pulling weeds out of the fields around the old wooden irrigation flumes," he remembers. "The rats and the rattlesnakes would hide beneath the long wooden troughs. Every time I reached in to pull out the weeds and garbage, I was afraid a rat would bite off my finger or a rattlesnake would clamp his fangs into my arm.

"By the time I was fifteen or sixteen, I could hoist a one hundred-pound bag of potatoes on my shoulder and toss it around the loading dock. Eventually, after working in every job in and around that potato farm and processing plant, the owners promoted me to manager. Soon after, I married Rita, a farmer's daughter raised on the plains of Nebraska.

"Being manager of that plant was an achievement far beyond what anybody in my family would have expected of me. And I ran the place just like I owned it. I came early and stayed late. When everybody else dived out the door at the five o'clock whistle, I spent the next four or five hours being sure that everything was ready for the early morning shift. After all, I was a migrant worker's kid. I had a work-from-daylight-to-dark mentality.

"It wasn't long before I had to admit that Rita was right. I seldom saw her. We had a twelve-hour divorce every day. She was working double hours as a beautician. I practically lived at the plant. And down inside, I was growing more and more discontent. I was failing as a husband and a father, so how could I love myself? I was putting in a twelve- to fourteen-hour day and getting no thanks for my labor from my employers or the workers in my charge, so how could I love them? And God was growing more and more distant. I had no time to love or hate Him. He just kind of disappeared from my life."

Jack and Rita began to search for a business of their own that could help them claim a life of their own. When they found it, they embraced it and gave their lives full-time to it. Their sponsors in the Amway business showed Jack and Rita a kind of love they had never known from their bosses in the cherry fields or the owners of the potato-processing plant. The community of friends and co-workers they discovered in the business reached out to the Daugherys to celebrate their victories and to give them comfort in their times of loss.

Making their new business succeed wasn't easy. They soon learned that they had to show the same kind of love to their customers and to the distributors in their new group that had been shown to them. In the beginning their new business took as much time, energy, and sacrifice as before.

"We lived in a little convenience apartment," Rita remembers. "You could sit in the kitchen and reach anything in the place. We invested twenty-nine bucks and a few years of hard work to see our dreams come true. At first we worked regular jobs in the daytime and our own little business at night and on weekends. Eventually we both worked full-time on our business. It was difficult at first, but at last we were together. And today that 'little' business does millions of dollars a year. And even more important, that little business does not belong to someone else. It is our own. Now we are free to help ourselves and to help others in ways we never dared to dream."

What are your goals? Where do you want to go with your life? Jack and Rita loved themselves enough to set some goals, to take some risks, to make some changes. In the process they learned how to love God and their neighbors. The migrant worker's kid has a six-figure income now. His children have their own pool to swim in. His church, his neighborhood, his town, and his world are better off because Jack and Rita Daughery have the free time and the money to love in practical, life-changing ways.

In a speech in 1959, when the cold war was heating to a boil, John F. Kennedy said, "When written in Chinese, the word *crisis* is composed of two characters—one represents danger and the other represents opportunity."

We live in a time when important institutions must be renewed and recreated. This is an age of opportunity, when we can forge new solutions, institutions, and approaches to the problems that confront us. In the past, great crises have created great opportunities and civilizations have surged forward with new vitality.

If we work hard to discover and practice love again in our churches, in government, in our homes, schools, factories, and offices, our economy could be turned around and our people could be set free to make life-changing goals and, with each other's help, to reach them.

Remember Jack Daughery, the son of migrant workers, who spent his childhood picking cherries in the hot sun and wanting something better! Remember Rita Daughery, who grew up on a farm in Nebraska hoping that one day she would have a business of her own. Compassionate capitalism reached out to the Daugherys, and their hopes for a better life came true.

4

Why Is Money So Important in Helping Us Get There?

CREDO 4

We believe that getting our finances in order—paying off our debts, learning to share with others, setting financial limits and faithfully living with them—is the beginning of getting our lives free to move forward.

Therefore, we need to get our bills paid and our financial priorities in order.

On a balmy North Carolina evening in the fall of 1972, Hal and Susan Gooch drove slowly by the Finch mansion in the center of Thomasville. Hal was just twenty-five years old and fresh out of military service. Susan was twenty-two, a computer operator in a large mirror company in an industrial park near their apartment. Hal worked for his father in the family furniture business. Often as the young couple drove past the twelve-acre Finch estate, they would ask themselves if they would ever be able to fulfill their really big dreams of home and family.

"The Finch family owned Thomasville Furniture," Hal remembers. "There were only sixteen thousand people in our little town, and six thousand of them worked for Mr. Finch. No wonder he could build such a mansion."

"They were one of the wealthiest families in our town," Susan recalls, "and on many of those warm Carolina nights we rode by their fifteen-thousand-square-foot house wondering if we would ever have enough money to live in such a wonderful place."

"I was making a decent income in my dad's little furniture business," Hal explains. "It wasn't much, but it should have been enough. And Susan had a good hourly job to help supplement our income. But by the end of each month—I should say at the beginning of the month, just after our regular bills were paid—there would be almost nothing left."

Hal and Susan Gooch still remember those nights long ago when they dreamed and wondered if they would ever have enough income to move out of their $55-a-month rental, let alone into the mansion of their dreams. Then, on one of those strange, wondrous nights, a dream began to grow in Hal's and Susan's hearts.

"We will not just own some big house one day," Hal whispered. "We'll own the Finch mansion right here in Thomasville." Susan smiled, squeezed her young husband's hand, and wondered if they would ever get all their bills paid and their finances in order, let alone own a multimillion-dollar mansion.

Do you know that feeling? You have a dream, but you wonder if you will ever be able to afford that dream? If you are employed, do you find it more and more difficult to stretch your paycheck for another thirty days? If you're unemployed, do you feel a wave of fear every time the postman comes? Do you see your dreams for a new house or a new car or a family vacation or even a small savings nest egg being eroded by the deluge of bills that flood your mailbox every month?

"We didn't have college degrees," Susan explains. "Our folks weren't rich. There were no wealthy aunts or uncles waiting in the wings. Costs kept rising and our net worth kept going down."

"If we were going to see our dreams come true," Hal remembers, "we would have to make more money. There just didn't seem to be any other way. Money seemed to be our only answer."

Money! Albert Camus, the French existentialist writer, wrote in his *Notebooks: 1935–1942:* "It is a kind of spiritual snobbery that makes people think that they can be happy without money." Dorothy Parker once told a fellow journalist that the two most beautiful words in the English language are "check enclosed." Margaret Thatcher, the former British prime minister, once said, "No one would have remembered the Good Samaritan if he'd only had good intentions. He had money as well."

Money! Whether you agree with St. Paul in his letter to Timothy that "the love of money is the root of all evil," or you applaud George Bernard Shaw's reply, "Lack of money is the root . . ." you will probably agree that getting and spending money (or worrying about getting and spending it) consumes a major part of our every waking day and often keeps us sleepless through the night.

The good news is this: there are plenty of ways to make more money. But the bad news follows: before you launch a new business or get ahead in the old one, you need to get your finances in order. There is an old saying that too many people refuse to heed: "If you can't get by on the money you're making, you won't get by on more." Jesus said it this way: "When you are faithful in little, you will be faithful in much."

"People don't solve old money problems by rushing into new ones," advises Bill Britt, one of Amway's most successful independent distributors with an organization that includes hundreds of thousands of people across North America and around the world. "First things first," he adds.

"People with financial problems must get their old bills paid, or at least have a plan and a schedule for paying them," adds Jim Janz, one of Amway's most successful distributors in Canada. "Then they are ready to move on, to take new risks, to begin new ventures."

Let's be honest. Most people make a mess of handling money. The problem is simple: they spend more than they earn. But solving the problem is not so simple, especially after the fact. Once an avalanche of bills has you buried, it seems impossible to dig your way out again. Once you've made a mess, fear, guilt, and feelings of helplessness tend to plague your every thought and action.

In *Of Human Bondage,* Somerset Maugham wrote, "Money is like a sixth sense without which you cannot make a complete use of the other five." Apparently, too many people have failed miserably to develop Maugham's sixth sense, and the consequences in their personal lives are staggering.

Let's look at the numbers. According to the experts, the average U.S. household owes $71,500 in total debt, including their home mortgage. Doesn't seem like much money to you? Compare it to German families, which owe on an average of $27,700, or—are you ready for this?—to the Swiss, whose average family debt comes to a staggering $800 total.

Credit card addiction and abuse have become a major source of new debt for the American spender. There are more than 1.3 billion credit cards in circulation just in the U.S., and eighty percent of all American adults have at least one credit card. And what a business credit cards have become! In one recent year, American Express alone had an annual charge volume of approximately $100 billion. At least 75 million Americans were behind in their credit card payments. A typical card holder owed $2,474 in card debt and annually paid $465 in finance charges at an average interest rate of 18.8 percent.

Unfortunately, there is no easy solution to millions of Americans being billions of dollars in debt. Credit card addiction and abuse can only be solved one person at a time. Are you addicted to the joy of using plastic? Have you dealt honestly with your own addiction? There is an easy way to find out. Answering the questions below should get you started.

How many credit cards do you have? How much debt is outstanding on each of them? Have you added it up? What kind of interest and penalties do you owe? Have you added that up? What is your total credit card debt today? If your income holds steady, how long will it take for you to pay off those cards if you don't use them again? If your income drops or ends, how will you pay them off, let alone keep up with the accumulating interest? How much more can you realistically afford to charge in the meantime?

College students are the new "priority market" for credit card companies. Already 3.9 million students have at least one credit card—that is, 70 percent of the nation's 5.6 million full-time students at four-year colleges. That's an increase in youthful credit card holders of almost 40 percent in the past two years alone. Most cards are offered without requiring a co-signer; nor do applications have income or savings requirements built in. The plastic plague threatens to undermine the nation's economy, and the plague is spreading downward to younger and younger victims.

American students make an average $153 a week from their part-time jobs and from their parents. They may spend only $105 a week on entertainment, clothing, and other consumer goods, but when you total it up, that's $60 billion a year and credit card companies want their share.

An economics teacher at Texas Tech University told the *Washington Post* that she's found that students in her classes have as many as ten credit cards, each with a $1,000 limit. "I've seen kids with $50,000 to $70,000 in debt," she admits. "They spend the money on clothes, pizza, tuition, books, fun, travel, presents for girlfriends, shoes, watches, engagement presents, proms, formals. Kids just go haywire. There's no financial basis for these kinds of consumer transactions."

One of the parents interviewed for the *Post* article came to this interesting conclusion: "The best marketing agent for old-fashioned values was my first-grade teacher," she says. "Miss Billard handed out our savings books every Wednesday, so we could watch our pennies grow. Now our kids watch the government deficit grow. Why should they practice self-restraint?"

Blaming other individuals or institutions for our financial problems is a dangerous game, but in this case the frustrated parent may be on to something. The folks we've sent to Washington to represent us are not exactly setting a good example for Americans, young or old, to follow. If you think individual credit card users are acting irresponsibly these days, look at our government's use of their giant plastic in the sky.

Beginning in 1895, the U.S. had its first trade surplus, and that surplus continued until 1988. For decades we were the source of the world's credit. Now, suddenly, we've become the nation most in debt. In 1990 alone our trade deficit exceeded $100 billion. In 1991 it increased another $279 billion. Today the U.S. government's total debt is estimated to be in excess of 3.5 trillion dollars. We could pay it off if every man, woman, and child in America had an extra $12,000 to send to Washington. But we don't. Too many Americans owe too much on their own credit cards.

So, how do we get started on the road to personal financial recovery? During our interviews with Amway's most successful distributors I found them to be in general agreement with the following five steps: first, pay off your debts; second, learn to share; third, save at least a little money every month; fourth, set strict limits on your spending; and fifth, learn to live within those limits.

Aristotle said, "What we have to learn to do, we learn by doing." The best plan for paying off your debts and getting your financial life in order will be the plan you discover for yourself by doing it. But maybe one or two ideas will help you along the way.

Pay Off Your Debt

There is a story about an English nobleman who had fallen on hard times. When approached by his tailor to pay his debt or at least to pay some interest on it, the Englishman answered, "It is not my interest to pay the principal, nor my principle to pay the interest."

Although it isn't as easy for you to get a creditor off your back as it was for that pompous lord, it may be easier than you think to get your debts paid and your personal finances in order. Recently I had a long conversation with the credit manager of a department store in Grand Rapids. She was quite positive about the way most of her overdue customers were handling their debt.

"A good customer will notify us when she is going to be late in making the full payment," she told me. "Then, to show good faith, she will enclose a check or money order with that written notice to cover at least a percentage of the amount that is overdue. We see that kind of person as a responsible customer worthy of our trust. And we will do everything in our power to help that customer get through her difficult financial times. However, when customers don't write or call us, when they don't send us at least some small amount every month, eventually we have to call in the professional collection agencies. And those folks don't mess around."

When I asked her what steps she would advise people to take in order to get their debts paid, she answered: "First, get people to add up what they owe. Second, have them figure out the weekly or the monthly payments that they can afford to make. Third, be sure they notify (or negotiate with) their creditors to see that the payments are adequate. Fourth, remind them to make those payments faithfully. And fifth, tell people to start living within their means so that they won't get into this kind of mess again."

It seemed like good advice to me. What do you think? Do you have considerable debt? Do you have a plan in place for paying it off? Have you been in contact with your creditors to get them on your team? Have you been making your payments faithfully? Are you living within your means? I know this little plan seems simplistic. But it is a plan. And any plan is better than none.

After Ron Rummel got his degree in architecture from Texas Tech, attended Cambridge on a Rotary scholarship, and spent a year living abroad, he returned to America excited about his future and eager to begin. Ron soon landed a good job with a prestigious architectural firm. About the same time Ron's wife, Melanie, signed a contract to teach language arts and science to fifth- and sixth-graders. Then, without warning, the world oil markets crashed. Suddenly the boom in Dallas turned to bust. Ron and Melanie found themselves out of work and deep in debt. Melanie's MasterCard was revoked, and every other credit card in her wallet was charged to its limit.

"It had taken me six years to get through college," Ron recalls, "with a lot of well-educated people showing me how to make eight hundred dollars a month as an architect. Then, when everything crashed, I found myself listening to a twenty-six-year-old dropout's presentation of the Amway marketing and distribution plan. I signed on," Ron admits, "with just two goals: to pay off Sears and to spend more time with my family."

He isn't joking. To pay off credit card debts is a major goal for tens of millions of Americans. Taking on a second job to accomplish that goal has become commonplace. "I worked my Amway business just like I worked my other job," Ron explains. "We postponed buying almost everything we wanted or even needed and worked seven nights a week, twelve hours a day to pay off that debt."

In the process, Ron and Melanie Rummel have accomplished far more than getting their bills paid and their credit cards back on line. They have built a hugely successful business that allows them the freedom to spend quality time together with their children, to be compassionate with the needy in their neighborhood and around the world, and to never again feel the stress of credit-card or any other kind of debt.

Before we can take any step forward into the future, we must be responsible for the steps we've taken in the past. If you need a more complex plan to get you out of debt, your banker or a local credit manager will help you. There are all kinds of books and tapes, seminars and counselors, to assist you along the way. But accomplishing solvency is no different from accomplishing any other goal. You have to have a plan and then work at it.

There is one plan that will not work. The American humorist Artemus Ward described it: "Let us all be happy and live within our means, even if we have to borrow the money to do it." Borrowing money is not the way out of debt. It is the way in. And credit cards have become the nation's primary way to increase personal debt. Solving our individual credit card problems may not be a cure-all for personal debt, but it is an excellent place to begin.

Add up your credit card debt. If you don't know what you owe on every card, call the bank's 800 number and find out your current balance. Then add up what you owe on all your cards together. Next, add that figure to your mortgage payment, car loan, old student loans, and any other debts you have outstanding.

With so many credit cards in our wallets and purses, it's hard to keep track of totals. But once you get that awful number written down and in your head, once your bottom-line deficit is really clear, then you may be motivated as you have not been before to quit using your cards and to come up with a realistic plan to pay off that debt.

Write the total amount you owe on pieces of marking tape. Stick them on every credit card you carry. Use Post-its to attach the total amount you owe to your refrigerator or dashboard. You could even write it with soap on your bathroom mirror or carve it with a penknife into those rubbery covers of your checkbook.

Ignorance may be bliss, but it's also the last step before bankruptcy. Once you're aware of what you really owe, you're on your way to controlling your spending and to the end of your debt. Just for fun, the next time you are tempted to use the little plastic card, read the sign taped across its surface (or quote it from memory). "I owe $4,321 on this card alone and $74,000 all together."

Then, before you use your card again, close your eyes and ask yourself these questions: "Is this purchase worth it? Do I want to add to the debt I already carry? Or can I get along without it?"

Locate and examine all the credit cards you currently own. Place them in long lines on the floor of your living room. Now cut up the cards that are out of date. Even though they have expired, keeping them around is dangerous. Crooks love to fiddle with other people's plastic. Dump them.

Find out which of your active credit cards carry the lowest interest rate. Sometimes you really have to search to discover the rate of interest you're paying, but usually you can just phone the bank's 800 number and ask. Shopping for a low-interest card can save you thousands of dollars over the next ten years.

Teresa Tritch, writing in *Money* magazine, reminds us that if you maintain a credit card balance—that is, if you don't pay off the card every month—"you'll nearly always save more during the year by choosing a low-rate card, even one with an annual fee, over a high-rate card with no fee."

When you add up the costs for maintaining credit card debt, they are staggering. "On a $1,200 average balance," Tritch points out, "your annual interest cost on a major bank card at 19.8 percent comes to $237.60." She adds, "You're probably paying an annual fee from $18 to $20 as well."

Refuse to pay annual fees. Don't worry, the bank is still making money from the merchants. If you find a fee on your bill, call the toll-free number and ask to have the annual fee waived. If they won't listen, tell them you're going to cancel their card. Then watch what happens. However, if they insist on collecting the fee, dump them.

Carry no more than two or three credit cards. Robert McKinley, publisher of "Ram Research's Bankcard Update" newsletter recommends one no-annual-fee card with a grace period for purchases you plan to pay off in full each month and a low-interest-rate card for purchases you want to finance, ideally also without an annual fee. Keep a third low-rate card for business use only.

Don't just cut up your surplus cards. Pay what you owe. Notify the bank that you are canceling their card. Watch your bill carefully to make sure they don't add a fee to your monthly payments that keeps the card active even after you've said you want it canceled. Then cut up the card and mail it to them.

Do you think I'm going overboard on this credit card issue? Not on your life. Turn to the business page in your local paper. Read the headlines. Credit Card Delinquencies Increase 30%. Credit Card Delinquencies Hit Four-Year High. Moody's Investors Service in New York reported recently that 6.13 percent of all credit card users were at least thirty days behind. That means roughly 82 million of the nation's 1.8 billion credit cards are in arrears.

How many individuals or families does that represent? The Moody analyst explains one of the reasons for the continuous rise in delinquencies. "Many of the recently unemployed are using credit to get through until they get their next job." When their credit limits are reached and there is no new job on the horizon, the debtors are forced into personal bankruptcy.

"That surge in delinquencies and personal bankruptcy filings," warns Moody, "has precipitated a forty-two-percent increase in the amount of card debt that banks have charged off to uncollectable." The credit card divisions lose huge sums of money for their sponsor banks. The consequences for the financial future of the nation and even of the world are really frightening. Even as I write, bank examiners are warning that hundreds of American banks with more than $600 billion due from their customers are teetering on the edge of failure.

Are you a credit card junkie? Do you need a division of Credit Card Users Anonymous established in your town? It seems so easy to get a $100 cash advance every few days with your credit card at a local ATM machine, especially when you need the money. But what is going to happen when you have no way to repay what you owe, let alone the eighteen to twenty percent interest that is accumulating daily on your debt? What will happen to you and your family when the bank fore-closes?

Don't think for a minute that just because bankers write off certain bad debts as uncollectable they won't come after you. They will! And once your banker sees you as an enemy, he can make your life miserable. He or his collection agent will try to repossess everything you own. Not only can your credit be ruined, sometimes for life, but you may end up in deep trouble with the law and even serve time in jail.

So, a word to the wise. Using a credit card for a purchase or a cash advance when you don't know how you will repay it is bank robbery pure and simple. When we spend money that isn't ours, we take a terrible risk for our future and the future of our children. Whatever we do as individuals or as a nation to create debt must be faced responsibly. We cannot move forward effectively until that debt is paid.

Share with Others

Most of my friends and co-workers in our business agree that paying off your debts is one of the first steps you take toward success as a compassionate capitalist. That's no surprise. But a large majority of them also agree that learning to share with others, even before we can "afford" it, is something a compassionate capitalist does even while paying off debts.

Paul Miller, a friend in this business from Raleigh, North Carolina, believes that ninety percent of the American people wind up financially under the gun at age sixty-five. "We're victims of the 'acquiring syndrome,' " he said with a grin, "and getting out of debt is the first thing we have to teach our people." Then he added something that surprises almost everyone who hears it.

"The first step at getting out of debt," he said, "is tithing." To illustrate his point, he leans over his desk, picks up a rather worn-looking Bible, thumbs through its heavily marked pages, and turns to the last book in the Old Testament.

"God is angry with His people," he says, creating the context for what he is about to read. "They have not fed the poor, housed the widows and orphans, or cared for the oppressed," he explains. "In the third chapter of Malachi, the old prophet hears God say, 'You are robbing me!' When the people ask God, 'How?' God replies, 'In tithes and offerings.' "

Then Paul read those words of promise and warning from the great Judaeo-Christian tradition. "Bring the whole tithe into the storehouse, that there may be food in my house. Test me in this, says the Lord Almighty, and see if I will not throw open the floodgates of heaven and pour out so much blessing that you will not have room enough for it" (Malachi 3:6-10).

"People can't believe their ears when we share what happened in our lives," Debbie Miller says, "when we started giving ten percent of our income to our church and other offerings to the causes we believe in all around our community."

Later I'm going to share the story of Paul and Debbie Miller and their business success, but now it's important that we pause long enough to take seriously what they are saying about giving. "Don't wait to be generous until that time when you can afford it," Paul reminds us. "Be generous now and be surprised at what you receive in return."

The apostle Paul gave us these important words about sharing: "Every man according as he purposeth in his heart, so let him give; not grudgingly, or of necessity: for God loveth a cheerful giver" (II Corinthians 9:7).

I was tempted, as you may be, to talk about sharing at the end of the process, when there's food on the table and money in the bank. But Paul and Debbie Miller remind us that sharing is not the end of capitalism but the beginning, and it is found at every step along the way.

When we talk about sharing, about compassion, we're not just talking about donating a percentage of our profits. We're talking about an attitude of compassion that affects everything we do: the products we choose to develop and market, the plants we build and the machinery we place in them, the raw ingredients we use and the wastes we create, the advertising and marketing campaigns we approve, and above all the people whose lives we touch, our families, our personnel, our customers, even our competitors.

If we are always waiting for that day when we'll have extra money to share, we may never do it at all. Paul and Debbie's idea that we should be generous from the beginning, because in the long haul we will receive in kind, should be taken very seriously.

You don't even have to be a Jew or a Christian to practice the art of sharing. You don't have to read the Old or the New Testaments to have experienced the good that sharing brings to those who receive and to those who give alike. The American poet Ella Wheeler Wilcox wasn't quoting Jesus when she wrote these words

> So many gods, so many creeds,
> So many paths that wind and wind,
> While just the art of being kind
> Is all the sad world needs.

In my experience, whatever their religious background, those people who share generously from the beginning of their business are the ones who succeed at it. They are the ones who are thought of with affection and gratitude by customers and competitors alike.

After all, when it's all over, how you are remembered makes all the difference, and we determine those memories from the beginning. "The purpose of human life," wrote Albert Schweitzer, "is to serve and to show compassion and the will to help others."

You remember Schweitzer's story. He was an accomplished doctor and research scientist. He was one of the world's great interpreters of Bach and gave organ recitals in cathedrals all over Europe. His philosophical speeches and writings were revered even while he lived, and yet he spent most of his life as a missionary doctor in the tiny village of Lambarene in the Gabon province of French Equatorial Africa.

There on the banks of the Ogowe River, Dr. Schweitzer built a hospital for his "forgotten people." The world remembers him not for his achievements in music, not for the books he wrote or the Nobel Peace Prize he won, but because he shared his life generously with those in need. You don't have to be a missionary doctor to do that. A compassionate capitalist has the same opportunities presented to her every day of her life.

"That best portion of a good man's life," wrote Wordsworth, "his little, nameless, unremembered acts of kindness and love." Few of us will ever achieve Schweitzer's fame or Wordsworth's eloquence. It doesn't matter. Even they point out that fame is an illusion. What's really important is sharing just for the joy of it. Most of our little acts of sharing will go unremembered, but we still do them. Not just because they are good business, but because they give honor to our Creator. They give hope and help to those in need and a sense of joy and self-worth to us. The radical social critic Ivan Illich said these unforgettable words: "Man must choose whether to be rich in things or in the freedom to use them." Every little act of sharing, especially when we "can't afford it," sets us free!

Save a Little Every Day

My mother gave me my first bank, one of those hand-painted cast-iron beauties with moving parts. I could roll the coin down a little trough or place it in the bird's beak and press a lever that sent the coin tumbling through the slot. Once a month after school, Mom and I marched down to the local branch of the First Kent Bank and made a deposit into my very own savings account. I loved to watch the bank teller add up my deposit and write it in my little red bank book. Then she signed the book and stamped it.

Did you have a bank when you were a child? Maybe it was a decorated glass canning jar with a slot cut out of the metal top, or a colorful plaster of paris pig with *"Hecho en Mexico"* printed in purple ink on the bottom? In those days we were a generation of savers. Every family had a savings account no matter how small. And every payday the father went down to the bank to make his deposit. Even in the hardest times, every family tried to put something away every month.

Now times have changed. Americans save at a rate lower than that of any other industrial nation. In just one generation our average savings rate has fallen 6 percent. Whereas the Japanese save an average of 19.2 percent and the Swiss save 22.5 percent of their monthly income, Americans save only 2.9 percent. That means the average American household has about $4,000 put away for a rainy day while the Swiss have $19,971 and the Japanese have $45,118.

What percentage of your income do you save each month? How much money do you have in the bank to cover emergencies? Remember the basic savings rule. You need at least one month's salary in your savings account to protect you from disaster. Given that standard, are you ahead or behind?

The editors of *Where We Stand* conclude that "in the long term, diminished savings not only undermine a family's security, but also severely lessen the amount of money available for investment in a nation's future."

I know it may be hard, especially when you are in debt and your cash-flow needs seem to increase every day, but in the long haul you might be surprised how much money you can save even in the worst of times if you put a small amount into the bank faithfully every month.

The editors of *Black Enterprise* magazine recommend that every family have at least three months of expenses in a cash emergency reserve. They also suggest that families with children start a college fund by spiriting away twenty dollars every week in a "conservative growth mutual fund" yielding about ten percent a year. In fifteen years, they say, you will have earned thirty-five thousand dollars.

Unfortunately, money from your savings account may be needed before the kids get to college or before your retirement begins. Health-care costs are staggering. The costs of home or auto repairs are going up every day. Who knows what extra money you will need to get you through the next crunch? Whatever the needs, most people aren't prepared to meet them because they've lived beyond their means and there is nothing in the bank.

Do you remember the name S. S. Kresge? He was born to a poor family in the heart of the Pennsylvania Dutch country just after the Civil War. He began his career as a traveling salesman for a hardware company. Kresge was excited by the plan of Frank Woolworth to do cash-and-carry merchandising in little stores across the country, and by 1932 Kresge owned more than several hundred stores of his own.

Kresge was a strong advocate of savings. According to his biographers, he had "a lifelong ambition to make money and an obsession to keep it." At the end of his life he was one of America's wealthiest men, and yet he gave up playing golf because he couldn't stand to lose the balls. He would wear a pair of shoes until they almost fell apart. And when the soles got so thin that water would leak in, Kresge would line his shoes with old newspapers. His first two wives divorced him, citing his stinginess as their major complaint.

Today the Kresge Foundation is a giant among America's philanthropic institutions with a reputation for generosity and vision second to none. Years after his death, Kresge is giving his money away. Universities, hospitals, and service organizations across the nation are benefiting now from his frugality then. Still, I can't help asking, wouldn't it have been more satisfying for Mr. Kresge to learn to share while he was still here to reap the joy of it? At least that's a question we all need to ask ourselves, especially during these difficult times when so many individuals and charitable institutions are in need.

Set Financial Limits and Live Within Them Faithfully

In one of her speeches to the House of Commons, Margaret Thatcher said it simply: "I belong to a generation that doesn't spend until we have the money in hand." Whatever you think of the prime minister's politics, it's time we seriously considered the wisdom of her words.

Two problems follow. First, most people don't know whether they have the money in hand or not. How could they? They usually don't have a clear idea of their bank account balance, let alone of what they owe. Second, they never make up a personal or a family budget, and if they do, they don't live within its limits.

So without a budget, even if they have the money in hand, they don't remember that most of that money is already designated to pay off debts, to share with others, or to add to savings. So they go on spending, like drunks on a binge, and wonder in the morning why they find themselves with such a terrible headache.

If you don't have a budget, why not spend a Friday evening or a Saturday afternoon having a budget party? The rules are simple: to set financial limits and to live within them.

Sit down with your family. (If you are single, you can even play the game alone. If you are married without children, play it as a couple.) Be creative. Make it fun. Have refreshments. Give prizes. Reward the players (or yourself) with a special event like going to a movie or to the beach when it's done. (Be sure it's in the budget.) Money talk doesn't have to be torture. It can be fun. Try it!

Level 1. Add up all your regular monthly expenses, including those bills like insurance or taxes that may be paid every six or twelve months but that need to be included in the budget now.

Level 2. Add in the amount you need to pay on past debts, the amount you want to share with others who have needs even greater than your own, and the amount you want to put into savings.

Level 3. Subtract the total of those items in levels 1 and 2 from your monthly income. If you have any money left over, you can allocate some to each member of the family for discretionary spending or for paying off your debts more quickly or for sharing it with others in need.

If you don't have any money left—or worse, if you don't make enough money to cover the costs—then it's time to bite the bullet, to reduce spending. At this point you may be tempted to think about making more money. Don't yield to that temptation, because you'll be tempted to spend money you haven't earned yet. And that's exactly how we got into this mess in the first place.

Level 4. Get the family in a circle. Bring out the old family Bible. Have everybody put his or her hand on the Bible and right hand in the air. Then repeat these words one by one around the circle: "I (add your name) promise that this month I will spend only what I have agreed to in this budget. So help me, God."

At the end of the month, when the money has been spent and the totals are in, you reconvene for the next level of play, the follow-up. It's easy to make up a budget. It's difficult to follow through faithfully to live within its limits.

Level 5. Honor those who have kept their promise to the family to spend only within their limits; question those who have overspent; discuss their reasons until everyone is satisfied; penalize those who have spent beyond their limits from their next month's allocations; decide together what budget items should be added, dropped, increased, or decreased; pledge again your promise to be faithful in the month ahead.

To avoid end-of-the-month conflict, you might consider calling emergency family meetings during the month to discuss expenses that arise that are not included in the budget and to come to some kind of compromise agreement.

OK, I admit it, the whole idea of a couple or even a family working this closely and this carefully on a monthly budget is somewhat of a fantasy. Nevertheless, something has to be done to set our limits together and to monitor whether or not we are living within those limits faithfully.

Too often we don't talk about money until it's too late. We spend and spend and spend until suddenly the debt and its interest threaten our future. Then we begin to blame each other for spending too much. We shout. We call each other names. We curse and leave the room or even come to blows. Money talks should be held early on because when they come too late, they may lead to the end of our most cherished relationships. They may even lead to violence and to death. The data are clear. More relationships are ruined and even ended over money than over any other issue including sexual infidelity.

Remember Hal and Susan Gooch? I began this chapter with them standing beneath a great oak tree looking up at the Finch mansion, wondering if they would ever have enough money to pay their bills, let alone to live in that great house. I wish you could see them now, just twenty years later. They got their bills paid and their finances in order. They started their own little Amway business and worked hard to make it grow. Today that business has spread across all fifty states and fifty-four countries. And that house of their dreams that began as a small summer cottage for the owners of Thomasville furniture, that grew into a sprawling mansion, is now the home of Hal and Susan Gooch and their eighteen-year-old son, Chris.

Their story is not unique. I've seen it happen time and time again. People dream big dreams. They begin to take money seriously. They don't spend more than they earn. They get their bills paid and their finances in order. They start a savings account and put something away, even a small amount, every week. And they learn to share their blessings, to give money away to those in need even when it isn't easy or convenient. And in no time at all, they see their dreams come true.

Of course, there are sacrifices along the way. Hal Gooch loves to fish more than any man I know. His one prized possession in those early days was a little fishing boat that he had to trade for a used motor home so that he and Susan could travel back and forth across the state and around the country helping their business take root and grow.

"Hal's friends all teased him when he sold that boat," Susan remembers. "They predicted that the business would fail and that Hal would never fish again, at least not from his own boat. But we needed that motor home," she explains. "We couldn't travel with our small son and not have a regular place to stay. The hotels and motels were too expensive."

"I had to fish from the beach for a while," Hal remembers. "I had to be satisfied with flounder and channel bass in those days. Selling my little boat wasn't easy, but it was worth it. Today, Susan, Chris, and I own a sixty-foot Carolina cruiser named *Diamond Lady*. Now, we're fishing for five hundred-pound marlin together as a family because we dreamed big dreams and paid the price to see those dreams come true."

Like the Gooches, Larry and Pam Winters, who live in Raleigh, North Carolina, had little or no money when they began to dream. Larry ran a car wash and Pam was the car wash cashier. They still remember those lunch breaks long ago, sitting on a bench overlooking the car wash, eating egg salad sandwiches, wondering if they would ever have enough money to move out of their $225-a-month rental in a rundown neighborhood of Raleigh, wondering if they would ever get their bills paid and their finances in order.

Last Christmas, less than seven years later, Pam Winters stood in the kitchen of her new home in a beautiful residential district of Raleigh. Her daughter, Tara, eight, and her son, Stephen, four, were helping her cut and wrap another dozen fresh-out-of-the-oven brownies. Larry entered the kitchen carrying a bundle of new winter clothing in one hand and their two-year-old son Ricky in the other.

"For the past five years," Larry told us recently, "Pam and I have collected gloves, warm socks, thermal underwear, blue jeans and khaki pants, flannel shirts, and knit hats to give away at Christmas time. Pam puts together holiday food baskets topped with her own special home-made brownies. Our kids help us load the van with all the goodies we've collected. Then, along with other friends and families in this business, we drive to downtown Raleigh or Charlotte looking for people who are not going to be sleeping indoors on Christmas Eve."

Less than a dozen years after their car wash days, Pam and Larry Winters are financially independent. Now they own their own business and they are free to spend their time and money at Christmas and throughout the year doing what they always dreamed.

"We couldn't help anybody back in those car wash days," she adds. "We had too many money problems of our own. And like everybody else we were bombarded with ads for those get-rich-quick schemes that you see marketed on late-night television or in the Sunday classifieds. How quickly we learned to avoid those folks who promise you almost instant wealth by selling you foolproof kits and promises. Beware! The promises may be half-truths, hyperboles, and even lies, while the kits are expensive, difficult to use, and almost impossible to return."

"When we first heard about beginning our own distribution business," Larry adds, "we thought at last we found the quick and easy way to make some extra money. We liked the products and the marketing plan. We thought people would rush to buy those products and to join me in starting businesses of their own. We spent money on equipment and supplies. We furnished a little office and put in new telephone lines. I quit my old job in the car wash, made a few presentations, and waited for the phones to ring."

"We began our little business in 1980," Pam continues, "and by

1985 we were worse off than we had been before. Instead of instant success, we couldn't even pay our phone bill.

"Before we could reach our financial goals," she continues, "we had to listen more carefully to our mentors. From them we learned that Amway or any other new business is not an easy way out of the money problem, that there is no easy way out. We had to learn to live with the money we were making before we could trust ourselves to live with more. We had to make our budgets and pay our bills. We had to get our finances in order and they helped us do it."

"Whenever we got afraid or discouraged," Larry recalls, "we went to our new friends and mentors in the business. They taught us these three amazing principles: first, that we live in a country where anything is possible; second, that the opportunities are out there if only you're willing to look for them; and third, that God is no respecter of lazy persons. If you give generously and work hard, if you treat people right, then God's laws of prosperity will work for you, whether you're black or white, fat or skinny, rich or poor, tall or short, ugly or good-looking. It doesn't matter. If you go out and give yourself away, if you do good things, good things will happen to you.

"So we quit hoping that other people might save us from our financial difficulties," he says, "and we went to work to save ourselves. By 1988 we had paid off every debt. By 1989 we bought a new car and moved into our new home in one of Raleigh's best neighborhoods. By 1990 we were financially independent and free to use our time and money in any way we wanted."

"Once we learned how to help ourselves," Pam says, "then we could teach other people to help themselves. Again our friends were teaching us that if we wanted to really help someone, we shouldn't just give him money. We should help him help himself. In the past few years we have had the opportunity to help hundreds, maybe thousands of couples in their 'car wash' stage to find their own way to financial independence.

"Still, there are people out there," she reminds us, "who need help. That's what is so wonderful about having money. You can help people who cannot help themselves."

On Christmas Eve, 1991, Pam, Larry, and their three children set out for downtown Raleigh. They drove through the colorful, well-lit neighborhoods with holly wreaths on the heavy paneled doors and decorated Christmas trees in the draped and leaded windows. They passed the last-minute shoppers loaded down with gifts wrapped in gold and silver paper rushing toward their high-rise condos. Larry finally slowed the van when they entered that part of town that is shadowed from the sun by tall buildings and dark clouds of despair.

"The children were the first to notice the small, ragged group of men standing around a flaming barrel," Pam remembers, "their cold bare hands held out to the orange flames."

"Gloves," little Tara said excitedly.

"Gloves," Larry answered, slamming on the brakes and rushing around to the back of the van to get the bag of lined leather gloves he had purchased from an army surplus store.

"Don't forget brownies," Stephen said, climbing down to help.

"Brownies," Larry repeated, digging out some food bags that would get these men through Christmas dinner.

For several hours the family drove up and down the streets of Raleigh's skid row, stopping here and there to drop a load of Christmas cheer to those in need. Then they saw an African American woman with two children huddled on a steaming grate near a Chinese laundry.

"For a moment," Pam remembers, "we just sat there looking at this poor woman and her children. It was a cold night. They were bundled together trying to keep warm. I wondered how I would feel if I were in her shoes, sitting there on Christmas Eve with nothing to give my children, no way to keep them warm. I felt angry that this kind of suffering could go on right here in the richest country in the world. Then our little daughter whispered once again to her daddy."

"Gloves," she said with a catch in her voice.

"Gloves," Larry repeated, and the two of them walked to the back of the van, loaded their arms with food and clothing, and stepped up to that cold cast-iron grate. The woman just sat there staring as the packages were opened. Then, quickly, as though wakened from a dream, she began to dress and feed her children. Larry took his daughter in his arms and started to move back toward the van.

"Thank you," the woman said quietly. For a moment nobody moved. Our daughter said, "You're welcome." The woman smiled. Larry could see the sun's last rays reflected in her tired, wet eyes, and the mixed joy and sorrow of that moment reflected in the faces of his children.

PART II

Get Set!

5

What Is Work and How Can It Enrich Our Lives?

CREDO 5

We believe that work is good only if it leads the worker to freedom, reward, recognition, and hope.

Therefore, if our work is not satisfying (financially, spiritually, psychologically), we need to end that work as quickly as we can and begin work that is.

Dark rain clouds hung low over the Hanford Nuclear Reservation. A summer storm was brewing. Ron Puryear drove his 1963 Rambler station wagon toward the guardhouse just as lightning lit up the morning sky and thunder rolled in the distance. Clipboard in hand, a uniformed security officer spotted Ron's security badge, stooped to get a confirming eyeball ID, and waved him through.

"I was an accountant," Ron recalls, "with a government contractor in the Tri-City area of Washington state. I had advanced through the ranks and held a responsible middle-management position. All my life I had been taught that success and security would come if I got a good education, found a good job, and worked hard at it. That morning as I drove to my parking place in that giant nuclear-research facility, I was convinced that I had paid my dues and found the American dream."

As Ron entered the massive office complex that Friday morning, he saw shock in the faces of his co-workers and heard anger in their voices. On most Fridays, friendly greetings echoed down the long, gleaming corridors. Anticipating the weekend, workers normally waved and smiled across the chest-high office dividers. That morning they were clustered in small groups, whispering among themselves as though the president had died or war had been declared.

"I remember sitting down at my desk with a sudden sense of dread. A long envelope from personnel relations lay on my desk with my name typed on it in bold print. The pictures of my beautiful wife, Georgia Lee, and our two children, Jim and Brian, smiled up at me."

That morning, along with 2,100 of his co-workers, Ron Puryear learned that his services, "though valued by his employers," were no longer required. The private nuclear company had lost its government contract. No one had believed that day would ever come. Nuclear energy was the wave of the future. Ron had felt uniquely blessed to have a job that was so secure.

"Then, out of the blue, reality dawned," he remembers sadly. "After all those years of hard work, they just handed me a pink slip and it was over. I was good at what I did. I was loyal. I had donated hundreds of extra hours to the cause. I took work home to meet their deadlines. But none of it mattered. 'Dear Mr. Puryear, we are sorry to inform you that . . .' "

At the end of the day, Ron said sad good-byes to old friends, collected his severance check, walked through the corridors one last time, and drove home to face his wife and family with the bad news.

Ron got his pink slip over twenty-five years ago. Today, as I write, the U.S. Post Office has announced the layoffs of thirty thousand people, and General Electric has handed notices to another forty-five thousand workers. Unemployment in the United States has reached almost eight percent of the work force, and more than fourteen percent of this nation's population live below the poverty line.

With more Americans applying for unemployment checks this month than last, it may seem a strange moment to suggest Credo 5, "We believe that work is good only if it leads the worker to freedom, reward, recognition and hope." Who cares about quality work? When you're unemployed, you're glad for any work at all.

And the action premise that completes this credo may seem totally ridiculous in these troubled times. If I'm getting a regular paycheck and I'm meeting my monthly bills, who cares if work "is not satisfying (financially, spiritually, psychologically)"? With so many workers unemployed and so many jobs disappearing, who would dare "to end that work as quickly as you can and begin work that is"? I'm working, you might say, and that's all that matters.

Only, it isn't all that matters. Being unhappily employed may cost you in the long run far more than your paycheck is worth today. But don't worry, if you are unhappily employed but hanging in there, you are among the majority of this nation's work force.

In a recent *Industry Week* survey, sixty-three percent of the respondents said that they did not get satisfaction from their work. As a popular bumper sticker proclaims: "A bad day at the beach is better than a good day at work."

In 1989, "American Demographics" reported that overall job satisfaction had dropped another five percentage points. Only forty-one percent of the office workers surveyed reported that they were "very satisfied" with their job. According to a 1989 Office Environment Index released by Steelcase, Inc., one of our Michigan neighbors, those with the lowest levels of satisfaction are "unionized workers, secretarial and clerical workers, younger workers, and those with lower incomes."

Since the beginning of time, work has been for many people a terrible, inescapable fact of life. The ancient Greeks thought that the necessity to work was proof that the gods hated them. The Romans felt the same way. The word for work, in both of those civilizations, came from a root which meant "sorrow." The Romans felt that work demeaned intelligent people. They thought that only the contemplative life (thinking, not working) deserved respect.

In the Middle Ages, work was dirty and difficult. Peasants spent their lifetimes shoveling dirt, getting it on their shoes and underneath their fingernails, smelling it on their skin and picking it out of their hair. And ordinary people didn't even get paid for all that shoveling. They worked because they had to. Life was work and work was life. They could not leave the jobs they had inherited from birth and go somewhere else. They usually were born, worked, and died on the same tract of land—land that they could shovel but could not own.

About the time of the Renaissance, ideas about work began to change. People like the Roman Catholic scholar Thomas Aquinas began to think that work wasn't so bad after all. Maybe God didn't hate workers. Work was a duty and a burden, to be sure, but perhaps it was a natural right as well. Gradually people's long-held negative feelings about work began to shift.

During and after the Reformation, attitudes changed more quickly. Martin Luther boldly proposed that work, instead of being a curse from God, was really a way of serving God—an act similar to worship. Luther helped give work dignity. He made it more than meaningless drudgery.

John Calvin, the Geneva reformer, advanced the revolution in thinking about work. In fact, he influenced ideas about work so much that he has been credited with planting the first seeds of capitalism. For

Calvin, work was like ministry. Work was good. He thought that people ought to work and use their abilities to the fullest.

That work could be good was a new idea in the days of Luther and Calvin. (It is a new idea for many of us still.) And if it was hard to believe that work was good, imagine people's surprise when they were told that they had a God-given right to do meaningful work, work they enjoyed, work that led to self-esteem!

People used to think that you could work only at those occupations your family or social class were supposed to do. Calvin liberated the idea of work from this bondage and encouraged people to take the greatest possible initiative, to explore their own gifts and talents and to put them to work.

Many of the ideas we have about work, including the freedom to choose any career we want, are fairly new. I am convinced that work—meaningful work—provides benefits to people that go far beyond just earning money to trade for food and shelter. And I thank Aquinas, Luther, Calvin, and the others who made it possible for me to think that meaningful work would enhance and ennoble our lives.

"When work is a pleasure," writes the Russian writer Maxim Gorky, "life is a joy! When work is a duty, life is slavery." If meaningful work makes us feel good about ourselves, then meaningless drudgery is only one step above unemployment in the misery it produces in the worker.

Think of Ron Puryear, for example. During those terrible months after getting his pink slip, he filled out endless application forms. Without work, meaningful or not, a man or a woman can lose the precious sense of self-worth. When self-worth is gone, so goes the power to face problems and to solve them. But work that isn't meaningful has its own painful price.

When Ron finally found another accounting job, as treasurer and office manager of a public utility, it soon proved unsatisfying at best. Worse, he had to take a thirty percent pay cut for working twice as many hours. In addition to Ron's regular forty-hour work week, he had to spend another twenty to thirty hours on evenings, weekends, and even holidays installing a computer program that management "desperately needed on line."

"Ron hated the grunt work," Georgia Lee recalls, "but he was willing to live with the long hours and reduced pay if his family didn't have to suffer. Unfortunately, during Ron's long siege of unemployment and during those first years of hard, unsatisfying work on his new job, we were accumulating a terrible debt. We were in debt up to our ears. Our credit cards were spent to their limits, and when the monthly bills were paid, we barely had enough money left to buy groceries. I don't think we were careless with our money," she adds, "but no matter how hard we tried, Ron's checks just barely paid the bills. Before long it became more and more obvious that even though I preferred to stay home with the children, I had to find a job."

"I grew up a latchkey kid," Ron explains sadly. "At the beginning of my marriage to Georgia Lee, I swore that my children would never come home to an empty house. I would pay any price to see that their mother would be there to greet them. I promised Georgia Lee that she would never have to work again unless she chose to work after the children were grown.

"When I got my pink slip," Ron continues, "and the savings account went dry as dust, on her own Georgia Lee took a waitress job in a Denny's restaurant. That decision broke my heart."

"In our new jobs," Georgia Lee admits, "we were making money, but in many ways it was costing us more than we were making. Neither one of us liked what we were doing. We hardly saw each other, let alone our children. We were tired most of the time. Our tempers were often short. The stress led to physical symptoms. Ron was downing Tums while I was popping aspirins. Neither one of us minds hard work, but it was agony to go on day after day working at jobs that were unsatisfying at best and demeaning at worst."

The Puryears' plight is all too common in America. In a 1991 survey, sixty-four percent of Americans ages twenty-five to forty-nine said they "fantasize about quitting their jobs to live on a desert island, travel around the world, or do something else for enjoyment."

Ron and Georgia Lee hated their new jobs. They were grateful to be employed and they earned every dollar in their paychecks, but they longed to have the chance to do meaningful work, work they enjoyed. Ever had that feeling? Do you have that feeling now? Maybe it's time for you to ask yourself the question: Am I happy in my work? What kind of work would be more meaningful for you?

In a 1981 study, forty-three percent of the Americans polled said "a lot of money" was the key to making a job worth doing. By 1992, a follow-up study showed that number had jumped to sixty-two percent. But is it really just money that makes work meaningful, or is there more to it than that?

The University of Michigan asked thousands of workers to list the most important aspects of meaningful work. They checked the following eight items in this order of importance:

1. Must be interesting
2. Must receive enough help and equipment to get the job done
3. Enough information to get the job done
4. Enough authority to get the job done
5. Good pay
6. Opportunity to develop special abilities
7. Job security
8. Must see the results of his work

What would you add to the list? What would you like changed to make your work more meaningful?

Meaningful work always pays dividends beyond the paycheck when we embrace it with energy and commitment. Freud said that the urge to undertake meaningful action provides us with a sense of reality. He thought that we get in touch with the world and others through meaningful work. He taught that the urge to engage in meaningful work responds to something essential in our human nature. In fact, Freud's successors went on to speculate that this urge to meaningful work is what distinguishes us from animals.

Psychologists say that work helps us meet our needs for food, shelter, and material goods. But they also point to the benefits of meaningful work in building self-esteem. Successful people gain a sense of mastering themselves—overcoming their fears and doubts—and of mastering their environment—gaining a sense of independence and freedom from want. Work is a powerful force in shaping a person's sense of identity.

Meaningful work also gives people the knowledge that they are making a difference in the world, increasing the wealth and welfare of their nation, and achieving a better standard of living for themselves and their children.

Meaningful work provides the opportunity for people to grow and broaden their horizons: to travel, to expose themselves to the arts and music, to meet interesting people, to have experiences they could not have without the benefits of work.

Theologians have said that the need to perform meaningful work is rooted in the God-given urge to be co-creators of the earth—that by undertaking to improve our world or serve our fellow humans, we share in God's activity. Thus our work assumes a kind of holiness that permeates even the most ordinary of everyday activities.

Social scientists have said that meaningful work is a response to the needs of society. People who work provide the means by which we get the goods and services we want. In other words, when we work, we provide something of value for other people. In this sense, successful people are not just opportunists out to take advantage of the public. They succeed because they operate with values that go beyond opportunism. They have a vision broader than their own needs, and they feel better about themselves in the process.

Entrepreneurs say that their enjoyment of meaningful work often springs from a deep interest in some hobby or other pursuit. We are spurred to action when we notice that something is missing in the world, and we begin to think about undertaking a project or business to fill that gap. Modern entrepreneurs often find meaningful work to be play. They take action in order to discover, or to serve, and in the process transform or improve the world.

American entrepreneurs in particular seem to be motivated to do meaningful work by the spirit of free enterprise, by the freedom of choice we enjoy and the opportunity to go as far as our ambition and hard work will carry us. At the worst financial moment in their lives, Ron and Georgia Lee Puryear discovered their own entrepreneurial spirit, and what a difference it made.

"About that time," Ron recalls with a grin, "some old friends we hadn't seen for five years called us out of the blue. They wanted to show us a business opportunity. I guess it's proof of the old axiom: Success occurs in a person's life when opportunity and preparedness meet at the same time."

"If they had called at any other time in our lives," Georgia Lee adds, "we probably would not have listened. But we had a need and they just happened to call at our time of need."

"I wanted with all my heart," Ron admits now, "to bring my wife home again. I had broken my promise. When I saw the sales and marketing plan and heard what we could make to supplement our income, I decided I would try it. Anything to get Georgia Lee out of Denny's restaurant and back with our children once again."

"I hated the whole idea of selling soap or presenting the sales and marketing plan," Georgia Lee says, grinning. "All I needed was something more to do. I was already exhausted. It was hard enough to be a waitress eight hours a day, but to go on being wife, mother, homeroom parent, cook, and cleaner had worn me down. I didn't see how it was possible to fit another thing in. Besides, I thought Ron would do it for a while and then lose interest."

But the presentation awakened Ron's entrepreneurial spirit. He realized this business opportunity just might provide the way to bring his wife home from Denny's forever. He would keep his job and work his new business only one or two nights a week. He set a realistic goal. If he could make four hundred dollars extra a month, he would be satisfied.

"When I reached that goal," Ron remembers, "I asked Georgia Lee to quit her waitress job and join me in the business."

"Scared me to death," she says. "Talk about a small thinker: that pocketful of tips had me by the throat and wouldn't let go. But Ron was very persuasive. The next thing I knew, working together we were supplementing Ron's income by a thousand a month, then two thousand. I was no salesman," Georgia adds, "but Ron asked me to establish some retail customers and I did it."

"We had reached our first goal," Ron recalls. "Now we needed to solve the second biggest problem in our lives, paying off the credit-card and installment debt. So, Georgia Lee and I set a goal together for the first time in our business to pay off all the bills and get ourselves out of debt. When that goal was reached, we thought about a family vacation. We had earned one. Our savings account came next. It wasn't overnight. It happened one small step at a time. But it happened and our little business showed signs of growing big."

"We bought a Cadillac," Georgia Lee remembers, "and driving that Cadillac to work was the beginning of the end for Ron at the public utility. Even though he was being praised for his performance at work, his boss made Ron choose between our new business and his job."

"I chose freedom," Ron says quickly. "It wasn't easy to quit and to walk away from the limited security that my job provided. But I did it. With fear and trembling, we let go of our security blanket and followed our dream."

What is it about meaningful work that is so satisfying, that inspires people to take great risks? Cynics might say it is only the love of money—the lust for material possessions. But they are wrong. Meaningful work is satisfying because it is rooted in basic human needs. In my speeches around the United States I like to talk about four of these needs: freedom, reward, recognition, and hope.

Remember Ron's words: I chose freedom. He had set his wife free from a job she didn't like. He had set his family free from debts that dragged them down. Together they had increased the family income to the point they were free to take time off for a family vacation and free to put money in a savings account for future needs.

Meaningful Work Brings Freedom

Confucius and a handful of his disciples were once walking through a remote region of China when they came upon an old woman weeping beside a grave. "A tiger killed my only son," she said. "And now he lies here beside my husband, killed by the same terrible beast." "Why do you live in such a savage place?" Confucius asked. "Because there is no oppressive government here," she replied. "My children," said Confucius to his followers, "remember that oppressive government is worse than a tiger."

Ron and Georgia Lee would not have had the freedom to flex their entrepreneurial muscles under the old communist system. People had few rights in the Soviet Union, China, Cuba, and other communist countries. They didn't have the right to own their own businesses. They didn't even have the right to own property that would make a business possible. And yet private ownership is basic to freedom. Take it away and an economy is doomed to failure. Deny people the freedom to be what they want and to do what they want, and an economy will collapse.

It's useless to talk about economic freedom as separate from political or social freedom. They're not separate. People in Hungary, Poland, Rumania, Lithuania, Czechoslovakia, East Germany, Russia, and China know that the extent to which freedom is available in the marketplace is related to the extent to which freedom is available in all other areas of life. The freedom to work at whatever you want to goes hand in hand with freedom of every kind.

Meaningful work and free enterprise are part of one big package of freedoms and responsibilities—freedom to speak out, freedom to assemble, freedom to vote and to conduct political process, freedom to pray and worship as you choose, freedom to live and love without fear of interference or persecution.

Meaningful work flourishes in settings where power is distributed widely and there is opportunity for all—where there is a chance for everyone to get ahead. Citizens in formerly communist countries had virtually no freedom in any part of their lives. Become an entrepreneur? Start a business in your own home, as tens of thousands of our friends and associates have done? It just wasn't possible. Within the communist state, all of the personal economic choices we take for granted were made by someone else.

The free-enterprise system is inclusive and should embrace all people. We all have the right to work regardless of our race, nationality, skin color, regional or tribal background, religious beliefs, age, physical illness or disability, gender, or sexual orientation. Wherever freedom is denied to anyone for unfair or unjust reasons, capitalism cannot thrive.

The freedom to choose meaningful work is so fundamental that we don't reflect on it much anymore. But people who haven't had that freedom think about it all the time. When I was in school I learned about two kinds of freedom. But when I became an adult, I began to see the importance of those abstract principles in a personal way. The principles of freedom are not just words in a textbook.

I learned that one kind of freedom was "freedom from." This is the kind of freedom that we find in the Bill of Rights. It's the idea that everyone ought to have freedom from coercion by their government. Governments should not have the right to either force or prevent us from certain important acts ("Congress shall enact no law . . .").

I also learned about a second category, "freedom to." True liberty exists only when we have the freedom to achieve our goals and dreams. "Freedom to" gives us the right to exercise initiative and do something with our lives. The freedom to become an entrepreneur or choose our occupation is a freedom of immeasurable value.

True freedom encompasses opportunity, the ability to work and enjoy the fruits of our labor. True freedom provides the means to realize our dreams—not the guarantee that we will succeed, but the promise that our efforts will not go unrewarded. In countries where the government is the sole legal supplier of all goods and services, there is little or no opportunity for people to enjoy the benefit of their own work and initiative.

It has been said that freedom is "the capacity for continuous initiative." To put it more simply, when we are really free, we can always do something about seeing our dreams come true. Ron and Georgia Lee had a dream. They lived in a nation where they were free to pursue their dream, and in pursuing it they found personal freedom.

"When our business income more than doubled my take-home pay," Ron remembers, "we realized the limitless possibilities of our new business. The next thing I knew, Georgia Lee and I were treating our 'little business' like we once treated our work: full-out dreams, full-out time, full-out energy."

"We treated our business like we had treated our careers," Georgia Lee says. "We shared the sales and marketing plan four or five nights a week, and we maintained that effort for two and a half years. During that short time our income skyrocketed. We were shocked. We had no idea it would be that good, that we could get that much reward out of sharing the products and the plan that made us proud."

Isn't it amazing what earning a little money will do to liberate our entrepreneurial spirit? Let me make it clear that I'm not trying to persuade anyone to go into our business. People should go where their entrepreneurial spirit leads them. What kind of rewards would follow if you gave time, energy, and hard work to your dreams?

Meaningful Work Brings Rewards

In the 1920s, the famous American lawyer Clarence Darrow was approached by a female client whose legal problems he had solved. "How can I ever show my appreciation, Mr. Darrow?" she asked. "Ever since the Phoenicians invented money," Darrow replied, "there has been only one answer to that question."

When do people work hard? When it pays. When do people not work hard? When it doesn't pay. It's that simple. Reward is the second major pillar on which meaningful work is built. Reward people for their labor, and they will continue to produce. Take away those rewards, and production will grind to a halt. The most effective reward is money.

Individuals have financial needs. Families have financial needs. But we don't need to be reminded of that. We know from personal experience how quickly the stream of bills from our mailbox becomes a flood: taxes, mortgage, car and credit payments, loan principal and interest, food, clothing, gas, electricity, insurance, home maintenance and improvements, tuition, board and room for students, tithes, offerings, and gifts to charity, a vacation or even a night at the movies.

"Father," says Junior, "what is a financial genius?" "A financial genius, my son," answers the harassed parent, "is a man who can earn money faster than his family can spend it." The list of financial needs goes on forever. And they are not met with prizes, promises, or pats on the back. They're met with money.

You can be as idealistic as you want. Of course there are other reasons to work, important, life-enhancing reasons. Ask yourself: What's the main reason I work? For money. Communism forgot that basic truth and the system collapsed.

People work for rewards. And when they are not fair, or when they come too little and too late, or when they dry up altogether, it is impossible to keep workers enthusiastic about working. Without adequate rewards, workers grow discontented. Eventually they will put down their tools and walk away. And when that happens, the whole system goes down in flames.

Workers Should Be Rewarded for Their Work. Under communism, party bosses said, "Work hard!" And for a while the people obeyed. Then one day somebody asked, "Why? Why should we work hard when there is nothing in it for us, when there is no significant reward?" Oh, the bosses had their answers ready:

"Work for the people!"

"Work for the state!"

"Work for the future!"

But the people were neither blind nor stupid. The benefits of their labor didn't go to the people or to the state or to the future. The rewards that were supposed to go to the worker went to the communist elite. While workers suffered and sacrificed, party bosses often lived like kings and queens. They had private homes or apartments, country estates, special restaurants and shops. Meaningful work is built upon the principle of rewarding performance at every level. In the history of our great system, there have been capitalists, too, who have been greedy, who have refused to share profits fairly, who have refused to reward working people for their labor.

This takes us right back to the first pillar of meaningful work: freedom. Under free enterprise, workers have the right to organize when necessary, to fight back against unfair rewards and unhealthy working conditions. I believe in that right.

Last year Jay and I passed out bonus checks to our independent distributors and employees that totaled in the millions. Those checks were not expected. They were a special reward based on reaching various outstanding levels of performance. They were over and above all the other rewards built into our system.

Why didn't Jay and I pour all those extra profits back into the business? Because that wouldn't be fair to the men and women who helped make those profits. It was an exceptional year for our company. Our distributors worked hard to sell our products. Our employees worked hard to produce and distribute those products efficiently. Therefore, our distributors and employees deserved a reward for their success. What fun it was to surprise them with those unexpected checks. That's the way capitalism ought to work.

Rewards Are Earned in Proportion to the Amount and Quality of the Work Done. Meaningful work is built on the principle of reward, but those rewards are not handed out equally. When we gave away this year's extra bonus checks, they were not all the same size. Some checks were huge. Other checks were small.

A reward is not something you get for being born. A reward is something you earn for work accomplished. Communism, ostensibly, tried to reward all workers equally. Sounds good on paper, but in the real world it doesn't work.

If You Don't Work, You Shouldn't Be Rewarded for It. I know there are exceptions to this basic rule. Our society has people who cannot work and need to be taken care of. In that regard free enterprise has proven the most compassionate system in the history of the world. But too many able-bodied, able-minded people want to be cared for simply because they are alive, and that is not what the principle of rewards is all about.

I am thankful every day for the rewards the free-enterprise system has provided to me and my family. I have worked hard, and I have enjoyed the rewards of my labor. Americans believe deeply in the benefits of hard work. It's part of our national psyche. And we believe, in general, that a person is rewarded in proportion to her effort.

But what if you worked hard and everyone around you said, "Don't do that!" That is exactly what happened under communism. If you worked too hard, other people became angry because you made them look bad. If there is no reward for working hard, why do it? This kind of situation only promotes an equality of poverty.

Maria Sandoval and her husband, Eliseo, lived in a small village in the mountains near Saltillo, Mexico. For the first seven years of their married life the Sandovals lived in semi-poverty. Eliseo worked in a large state-run factory for a very small wage. Maria tended home and family, trying to stretch the pesos to meet her family's needs. In the depressed and managed economy in which they lived, there were few jobs available and no way to escape the cycle of poverty that had enslaved their parents and grandparents before them. Then President Salinas opened the doors to free enterprise, and Maria and Eliseo eagerly walked through.

"We are the Sandovals," Maria said softly, facing a banquet hall filled with our new Mexican distributors. Eliseo grinned broadly as his young wife described how they had become two of our first direct distributors in Mexico. Less than eighteen months before, they had been recruited by friends in Monterey. In that short time the Sandovals had worked day and night to build their business with the people in their villages and with the farmers whose thatched adobe farmhouses dot the mountainous landscape.

When Maria and Eliseo had finished their short, moving testimony, four hundred Mexican distributors jumped to their feet and began to cheer. Maria's eyes filled with tears. She clutched Eliseo's hand tightly, and together they walked across the platform in my direction.

"Señor DeVos," Maria said, taking my hand and shaking it. Then she spoke a sentence in carefully practiced English that I will never forget. "This is my first new dress," she said. "I buy it for today."

Maria was wearing a simple cotton dress and sandals. I smiled and nodded. "It is very beautiful," I said, shaking her hand and then turning to greet her husband. Maria could see by the blank look in my eyes that I didn't understand. She turned to my interpreter and spoke a few sentences in earnest Spanish. When Maria was finished, both she and Eliseo turned to watch me as the interpreter translated.

"She wants you to know that this is the first new dress she has ever bought in her lifetime," the interpreter explained, "and she wants to thank you." Maria and Eliseo were holding hands and grinning at me. Finally I understood.

For generations the Sandovals, like millions of their fellow countrymen, had suffered from grinding poverty and deprivation. Then suddenly free enterprise had entered their lives. Finally the Sandovals were experiencing the rewards of their own labor. For the first time in her life Maria had enough money in her purse to walk into a store and buy something of beauty for herself with money she had earned. Now she was standing in front of me wearing a bright yellow dress, a colorful symbol of her new freedom and the rewards it had brought her.

There was nothing to say. I just reached out and took both of them in my arms.

Meaningful Work Brings Recognition

Closely related to the idea of reward for effort is that of recognition. Without reward there is no recognition of excellence. All of us need recognition, what psychologists call "positive reinforcement." The money in Maria Sandoval's purse made her feel proud, independent, and free. But the power of a standing ovation from four hundred of her colleagues should not be underestimated.

I saw the tears well up in her eyes as she accepted the first real recognition for a job well done in her life. I saw her smile as she walked among us receiving our congratulations. It is my strong belief that reward and recognition go hand in hand. Neither is really adequate without the other.

"At the heart of this company's success," Ron Puryear explains, "is people's need to feel good about themselves. We are a stand-on-your-feet-and-cheer-each-other's-victories people," he adds, smiling. "And our cheering isn't phony or contrived. We know how hard each of us works. We know what it takes to stay motivated, to go out night after night when it's easier to stay home and watch television. We know what those first hard years cost in time, energy, and commitment. And when people achieve, we think it only fair to recognize those achievements until our palms are sore and our throats are raspy."

Ron and Georgia Lee reached one of our highest levels of achievement because they knew how to appreciate and recognize people. Financial reward may be the primary reason we work, but even great wealth will not keep us working if someone doesn't praise us occasionally. All of us need recognition.

A few months ago I flew to Bangkok, Thailand, to attend a sales conference in a local soccer stadium. That night we would honor our new distributors and recognize the accomplishments of the old ones who had achieved new sales or sponsorship levels. Six hours before our meeting began, the city was deluged with torrential rain. I thought no one would show up in that downpour. Our Thai leaders smiled and said, "Don't worry. They will come."

An hour before our meeting was scheduled to begin, I stood on the platform and watched as thousands of people began to arrive. When they found the stadium floor deep in mud, they simply removed their shoes, rolled up their pant legs, and waded out onto the field. Later, as their names were called and they walked across the platform to the wild cheers of their friends and neighbors, I knew without doubt why they had braved flooded streets and muddy fields to attend that meeting. They were there to recognize one another's accomplishments, to applaud and to be applauded for what they had achieved. No tropical monsoon could stop them.

I believe in the power of recognizing people's accomplishments. Throughout the world today, people are dying to have somebody notice what they are doing and praise them. The reason for this is not difficult to understand. Recognition builds self-esteem and confidence. It's not just puffery. The need for recognition is part of human nature, and when people don't get it, they frequently don't succeed.

When we give recognition, we say to other people, "You matter, you are doing something important." Without recognition, people lose interest in success. Without recognition, people become depersonalized and anonymous.

During a recent meeting with a government minister in Malaysia, I reminded him that in just a few weeks, four hundred Malaysian distributors would be flying across the Pacific to visit Disneyland at our expense. "Why would you do that?" he asked. "Because we recognize achievers," I answered. "It's the way we grow." For a moment he just stared at me, looking rather perplexed. Then he nodded his head and said, "We have a lot to learn."

It doesn't matter whether you are an employer or an employee. We all need to help one another become achievers. Imagine the power in a simple thank-you card or a telephone call. Pay attention to your fellow workers' accomplishments. Cheer them on. Applaud them for their victories and they, in turn, will give you the rewards and recognition that you need.

Meaningful Work Brings Hope

No freedom? No reward? No recognition? What does it add up to? No hope. Communism failed and capitalism will falter if we do not give people the ability to make their dreams come true. How long can you hang on to an impossible dream? Hope dies when there is no way of realizing our dreams. But where there is hope, anything can happen.

It has been said that there is no medicine like hope—no incentive so great, no tonic so powerful. Free enterprise and hope are inseparable. The hope that your quality of life can be improved—that you can do better financially, that you can get a raise or promotion, that you can start your own business—this is at the heart of free enterprise.

If everyone is treated like a number on a computer printout, with no realistic hope of getting ahead, what will happen? People will revolt. And as we have seen in recent years, people did. But not the kind of revolution that Karl Marx envisioned. It was an anti-communist revolution. People needed hope, and communism couldn't deliver it.

People must have hope for tomorrow or they won't work effectively. It's easier to cope with an uncertain present when you have hope for the future. If the present moment is precarious and there is no hope for the future, what are you left with? Despair.

I remember those live television broadcasts from Beijing, China, when the youth of that great land were demonstrating for democracy and free enterprise. I will never forget a Chinese teenager I saw riding on the back of a truck. He was wearing a white headband and dropping flyers into the crowd's eager outstretched hands.

"Why are you protesting?" an American journalist shouted above the noise. "We want to be free," the young man shouted back. Suddenly the truck jolted forward toward Tiananmen Square. The boy grabbed hold of a wooden railing and leaned down toward the journalist. "We want to do it like you do it in America," he shouted. Then in a cloud of dust he was gone.

Soon the brave young man and his friends would face tanks, bullets, and bayonets. Was he killed during that bloody massacre that followed? Was he imprisoned? Did he perhaps escape to Hong Kong? For a brief moment that brave young Chinese man had expressed his hope for all the people of China.

We must keep hope alive, not just in the hearts of those who still live under totalitarian regimes, but in the hearts of everyone whose dreams are struggling to come true. No longer can we speak of first-, second-, or third-world nations. Wherever there is poverty, homelessness, unemployment, or despair, we must bring real, practical, life-giving hope, or capitalism too will fail.

In the first century the philosopher Pliny wrote, "Hope is the pillar that holds up the world, the dream of every waking man." Our future, the world's future, depends on great doses of hope administered liberally wherever people, young or old, teeter on the edge of hopelessness.

In Europe, Asia, North and South America, in hotel ballrooms, large convention centers, and stadiums, I have heard the cheering voices of those who have welcomed the good news of hope. We all long for freedom, reward, recognition, and especially hope. These are the pillars that undergird meaningful work and make the free-enterprise system strong. Above these foundation stones compassionate capitalism rises like a beacon.

Almost twenty-two years ago, Ron and Georgia Lee Puryear found their career plans shipwrecked. Scared and desperate, they swam toward the light. Amway is not the light. America is not the light. The light is democracy and free enterprise, and that light is shining brighter and brighter in the most unusual places. No one nation has an exclusive on compassionate capitalism. No one people owns the map that shows the way.

Perhaps you haven't discovered your own pathway to freedom. Perhaps you don't feel adequately rewarded or recognized for your hard work and creativity. If you don't feel hopeful about your future, follow the example of Ron and Georgia Lee Puryear. What are your dreams? What kind of work would give you the chance to see those dreams come true? What do you need to change in your life to begin that kind of work? What would make you courageous (or desperate) enough to make those changes?

After a large rally in Portland, Oregon, Georgia Lee noticed a young couple standing near the empty stage. The arena was silent. Almost fourteen thousand people had come and gone. Long lines of proud, smiling couples had walked across the platform to receive hugs and handshakes from Ron and Georgia Lee. The standing ovations were over for a while. The cheering and applause had ended.

"Can I help you?" Georgia Lee said to the two young people standing there.

For a moment the two strangers just stood there holding hands and blinking back their tears. Without hesitating, Georgia Lee took their hands in hers and said softly, "It's OK. I understand."

After another long moment of silence, the young man began to speak. He shared an all too familiar story about shattered dreams and growing fear. After all those expensive years in college, after being recruited by a large engineering firm, after buying a house and starting a family, he had found a pink slip in his mailbox that same afternoon.

Suddenly the young man was almost overcome with his feelings of disappointment and anger. His wife reached out to comfort him. Ron Puryear noticed what was happening and joined the little circle.

"What am I going to do?" the young man whispered. "How are we going to begin again?"

Ron looked at Georgia Lee and smiled. Their eyes, too, were wet with tears. But their tears were tears of joy and gratitude. Ron put his arm around the young man's shoulder and quietly, confidently he began to tell the story once again.

6

What Is Capitalism and Why Is It "The Best Place to Work"?

CREDO 6

We believe in capitalism (another name for free enterprise) because it provides us and our world our one great hope for economic recovery.

Therefore, if we don't know what capitalism is or how it works, we need to find out now. Our financial future depends on it!

Ken and Donna Stewart approached a long line of travelers waiting for service at the TWA airport ticket counter in Springfield, Missouri. An agent walked up to Ken and smiled broadly. "How's your dad?" he said. "We still remember him around here, you know!" As the agent printed up boarding passes and checked the Stewarts' luggage, the two men chatted about Ken's father and all that had happened in the past twenty-five years.

"That particular agent came to work for Ozark about the same time as my dad," Ken recalls. "They worked the airline counter together when I was just a child. They were both young men with new wives and families. Apparently, they both had dreams of owning their own businesses one day. My father saw his dreams come true," Ken explains, "while that other man spent the rest of his lifetime pulling tickets and checking baggage."

Ken's father saved enough money after eleven years at Ozark Airlines to make a down payment on a laundromat near their home. About a year later, he took the profit from that laundromat and bought an empty lot across the street. "What do you say we build a house in our spare time?" he told his family. "We all chipped in to build that house," Ken remembers, grinning. "I was thirteen, with two sisters eleven and nine years old, and my father put us all to work."

One house lead to another. Ken's father worked slowly, carefully as he learned the business. Consequently, they were well-built, inexpensive homes, and they sold quickly. In a year Ken's dad had made enough profit to buy a Dairy Queen near their laundromat. More houses followed. In just a few years Mr. Stewart quit Ozark Airlines. He was his own boss now, a builder with several small businesses and houses springing up all over town.

"When I told the agent about my father's success," Ken remembers, "he smiled and said, 'I wish I had the courage to do what your dad did.' Then he shook my hand and walked away."

Both men had dreams for themselves and their families. But only one had the courage and enough understanding of how capitalism works to see his dreams come true. It's an old story. Maybe you are standing at the crossroads now, wondering which way to turn. Will you spend the rest of your life working at a job you don't like?

One way to discover what capitalism is and how it works is to try it for yourself. Ken's dad probably learned the hard way, as Jay and I did. We didn't study economics in high school, let alone get an MBA degree. I have a dozen or more honorary degrees now, but I spent my lifetime feeling bad about not finishing my college degree. Jay and I were young and enthusiastic. We just jumped into water that was over our heads. We had to learn to swim or drown. Experience was our teacher; however, if I were to do it all over again, I would spend more time reading the history of free enterprise and the stories of courageous men and women who led the way.

Maybe you didn't awaken this morning with the need to find out about capitalism or how it works. Tolstoy said it this way: "Historians are like deaf people who go on answering questions that no one has asked them." Maybe you've always hated history or found it boring. It's like the telephone yellow pages. They're boring until you need to find something in a hurry. Looking at the economic mess this country is in demonstrates clearly that we need some guidelines and we need them fast. Looking back at the history of this great economic system helps us understand the rules of the game and understanding the rules makes playing the game successfully a whole lot easier.

Worse, if so many of us go on playing it badly, we're apt to find our personal finances in ruin and our nation bankrupt. Ignoring how the system works has already cost millions of people their financial dreams. The philosopher George Santayana sounded the warning: "Those who cannot remember the past are condemned to repeat it." So, before we try to guarantee our future, let's try to understand our past.

The word *capital* comes from Latin and means "wealth." Capitalism is an economic system based on the free accumulation of capital or wealth. Ken's father accumulated two thousand dollars to make a down payment on a laundromat. The rest is history. But money isn't the only kind of capital. There is *physical* capital: natural resources and manufactured things like machines that are used in the production of other goods. There is *financial* capital: cash, stocks, bonds, etc., which can be exchanged for, or invested in, other capital goods. And I'd like you to think about a third kind of capital—one that isn't always in the books—*mental* capital. Ideas. Ingenuity. The human element in the production of physical and financial capital.

The main characteristics of capitalism are *private ownership of capital* and *freedom of enterprise.* To oversimplify, a capitalist is (1) free to own wealth and (2) free to use it. Ken's father saved a few dollars and used them to buy an empty lot. If you own capital—anything that can be used to create wealth—you are halfway to becoming a capitalist. A home, a car, a few dollars, a computer, a hammer, a telephone, stocks or bonds, a violin, a football, a paintbrush, a shovel, a notepad and a pen, are all potential tools for creating wealth.

It's a fairly new idea in history that everyone can be a capitalist. Until a few centuries ago, only a handful of privileged people had that right. In ages past, Ken's father would not have been paid for his labor, he could not have saved money, let alone invested it to buy property or improve the quality of life for himself or for his family. Let's look back at the fascinating evolution of capitalism to better understand how we ordinary men and women inherited such a priceless birthright. During our century whole nations and peoples have lost their right to participate in the free-enterprise system. By looking back at history, we help guarantee that no one will ever be able to take that right away from us again.

Using a broad definition, we could find examples of capitalism even in ancient civilizations. Egypt, Babylon, Greece, and Rome all had some form of private property and free enterprise. Early examples of capitalism are not widespread, but they seem to have been around from the beginning of time. Talent, incentive, resources, and opportunity soon create capitalists in just about any society, in any age.

Feudalism. However, it was not until the end of the Middle Ages that the type of capitalism familiar to us began to develop. Feudalism characterized most of the world during the Middle Ages. People lived in small communities spread throughout the countryside, under the authority of feudal lords whose land they worked as tenants. People in these communities had to be self-sufficient. They had to grow, make, or barter for most of what they needed.

In the late feudal period, people began to move into towns, and an economy based more on money than barter started to develop. One of the many things that happened when people moved into towns is that they began to be more specialized in what they did. Instead of, for example, raising sheep, spinning yarn, weaving cloth, and sewing the finished garment, people began to do one particular thing. They became weavers, or tailors, or wool merchants.

If feudalism is by definition disorganized—in the sense that people were spread out and there was no central government—then the movement into cities was a process of organization. Two of the many ways that cities organized themselves were to establish ruling councils and to issue coins. The use of coins for trade is a monetary system, and this made the accumulation of capital much easier and greatly facilitated free commerce.

There were no laundromats or Dairy Queens in those days. Let's say Ken's ancestor was a dairyman specializing in Limburger cheese. In a monetary system, he could sell his cheese to a merchant for money, who could in turn sell it again to others. It was no longer necessary for him to find another person who happened to have a specific good that he needed—say, milk buckets—who happened, at that same moment, to want Mr. Stewart's cheese. He could use coins to buy anything he desired, whenever he desired it. This was an advantage over the old way of exchange.

Mercantilism. As cities and their monetary systems organized further into city-states and then into nations, an economic system called mercantilism developed. The system takes its name from merchants and business people—usually small entrepreneurs like cheese sellers, cloth brokers, and grain dealers. Mercantilism became the dominant economic system in Europe from about the sixteenth to the eighteenth century.

The accumulation of gold and silver was the goal of every mercantilist, especially of the rulers of the newly emerging countries. These monarchs were increasingly anxious to accumulate gold and silver because they needed it to maintain power. Power was dependent on maintaining a stockpile of arms and professional soldiers. This took a lot of capital. And the way to accumulate it was to maintain a favorable balance of trade. When exports exceeded imports under the mercantilist system, the balance was paid in gold and silver (in the form of coins or bullion), and the exporting nation would add to its capital. Consequently, rulers encouraged people to produce goods for export and devised high tariffs to discourage imports.

Mercantilism was an improvement over feudalism. In general, it raised the standard of living, made more goods available, and began to allow the development of a middle class. But mercantilism mostly benefited a powerful elite, an aristocracy—the vast majority of people lived in poverty. Ken's ancestors, yours, and mine were still centuries from having any rights of their own to practice free enterprise or to improve the quality of their lives. Mercantilism wasn't a particularly compassionate system, but at least it was heading in the right direction.

What happened to mercantilism? It faded away due to many social and historical changes that were taking place, in addition to built-in flaws in the system. A major flaw was the assumption that the measure of real wealth was the accumulation of money and not the enhancement of individual and community life. Just owning gold became important, and it didn't matter whether you did (or didn't) do anything beneficial with it.

This is an old and persistent assumption—as old as the Bible—which long ago warned against such ideas. Some extreme believers in the gold-is-everything notion even argued that agriculture ought to be limited to export crops like tobacco, because food crops were consumed domestically and didn't generate foreign exchange. Some people didn't even bother to ask the question: If we only grow tobacco, what will we eat? Real wealth is achieved when human needs are met. *Human welfare* is the ultimate goal of economic activity. It doesn't matter how much gold is in the treasury if people's needs are not met!

Who Shaped Modern Capitalism and with What Ideas?

Adam Smith: The First Economist. The ideas that shaped free enterprise, the same ideas that guided Ken's father, that led to our success in business, came from an oddball Scotsman named Adam Smith. He was a great thinker—and something of a character. There was nothing ordinary about him, not even his appearance. He had a large nose, protruding eyes, and a prominent lower lip. He didn't have charisma and was an inarticulate speaker. He had a nervous twitch and a speech impediment. As Smith himself said, "I am a beau in nothing but my books."

Smith was born in 1723 in a little Scottish seaport named Kirkcaldy, near Edinburgh. He entered the University of Glasgow at the age of fourteen and then won a scholarship to Oxford University, where he spent an additional two years. After Oxford, he was appointed to the faculty at the University of Glasgow.

While still a teenager, Smith began to ponder this question: Why are some nations richer than others, and how do those richer nations produce more to eat, wear, and use than the others? His answer to this question led the world to the development of the free-enterprise system. A nation's wealth was not increased by the accumulation of money, said Smith, but by the *division of labor.*

The world was about to learn that the energy, ideas, and skills all waiting to be discovered in millions of people were more valuable than gold. To paraphrase Smith: the division of labor is the main cause of the increase in public wealth because a nation's wealth is in proportion to the different creative abilities of people and not the quantity of gold.

What exactly does this mean? You can find Smith's ideas in his *Wealth of Nations,* without a doubt the most famous and influential book on economics ever published. At the beginning of that book, Smith told a story to illustrate what he meant by the division of labor.

The subject of this celebrated story is a pin. The story goes something like this: A person not trained to be a pin maker might—by working very diligently and carefully—succeed in making one pin per day, from scratch. At the most, a person with some experience might make twenty. But even in Smith's day, the pin business didn't work that way.

A pin manufacturer was typically made up of workers who specialized in certain tasks. In Smith's illustration, one person might make the wire, a second person straighten it, a third cut it to length, a fourth sharpen one end, and a fifth prepare the other end to receive the head. Another two or three people might be involved in fabricating and installing the head. A typical pin might be the result of many individual workers, each with a specific task to do. In the 1700s, a small company with ten workers could turn out 48,000 pins a day. That's 4,800 each. But if every worker made pins separately, the factory might make as few as 10 or at the most 200.

Smith's little story clearly illustrates his point. When the labor necessary to complete a task or make a product is divided into specific, distinct operations, productivity soars. When it does, a nation's wealth is increased. This is how the division of labor increases a nation's wealth. But that's not all. When workers specialize, they learn to solve problems better, and the more likely it is that they will invent machines that can help increase productivity. In other words, the division of labor is also a key factor in the development of new technology.

In two words: people matter. They have a variety of gifts to contribute to the manufacturing process. Free them to develop and exercise those gifts. Smith's insight was fundamental, and it made sense of a complex system that people really didn't understand very well. But his insight didn't stop with pin factories. He had a lot more to say, not only about nations and their economies, but about people and their importance to the economic process.

Smith was curious about how people made economic decisions. This was a result of his puzzling over how they made moral decisions. Like most serious-minded people in his day, Smith started out studying for the ministry. He didn't plan to be an economist. In fact, in those days there weren't any economists. When Adam Smith got interested in what we would now call the study of economics and psychology, he pursued a major they called "moral philosophy."

Adam Smith's Invisible Hand. He had a theory about how economics and psychology work together in the marketplace. It's called the theory of the invisible hand. Smith was concerned with how people could make good moral judgments in the face of powerful, conflicting motives like self-interest and self-preservation. Also, he was also concerned with how people make good *economic* judgments under the same kind of pressures.

He argued that people do the right thing—most of the time—because each of them possesses an "inner person" who plays the role of an "impartial spectator" who approves or disapproves their actions. Smith considered this impartial spectator to be a powerful voice—a sort of loud-spoken conscience—that is tough to ignore. He saw people driven by their passions, but self-regulated by their ability to reason and their uniquely human capacity for compassion.

What's more, self-seeking people are often led by an invisible hand—without knowing it or intending it—to advance the interest of society. In the economic arena, as opposed to the moral arena, he substituted for the impartial spectator another regulating force: competition. In a free marketplace, a person's passion to get ahead is kept under control by competition.

The Role of Competition. Smith considered the competitive urge to be a basic part of human nature. And this is not bad, because it is turned into a socially beneficial force *if it is allowed free expression.* Why? Because in pitting one person's self-interest against another's, the invisible hand comes into play. The invisible hand influences what products will be produced and at what price. Smith argued that the invisible hand is a powerful force in ensuring that society gets the products it wants at a price it's willing to pay.

Smith believed that society should give free reign to everyone's desire to get ahead—to compete. Above all, he said, the government should not interfere with the expression of people's self-interest. Government should not try to legislate goodness or generosity. People are much more likely to do the right thing if they can see some personal advantage to it. He believed strongly in economic incentive.

The Need for a Free Marketplace. Smith had a well-developed conscience and a low tolerance for exploitive business practices. He was not naive, nor was he blind to the greedy practices of some merchants and manufacturers in his day. In fact, he said once that when people in the same trade got together, even for a party, the conversation always seemed to turn into a conspiracy to cheat the public. Still, he believed that the power of the invisible hand would overpower "devilish pacts" concocted by business people who were dishonest.

When businesses did make exorbitant profits, Smith usually looked to see whether government was playing a role in supporting them with some kind of law or regulation. According to him, greedy business people often looked to the government for help in maintaining their position. The government was in a position to render the invisible hand ineffective. The government could impose restrictions on trade, grant monopolies to some industries, or favor others with protective laws.

Smith did not believe that anyone should have special privileges. If businesses gave themselves preferential privileges by conspiring together, or if government granted them legislative favors or interfered in any way with competition, then the invisible hand could not work. It had to work in a context of "natural liberty," in which everyone's best interests were served. But the government had to stay out of business and vice versa. It's another Adam Smith idea we need to rediscover and rediscover fast.

Smith particularly feared unholy alliances between business and government. The government should not, he said, heed "the mean rapacity, the monopolizing spirit of merchants and manufacturers, who neither are, nor ought to be, rulers of mankind." Smith was realistic about human nature and idealistic about the necessity for the exercise of conscience in the marketplace.

Smith and Laissez-Faire. He advocated a policy of laissez-faire, meaning literally, "allow to act." In other words, in economic matters you ought to leave well enough alone. His economic philosophy was based on the assumption that the invisible hand would guide people, businesses—entire industries—with impartial efficiency, *only if they were left alone.* But in the absence of governmental interference, how does it help us prevent runaway greed?

Let's say a powerful merchant has developed a food product that is a smash hit at Mercantile High: banana Popsicles. Or, as the merchant decides to call them, Banana on a Stick. Suppose the students at Mercantile High develop a craving for Banana on a Stick and buy out his entire supply every afternoon. But the merchant—because he is both powerful and greedy—decides he doesn't want to go to the trouble of making enough of these frozen treats to meet demand. So he starts charging more for those he makes. A lot more. He's the only one making the product, so he can charge what he wants.

Along comes Ken's imaginary ancestor. He may be poor and powerless, but he notices that this greedy merchant is making a lot of money charging high prices for something that's not hard to make. What's going to happen? Competition. He is going to give that merchant a run for his money. And do you think he's going to charge more or less than the greedy merchant? Less, of course. This new competitor wants the students' business. So, as Smith might say, a man who lets his greed get out of control is soon going to find his competitors taking his business away!

Now about that laissez-faire issue. What if the principal of the school decides that only one merchant can sell banana Popsicles? Banana on a Stick becomes the official Mercantile High Popsicle, and Stewart's product, Chimp's Choice, is banned. There could be a lot of different reasons for the principal to limit sales to one merchant. Maybe he's concerned that the sidewalk in front of Mercantile High is getting too crowded with merchants and carts blocking the entrance. Or maybe the greedy merchant is a personal friend.

Whatever the motivation—safety, favoritism, altruism—the results will probably be the same: higher prices. One thing to remember about the invisible hand is this: it doesn't matter whether interference in the marketplace is for good reasons or bad, the effect is identical. In Smith's view, the invisible hand is indifferent to moral issues—it is completely unbiased. Smith believed that people have to make their own moral choices. Any attempt to legislate goodwill in the marketplace is doomed to failure. Self-interest is just too powerful, and the *only* thing that can contain it is competition.

The age of capitalism really began after the publication of *The Wealth of Nations.* Smith provided a rational basis—a way of thinking—that was a conceptual breakthrough. Up until this time, people hadn't always thought of themselves as individual agents, free to make decisions on their own. They thought of themselves as members of a community or class. With the old way of thinking, decisions were made by consensus or fiat, and the individual didn't count for much. In the world before Newton, events often seemed to happen for mysterious, unknown reasons. The world seemed to be a chaotic place. If someone was wealthy, or acquired wealth, it was because God ordained it.

How economics functioned—the process by which wealth was accumulated or acquired—was not understood. Because of this people were willing to accept poorly formulated religious explanations which had little or nothing to do with the Bible. The poor simply accepted their economic status as God's will. The powerful claimed God's authority for their carefully guarded special privileges. These explanations were seldom more than rationalized excuses for the status quo.

The idea that it is honorable to be motivated by profit—the concept that work might be a means to an end, *and not the end itself*—is relatively new. Society and the church used to condemn the profit motive as sinful and wrong.

The writer Charles Van Doren has said, "It is astonishing to realize that, until quite recently, most human beings, otherwise much like ourselves, lacked the conception that is so obvious to us of how to earn money. The phrase 'to earn a living' would have been incomprehensible to them." The only money they ever received came from selling a small portion of their produce to townspeople. This money was then used to purchase items they could not produce themselves, like salt.

Before the Enlightenment began to change ideas, there was no concept of labor as some kind of thing you could sell or attach value to. In fact, the value that was attached to a person was the kind you would attach to a cow or piece of merchandise. Your "value" was often determined solely by your status in life. For example, if someone was murdered, the murderer could either be executed or pay what was called the "body-price" of the person murdered. A noble was worth 1,200 shillings, a free peasant (like a craftsman) was worth 200, and a serf was worth nothing!

People weren't free agents who could move from job to job or company to company. If you were a serf, you were tied to the land, which you worked as your duty. If you were an artisan or craftsman, you pursued the occupation your father had. If you were a woman, you had even fewer opportunities.

Smith put things together in a brilliantly simple and powerful concept built around self-interest. His theory has the same kind of elegance that Newton's theory of gravity does. While Smith was an advocate of laissez-faire—he opposed policies of legislating morality—he was also an advocate of the highest personal standards of morality and conduct. He did not turn a blind eye to corruption or greed. It would be a mistake to use Smith's ideas as a way to rationalize or excuse those who abuse the capitalist system. Conscience was at the center of his concern. He assumed that people had inside them an urge to do the right thing—an inner voice. And upon that assumption capitalism was based.

Capitalism Under Fire

The changes in the Western world that began to occur about the time of Adam Smith were exciting and overwhelmingly positive. Unfortunately, then as today, capitalism also had a dark side, dark enough that some people thought capitalism was evil and had to be destroyed. Karl Marx was one of capitalism's most eloquent critics. Let's take a moment to look at capitalism as he saw it.

We can't blame Adam Smith for capitalism without a conscience. He argued for laissez-faire, but we know that he did not confuse the right to freedom of action with the license to exploit workers or engage in unscrupulous business practices. Some capitalists didn't get this message. In fact, a few didn't care at all about the conditions under which their employees worked. They got caught up in an atmosphere of greed. This is a legacy of suffering that we have to be on guard against. It's another one of those lessons from history to which we must pay attention.

Crisis in the Cities. Along with the rise of capitalism and the Industrial Revolution came an unprecedented rise in population. From 1750 to 1850 the population of Europe almost doubled, from 140 million to about 266 million. Improvements in hygiene and disease control reduced the overall death rate, and most of the new population growth was experienced in the cities. Millions of people either moved there or were born in new industrial centers where factories and mills were located. This created terrible slums, full of people living under horrible conditions. The cities just could not accommodate the hordes of new men and women moving in to work.

Housing in the inner cities was completely inadequate. Home-building technology lagged behind industrial technology. People were crammed into old, dilapidated buildings or flimsy shantytowns or crudely built new housing. Moving into the city could be very stressful. Even though many people were actually better off—the places they moved from were even worse—it did not seem so in a psychological or spiritual sense. The old hometowns were familiar and felt secure. People often came from small villages, with parish churches, long-established social groups (like guilds), and extended families. Living in an unfamiliar environment, surrounded by strangers, people felt uneasy, lost, and disoriented. The novels of Charles Dickens contain moving descriptions of the terrible difficulties people faced during this time.

Cities were formerly thought to be centers of civilization and culture. Some people moved to the city to escape the narrow-mindedness of country villages, to experience freedom of mind. But during the Industrial Revolution it was not unusual for people to think of cities as places of alienation. Some felt like insignificant ants in a great mass of urban workers. Cities became associated with disrupted values, anonymity, facelessness.

Even though technology raised the standard of living for most people, it also changed the quality of life in negative ways, too. For one thing, it made many feel cut off from nature, community, and even God. Writers of the time talked about how factories and mills dehumanized workers. Some people felt that machines exercised a new kind of tyrannical power over them. It was as though they existed to serve machines instead of machines serving them.

Alexis de Tocqueville thought that the increasing specialization of work was more degrading to the worker than the dictatorial policies of political tyrants. Adam Smith thought that specialization had the potential to degrade workers, too. He feared that in the absence of moral standards, workers could be abused and exploited. His fears were sometimes well founded.

Child Labor. For the first time, large numbers of people—men, women, and children—worked away from home. They worked long shifts, twelve, fourteen, even sixteen hours a day. The average work week was nearly eighty hours of either backbreaking labor or mind-numbing tedium. Sometimes workers lived away from their families altogether, in miserable dormitories.

A few cloth mills in particular were notorious for exploiting women and children. It was not uncommon for young people under the age of ten to work long hours under the less than compassionate supervision of strangers. Children were routinely beaten for insignificant violations of strict company rules. Sometimes they were beaten just to keep them awake. The story of one child worker, Robert Blincoe, who was severely abused by factory foremen, was widely written about in the 1820s. Factories were often dirty, poorly lighted, and unheated in winter. There were few laws or regulations to ensure worker safety. Industrial accidents were common.

Worker Unrest. Because people were pressed together in cities, factories, and slums, old connections broke down. Instead of feelings of loyalty to a parish church, an aristocratic lord, or a guild of craftsmen, some people came to feel bound together only by the common misery of their working conditions. People became politically active. In the early 1800s people complained, rioted, and organized. Factories and mills were wrecked by mobs.

At the height of all this activity, rumors spread among working-class people in England that someone named Ned Ludd, who was supposed to be a general or a king, was leading mobs of laborers. This was probably not true, but the rioters soon became known as "Luddites." They were bound together by their hatred of the factories in which they worked—places that seemed to them like prisons. In the midst of all this some other people turned their anger inward and wrote newspaper articles, pamphlets, and books. The most famous of those angry people was Karl Marx.

Who Was Karl Marx and Why Was He So Angry About Capitalism?

It's difficult to discuss Karl Marx without stirring up a lot of conflict. Some people think he was the devil incarnate; others think he was a great social critic. Today his dreams for a new society lie in ruin. But his critique of capitalism is still worth serious consideration.

So who was this man? To begin with, he was, like Adam Smith, a man of his times, a child of the Industrial Revolution. He was born in a small town in Germany twenty-eight years after Adam Smith died. By his early adult years Marx had come to consider religion as a tool of oppression. There were unconscientious capitalists who hid behind the facade of the organized church, but Marx did not distinguish between what they did and what the Bible said they ought to do.

If Adam Smith was the perfect example of the absentminded professor, Marx was the perfect example of the single-minded revolutionary intellectual. He lived to research, think, and write. He cared little about his living conditions, his personal appearance, or social amenities. An undercover policeman once wrote a description of Marx's apartment in the Soho district of London: "He lives in one of the worst and cheapest neighborhoods in London. He occupies two rooms. There is not a clean or decent piece of furniture in either room, everything is broken, tattered and torn, with thick dust over everything and the greatest untidiness everywhere."

Marx may have had a messy apartment, but he didn't have a disorganized mind. His ideas are challenging, and demand from us a response. And indeed, he has received many responses. There is not much middle ground when it comes to opinions about Marx's ideas.

To begin with, he was diametrically opposed to the economic ideas advocated by Adam Smith. Marx's view of the world is called dialectical materialism. He did not believe in a spiritual world. He believed in the here and now. Marx wasn't interested in talking about God, creation, or anything heavenly. He said, "For man, man is the supreme being." Marx borrowed one of German philosopher G. W. F. Hegel's methods of arguing philosophy, called the dialectical method.

Dialectic is a word borrowed from Greek, which means something like "the art of arguing." According to Hegel, the world is in a continuous process of development and change, a result of the clash of ideas, in which one particular viewpoint challenges another, and in turn a new idea is produced. For example, the idea that the good of the community should always be valued above the individual ("the thesis"), might clash with the idea that an individual's rights are always preeminent ("the anti-thesis"), and produce a "synthesis": a society that values both community and individual rights.

For Hegel, material things were less real than ideas. He believed that the mind, or thought, is the essence of the universe. But Marx's materialist mind-set focused on things that you could see and touch. For Hegel, thought was primary. For Marx, *action* was primary. He took Hegel's dialectic out of the university and put it on the street. Marx thought that scholarly contemplation was a waste of time. The prevailing economic order had to be challenged, and out of the conflict a new world order would emerge.

Marx viewed the Industrial Revolution and capitalism with the eyes of a revolutionary critic, and he did not like what he saw. He was an angry man. He did not believe that capitalism just needed a little tuning up—an adjustment here, a couple of new parts there. He believed the whole vehicle had to go: private property, private ownership of factories and the machines inside them, the political system, religion, everything.

Marx believed that competition, one of the foundations of capitalism, caused crime, discontent, inequality. He expected that people would be morally transformed when communism replaced capitalism, and competition was abolished. Marx believed that the invisible hand of capitalism had to be replaced by the strong arm of centralized control, which he called the "dictatorship of the proletariat."

In ancient Rome, the lowest and poorest class of people were called *proletari*. The idea is that these poor, working-class people—who did not own land—had nothing to contribute to the state except the labor of their children. They were like breeding cattle. Marx wanted to identify the common working people of his day with the *proletari* of Rome.

He did not care if people liked him or not. He was not interested in making it easy for anybody. He was self-assured, even arrogant. His ideas were, and are, very controversial. So what is a compassionate capitalist to think? Ultimately, this is a question you will have to answer for yourself.

But as you consider Marx and capitalism, perhaps one piece of advice will help. A theology teacher once advised his class to read one good book of heresy a year. Why? Because it helps to keep you honest. Heretics sometimes have a few insights into inconsistencies or problems in our beliefs. We don't have to buy their solution at all, or even their analysis of the problem. But neither do we have to be defensive if they occasionally have a valid criticism.

Marx was so aggressive in his criticism of capitalism that we have a hard time listening to him. Some find his religion bashing so offensive that they can't hear anything else he says. Marx is easy to dislike. Most of his assumptions have proven to be completely false. But he had important ideas that are still worth thinking about.

For example, he believed that all things in life—economics, politics, and religion—are interrelated. In rejecting his analysis of these things, we have to be careful not to overlook the importance of his wide-ranging view. Some of us may have lost touch with our consciences because we somehow have managed to forget that our business behavior and our religious beliefs are interrelated. If our business behavior is bad, it may be because our religious beliefs need to be overhauled, or if not overhauled, listened to. The same goes for our political system. We can't talk about any one aspect of capitalism as though it is isolated from the other parts of our lives.

The honest capitalist, while rejecting Marxism, needs to acknowledge that there are important things we can learn from this angry man.

First, Marx was a dedicated scholar. He wasn't always right, but he was widely read and he presented his views in thoroughly researched, carefully reasoned arguments. We can't afford to do anything less.

Second, the social conditions that motivated Marx to write were terrible. Although all the poverty and despair cannot be blamed on greedy capitalists, the desire to improve people's lives was absolutely necessary then and is absolutely necessary now. You don't have to be a communist to have this concern.

And third, Marx was single-minded and relentlessly determined to bring about change in his day. We need that same kind of determination. It is not enough to think about compassion. We must act compassionately.

Summing It Up

Guided by the principles of Adam Smith, capitalism has produced the greatest prosperity the world has ever known. There have been failures. Karl Marx was just one of the critics of capitalism who made that perfectly clear. We all know the stories of greedy capitalists, child-labor exploiters, and robber barons. Nevertheless, these are the exceptions and not the rules. Capitalism remains the only economic system that gives us hope that we can pull the world and all her people back from the brink of bankruptcy and forward into an age of prosperity and peace.

When Ken Stewart's father set out to buy that laundromat twenty-five years ago, he probably hadn't heard of Adam Smith. When Jay and I started Amway, we hadn't read *The Wealth of Nations* or thought about Smith's invisible hand. It has taken us a lifetime to understand free enterprise and the principles that make it work. But most of what we learned the hard way, Adam Smith had explained three hundred years before.

1. If you want to succeed in business, liberate other people's gifts.
2. Serve other people's needs and you'll find your own needs being met.
3. Be glad for competition. It makes the system work.
4. The profit motive is good. Accumulating wealth is necessary for a business to succeed and for a nation's people to prosper.

5. Understand and respect each individual's conflict between self-interest and conscience. Examine and re-examine your own heart and your own business practices to keep both sides in balance.
6. After the government ensures all people's basic rights to life, liberty, and the pursuit of happiness, encourage politicians to stay out of the business of business.
7. Don't be afraid when other countries begin to compete. Learn from their success. Work harder. Don't ask for favors. Pull down the walls governments would build between us.
8. Give everybody an equal chance regardless of race, creed, sex, or color.
9. And remember, *human welfare* is the ultimate goal of economic activity. It matters little how much gold is in the treasury if people's needs are not met!

The principles stated by Adam Smith made it possible for Ken's father to buy a laundromat and to succeed at his home-construction business. Those same principles are at the heart of our success, the success of Ken and Donna Stewart, and the success of millions of people like them who own successful businesses.

But that's still looking back. Let's look ahead now. Adam Smith developed those principles in the not so ancient past. How can we use them to help guide us into our not so distant future? Read them again. Ask yourself what might happen to you and to your family if you rediscovered these old principles and put them to work in your own life and business? What could happen to a world poised on the brink of bankruptcy if we all rediscovered these principles and let them guide us in the future? What will happen if we don't?

I am not a prophet of doom. I believe in the future. This is the greatest moment the world has ever known. There has never been a better opportunity to succeed in business, to see your financial dreams come true. Go for it. The principles on which capitalism is built have been trustworthy in guiding us in the past. Let us go on trusting them to guide us in the future.

The true story of Charles and Laquetta Prince from my company of friends illustrates the power of Adam Smith's capitalism to help people's dreams come true and, at the same time, the obstacles that must be overcome along the way. Charles Prince did all the right things. He went to high school, worked hard, got good grades, and graduated with honors. He had dreams of becoming a doctor, and he was convinced that in this great, free country, he would see his dreams come true.

"But I had the wrong skin color," Charles confides. "When my white classmates went to work as cashiers in our neighborhood supermarket, I was stuck bagging groceries at half the wage. By the time I got my chance at the cash register, my white friends had been promoted to management. Finally, when I struggled up the ladder and over the wall into a white-collar job, my black face guaranteed that I would always be at least one step behind in promotions, raises, and opportunities common to my white brothers and sisters."

Charles Prince was willing to work long and hard to get his medical degree. But once enough money was in the bank to begin his education, he stumbled into another barrier. Charles applied to more than fifty medical schools across the country. Even with his good grades, proven determination, and obvious gifts, his application was rejected by every one of them.

"By then I was angry," Charles remembers. "At a baseball game or civic event when the 'Star Spangled Banner' had the crowd leaping to its feet, I refused to stand. When my friends or classmates pledged allegiance to the flag, I remained seated and silent. How could I say those words in good conscience, 'with liberty and justice for all,' when I was being denied the very principles this country stood for?"

Laquetta Prince, Charles's young wife, graduated from the University of Houston with degrees in psychology and African American studies. She had been sheltered from prejudice and injustice by her family until she went to work as a child therapist. In those intimate sessions with her patients, Laquetta began to discover why so many families were plagued by instability, separation, divorce, even violence and abuse.

"When you work hard but still can't pay the bills," Laquetta reminds us, "you begin to feel helpless and angry. Though you try to keep a lid on those growing feelings, eventually they erupt, affecting those you love the most. Fathers feel humiliated and demeaned when discrimination keeps them from earning enough to support their families, let alone from becoming all they were meant to be. Mothers feel sad and helpless when they have to cart their small children off to baby-sitters while they work to help support the family. Children are left to fend for themselves and often get in trouble in the process. Slowly and painfully the family dies along with its dreams."

"People need the chance to get ahead," Charles adds. "When they can earn enough money to pay their bills and see even a handful of their dreams come true, their sense of helplessness and anger is replaced by feelings of hope and self-worth."

Charles and Laquetta Prince realized early in their marriage that free enterprise was the only sure route to financial independence. But they had to find a business based on compassionate capitalism where they wouldn't face discrimination because of race, or age, or religion; where they would be judged only by what they were able to produce; and where there were no limits built into the amount of money they could make or the power and influence of the position they could attain.

"When we saw that potential in this business," Charles recalls, "and when we realized that the start-up costs were less than one hundred dollars, we were convinced." After a decade of hard work and sacrifice, Charles and Laquetta Prince while still using their unique gifts have also built a successful Amway business. And in the process they have proved once again to racists and skeptics that people of color are equal to any challenge if only they are given the chance.

I will never forget meeting them for the first time at one of our distributor seminars in Seven Springs, Pennsylvania. At the close of my address, this attractive black couple walked across the stage in my direction. Charles Prince grabbed my hand and looked me straight in the eye. I noticed that his hands were trembling slightly, and he seemed to be blinking back tears. The crowd grew silent.

"Mr. DeVos," he began quietly, "when I first heard you talk about free enterprise, I didn't believe a word of it. Capitalism was for white, middle-class men with a degree from the right college and daddy's money in the bank. Because I was black, there was no room for me."

For a moment he paused. His wife looked up at her husband and smiled. She, too, was deeply moved by the moment.

"I couldn't pledge allegiance to this country or its flag," he said, "because I didn't think there was 'liberty and justice for all,' " he said. "But you didn't notice my skin color or ask me for a resumé. You just said, 'Come, join us.' You only asked one thing, that I produce, and you rewarded me on the same scale and by the same rules that you rewarded all the others."

Suddenly, Charles and Laquetta were standing on either side of me with their arms entwined in mine. Charles faced the crowd and said, "Now at last I can say it: 'With liberty and justice for all . . .' "

With his hand on his heart and tears spilling down his cheeks,

Charles Prince pledged his allegiance to the flag. As I stood watching, I wondered how many young people in this country or around the world who have hoped and dreamed of the promises of Adam Smith's compassionate capitalism, but have experienced the same kind of uncompassionate capitalism that Karl Marx ridiculed and reviled. We cannot afford to waste another life. The rules must be fair. The same opportunity must be offered everyone. The proof is in what happens when compassionate capitalism prevails, when we refuse to let race, creed, color, sex, physical limits, or anything else stand in the way.

Today, Charles and Laquetta Prince are recognized leaders in their community. They have succeeded in business and are using their unique gifts to help and heal a wounded nation. They are models of compassionate capitalism at work to black and white alike. I wish I could have been there that day several years ago when the chairman of the board of one of this nation's great hospitals called Charles Prince on the telephone.

"We would like to invite you," the man began, "to serve on the hospital's board of directors." For a moment Charles remained silent. Then he smiled broadly to himself and replied, "Of course. I would be delighted to serve."

Charles Prince, the man who had been rejected by almost every major medical school in this nation, served on that prestigious hospital board for four successful years and ended up its chairman. Today, in their box at the stadium, when the crowd stands before a game or concert to pledge allegiance to this nation's flag, he stands with them. And often when he says those words, "with liberty and justice for all," his eyes fill with tears of gratitude for what has been and tears of determination for what must yet be.

7

What Is a Compassionate Capitalist and Why Should I Be One?

CREDO 7

We believe that practicing compassionate capitalism is the secret to real financial success.

Therefore, we need to ask ourselves daily: "How compassionate am I in caring for my co-workers, my supervisor, my employer or my employees, my suppliers, my customers, and even my competitors, and what difference does it make?"

At sunrise, sixty-three-year-old Isabel Escamilla closed the heavy wooden door of her thatched adobe home in the mountains of northern Mexico. Wearing sandals soled with rubber from an old truck tire and a dress she had made herself from a bolt of bright yellow cotton, Isabel walked the two miles into town to buy her family's supplies for the coming week.

In the morning light she looked down the narrow, twisting road and saw clouds of dust kicked up by her neighbors on their way to work in the tile factory at the edge of town. Generations of her family and friends had given their lives to mixing the rich red clay, forming, painting, and glazing the tiles, and baking them in open kilns.

The owner of the tile factory lived in Mexico City. Isabel had heard that he and his family lived in a penthouse at the top of a building that reached to the sky. She smiled to herself imagining what it would be like to ride in an elevator fifty stories just to go to bed. In all those years she had seen the patron only one brief time as he sped by her in a cloud of dust in a long black chauffeured limousine.

Isabel and her family were very proud of the glazed tiles handcrafted in the factory. They were glad to be working, especially in these years of drought when so many people were unemployed. But Isabel often dreamed of a better life for herself and for her family, especially her beautiful grandchildren. Often at night she would toss and turn on her straw mattress unable to sleep, worried about their future, wondering if they would spend their lives as she had, walking the dusty road to the tile factory below.

She didn't want to seem ungrateful, but the pay at the tile factory was meager. What little schooling they could afford for the children had ended at the sixth grade. The young ones worked for the tile factory, collecting hard manzanita branches to fuel the kilns and digging and hauling clay. Inevitably the older ones, like their parents and grandparents before them, would spend their adult lives in the huge factory at the foot of the mountain.

Capitalism had reached Isabel's village in northern Mexico, but her life and the lives of those she loved had not been touched by its benefits. You don't have to go back to the days of Adam Smith and the Industrial Revolution to find failures of our great system. But there are also signs of compassionate capitalism breaking out all across the world and that is the story I want to tell.

What Is Compassionate Capitalism?

What is compassion? Is it only for people like Albert Schweitzer or Mother Teresa? Doesn't compassion just get in the way of business and make trouble for the rest of us? Aren't the ideas of profit-making and compassion diametrically opposed? No. Compassionate capitalism is not an oxymoron. Those two words go together for owner and worker alike. Compassion is in everyone's interest.

The dictionary defines *compassion* as "a feeling of deep sympathy for another's suffering or misfortune, accompanied by a desire to alleviate the pain or remove its cause." The opposite of compassion is mercilessness or indifference. You can see from the dictionary definition that compassion involves both a *feeling* and an *action.*

One of my favorite forums for social commentary is *Peanuts.* I remember one strip in particular. On a "dark and stormy night," Snoopy lies on the top of his doghouse almost covered in newly fallen snow. Lucy looks out the window and feels sorry for the little dog, who is hungry, thirsty, and almost blue with cold. "Merry Christmas, Snoopy," she shouts above the blizzard. "Be of good cheer!" She returns to the warmth of her blazing fire, slurps her hot chocolate, and says to Linus, "Poor Snoopy."

Linus looks out that same window, sees Snoopy's plight, feels compassion for the puppy, bundles up in a coat and mittens, and rushes a dish of warm turkey and dressing to Snoopy's aid. Both Lucy and Linus feel compassion, but only Linus acts compassionately. His spontaneous action leaves Charlie Brown's little spotted dog dancing with joy in the drifts of snow piling up on his doghouse roof.

It holds equally true that a compassionate act needs to be spurred by a feeling of compassion to be effective. Imagine how differently the "act of mercy" would have been received if Linus had thrown the plate of food down into the snow, yelling at poor Snoopy, "You dumb dog. Why can't you get your own food next time? I'm sick and tired of feeding you."

After a cold, merciless act like that, would it be surprising if Snoopy ignored the food and lay there under the blanket of snow suffering even worse despair? How would you feel if someone helped you but obviously hated doing it?

Doing something you feel obligated to do is not bad. It just isn't the same as compassion. Real compassion involves our whole being. It means to feel sorry about someone or something and to act with passion to help end the suffering and even alleviate its cause. A compassionate act comes out of a compassionate feeling. Compassion is feeling and acting together.

Now, let's ask the hard question: Why are there so many Lucys in the world, who feel sorry when they see suffering but never do anything to help, and so few people like Linus, who see a need and act creatively and courageously to meet it? Why do some people care enough about other people's suffering to act compassionately while others could not care less?

Why Compassion Is So Rare

Moses, the Hebrew leader and lawgiver, writing more than twelve centuries before Christ, described the problem clearly. According to his powerful, poetic vision of creation, the Creator gave Adam and Eve the freedom to choose between God and Satan. The Old Testament writers see life as warfare, not on a battlefield but in human minds and hearts between God's call to obedience and Satan's call to sin. The Bible's ancient stories illustrate how easy it is to follow the promptings of evil toward self-centeredness, indifference, hatred, greed, lust, jealousy, and murder, and how difficult it is to hear the voice of God calling humankind to compassion.

Jesus, the young Jewish prophet whose life and teachings led to the founding of Christianity, called his followers back to obedience and to compassion. "Love God," he said. "This is the first and great commandment. And love your neighbor as yourself." When Jesus described the final judgment, he made it clear that the righteous shall be rewarded for acting with compassion toward the hungry, thirsty, naked, sick, strangers, and people in prisons. "When you have done it unto one of the least of these," he said, "you have done it unto me."

Gautama Buddha, the Indian philosopher and founder of Buddhism, lived five centuries before Christ. Buddha abandoned a life of wealth and privilege to seek "enlightenment." At the heart of that process was a terrible struggle to free one's self from the influence of Mara, the evil one. Buddha described Mara's army of tempters as lust, dislike for the higher life, hunger and thirst, craving, sloth, fear, doubt, hypocrisy, false praise, exalting self and despising others.

Like Jesus, Buddha called for his followers to perform acts of compassion. While nursing to health one of his followers who had been neglected by the others, Buddha said, "He who attends on the sick attends on me." Buddha was a social reformer who condemned India's caste system. He argued against trying to suppress crime through punishment, arguing that poverty caused crime and that his followers should help eliminate the injustice and inequality that led to poverty and thus to crime.

Confucius, a Chinese philosopher who also lived five centuries before Christ, taught his disciples that they should direct their lives by this one Golden Rule: "Do not do unto others what you would not want others to do unto you!" In the *Analects,* the most revered scripture in Confucian tradition, this thoughtful Chinese scholar and teacher described compassion this way: "A man of humanity, wishing to establish himself, also establishes others, and wishing to enlarge himself, also enlarges others."

Muhammad, the Arab religious leader and prophet in the seventh century after Christ, also saw human life as a struggle between good and evil. He taught his followers that one's goal is to submit to the will of God in the war against evil. Alleviating suffering and helping the needy was an integral part of Muhammad's teaching. He thought praying and other religious acts were worthless and hypocritical in the absence of active service to the needy.

In the Koran, the prophet writes: "Man is by nature timid; when evil befalls him, he panics, but when good things come to him, he prevents them from reaching others." It is Satan who whispers, "Keep it." It is God who replies, "Give it to the poor." In exchange for "noble sacrifice" God promises prosperity.

Out of which great religious or philosophical tradition does the call of compassion come to you? I am called to compassion by my deep family roots in the Christian faith. But let's face it. Throughout history, millions of people have been starved, tortured, killed, and enslaved because of the misuse and misunderstanding of that same faith. But the abuses of our religious traditions should not keep us from affirming their call to compassion.

Paul, the apostle of Jesus, said it this way: "I have the desire to do what is good, but I cannot carry it out . . . and the evil I do not want to do . . . this is what I keep on doing." For those of us who honor the Judeo-Christian tradition, both Old and New Testament writers call us to compassion. Still, we fail. And in our failure we turn to God for forgiveness and for a second chance. For the followers of Buddha, Confucius, and Muhammad, also called to compassion, there is a similar history of a failure in their struggle between the forces of good and evil and a similar need to be forgiven and to begin again.

Augustine, the fourth-century Christian bishop and theologian, described this tension between God and Satan, good and evil, in his classic work, *The City of God.* We live in two cities simultaneously, he said. The visible city of man is being built by human hands of wood and stone. At the same time God is building an invisible city in the hearts of humankind. The city of man will be destroyed because it is built on the false values of power and wealth. The city of God will live forever because it is built on love. The trouble is, we live in both cities at the same time, and all too often we are blinded by the city we can see (which is passing away) to the city we cannot see (which will live forever).

Even if you are an atheist or an agnostic who doesn't know if God exists, you have felt the pressure of living in Augustine's two cities at the same time. You are probably aware from personal experience of the war within. Call it whatever you will, but you, too, know firsthand that ancient struggle.

Haven't you made a New Year's resolution and failed to keep it? Haven't you felt sorry for somebody who is suffering and yet couldn't find the courage or weren't willing to sacrifice the time or money to help end that suffering? It is much easier to wish Snoopy well from the warmth and safety of our living room than to venture out into the storm with food and comfort.

I believe that compassion is the only foundation on which we can build a business or rebuild the world's shattered economies. If we are to find a way out of the current economic chaos, we must learn to love this planet and its people as they have never been loved before. Liberty and love are inseparable concepts. William Hazlitt said that the *"love of liberty is the love of others."* George Bernard Shaw said that liberty means responsibility—that's why most people dread it. Jesus said: "Greater love has no man than this, that he give up his life for his friend." Compassion means taking responsibility for the people and the planet no matter what the cost.

A Brief History of Compassion

In spite of all resistance, compassion has managed to get a foothold in every culture from the beginning of time. The ancient Jewish people put aside ten percent (a tithe) of every harvest to support their religious faith and to care for their poor. A corner of every field was not harvested so that the poor could glean what remained to support themselves. In fact, every seventh year the fields were left unplanted to rest the soil and to allow the poor to gather whatever crops might grow up from the previous years' plantings.

Jewish philanthropy included another wise method built around the "Cell of Silence." In every synagogue a room was set aside where people could sneak in alone and unnoticed to give donations to their neighbors, who then sneaked in, also alone and unnoticed, to receive them. That way neither the philanthropic nor the needy Jew would be given praise or shame for the act.

Buddha established his belief system built around the principles of self-restraint and caring for the poor. Buddha instructed his followers to minister to others "by generosity, courtesy, and benevolence, by treating them as he treats himself, and by being as good as his word."

One of India's first recorded philanthropists was King Asoka, the last major emperor of the Mauryan dynasty. During the second century before Christ, the king was so moved by Buddha's teachings on compassion that he gave up warfare, conquest, and greed and used his money and his power to spread the teachings of Buddha to Persia, to Greece, and even to Rome.

The spirit of compassion that guided good King Asoka can be summarized in his own words: "All men are my children," he wrote. "As for my own children I desire that they may be provided with all the welfare and happiness of this world and of the next, so I desire for all men as well."

In the fourth century B.C., Alexander the Great set a Western tradition for royal philanthropy. He donated Alexandria University to the people of northern Egypt. For the next thousand years, that vast and priceless library was the center of wisdom, art, learning for the Western world. Alexander also underwrote Aristotle's Lyceum (school and library) with such generous support that Aristotle could afford to hire a thousand scholars throughout Asia, Egypt, and Greece to search out and record ideas and illustrations to support his historic writings.

The teachings of Jesus and his followers are centered upon loving our neighbor as we love ourselves. Time and time again Jesus returned to his familiar theme: feeding the hungry, clothing the naked, healing the sick, and comforting the dying. Shortly after his death and resurrection, the early Christians began to collect church funds through voluntary offerings. Deacons were elected to use these funds to care for widows, orphans, and others in need.

In later years the churches were organized into districts, each with its own hospital, an alms office for collecting and dispensing donations, an orphanage, and a shelter for babies who were unwanted or whose parents were too poor to give them the necessary care. The word *hospital* comes from the French—*hôtel Dieu* or God's hotel. It was not really a hospital as we know it, but a place of refuge for the poor and of hospitality for strangers.

Modern hospitals have their roots in early Christian charity. They began as rooms in the house of a bishop set aside where the sick and dying could be cared for, usually by the bishop himself. The first documented hospital on record was established at Caesarea in A.D. 369 by St. Basil. According to one historian, "it was a veritable city, with pavilions for various diseases and residences for physicians, nurses, and convalescents. St. Gregory called it a 'heaven on earth.' "

Turning from these ancient examples to more modern times, let's consider the true story of Sir Walter Mildmay, Chancellor of the Exchequer under Queen Elizabeth. In 1584 the queen noticed that Mildmay was absent from the court, and demanded an explanation. Put off by her suspicions, he replied, "Madam, I have been away planting an acorn, and when it becomes an oak, God only knoweth what it will amount to."

Mildmay had just founded Emmanuel College at Cambridge University. The Reverend John Harvard was one of the first graduates of Emmanuel. When Harvard was just twenty-eight, he emigrated to America and two years later he died leaving his library and half of his small estate to help endow a small college that today bears his name.

"From Emmanuel College," writes Dr. Charles F. Thwing, "came the founders of Harvard, the founders of New England, in a special sense, the founders of a new nation." It is no wonder that Mildmay didn't admit to good Queen Bess what he had done. He founded Emmanuel College on behalf of England's Puritans, and the queen was definitely not a Puritan. But those same Puritans graduated from Emmanuel, emigrated to the New World, and started colleges of their own, among them Harvard, Yale, and Dartmouth, whose graduates include Samuel Adams, John Adams, Thomas Jefferson, and Daniel Webster, to name just a few of the founders and builders of this new nation.

Compassion in America

Benjamin Rush grew up in a "New Light" revival wing of the Presbyterian church in America with Quakers, Episcopalians, and Baptists leafing out his family tree. At fifteen, young Rush adopted a personal credo that still defines the goals of the social entrepreneur: "to spend and be spent for the Good of Mankind." Rush invested his life in practical, life-changing acts of compassion.

After finishing his degree in medicine, he wrote pamphlets against tobacco, strong drink, and slavery. In 1775 he urged his fellow pamphleteer, Thomas Paine, to write an appeal for American independence that helped precipitate the revolution that set the colonies free. After distinguishing himself in the Revolutionary War, Rush went on to found the Philadelphia Dispensary (the first free medical clinic in the U.S.) and to begin an important study of mental disease and experiments in humane treatment of the insane. Rush advocated cultivation of the sugar maple tree (to free the world from dependence upon slave-produced West Indian cane sugar), urged the establishment of free public schools across the nation, and nearly lost his life rescuing Philadelphia from a terrible yellow-fever epidemic.

Millions of social entrepreneurs have followed in the footsteps of Benjamin Rush "to spend and be spent for the Good of Mankind." But American philanthropy has been distinguished by another kind of caring as well. Without business entrepreneurs, social entrepreneurs would have no way to pay the bills. Thanks to the charitable foundations of the Carnegies, Danforths, Kelloggs, Fords, Rockefellers, and thousands of known and unknown businessmen and -women like them, compassionate capitalism has a two-hundred-year legacy of caring in this nation and around the globe.

Andrew Carnegie has been called the patron saint of compassionate capitalism. Mark Twain was the first to call him saint. He began a tongue-in-cheek letter to the ex-steel magnate requesting a $1.50 contribution for a hymnbook with the words "Dear Saint Andrew." I haven't discovered whether Carnegie sent Twain the money, but it is public record that after he sold his steel company to J. P. Morgan, Carnegie spent the rest of his life trying to give away his money to those in need. His own words set a very high if not controversial standard for today's compassionate capitalists.

"This, then, is held to be the duty of the man of wealth," Carnegie wrote, "to set an example of modest, unostentatious living, shunning display or extravagance; to provide moderately for the wants of those dependent upon him; and, after doing so, to consider all surplus revenues which come to him simply as trust funds, which he is called upon to administer ... the man of wealth thus becoming the mere trustee and agent for his poor brethren."

Practicing what he preached, Carnegie founded the Carnegie Institute of Technology in 1901, and from that base began sending gifts to institutions and educational enterprises in both his native Scotland and the United States, including Booker T. Washington's Tuskegee Institute. Public libraries were Carnegie's favorite cause, and by 1918 he had established more than 2,500 libraries in small towns and cities across America. Next time you visit your library, see if Carnegie was behind its founding gift.

Dr. John Harvey Kellogg (a social entrepreneur) and *Will Kellogg* (a business entrepreneur) were both sons of a poor Seventh-Day Adventist preacher. To help support his family, the senior Kellogg ran a small broom factory, making him a social and business entrepreneur simultaneously. Dr. Kellogg, the elder of the two brothers, became physician-in-chief of a Seventh-Day Adventist sanitarium in Battle Creek, Michigan, while Will worked in a back room as clerk, business manager, and general handyman.

A strict vegetarian, Dr. Kellogg began to experiment with various grains grown to develop food preparations that would be more attractive and palatable than the typical vegetarian fare. Will Kellogg soon proved to be his brother's most creative and energetic partner in these experiments, and together they developed a number of new food products, including peanut butter (which they didn't market because they didn't think the general public would like the taste) and the first precooked, flaked cereal. Later Will Kellogg flaked, puffed, crisped, fried, and exploded rice, wheat, corn, and rye into an amazing assortment of new food products. A genius at both management and promotion, he soon found himself the master of a multimillion-dollar business empire based on breakfast foods.

As his business began to grow, Will Kellogg wrote a friend his credo for compassionate capitalism: "It is my hope that anything I accumulate can be used for the benefit of mankind." For him, charity began at home. He sponsored recreational and social activities for the benefit of his workers. Early in the Depression he instituted a six-hour working day for employees on the production line, and in 1935 he made that practice permanent. He hired men and women on the basis of the number of their dependents, giving priority to wage earners with large families.

In 1925, when Kellogg was sixty-five years old, he established the Fellowship Corporation to distribute charitable gifts anonymously. Kellogg's first projects included the funding of an agricultural school, a bird sanctuary, an experimental farm, a reforestation project, a civic auditorium for Battle Creek, a day nursery, a city market for farmers, a Boy Scout camp, and hundreds of student scholarships. In 1930 he established a second foundation dedicated to the welfare of children. Today, the W. K. Kellogg Foundation ranks among the richest and most generous charitable organizations in the world with a corpus worth roughly six billion dollars.

"A philanthropist is one who would do good for the love of his fellowman," Kellogg wrote. "I love to do things for children because I get a kick out of it. Therefore, I am a selfish person and no philanthropist."

The Social Entrepreneur

In spite of every obstacle, history is replete with examples of people who have seen others in need and acted to meet those needs with courage and compassion. These people were entrepreneurs who undertook challenge not for financial gain, but for human service. You might think that being an entrepreneur is only about making money. Well, it can be, but not always. Being an entrepreneur is a way of fulfilling your creative potential. Wise entrepreneurs understand that what they do should improve the quality of their lives and the lives of everyone they touch.

Entrepreneurship is a way of seeing—seeing a need and filling it. It does not matter whether that need is for soap (a business entrepreneur) or compassionate service (a social entrepreneur); the same kind of vision is involved. In fact, entrepreneurship and compassion go hand in hand—or at least they ought to.

The *compassionate capitalist* sees herself as a business entrepreneur and a social entrepreneur at the same time. She is in business to make a profit but is guided by compassion at every step along the way. And though some social entrepreneurs support themselves with their business skills, most are supported by the compassionate capitalist's gifts of time, money, and ideas. Throughout history are examples of compassionate entrepreneurs in all walks of life.

Edward Jenner was a nineteenth-century English physician. In his day, Europe was plagued by the disease smallpox. Almost everyone caught it and almost a third of the population either died from it or had their faces permanently scarred. Jenner investigated a belief held by some dairy farmers that milkmaids who had been exposed to cows with a disease called cowpox never got smallpox. This turned out to be true, and Jenner was able to develop a vaccine. Jenner offered his vaccine to the world and made no attempt to profit from it. He literally changed the complexion of Europe. A grateful British Parliament eventually granted him a cash award.

Three years before Jenner's death, another of the great social entrepreneurs was born. Her name was Florence Nightingale. An Englishwoman born in Italy, she pioneered the development of nursing and hospital care. She was from a wealthy family and did not need to work. She felt nevertheless that God had called her to a career of compassion.

Shocked by the poor care people received in the "sick houses" of her day, Nightingale single-handedly reformed an entire system. Well educated, highly intelligent, and hardworking, she broke through the stereotypical role of women in her day and earned the respect of people all over England and Europe.

Too often we just remember the men throughout our history who have shown courage and compassion. The "gender barrier" has not stopped people with vision and energy for compassionate action. In our own nation's history the list of women who have been courageous social entrepreneurs begins before 1776 and continues to this day.

Abigail Adams, the wife of John Adams, second president of the U.S. and mother of John Quincy Adams, our sixth president, used her prolific writing skills (and her powerful lobby with two American presidents) to champion women's rights.

Jane Addams was awarded the Nobel Prize for her inventive work with underprivileged women and children. Addams founded Hull House in Chicago, a large settlement built to assist the poor, feed the hungry, house the homeless, and educate children. Others who continued to make their living in business or the arts came to live in Hull House in order to support Jane Addams's acts of compassion.

Susan B. Anthony was a pioneer crusader for women's suffrage. Her energetic and controversial work paved the way for the Nineteenth Amendment to our Constitution in 1920, giving women the right to vote.

Clara Barton, humanitarian and founder of the American Red Cross, was known for her Civil War work as the "angel of the battlefield."

Harriet Beecher Stowe, author of *Uncle Tom's Cabin*, was a committed abolitionist who wrote, lectured, and lobbied to end slavery. When Abraham Lincoln met her, he said, "So you're the little woman who wrote the book that made this great war!" Even the man credited with emancipating the slaves thanked this social entrepreneur for leading the way.

Pearl Buck, author of *The Good Earth* and other novels of life in China, won the Nobel Prize for literature in 1938 and committed her entire fortune to the Pearl S. Buck Foundation to continue her works of compassion, especially in China, long after her death.

Rachel Carson, a biologist well known for her writings on environmental pollution, passed on her loving concern for the world's oceans to an entire generation through her National Book Award-winning *The Sea Around Us.*

During my term on President Reagan's AIDS Commission, I came across the work of just such a woman. Ruth Brinker is a San Francisco grandmother who discovered her own power to make a difference when she was sixty-six years old. In 1984 one of her young friends, an architect, came down with AIDS. She was horrified to see how quickly the opportunistic infection took hold. One afternoon she realized that her friend was too weak to prepare his own meals. He couldn't even crawl to the refrigerator to get a frozen dinner or the microwave to defrost it.

That year Ruth founded Project Open Hand. Every morning at sunrise she would prowl the produce markets for "distressed" vegetables. She prepared meals in a church basement and delivered them door to door to people afflicted with AIDS. "Some of them were so emaciated," she recalls, "they would have to crawl to where the buzzer was." When her funds ran out, she began to beg donations from people in her neighborhood.

From seven grateful clients, Project Open Hand soon grew to a charity serving eight thousand meals a day. When I first heard about Ruth's commitment to compassion, she was struggling to raise more than a million dollars a year to feed the hungry people suffering from AIDS in her city.

In its salute to Ruth Brinker, *Time* magazine told the story of two men with AIDS sitting in a tiny apartment on New Year's Eve feeling gloomy, hoping they would have the strength to see in one last new year. Suddenly the doorbell rang. A volunteer from Project Open Hand was standing in their doorway holding a large box decorated with streamers and balloons. It contained donated champagne, pâté, cheese, truffles, a hat, and a noisemaker. The men broke down and cried.

All across America and around the world, there are women and men like Sir Walter Mildmay, John Harvard, Benjamin Rush, Andrew Carnegie, the Kellogg brothers, and Ruth Brinker who have discovered their compassionate side and reached out to rescue and renew lost and broken people. In later chapters I'm going to share more of the true stories of compassionate capitalists and their effects on my life and on the people whose lives they have touched. They have taught me by their example what it means to be a compassionate capitalist. But the real question is: What does compassionate capitalism mean to you?

Who are the truly compassionate capitalists that you know? What difference have they made in your life? How could you be more like them? What would you do differently if you suddenly decided to be guided by the spirit of love where you work? What are you doing now to show compassion to your co-workers, to your supervisor, to your employees, or to your employer, to your suppliers, your customers, even your competitors? How could you do it better? I wish I could hear your story and be inspired and informed by it.

In the meantime, let's go back to Isabel Escamilla, the sixty-three-year-old peasant woman living in a village in northern Mexico. When I met Isabel, her back was bent from decades of hard labor as wife, mother, and grandmother. Until recently her life had been an endless cycle of grinding poverty and growing hopelessness. It's not that people weren't compassionate. Quite to the contrary, over the years care givers sponsored by compassionate capitalists had come many times to assist Isabel and her fellow villagers in times of tragedy or to raise the quality of life in that isolated mountain region.

Isabel and her family were grateful for the Red Cross volunteers from Holland who set up and maintained a medical clinic in their village almost every summer. She would always remember the smiling young Americans who helped rebuild their village church after the earthquake of 1983. Isabel still gets teary-eyed when she recalls the Peace Corps volunteer doctors who landed their little plane in the football field, the UNICEF nurses who vaccinated the children, and the others from Mexico City and around the world who gave money, food, and expertise over the decades to help improve life in her village.

She was grateful for them all, but when their work was over and they said good-bye and drove down the mountain, the old woman felt more helpless than before. It's one thing to help people. It's another to help people help themselves. Isabel longed for a way to do something to improve her own life and the lives of those she loved.

Then one spring day Isabel Escamilla met Juanita Avalard, one of our independent distributors who was building a sales organization of mothers and grandmothers like Isabel who longed for a few extra pesos to supplement their meager incomes and for a modicum of financial security. Isabel sat in the shadows while the young women listened to Juanita share her story. The old woman never dreamed that she could do it, but as she looked through the catalogue and listened carefully to the plan, hope began to grow in her heart.

At the end of the meeting Juanita told the woman about a sales contest promoting a new car polish in her region. The first prize included a trip to the United States, first-class hotel accommodations, and VIP treatment at a championship auto race where the Amway car was running. "I will win that prize," that bright-eyed grandmother told Juanita in excited, broken English. "I will visit America."

Isabel had never been to the United States. She had never flown in a jet or stayed in a hotel or ridden in a chauffeured limousine. In fact, she had spent her entire life in that impoverished mountain village. Since childhood she had dreamed of visiting distant places, but never before had there been an opportunity to see that dream come true.

Her friends and neighbors smiled in disbelief. Why would a gray-haired lady even think about selling car polish in the mountains of Mexico? "It's good polish. That's why," she told them. "It's cheap, it helps protect the finish, and it makes old trucks and cars like yours look new." Neighbors laughed at first, but soon the battered cars and trucks in Isabel's village and in villages up and down the mountain were gleaming like the hope in her eyes.

When I met her, she was standing on the stage of the conference center in Monterey, Mexico, before hundreds of cheering Mexican distributors. When I handed her the first-prize certificate, describing her dream journey to the United States, she began to cry. *"Un sueño hecho realidad,"* she muttered. "A dream come true."

Why do I end this chapter on compassion with Isabel Escamilla's story? Because I am convinced that her life demonstrates both sides of compassionate capitalism. The volunteers from the Red Cross, UNICEF, the Peace Corps, and other mission and social service agencies demonstrated compassionate capitalism at work helping others. But Juanita Avalard was also a compassionate capitalist because she gave Isabel a way to help herself.

On October 3, 1991, a chauffeured limousine drove Isabel Escamilla to the airport in Monterey to begin her journey to the United States. Those who traveled with her told me later that she spent the entire journey wide-eyed and smiling. Today in the mountains of northern Mexico, a beautiful, gray-haired compassionate capitalist is hard at work seeing more of her dreams come true and in the process helping her children and her grandchildren to realize dreams of their own.

8

Why Should We Consider
Starting Our Own Business?

CREDO 8

We believe that owning our own business (to supplement or replace our current income) is the best way to guarantee our personal freedom and our family's financial future.

Therefore, we should seriously consider starting our own business or becoming more entrepreneurial in our current business or profession.

Eight-year-old Tim Foley and his ten-year-old brother, Mike, held their father's hands tightly as they walked toward the gates of Fun Fair in a large field near Skokie, Illinois. It was just ten o'clock, but already excited children were pulling their parents through the parking lot and into a long line of happy, impatient boys and girls waiting for the kiddie park to open.

Tim's father unlocked the back door of the ticket booth, turned on the p.a. system, and started the tape recorder playing. Instantly the small midway was flooded with the sound of amusement park music. Like soldiers responding to the bugle's morning reveille, the Wild Mouse, the Merry-Go-Round, the Ferris Wheel, the Big Dipper, and all their merrymaking allies sprang to life.

Tim loved those Saturdays at Fun Fair with his family. "If I wanted to be with my dad during those busy summer months," he remembers, "I had to be with him there. My father was a staunchly independent human being. Like his father and his grandfather before him, my father had the entrepreneurial spirit. He had to work for himself. It was the tradition in which he had been raised.

"During the daytime hours, Monday through Friday, Dad sold real estate. In the evenings and on weekends he assisted his brother and brother-in-law in the operation of an amusement park and golf range. It wasn't Disneyland," Tim adds, smiling, "but it provided a good living for our family and an excellent opportunity for me to see a family working together in a business of their own."

"Like father, like son," the saying goes. At age eight Tim was already a pint-sized entrepreneur. He didn't just sit around on those Saturdays at Fun Fair. He remembers selling balloons, pinwheels, and fireman hats to eager youngsters. Neither Tim nor his siblings, Mike and Sheila, were forced to work. But in the spirit of their enterprising family, they always took advantage of the opportunity.

At twelve, Tim had worked his way up to the refreshment stand, where he sold milk shakes, snow cones, hot dogs, and even mastered the art of making cotton candy. From there he climbed the ladder of amusement park success until he was operating the Wild Mouse, the "ultimate responsibility" in his father's eyes. "If I didn't pull the brake on time," Tim explains with a grin, "the riders would end up in the parking lot."

During all those formative years Tim watched his father at work. "He was the owner of the park," Tim remembers, "but he was never too good or too busy to do whatever was necessary to keep it running smoothly. He wanted to be sure that his customers were never disappointed. Working behind the scenes, his hands were always dirty. If something needed to be fixed, Dad fixed it. If it needed paint in a hurry, my father would paint it himself. His attitude and his work ethic were a tremendous example, not only for his children, but for all the young employees of the park."

Tim Foley went on to play football at Purdue University. Embodying his dad's whatever-it-takes attitude, Tim made All-American as an athlete and a student. In the third round of the 1970 NFL draft, he was selected to play for the Miami Dolphins under the leadership of coach Don Shula. Tim distinguished himself for eleven years in Miami, including the history-making 1972 undefeated season that climaxed in the 1973 Super Bowl. That year the underdog Dolphins beat the Washington Redskins for the football championship of the world. In his tenth season in the NFL, Tim Foley was selected for the Pro Bowl. When he retired from football, he went to work for Turner Broadcasting as the color analyst of their college football telecasts. Today he can be seen on the Jefferson Pilot Affiliated Network syndication football telecasts of the S.E.C. Game of the Week.

"It doesn't take a rocket scientist to realize that fame is temporary," Tim warns. "I knew I wasn't going to play for the Dolphins until I was sixty-five. So, even while I was an active player, I began to look for a business of my own to guarantee some kind of secure financial future for Connie and our family. During those eleven seasons in Miami I invested in real estate and lost some money. I invested in the stock market and lost some money. I invested in gold and precious metals and lost money there as well. Finally I invested in health clubs and racquetball courts, and though the business prospered for a while, interest rates rose to twenty-one percent and new memberships slowed and then finally trickled to a stop."

Today, Tim and Connie Foley own a successful Amway distribution business with a company of friends across fifty states and around the world. Tim and Connie have seen their dreams come true. The Foley family's future is financially secure. And it all began in that amusement park in Skokie, Illinois. Young Tim Foley's life and values were changed forever as he watched his hardworking, self-directed, value-driven father do whatever it takes to see his dreams come true.

The same entrepreneurial spirit that moved Tim Foley at Fun Fair can come alive in you. Have you felt that spirit in your own life? Do you see yourself as a capitalist or at least a potential capitalist? Or do you resist that label? All capitalists are not like the stereotypical tycoons: heartless moguls with cigars, double-breasted suits, and limos. Some of the most generous, loving, caring people on this earth wear the name proudly, but if it makes you uncomfortable to think of yourself as a capitalist, maybe calling yourself an entrepreneur, a free-enterpriser, or even a compassionate capitalist will help.

One way or the other, we all participate in this great free-enterprise system. We can benefit from its advantages or we can miss our chance forever, but we must never forget that the spirit and promise of free enterprise flow through our veins just as they flowed through the veins of the Rockefellers, du Ponts, and Carnegies. The entrepreneurial spirit was born in us right along with our need to eat and drink, to love and be loved, to learn, to grow and to achieve.

What Is an Entrepreneur?

The word itself is French. Literally, *entrepreneur* means "someone who undertakes a challenge." In France it originally referred to a person who organized music concerts, like the late Bill Graham (only on a slightly smaller scale!). But now it has come to mean anyone who undertakes a business venture, who sees a need and tries to fill it.

Entrepreneurs do not belong to a closed fraternity. Anyone can be an entrepreneur. Age is no barrier. Young people who organize a school play, have a paper route, a rock band, or baby-sit for the people next door are entrepreneurs. College students and adults of any age including senior citizens can be entrepreneurs. Gender is no barrier. Men and women are equally gifted with the entrepreneurial spirit. When it comes to entrepreneurship there are no insurmountable barriers except those we impose on ourselves.

The Entrepreneurial Spirit. Do you remember that time long ago when you first felt "the spirit"? Were you eight years old, like Tim Foley? Did the spirit of free enterprise move you to start a cold-drink stand on the sidewalk with a little sign that read *Lemonade 5 Cents a Glass?* Or did you bag walnuts or avocados, seashells or pinecones, and sell them from your front lawn? Maybe you shoveled snow, mowed lawns, pulled weeds, washed dishes, or bathed your neighbor's dog for extra money. Maybe you delivered papers or washed cars. Those are my earliest memories.

I was a child of the Depression. My father found himself without an income about the time the stock market crashed. My parents had built a pleasant little home for $6,000 in Grand Rapids, Michigan. Doesn't seem like much money now, but in those hard times Dad and Mom couldn't make the payments. Sadly, they were forced to rent their dream house to tenants for the $25 monthly mortgage. We moved into the attic of my grandparents' house. Dad spent those years after the crash sacking flour in a grocer's back room and selling socks and underwear in a men's store on Saturdays. From that day his advice was clear and simple: "Own your own business, Rich," he would say. "It's the only way to be free."

I was just ten years old when my entrepreneurial spirit kicked in. I suppose I began my first little businesses because my parents needed me to help pay the bills. That need for extra money is still the primary reason most people get into our business today. But something more was going on than just paying bills. I still remember the excitement, pride and even power I felt when my customers paid me for my work. I wasn't selling pinwheels or blowing up balloons, but I think I experienced the same joy that Tim Foley must have felt when children placed pennies in his hand.

During elementary school and junior high, I pulled weeds, mowed lawns, washed cars, and worked at a gas station to earn enough money to buy a bicycle. With that new black Schwinn Racer, I contracted with our local paper for a delivery route. I can still remember riding my bike up to the back of Mr. Bolt's dry-goods store to get my day's papers. It wasn't easy to learn how to ride my new bike loaded down with heavy newspapers front and back. At first my customers covered their eyes with fear as I wobbled up the road in their direction. But on Saturday mornings I stood in line with the other paper boys before Mr. Bolt's rolltop desk and could hardly hold in my excitement when he counted out thirty-five cents for the week's deliveries.

In high school, the baseball coach noticed I was a lefty. He wanted me to play first base and bunt left-handed. Although I loved the game, as I do now, I had to say no. There was no way to make after-school practice and still earn those extra dollars our family needed. I worked in a men's clothing store after classes Monday through Friday. On weekends I washed cars at a large gas station near our home. The owner charged a dollar, and I got fifty cents. The more cars I washed, the more profits I made. I worked fast. I wiped around the doors and the windows. I dusted off the doorjambs and under the dashboard, where most people never cleaned. Customers noticed. They tipped me for the extra care.

It was hard work, but I was making more money than I had ever dreamed and it was fun. The entrepreneurs I know have a positive attitude about work. They will tell you that sometimes "work is just work," but they will also tell you that—for them—most work is fun.

Work can be terrible, but it doesn't have to be. You can end up a slave to the system, putting in endless hours of tedium and hating it. Or you can decide today—whether you work for yourself or for someone else—that you will be an entrepreneur and turn your years of work into a lifetime of growth, discovery, financial reward, and opportunity for compassion.

Entrepreneurs of the Past

To understand how hard work and an entrepreneurial spirit can accomplish great things, it is helpful to begin by learning something about those who have seen past needs and worked to fill them. When we look back, we are inspired by those who had the courage, persistence, or genius to be entrepreneurs when the conditions were tougher and the opportunities fewer.

These people, some from the ancient past, deserve to be called entrepreneurs because in an important sense they are the distant relatives and "spiritual parents" of modern entrepreneurialism. Hardworking innovators have contributed immeasurably to our world and created opportunities for generations that followed them. So who were some of these "entrepreneurs"?

One of the earliest was a fellow named Ts'ai Lun, a Chinese official who invented paper in A.D. 105. Before then almost everything was written on bamboo. This made books very heavy and clumsy. Chinese scholars needed a wagon to carry around just a few books.

Ts'ai Lun's invention was recognized immediately for its great value. He was promoted by the emperor, made an aristocrat, and became wealthy. This invention changed China dramatically. Books became more available and, in turn, they spread learning throughout the country.

About 1400, in the city of Mainz, an innovative German goldsmith, Johannes Gutenberg, perfected a series of inventions that made modern printing possible. Gutenberg invented a practical way of making and using movable type, which made feasible the printing of a wide variety of books with speed and accuracy.

Although notable events happened between Ts'ai Lun and Gutenberg, the pace of progress in the world sped up tremendously after Gutenberg's invention. The development of printing was one of the most important events in the making of our modern world.

In one sense printing made entrepreneurship possible for the rest of us, because information could now be easily transmitted. How-to books were among the very first to be printed. They covered every imaginable subject from metallurgy to medicine, from good building techniques to good manners. People learned how to do things through books, and perhaps even more important, they learned to be innovators by combining others' ideas with their own.

One man who did this and filled a great need was James Watt. An Englishman, he designed the world's first practical steam engine, patented in 1769. Improving on a crude, steam-powered pumping device he had seen, Watt made some key modifications, added some entirely new features, and converted an impractical curiosity into a valuable tool. It is hard for us to imagine what a great invention this was. In

Watt's time there was no electric power—the electric motor had not been invented yet. Neither were there any gasoline engines.

If you wanted to do heavy work, like grind grain or run a cloth mill, you had to do it with water power. This was inconvenient, to say the least, and severely limited the amount of work that could be done.

Watt's invention was almost single-handedly responsible for the development of the Industrial Revolution. With a practical source of power, all kinds of things could be done. Soon entrepreneurs of every stripe thought of ways to put this new power source to work.

Thomas Alva Edison, the greatest inventor the world has ever known, had only three months of formal education and was considered by his teacher to be retarded. By the time he died, though, he had filed over a thousand patents and was a very wealthy man.

Edison perfected and patented everything from the first phonograph player in 1877 to the first practical light bulb in 1879. He set up the first electricity-distribution company, contributed to the development of the movie camera and projector, and made important improvements in the telephone, telegraph, and typewriter.

The light bulb is a good example of the entrepreneurial spirit alive and well in our early history. Perhaps you thought that Edison invented the light bulb when a light suddenly went on in his head. But in his time this expression would apply only if it were a gas light! In fact, Edison invented the light bulb not in a flash of insight, but over a *period* of time, in a very systematic way. His approach to invention is one of the earliest illustrations of a process that became known as "research and development."

Edison had six rules for invention. Even if you don't think that you will ever invent something as world-changing as the light bulb, notice how helpful his guidelines could be for all of us who have dreams we want to see come true.

1. Set a goal and stick to it
2. Figure out the steps you have to go through to complete the invention and follow them
3. Keep good records of your progress
4. Share your results with fellow workers
5. Be sure that everyone working on the project has a clear definition of their responsibilities
6. Record all your results for later analysis

This systematic approach to solving problems had been used by scientists for quite a while, but Edison adapted it for use in inventing things for the marketplace. He was as much an entrepreneur as he was an inventor. He wasn't interested in making things that didn't sell—he was interested in knowing what people wanted to buy. Consequently, he was very diligent in doing his marketing homework, too. And he did it very well. Edison's team of inventors became the world's first industrial research laboratory—a uniquely American institution at the time. His lab was the first of several to follow, including the Bell Laboratory and General Electric.

A few years before Edison patented the phonograph, two brothers were born—one in Indiana and the other in Ohio—who would eventually go into the bicycle business together. They did well as bicycle entrepreneurs, but it was their hobby that made them famous. The brothers were Wilbur and Orville Wright, and their hobby was aeronautics.

After several years of eagerly reading the latest research on the problems of flight, in 1899 the brothers decided to work on some solutions themselves. By 1903 their efforts resulted in the first manned flight. Having built many gliders, the brothers had become the world's most experienced glider pilots, with more than a thousand successful flights.

Based on this experience they came to an understanding of a fundamental problem of flight: control. After devising a way to maneuver their craft in the air, they added a lightweight engine of their own design and flew into history. They were granted the first patent on the airplane in 1906. Their total investment had been about one thousand dollars.

Alexander Graham Bell, an American born in Scotland in 1847, is another good example of how quickly capitalism developed new products and inventions in the last part of the nineteenth century. He patented the telephone in February 1876 and exhibited his new invention at the Centennial Exposition in Philadelphia that same year. It was an instant hit. At the time, the biggest communications company in the U.S. was the Western Union Telegraph Company. Bell offered the rights to his new invention to Western Union for a hundred thousand dollars—an offer that was promptly refused.

The next year Bell formed his own corporation, which was an immediate success. That company eventually became the American Telephone and Telegraph Company—AT&T. From March to November of

1879, stock in Bell's company went from sixty-five dollars a share to over a thousand dollars (by this time Western Union was eating its heart out). By 1892 New York and Chicago were connected by telephone. By the time Bell died in 1922, the telephone was common throughout the country. It went from being a new invention to a regular household item with remarkable speed.

In the meantime, Edison was busy developing a way to distribute electricity to power his new light bulbs. It's hard to sell light bulbs when no one has any electricity to fire 'em up! So in 1882 he established a small power-distribution system in New York. This was the first electric "utility" ever set up to serve households. It was a success, but Edison did have a few problems at first. The evidence is on nearly every electrical appliance you've ever plugged in. Did you ever notice that most of them say, "for use with 110-volt service only"?

Why 110 volts? Edison's first power-generating system couldn't maintain sufficient power throughout the system. The people near the power station had light bulbs burning brightly, but by the end of the line, things were pretty dim. Edison got complaints. So like any good entrepreneur—he wanted to sell *lots* of light bulbs—he decided to bump up the power from 100 to 110 volts. This new standard stuck, even when distribution systems became sophisticated enough to overcome the original problem.

Just think about the changes one invention brought about— electricity. Vast new areas were opened up for entrepreneurs and consumers—not only in telephones and light bulbs but radio, television, computers, and thousands of other products.

Many of the entrepreneurs who have had the greatest impact on our daily lives lived during the last century. One of them is the unknown patron saint of our "car culture," a German inventor named Nikolaus Otto. Otto invented the first practical automobile engine in 1876.

He had a junior employee named Gottlieb Daimler, who got together a few years later with a friend, Carl Benz. They started building cars using engines based on Otto's design and decided to name the cars after the daughter of a dealer who sold their cars, a girl named Mercedes.

Like the electric motor, the internal-combustion engine was soon used in all kinds of small factories and shops. Almost immediately after its invention it was being used to power pumps, sewing machines, printing presses, saws—all kinds of things. It was big and bulky by today's standards, but it was still an improvement over steam power. But how big was it?

Otto built a special racing engine in 1901 that weighed a thousand pounds and produced forty horsepower. A common Volkswagen "Bug" engine of the 1960s produced forty horsepower and could be picked up by two average men. A modern motorcycle engine producing that much power can be picked up by one person. Competition among capitalist entrepreneurs fostered these rapid advances.

By 1908, Henry Ford was combining Otto's internal-combustion engine, the production-line method of construction, interchangeable parts, electric lights, and scientific management to produce the Model T. Just five years later there were 1,258,000 cars registered in the U.S.! Ford made the automobile affordable for ordinary people, and they bought it in incredible numbers. In another twenty-five years there were thirty-six million cars on U.S. highways. Cars transformed the country, becoming in the process the most important product in the whole economy.

Cars created entrepreneurial opportunities for millions of Americans. Cars required a lot of raw materials—and people to produce them. These included steel, glass, chrome, rubber, wire, paint, upholstery fabric—all kinds of things. These cars required roads, bridges, and tunnels. Mechanics were needed to keep them running, gas stations to fuel them, insurance agents to insure them—the list is endless.

The mobility that people enjoyed in their cars created whole new industries: motels and resorts, roadside cafés, trailer parks, and tourist traps. The automobile introduced a new culture to America.

As we have seen, most of the consumer products that we take for granted are very recent creations. The entrepreneurial spirit is alive and working in our midst. And the pace of innovation and change has accelerated tremendously during our own century. Almost all of those thousands of products that our capitalist system manufactures so efficiently are the result of what has happened in the past one hundred years.

Today's Entrepreneurs

Don't think for a moment that the great entrepreneurial age is over. If it is true that the spirit of free enterprise has always been present in people, it is equally true that there has never been a better time to give wings to your own entrepreneurial spirit. The opportunities to become a successful capitalist have never been greater. There have been more new ideas brought to life and put to good use in our world during the past ten years than in all the past centuries put together.

In fact, the entrepreneurial spirit has spread throughout our country among people of every age. Some of our most successful entrepreneurs were young people when they started out. You are never too young, poor, or inexperienced to have a good idea. Here are some examples of young people I have read about who became successful entrepreneurs.

New Young Entrepreneurs. One successful enterprise was started by two high school friends who loved to eat. They considered making bagels, but the equipment was too expensive. As a second choice they decided to try making ice cream. They both signed up for a five-dollar correspondence course in how to make ice cream.

With their new knowledge they pooled their savings, borrowed from relatives and opened their first store in an abandoned gas station with low rent. Within a few years Ben and Jerry's Ice Cream had sales that were over twenty-seven million dollars.

Have you heard about the two students in California who were building circuit boards in their garage? They sold a Volkswagen and a calculator to raise their initial capital, about thirteen hundred dollars. They had hopes of selling a hundred boards to start. But when they took some boards to a friend who had a computer store, he said that he wasn't so interested in boards but would be interested in fifty fully assembled computers. This was a few years ago when personal computers were hard to come by. So they built some.

Sales got off to a slow start, and one of the partners became so discouraged he thought about joining a Buddhist monastery. However, they did not quit and their company finally took off. The company, Apple Computer, now has sales of more than a billion dollars a year. The student friends were Steve Jobs and Steve Wozniak.

Do success stories like this intimidate you? A billion dollars in sales? What are my chances of doing something like *that?* Don't be discouraged by the odds against it! You can succeed in ways you never dreamed, if you just give it your best try! And remember, you don't have to build a billion-dollar company to be successful. There are tens of thousands of successful entrepreneurs who have built much smaller enterprises.

One of those smaller enterprises was started several years ago in a very unusual way. You may have read the story in the press or seen it on television. It reminded me of the medieval stories about alchemists who tried to turn lead into gold. It was a story of some kids who succeeded in turning manure into gold.

These children noticed that people in their area needed fertilizer for their lawns and gardens. But because it was inconvenient to go and buy, they weren't getting it. With this simple but important insight, they had an idea. Why not package manure and sell it right there in the neighborhood?

With their parents acting as advisers, they learned what it took to process cow droppings into manure. Then they contacted some local dairy farmers who were quite happy to let the kids clean up their pens in exchange for the "unprocessed" fertilizer. So the kids took the manure home, processed it, bagged it and sold it around the neighborhood.

After some hard work the business began to grow, and pretty soon that manure started turning into "gold." Eventually they accumulated so much cash that they formed a corporation and named it KIDCO, Inc. With some help, they invested their money in real estate, and eventually ended up with an impressive portfolio of properties.

A few years ago, a young man named Roger Conner stopped at a local flower shop and asked the owner if he could work there for free so that he could learn the business. Roger was twelve at the time. The owner agreed, and Roger started working part-time after school and on Saturdays. Two years later, he asked for a small salary but was turned down because the owner didn't think he was good enough. Roger went to work for another shop but was soon laid off. This time he decided to go to work for himself.

At the age of fifteen, Roger started his own flower business with a sixty-five-dollar investment. He bought old refrigerators at garage sales and turned them into coolers for storing his flowers. Working out of his parents' house, he built a reputation for top quality and service. Within a short time his business became so successful he bought the shop where he had worked without pay. He renovated the place and made it so successful that he also bought the second shop where he had worked!

Paul Hawken, a successful entrepreneur, has said that good ideas often do not look very good at first—or even at second glance. He advises young entrepreneurs not to worry if their business ideas sound weird, crazy or obscure.

An important aspect of the entrepreneurial spirit that all of these young business people illustrate is the value of imagination. Enterprises, small and large, are not held back by lack of money but by lack of creativity. Rather than being limited by a shortage of funds, companies like Ben and Jerry's and KIDCO were successful in large part because they were unpretentious and down-home.

Their greatest assets were their honest and humble beginnings—it made people trust them. After all, these were just regular folks. Their ideas had obvious merit—after the fact. How many times have you wondered, Why didn't I think of that? Well, if you put your mind to it, you just might!

While we're on the subject of creativity, let's make one thing very clear. The entrepreneurial spirit is *not* about dog-eat-dog aggressiveness. Imagination and creativity are much more important. You can work yourself to death, you can roll over people, but if you don't have a good idea you will probably fail. Good ideas grow out of a recognition of *what society needs and wants.*

Your Entrepreneurial Spirit at Work

From our earliest childhood days until we grow too old to dream, we are hounded by important questions. Edison, Bell, Ford and the greatest entrepreneurs of the past asked and answered these same questions. Steve Jobs and Steve Wozniak asked them as did Ben and Jerry, Bill Gates, and the other young billionaires who dared to form businesses of their own while most people went on dreaming. Let's look closely at a sample list. Are the questions below ones you've been asking yourself? Where do these questions come from? God? Conscience? The entrepreneurial spirit? Finding the source of these questions isn't nearly so important as finding the courage to answer them.

1. How could I make more money and feel more secure?
2. What kind of work would make me feel better about myself?
3. What have I always dreamed of doing and why don't I do it?
4. Would starting my own business help me resolve these questions?
5. If so, what kind of business would I like to start, to own, to build?

Answering these questions with honesty and courage has led millions of people to take one of the most exciting, worthwhile steps a woman or man can take. They looked closely at their dissatisfactions and dreams. They wanted to be free, to be their own boss, to control their lives again. They wanted financial security for themselves and for the people they loved. They wanted to use their creativity to develop their gifts and end the cycle of boredom that had them feeling trapped and tired all the time. For our friends in this business and for tens of millions like them, the answer has been to start a business of their own.

Chris Cherest had a good job in retailing. His wife, Judy, was a teacher. She was free on weekends and holidays, but for Chris, these were the biggest sales times of the year. "We never saw each other," he recalls. "Our lives were going in separate directions. We began to dream about owning a business where we could work side by side. It took courage to quit what we both knew best, but we had plans for ourselves and for our children. Our two separate lives threatened our plans and undermined our relationship. Finally we swallowed hard, took the plunge, and the past years working together have been the best years of our lives."

Before I met Bob and Jackie Zeender, they owned their own business, an elegant and prestigious restaurant in Silver Spring, Maryland. Their dining establishment was a huge success, winning glowing reviews from critics and a large and loyal following of diners with good taste. The Zeenders had won ten Gold Cup awards from their peers in the food business. Bob's fellow restaurateurs recognized his talents and elected him president of the Washington Restaurant Association, the youngest president in that organization's history.

Bob Zeender should have been happy, but he was miserable and exhausted much of the time. No wonder, he was working day and night. He never had a few hours off, let alone a vacation. And every day the pressure began all over again: creating menus, finding fresh, quality foods, hiring and training new personnel, decorating and redecorating. "I had to find a business that gave me my life back," Bob recalls. "Sometimes success costs too much. It wasn't easy to begin again, but it was necessary."

Today, Bob and Jackie Zeender own a very successful Amway distribution business. But their success isn't measured in money alone. Now, at last, they have time to spend with each other and with their two kids, Rocky and Julie. And because they are free to set their own schedule, the Zeenders are also free to use their enthusiasm and their gifts for leadership in compassionate causes across the country.

Twenty-five years ago, Al Hamilton was a skilled tool and die maker with a salary approaching twenty thousand dollars a year. "It wasn't the most lucrative job," Al remembers, "but those were trying times and I was glad to be working even though we could never earn enough to get ahead. Finally my wife, Fran, and I sat down to figure out where the money was going. Once we subtracted the basics—day care for the children, a car, parking, lunches, taxes, etc.—we discovered that it didn't matter how hard or how long we worked, we would never get ahead."

"We didn't want to make a lot of money," Fran adds. "At first we just wanted enough to get me home with the children. Then our little business began to grow. Soon we were making enough to cover Al's income, too. It took courage for us to start a business, but with a little courage and a lot of hard work, we discovered financial security and better yet, our freedom."

Jim and Judy Head wanted to build a home in Lake Arrowhead, high above the smoggy Los Angeles basin. As a child, Judy spent summers at the lake with her parents, dreaming that one day she would have a home there of her own. Jim spent weekends with friends at the lake, whetting his own appetite to live one day on its shores. What's wrong with dreaming of living by a lake with all its quiet beauty and its happy childhood memories? Nothing!

For Val and Randy Haugen the dream was a home far from the city with all its stress and temptations, high atop a mountain looking out over the vast panorama of salt flats, the Great Salt Lake, and the city of Ogden, Utah, where mule deer move among the craggy gray rocks and mountain goat trails crisscross the canyon walls.

E. H. Erick was already a famous Japanese entertainer when he began to wonder if there weren't a better way to make a living. He was successful by everyone's standards, but he himself was dissatisfied. "When I performed, I was paid," Erick recalls, "but if I didn't perform, I didn't get paid. I couldn't get sick. I couldn't take time off for business, let alone to rest without paying for it. I wanted some way to go on making a good living, even if I weren't always there to perform."

Midori Ito, raised in a wealthy, powerful Japanese family, was very successful in her own vocation. "But my income was based solely on commissions," Midori recalls. "If I even slowed down to take a vacation, those commissions slowed down with me."

Erick and Midori left high-paying careers to start their own business. At first no one seemed to understand, but today it is different. E. H. Erick and Midori Ito's Amway business has become one of Japan's amazing success stories. They are wealthy. They are compassionate. And they are free.

Max Schwarz lived with his parents on the family farm in Langenmoosen, a village ninety kilometers from Munich, Germany. More than anything in the world, Max wanted to be an independent electrician with a business of his own. He had completed his studies to be licensed and was about to take the final exam when his family experienced a terrible tragedy. His beloved sister died. After her burial and a time of grieving, Max's parents came to him and said firmly, "There is no need for you to take the electrical exam. You are our only son. Now that your sister is gone, you must be responsible for the farm." To this day, decades later, Max remembers the agony of that day when "my dream was lost."

Picture that young German picking up a plow when he had dreamed of owning a business and eventually his own farm for breeding and raising horses. In spite of their disappointment, Max and Marianne Schwarz refused to give up their dream. To their small potato farm they added a thousand geese, then two thousand rabbits, then hogs and grain to feed them. Still unsuccessful, they built and sold houses. For years they saw their dreams frustrated, their goals just out of reach. But they refused to quit. They learned from each new business experience. Now they own an international distribution company and have reached the highest levels of achievement in our business. Instead of a family farm raising potatoes and grain, they also own the horse-breeding farm of their dreams. Their first championship colt, Crown Ambassador, has won nine races already.

Marshall Johnson, an African American, grew up in Jacksonville, Texas. When he was just a child, his father abandoned the family. To support her five children and her invalid mother-in-law, who was paralyzed from the waist down, Marshall's mom went to work cleaning other people's houses for seventeen dollars a week. Marshall remembers how his father used to resist paying even five dollars weekly for child support. Desperate to make enough money just to pay the bills and dreaming of a better life for herself and for her family, Marshall's mother finally took a dangerous and demanding job on a factory assembly line.

"She never seemed angry or bitter," Marshall recalls. "But even as a child, I remember how hard my mother worked to support us. She left home early in the morning and often returned late at night. She was constantly tired in mind and body. On two terrible occasions Mom's machine malfunctioned in the factory and crushed her hand each time, taking a different finger off in the process."

In spite of everything, Marshall's mother managed to provide for her family. Their hand-me-down clothing was patched but clean. At every mealtime there was food on the table. And after church on Sundays, when his mother gathered her family for their weekly time together, she always remembered to remind Marshall that one day he would go to college and on that day she would be the proudest woman on earth.

"Mom saw her dream for me come true," Marshall remembers. "I attended the University of Houston on an athletic scholarship, playing four years of football, two years of basketball, and one season of track. After receiving a degree in education, I was drafted by the Baltimore Colts. During my senior year I met and married Sherunda, a beautiful Texan with a degree in psychology and an endearing habit of bringing home stray animals and stray people to feed and care for them. In those days I still believed the old notion that education and athletics would be my guarantee to a better life, not just for Sherunda and our children but for our whole family."

Soon Marshall Johnson was making more money than anyone in his family had ever made, but he saw the handwriting on the wall. One day he would not be with the Colts. You can't play professional ball forever. And he would have no way to meet the wider family needs even on two teacher's salaries. "Besides," he remembers, "I wanted to be an example to my community, to show young black men and women that we, too, could make it in the business world."

Marshall and Sherunda began their distribution business in 1978. Today it prospers and because of the financial independence that business brings, the Johnsons' dreams are coming true. Today they are a model not just to African Americans, but to all of us.

When a fellow Air Force officer offered John Vaughan a chance to have his own part-time business, John was finishing his ninth year of full-time college, completing his Ph.D. in engineering from Purdue. John's wife, Pat, was finishing her master's degree in education, was raising three small children, and was pregnant. As busy as they were,

John and Pat decided to begin their own small business. "We decided that our part-time business would be fun," John remembers. "We already had enough stress in our lives." The Vaughans turned work into play. In just one year, they had doubled their income. What a wonderful surprise it was when Pat could stay home to be a full-time wife, mother, and business partner.

There are endless stories like these, inside and outside our business. In good economic times and in bad, millions of people dream of owning a business one day, and thousands see their dreams come true. If the spirit of free enterprise has been raising questions in your mind, if you're longing for financial security, if you don't like what you're doing, this is a great time to make the change. I'm not just pushing Amway here. Some of my best friends don't even use our products. Look at the evidence. Capitalism is alive and well in North America and around the globe. Opportunities for entrepreneurs to see their dreams come true are abundant even in these difficult economic times.

Follow Your Entrepreneurial Spirit

In the U.S., for example, in 1980 there were only 13,022,000 small businesses. Just ten years later there were 20,393,000. In 1990 alone, 647,675 new businesses were incorporated nationwide, accounting for ninety percent of the net job growth. The number of women-owned businesses increased by fifty-seven percent between 1982 and 1987, and the receipts of those businesses rose by eighty-one percent. The number of black-owned businesses increased by thirty-seven percent from 1982 to 1987, and the receipts of these businesses increased by more than two hundred percent.

Some people start a business because they've lost a job after a lifetime of service. They want to feel secure the second or third time around and they've found that owning their own business—though risky and difficult at first—meets that need. Others are leaving their jobs and starting their own businesses because they are bored, disappointed, angry, exhausted, or just plain tired of corporate life. Young people fresh out of colleges and universities are starting their own businesses. In a recent Roper survey, thirty-eight percent of twelve hundred students in one hundred different colleges said "owning a business represented an excellent opportunity for a successful career."

"They want to maintain some autonomy," reports the *Wall Street Journal.* "They're looking for greater job satisfaction and independence. They want to channel their energies in any direction they want, to do things their own way. They want to find a need in their communities and create business to fill it. Ultimately, they want to be free," the article concludes, "to do what they want to do with their lives."

Don't get me wrong. There are plenty of business failures. There were 60,400 in 1990, up twenty percent from 1989. That's why we encourage most people who are thinking of starting a business to do the following:

1. If you have a job, keep it while you start your own business. (You'll be surprised how much extra time and energy you have left in the evenings and on weekends to get a new business going without ever taking time from your current employer.)
2. Quit your old job when you have enough money stockpiled to keep you through the low-income days ahead.
3. Try to find or create a business opportunity that takes the smallest possible amount of start-up capital. (Don't go deep into debt on a whim. Businesses don't need fancy office space, expensive equipment, and dozens of workers in the beginning. Think small. Think inexpensive.)
4. Be sure that the goods or services you want to manufacture or market are first-class in quality. (Don't cheat your customers. It leads to certain business failure.)
5. Be sure that you know what you are doing, that you have read every possible resource about your new business, that you have talked to a banker, a lawyer, and a friend or two you trust for their common sense. You will learn plenty by trial and error, but know all you can before you start.

Don't be afraid to try. Remember, in spite of the economic downturn, small business income increased six and a half percent in 1990, and all across this nation and around the world new businesses are booming.

In the next few chapters, I'm going to share some practical, step-by-step suggestions for starting your own business. It isn't easy, especially at first. Ann Landers was right when she said, "Opportunities are usually disguised as hard work, so most people don't recognize them."

But with that hard work comes a sense of achievement and security that can raise the quality of your life in ways you only dreamed.

Let me repeat: before you seriously consider any job or business, including our own, check it out! Be sure that the business and its people have integrity. Today, for example, Jerry and Cherry Meadows have a successful international Amway business, but in the beginning they weren't so sure that we would deliver on our promises.

After graduation and marriage, the Meadowses moved to North Carolina, where Jerry had accepted a job in chemical engineering. Cherry went to work as a home economist. Part of her job was to do a weekly television show on clothing design and construction. When their son, Greg, was just six months old, the Meadowses heard a presentation of the Amway marketing and distribution plan.

"I understood what I heard that night," Jerry remembers, "but I didn't believe it. Cherry believed it, but she didn't understand exactly how it works. So we did our homework. We checked it out."

"He made me call a whole bunch of people about Amway," Cherry recalls with a grin, "including the state attorney general's office. The woman I talked to there said, 'Gosh, I think the last attorney general went into Amway himself.' That's when we both decided that Amway had passed the test and that we could trust the company and its independent distributors to deliver on their promises."

The *Intra*preneurial Spirit

Maybe you don't want to own a business, but you still feel the entrepreneurial spirit moving inside your soul. Good for you! Too many people think that entrepreneurs have to own their own businesses, that the entrepreneurial spirit dies or at least grows limp when they're working for someone else. That isn't true. In fact, there are very creative, gifted people who like working in other people's businesses large or small. They don't feel comfortable with the responsibility that comes with going out on their own. They like the regular monthly paychecks more than the risk that goes with starting one's own business. They'd rather be in a large community of workers than alone.

Just for the sake of clarity, perhaps we should call employees who do more than punch their time card *intra*preneurs. More and more businesses and even professions are beginning to find new and creative ways to honor the contributions made by these employees who let their entrepreneurial spirit lead the way. *Intra*preneurs also ask questions and act on them:

- What can I do in my current job, business, or profession to grow, to use my gifts and talents more creatively, to feel more satisfied with what I do each day?
- How can I help make this business stronger, more successful?
- What would make this task more efficient, less time-consuming, and thus less expensive?
- How can we improve the workplace to make it safer, more relaxed, more comfortable for me and for my fellow workers?
- What are we doing wrong? How could we do it better?

We can spend our lives just putting in our time on the job, but the entrepreneurs and *intra*preneurs see work every day as an opportunity to grow, create, discover, challenge old ideas and come up with new and better ones.

Our company of friends is made up of two different groups. There are distributors who own their own businesses and employees who work in our offices and plants around the world. So far only the stories of the entrepreneurs have been told. But, let's remember the intrapreneurs, without whose commitment and creativity we could not survive.

Bob Kerkstra has been a creative and committed employee of the Amway Corporation for more than a quarter of a century. He has all the skills and gifts to own his own distribution business, but we have been grateful that Bob and thousands of other employees like him have chosen to share their talents with us. They have a unique perspective on compassionate capitalism. They see us as no others see us, and in the process of dialogue and confrontation we learn from them how compassionate capitalism works in the stenographic pool or on the assembly line.

"When I first came to this company," Bob remembers, "there were only five or six hundred employees, but we had 450,000 square feet of office, manufacturing, research and warehouse space sprawling across a 281-acre complex. Still, Rich and Jay found their way through that maze to welcome each of us one by one."

I don't remember that Jay and I ever really made an official policy to greet each worker in his working space during the first week on the

job, but we saw in their eyes and heard in their voices what a difference it made to be recognized from the beginning as being important
to this company. We took only a few moments out of every day to
greet these folks by name, and the immediate and long-range benefits
to our company in loyalty and productivity still amaze me.

"During my first two years at Amway," Bob recalls, "I came into
conflict with one of my key managers. When it got more and more
painful to put up with him, I quit. That happened without warning late
one Friday afternoon. Rich was out doing a meeting somewhere, but
on Monday morning when he found out that I had left the business, he
called me on the telephone, apologized for the misunderstanding and
urged me to reconsider. I didn't go back right away, but I still remember being amazed that the owner of the corporation had learned about
the incident so quickly, let alone that he had cared enough to call me
and try to make it right."

Sometimes we confuse people with numbers. How many hired?
How many fired? How many still on the line? But from the beginning
of our corporation's history, Jay and I have tried to remember that it
is as important to handle people with dignity and understanding who
are leaving us as it is when they are just coming on board. Now we
have ten thousand employees and more than two million distributors.
It is impossible to keep track personally of every one of them. Still, we
try.

Bob says, "Even today Rich and Jay practice what we call the
'walkabout.' You never know when or where they will show up. It
isn't like spying, although their sudden, unexpected appearances keep
us on our toes. It is far more jovial than that. 'Hi, guys. How'ya
doing?' they might shout across a production line as they walk slowly
through a plant. Then they pause long enough to really hear the answer. 'Anything we can do to make this work go smoother?' Rich or
Jay will ask, honestly wanting to know the answer as they stand beside
a conveyer belt operator or research technician. And when a suggestion
is made or a criticism shared, we are sure that Jay or Rich will hear
it and that something will be done."

Bob is putting a very positive spin on his memories and I am grateful, but I'm afraid that Jay and I may have failed many times in staying tuned to our employees and their needs. Still, compassionate
capitalism demands that we continue to try. Compassion works both
ways. When we reach out to employees, they reach back to us. Without their loyalty, their creative ideas, and their hard work the company

will not succeed. The larger we grow, the easier it becomes to take people for granted and the harder it becomes to stay in touch. Now, for example, it's impossible to walk through just one of our maze of buildings, let alone even dropping by the production and distribution centers across America and around the world. That's why we try so hard to find managers who understand compassionate capitalism and then to release them to that task.

"As we grew," Bob continues, "Rich and Jay began to invite men and women from every department in the company to represent their fellow workers at Speak-Up meetings. They are still convened weekly on an informal basis in a cafeteria or auditorium for a different group of employees from across the company. Any question is fair game. Every answer is carefully and sometimes critically heard. Through the years, Rich or Jay or both were always there and available."

In those sessions employees have shared ideas that have become company traditions. Our employee magazine (once called *Ambit,* now titled *Friends)* was one of those ideas. Now fairly standard practice across the country, the employee magazine was new to us when it was suggested. Published every month, it features pictures and stories of employees at work or play. We learned to honor personal and professional achievements through those magazine stories, on posters and displays around the offices, in banquets and at special tributes and events.

"Instead of sick leave," Bob says, explaining another of the creative practices that were developed out of employee discussions, "we get 'comp' days. Accumulating days for sick leave proved to be a trap. Employees had to get sick to use the days we earned. If we didn't get sick, we had to fake it. It wasn't fair to the employer or to us. Now an employee can earn up to four comp days a year just by appearing faithfully on the job. We use those days not just when sick or troubled, but to enjoy an extra day in the sun or an extended family vacation. That way we don't have to fake sickness to use the days we've earned."

The best ideas often come from a friendly confrontation with employees. Our people in Ada reminded Jay and me that since we trusted managers to arrive on time and to put in a full day's work, employees should be trusted in the same way. And since we dumped time clocks, work performance and attendance have not slackened for a day.

"The year I returned to Amway," Bob told us, "one of our employees was blamed for a serious auto accident in which one man was killed and several were severely injured. At the employee's trial Rich showed up just before the judge rendered his verdict. In his appeal Rich promised to supervise the employee's 'rehabilitation,' and the judge ended up being convinced and placing the employee in Rich's hands."

Compassion is good business. Whether you are an employer with a business of your own or an employee lending your creativity and commitment to someone else's business, you must give your entrepreneurial spirit free reign. With compassion as our guide, there is no limit to what we can achieve together.

More than a half century ago, a six-year-old child rushed down the main street of his hometown, Three Hills, Alberta, Canada. He strained to open the candy store's heavy leaded glass door and walked quickly to a large discount barrel. The sign read "25 JAWBREAKERS 25 CENTS." The boy reached into his pocket, pulled out a Canadian quarter, bought the jawbreakers, and rushed from the candy store toward a children's park and playground in the center of town.

The boy noticed that a large crowd of children and their parents had gathered around a new set of metal swings and slides. He approached them opening the bag of jawbreakers noisily and slowly unwrapping the plastic tissue from the largest jawbreaker of them all. At the sound of his contented slurping, one by one the children gathered around him and his bright green plastic bag of goodies.

"Would you like one?" he asked, and a dozen tiny hands waved in his direction. "They're only two cents apiece," he said, reaching into the bag and pulling out a handful of red, green, yellow, and black jawbreakers.

In just seconds, children were finding pennies in their pockets or running to their parents for change. Within minutes all twenty-four remaining jawbreakers were sold, the bag was empty, and the little boy was trudging home with a smile on his face and twenty-three cents' profit in his jeans.

Years later that child, Jim Janz, together with his wife, Sharon, heads a successful business in Canada and the U.S. After a lifetime of successful entrepreneurship, Jim still recalls fondly those childhood memories. Standing in the park that day with a bag of jawbreakers in his hand, six-year-old Jim Janz was a capitalist and he didn't even know it.

What if some adult had destroyed the entrepreneurial spirit in that little child? "They tried to crush it," Jim remembers more than half a century later. "I was raised on the campus of a Bible institute," he explains. "If you wanted to be a missionary, you ranked a high ten on their scale of importance. A pastor in North America came in around five or six. But if you wanted to own a business, you didn't even rate a zero."

All my life, too, I've heard the word capitalism spoken with a sneer. I suppose that's one of the reasons I tended toward using free enterprise as a less inflammatory way of describing our great economic system. Whatever you choose to call that spark of entrepreneurial life in the children of this world, do everything in your power to keep it burning. When that little boy bought his jawbreakers in bulk for one cent and sold them for a profit on the streets, he should have been praised and encouraged for his creativity and labor.

Jim and Sharon Janz stayed true to their calling. They followed the lead of their entrepreneurial spirit, and as a result they have succeeded as capitalists. They have given thousands of other people opportunities to succeed, and with their wealth Jim and Sharon have gone on to perform acts of compassion that have influenced the world for great and lasting good.

That little boy with the red jawbreaker juice running down his face went on to become the Chairman of the Foundation of Trinity University, the Founding Chairman of Bibles International in Canada, and the Chairman of the Board of Robert Schuller Ministries. He didn't follow the dreams others had for him; he followed the dream that God had planted in his heart and as a result, his dreams for himself and the dreams the others had for him *both* came true.

Jesus said almost two thousand years ago, "A little child shall lead them." Remember that little child in you who ran a lemonade stand. Feel again that spirit of free enterprise that you felt then. Dare to dream those old dreams again. General Douglas MacArthur said, "There is no security in this life. There is only opportunity." What would you like to do with the rest of your life? Do it! Take the first step today and everything else will follow.

After his eleventh year with the Miami Dolphins, Tim Foley allowed his entrepreneurial spirit to lead him into our business. He was seeking financial security for Connie and the family, but he was seeking so much more. Believe it or not, most successful entrepreneurs aren't in it just for the money. Once you've been captured by the true spirit of free enterprise, you will discover that freedom is something you will want to share.

"I never cared about buying a Mercedes," Tim remembers. "And though we have a beautiful home in Tavares, Florida, and all the comforts a family could dream, what really makes Connie and me happy is helping other people see their dreams come true as well."

Last summer at a huge rally in the Hoosier Dome in Indianapolis, Tim and Connie Foley sat on the stage before forty-one thousand people. After Dolly Parton entertained the enthusiastic crowd and former President Ronald Reagan delivered a moving address on behalf of free enterprise, a handful of men and women who had reached new levels in this business accepted a thunderous standing ovation from the crowd.

"Louie and Kathy Carrillo were one of the first couples to walk across the stage that night," Tim recalls. "Until 1981 Louie had been a successful air-traffic controller. When he and hundreds of his co-workers were fired, Louie pounded the sidewalks for many months looking for a new job. When I first met Louie, he was parking cars for a hundred-fifty dollars a week, and his wife, Kathy, had gone from being the wife of a successful air-traffic controller making fifty thousand dollars a year to being a maid and waitress trying to help save their little home from the bank by cleaning other people's houses."

Louie Carrillo had lived a difficult life. He had worked hard and sacrificed much to win a place in the nation's air-traffic-control system. When he was fired, there was almost no money in the bank to see the Carrillo family through their personal disaster. And by the time Louie and Kathy decided to enter our business, the money was long gone. Louie was a good man, but he wasn't gifted as a communicator and had no people skills at all. And when he drove his rusted yellow '75 Datsun to the homes of his old friends and acquaintances to make his first presentations, he parked it down the block to hide his shame.

"But Louie Carrillo still had dreams for himself and for his family," Tim remembers, "and night after night he packed his materials and his sample products into the '75 Datsun and drove across Florida making his presentation as best he could. We spent hours together," Tim recalls. "I tried to pass on to Louie everything I knew about the business. Connie and I helped him make his first presentations. We sat beside him and encouraged him when he stumbled or went blank. One night when Louie was about to venture out alone for the first time, I drove to his house and placed a note on the windshield of his ugly mustard-colored car: "Don't forget, Louie, you have a partner. We'll do it together! Love you, Tim."

Louie Carrillo's eyes still fill with tears when he remembers that note from Tim Foley. Thanks to Tim and other compassionate capitalists whom Louie met in this business, he has created his own company of friends that now stretches across Florida and the southern states into Mexico, South America, and England.

I wish you could have seen Louie and Tim together after that triumphant rally in Indianapolis last summer. After seeing his dream come true, Louie walked through the cheering crowd, trying to find Tim's eyes, struggling to express his thanks. When words failed, Louie grabbed Tim in his arms and hugged him. It is a fairly normal sight in our company of friends to see grown men and women hugging and weeping in gratitude to God and to each other for what they have seen accomplished together.

Somewhere down inside of you your own entrepreneurial spirit is struggling to be free. Don't be afraid to try. Go for it. The journey begins with that one first step. Find a company of friends who will help you see your dreams come true. And one day you will know what Tim and Connie Foley and Louie and Kathy Carrillo know, that the real joy of compassionate capitalism is not just finding your own personal fulfillment and financial security. The real joy is helping other people to find personal fulfillment and financial security for themselves.

PART III

Go!

9

What Attitude Do We Need to Succeed, and How Do We Develop It?

CREDO 9

We believe that developing a positive, hopeful attitude is necessary to reach our goals.

Therefore, with our mentor's help, we should design a program (using books, tapes, special meetings and events, associations with friends and co-workers, recreation, and worship) that will help us develop a positive, hopeful, productive attitude about our life and its potential.

The young salesman drove his West End Brewery company car up Route 49 from Utica to Rome, New York. As he crossed the Mohawk River on the East Dominick Street bridge, the sky turned black and lightning lit the distant horizon. Hoping to beat the late summer storm, the driver jammed down the accelerator, swerved onto James Street, and screeched to a halt in front of Gillette's Food Market on Turin Road.

The first raindrops were beginning to splatter the windshield as the young man grabbed his briefcase and a cardboard display and ran across the parking lot toward the waiting manager. He had already visited forty different accounts that day on five different routes across Oneida County, making sales, taking orders, delivering displays. He was working eighty-hour weeks that summer of 1964, doing everything required of him and more. In spite of hard work, his skills as a salesman and his endless hours on the road, Dexter Yager was not getting ahead.

Dexter and his wife, Birdie, still drove a rusted 1955 Ford station wagon, and they still lived with their four young children in an old row house that fronted on an alley. "When we stepped out of our front door," Birdie remembers, "we were standing on the street. There were no green lawns, no place for our kids to play safely, no peace and certainly no quiet."

"I had big plans for me and for my family," Dexter remembers. "Since childhood, I had dreamed of owning my own business. Mom used to say, 'The name Yager means you don't work for someone else.' But I had no money to begin a business, and every night when I read the local paper, I got more and more frustrated. There were no start-up business opportunities that I could afford. So I mistakenly thought it was my lack of money that was holding me back."

"I didn't have a college education either," Dexter explains. "I thought that was another major handicap. Anytime I applied for a better job, the gray suits and striped ties would throw it up to me. 'No college, son?' they mumbled, looking over my job application and clucking to themselves. I'd shake my head and feel even more frustrated. After scanning my brief resumé they would smile, hand me back the form, and show me to the door, muttering something like 'Well, come back when you get that degree and we'll talk.'

"I didn't have a great vocabulary, either," Dexter admits. "For a while I thought that, too, was standing in my way. I'll never forget the day someone said to me, 'With your limited vocabulary, who will want to know you?'

"And vocabulary or not, I had to admit I just didn't seem to fit in anywhere. I was raised in upstate New York in a little town called Rome. I was a Protestant in a Catholic community. I was a German-Scot 'mongrel' surrounded by full-blooded Italians. I was a plumber's son in a neighborhood of doctors, lawyers and politicians.

"There were plenty of reasons for me to look down on myself. There were plenty of excuses I could have used to feel depressed about my future. But something down inside me refused to give in. I believed in myself, and through the years that belief has made all the difference."

How to Become a Successful Entrepreneur. Believe in Yourself!

I hope that some of you are saying, I now know something about entrepreneurs, but how do *I* become one? For Dexter Yager and for millions of businessmen and -women like him, success begins with a positive attitude.

When we say someone has an "attitude," we often mean they are arrogant. That's not what I am talking about. Arrogance and confidence are different. I am talking about a positive attitude about yourself that says, I can do it! And because he displayed this type of attitude, he was off and running toward one of the greatest success stories in our company's history.

Not feeling very confident? When someone says to you, "You can be a successful entrepreneur," is your first instinct to say, "No way"? Well, you are not alone. Most of us, at least in the beginning, think we don't have the right stuff. But we are wrong. Often the right stuff is buried under an avalanche of garbage. All our lives we are told—sometimes in subtle ways, sometimes not so subtly—that we are not adequate, that we have weaknesses, we will never get ahead. As the computer expert says, "Garbage in. Garbage out!"

"You need a college education to get ahead" is one of those lies. I believe in education. I've served on various university boards and received more than a dozen honorary degrees. My children are all college graduates, but I didn't have a college education. Dexter Yager didn't have a college education. The list of Fortune 500 companies whose founders or chief executive officers didn't go to college is long and impressive. Karl Barth, one of the most important theologians of the century, didn't even go to a seminary, and yet his collected writings are used in every seminary in the world.

I'm not saying that a university degree is unimportant, but don't you believe for a moment that you can't succeed without one. One of Dexter Yager's heroes was his uncle. "I knew Uncle John when he was a dishwasher," Dex remembers. "He quit school in the eighth grade. Then, while he was working for minimum wage as a laborer, he hung around skilled carpenters and learned their trade. When the construction company that he was working for went belly-up, he started his own little building business. Then he borrowed money to buy land and became a developer. With his profits he bought his favorite restaurant. He was always starting something. By the 1960s he had at least a dozen businesses and was successful beyond his wildest belief. I wanted to be just like him.

" 'But you need to go to college first,' Uncle John warned me. 'Get your degree,' my dad chimed in. 'But I want to be like you,' I told them both. Like Uncle John, Dad quit formal schooling in the eighth grade. And yet they never stopped learning, growing, and changing. I knew a lot of people with college and graduate-school degrees, but I respected my father and Uncle John the most for what they had accomplished and for the ways they had accomplished it. And though they didn't beat up on me like my teachers and academic advisers with the constant demand that I go on to college, still both my father and my uncle encouraged me at various times, 'You can't be a success unless you get a college degree.' "

Even our heroes can mislead us. Dexter learned that early on. "By the time I was working for the brewery in Rome, New York," he remembers, "I was convinced that without a college degree I could never succeed. But I was too old to start college. I had a wife and four small children. I couldn't become a freshman with my responsibilities even though people thought I should."

The next thing we know, bad advice becomes a self-fulfilling prophecy. It echoes in our brains and clouds our dreams. "You'll never make it without a college degree." "With your limited vocabulary, nobody will give you a chance." "There's no room at the top for a Protestant or a Catholic or a Jew, for a Hispanic or an African American, for a bald man or a plump woman." The list goes on and on until there isn't anyone who can succeed.

Such advice begins early in our lives. It starts with a joke or a whisper. It grows with every quiet aside or "friendly" bit of advice. And it may end with the destruction of our potential and the death of our dreams. Don't let past lies about your limits threaten your future one more day. Instead, list your gifts. Find one positive quality that you recognize about yourself and use that quality as a wedge to open up yourself to all the potential within you. Today is the day to begin developing a new, positive, life-enhancing attitude about yourself.

Not long ago, I was rushed to the intensive-care ward of Butterworth Hospital in Grand Rapids, Michigan, after suffering classic heart-attack symptoms. My doctors performed a bypass operation to clear away a blockage in the blood vessels that supply my heart. During that long hospital stay, it became painfully clear that I had two choices. I could go on exactly as before and probably end up back on the operating table if not buried in the family plot. Or I could make serious, long-term changes and hope to live to a ripe old age.

As I lay in my hospital bed, all hooked up to life-support systems that blinked and buzzed in the night, I thought seriously about my doctor's advice. He said that three factors had caused my arteries to be blocked: heredity, poor diet, and lack of exercise. Those three factors were trying to teach me lessons that could save my life. Those same lessons apply to changing our attitude from one that leads to failure to one that leads to success.

Dexter and Birdie Yager's positive attitude led them to the top. They have inspired millions who never dreamed they could do it too. What if we think of that can't-do attitude as a kind of blockage? Would the same factors—heredity, poor diet, and lack of exercise—apply? Could it be that not believing in ourselves is something we inherit? Is it possible that a new thought diet could make a difference? Are there ways to exercise our minds that will break through the negative conditioning and get our entrepreneurial spirits flowing freely once again?

Heredity. My father, Simon C. DeVos, suffered several heart attacks before his premature death at the age of fifty-nine. Many of the attributes that led to my success I inherited from him, and I am grateful for every one of them. At the same time, though, inherited psychological and physiological traits had their dangerous downsides. By not taking my inheritance seriously, I found myself in the hospital wondering if I, too, would follow my father to an early grave.

Trying to find someone to blame for our weaknesses is not the point. Just remember, whoever or wherever it comes from, a can't-do attitude can be "inherited." Not genetically, but in the sense that one generation can pass a trait on to the next.

If your parents thought of themselves as losers—if they didn't have the confidence or desire to succeed—what kind of attitude did they pass on to you? Chances are, you may have been taught to think of yourself as a loser too. It isn't necessarily your parents' fault. They had their own "heredity" to contend with. For better or worse, we have inherited many of our parents' strengths and weaknesses. But that does not mean you cannot change. Forgive the bad traits you have inherited and cling gratefully to the good.

"My mother was a very determined woman," Dexter recalls. "All her life she was troubled by a weak and painful back. Her doctors told her she could never have children. She had five. They warned her against lifting and holding us. She ignored them and hugged us long and often. When we were young kids, the doctors discovered Mom's high blood pressure, and they tried to prepare us for her untimely death. She smiled and went right on believing in herself and in her frail body. She never took the doctors seriously, and at eighty years old she had outlived them all.

"Shortly after her eightieth birthday, Mom had a stroke. Her right side was paralyzed. The nurses lowered her gently into a wheelchair. 'She'll never walk again,' they said. But those well-meaning nurses didn't know my mother. 'I want a cane,' she said during her first week in therapy. 'I will walk again.' On a visit shortly afterward, I stood in my mother's room and watched with amazement as she struggled up out of her chair. 'Good morning, son,' she said. 'Come give your mother a hug.' And with that she started toward me, walking, smiling, believing in herself, determined to overcome everything and everybody whose dreams did not match her own.

"My dad was just five feet, six inches tall," he also remembers, "but he was tough and he could hold his own in Rome, a rough-and-ready town. One Saturday a couple of young punks decided to start a fight with my father. He tried to avoid it, but after the first blow struck, he went after them like a tiger. The last time we saw those two guys, they were heading south as fast as they could run.

"For a long time, I had a little plaque on my desk that read: *'It isn't the size of the man who's in the fight, but the size of the fight in the man.'* Every time I see those words, I think about my father and of the size of the fight he passed on to me."

Like Dexter, we've all inherited good and bad from family and friends, but we must not be satisfied with what we've been given. *Build* on it. If you've inherited a low view of your potential, fight back. Say to yourself, I'm not a loser, I *can* and I *will* succeed. The circumstances that have held back my parents or grandparents are not going to limit me. Be thankful that someone is saying to you—right now—what no one may have ever said to them. *You can do it!*

Diet. We may have inherited strong, lithe bodies, but if we constantly feed ourselves a diet of French fries and cheeseburgers, chocolate cake and beer, you know what will happen. Unless we are very lucky, we will end up with clogged arteries. The inside of our blood vessels will look like rusty old pipes. But if we eat a balanced, low-fat diet (and it's not as boring as it sounds), chances are our arteries will remain in good shape.

The same holds true for our minds. If we're constantly fed a diet of unhealthy ideas, what's going to happen? We're likely to develop an unhealthy attitude about ourselves. A little poem by Walter De la Mare has the right idea:

> It's a very odd thing—
> As odd as can be—
> That whatever Miss T eats
> Turns into Miss T.

It's that old idea: you are what you eat. If you take in a constant diet of negative, can't-do thinking, sure enough, you will fail!

During the interview with Dexter and Birdie Yager, he suddenly leaned over and picked up a glass. "See this glass," he said. "Right now it's full of Coke and ice. When I drink it down completely, it will be full of air. There is no such thing as an empty glass.

"There is no such thing as an empty mind, either," he continued. "Our minds are full of negative thoughts, positive thoughts, or a mixture of the two. There are happy memories and there are sad, all floating in our minds together. There are feelings of hope and of hopelessness bobbing about side by side. But our minds, like this glass, are not empty. We have to learn how to flush out the poisons and the waste, just like we have to flush a toilet. And we have to learn to refill our minds again with good, positive, hopeful, helpful, encouraging thoughts."

Picture Dexter and Birdie Yager in those early days in the 1960s when they risked their financial future on a brand-new business. They still lived in the row house with their 1955 station wagon. But every night, just before Dexter went to sleep, he drove down Dominick Street to Rome's only Cadillac dealership and garage.

"I sat there in the darkness," he remembers, "staring at the brightly lit Cadillacs in the showroom window. I focused on a light red DeVille with plush leather seats and electric windows. We didn't have a dime extra in the bank, but standing in the darkness I told myself over and over again that one day soon, that car would be mine."

"Dexter wasn't the only one with dreams," Birdie reminds us. "While he was dreaming about trading in the Ford for a Cadillac DeVille, I had a dream house in a neighborhood on the outskirts of Rome. I dreamed that our children would have a backyard with a lawn and a little stream on a street that was peaceful and safe. Once I shared my dream with Dexter, he would park the old Ford in front of my dream house for fifteen minutes at a time, claiming it for me and for our family. It's a wonder the neighbors didn't call the cops while Dexter sat there staring and dreaming and claiming that place for his own."

"I learned to focus on what I wanted," he explains. "It was the best way to flush out all the junk that other people wanted or didn't want for me. I had to claim my own life back from all those well-intentioned folks who thought their dreams for me were better than my own. Day after day, night after night, I fed on my dreams for the future."

Today, Dexter and Birdie Yager enjoy their ultimate dream house on Lake Wylie near Charlotte, North Carolina. The old row house is just a memory. The rotted-out Ford station wagon has been replaced. Besides a long list of Christian causes and local and national charities that they support, they are creating a camp for children to learn about the free-enterprise system and how they, too, can succeed at it. The Yagers are trying to help reprogram a whole generation from "I can't" to "I can do it if I try."

One important way to improve your "diet" is to *listen to tapes and read books.* From the earliest days of childhood, our brains act like tape recorders with the built-in microphone always on Record. Voices we hear—some experts say even before we leave the womb—are stored permanently in those mysterious archives encased somewhere between our ears. Some of the voices give good advice, others not so good. But all the voices are recorded, and whether we like it or not, those old tapes—especially the bad ones—play over and over again in our heads.

"You're ugly!"

"You're stupid."

"You're just a girl."

"You're accident prone, you know."

"Once a failure, always a failure."

And the tapes play on, old tapes, tapes we no longer believe but tapes we can't stop playing. Take a minute and ask yourself: What are the tapes that you play that undermine your self-esteem and cause you to underestimate your potential? For Dexter it was college degrees, limited vocabulary, and growing up on the wrong side of the street. What tapes are you playing that take you down and what new tapes could you play to bring you up again?

A few years ago, in Innsbruck, Austria, my special friend and confidant, Billy Zeoli, the president of Gospel Films (and the man most responsible for urging me to write this book), made a speech in the Olympic Stadium. To thousands of Europeans who were just discovering free enterprise and its benefits, Billy told the story of a speech Winston Churchill made shortly before his death to the graduating class of a great English university.

Churchill arrived at the occasion a little late, Billy related. He walked to the front of the large auditorium still wearing his heavy coat and black felt bowler. While the students cheered, the former prime minister slowly removed his hat and coat and placed them on the stand beside him. He looked old and tired, but he stood proud and erect before them.

The crowd grew silent. They knew this might be the last speech the old prime minister would ever make. One thousand pink, scrubbed faces stared up at the man who had valiantly led the fight to deliver England from the Nazi threat. His rich, full life as a statesman, poet, artist, author, war correspondent, husband, and father was almost over. What advice would he give them? How would he condense all that experience into one sixty-minute speech? Churchill looked down on them for one long minute and then spoke these three words:

"Never give up!"

The students looked at the old man, waiting for him to say more. For at least another thirty to forty-five seconds the former prime minister just stared back at them. His eyes twinkled. His face glowed. Then he spoke again. This time he growled it louder.

"Never give up!"

One last time Churchill paused. Around the room, faculty eyes were filling with tears. They remembered the Nazi aircraft over London and the bombs falling on their schools, homes, and cathedrals. They remembered Churchill walking through the rubble of their dreams with that cigar clutched tightly in his left hand, while his right hand reached out over them with the sign for victory. In his endless silence that day, even the youngest of them were moved to tears. Finally the old man spoke one last time.

"Never give up!"

This time he shouted it. His three-word graduating speech echoed up and down the auditorium. At first the crowd was silent, surprised, waiting for more. Nobody moved. One by one they realized there was no need for more. He had said it all. In his lifetime of crisis he had never given up. And the world was changed forever by his presence.

Slowly, Churchill put on his hat and coat. Before they realized the speech was over, he turned and began to walk from the stage. At that moment the cheering began, and it didn't end until long after the old man was gone.

Billy Zeoli used the Churchill story to finish his speech, which was taped on audio and video. Thousands of people requested the tape, among them a young German, Wolfgang Backhaus. He took the video back to Germany, where he and his wife were building a new business.

"I can't tell you how many times my wife and I have listened to that tape," Wolfgang tells us. "When the Berlin wall went down, we knew it was time to bring our products and our plan to East Germany. Still, it wasn't going to be easy. We took the chance! We invited people in for our presentation. Few understood how free enterprise could work. Few would take the chance. But whenever we considered quitting, we played the tape of Billy's speech and heard Churchill's words again, "Never give up!"

Today, the Backhauses own a distribution organization that stretches across Europe. They drowned out the "We can't do it" tape in their own minds with Churchill's famous words, "Never give up!"

Early in their own business venture, former Colt football star Brian Herosian and his wife, Deidre, decided that listening to audio tapes that would inspire and inform them would be the key to changing their attitudes. "We listen to one inspirational tape a day," Brian claims. "We have a playback unit in our car, in our living room, and in our bedroom. We take a tape player on vacations and even listen while we walk in the morning or exercise at the gym."

Brian and Deidre have a habit of listening to helpful tapes and reading motivational books and pamphlets. "We read or listen to something positive every day," Brian tells us. "We especially love testimonials of people who overcome tough times. It makes us feel more confident about the tough times we're facing."

Dexter and Birdie Yager agree. They're dedicated their lives to teaching countless others like the Herosians this philosophy. "My mother was a reader," Dexter recalls. "Almost every evening of her life she sat down to read the Bible. When I asked her why she read it so faithfully, Mom answered without a pause, 'Some people sit down every night to watch television. But television doesn't make me feel better about myself or the world. So I read God's Word instead.'

"When I look back on my mother's life," Dexter concludes, "I realize how much of her strength came from those evenings alone in that ancient book. She read the stories of creation to find her own spiritual roots. She memorized the Psalms when she was troubled or afraid. She was inspired and informed by the Old Testament stories of Moses' sister, Miriam, of Queen Esther and the prophet Deborah, of Ruth and Naomi, and by the New Testament stories of Mary, the mother of Jesus, of his friends, Mary and Martha, of Lydia and the other brave Jewish women who helped change the world. And she read the life and teachings of Jesus to find forgiveness and grace and to strengthen her for her own difficult journey."

Grandma Yager passed down to her children and grandchildren a love for reading, not just the Bible but all kinds of books. Dexter did not go to college, but inspired by his mother he has read consistently for the past thirty years. What better education could we get? What good is a degree if it isn't backed by a lifetime of reading?

"Birdie tries to read at least one new book a month," Dexter says. "There are personal-development books, inspirational books, spiritual books, skill-developing books, success and organizational principles books. It doesn't even hurt us to read books about successful business practices," he adds, grinning. "After all, we're in business. Why not be successful at it? A doctor has to keep up with scientific research. A lawyer has to know all the new cases coming down. A minister goes on reading the Bible and theology until the day he dies. Why should compassionate capitalists do any less?"

What books are you reading, what tapes are you listening to, that help you build a more positive attitude about yourself and your potential as an entrepreneur? Across our organization the one-book-per-month practice is pretty well established.

Since we're talking about feeding our inner spirit and thus building a more positive attitude about ourselves and our potential, remember the power of friends. The people we hang around with have more influence on our attitudes than we imagine.

The secret to our company's success is people like the Yagers, Herosians, and Backhauses who are drawn together by their common dreams. In seminars and rallies, across kitchen tables or seated around the fireplace, these men and women share and dream together. In the

New Testament the apostle Paul writes this advice to the new young churches: "Forsake not the assembling of yourselves together." Two thousand years later the Beatles sang a song about how "I get by with a little help from my friends."

Unfortunately, too many of us inherit friends who don't help us build new life-enhancing attitudes. They drag us down. When a politician complained to President Charles de Gaulle that his own friends were bringing him down, de Gaulle replied, *"Changez vos amis."* Change your friends. Another Frenchman over one hundred years earlier, Jacques Delille, spoke words we all need to take seriously: "Fate chooses your relations," he said, "but you must choose your friends."

In talking about changing our diet, we're not worried about calories or carbohydrates, fat grams or sodium. In this case we're talking about our intake of thoughts and hopes and dreams. Are you surrounded by bad-mouthers, doomsayers, nitpickers, and gloom slingers? Or do you have a growing list of friends whose very presence makes you feel better about yourself and more hopeful about your future. Garbage in. Garbage out. Beware!

Exercise. To be really fit, you still have to exercise. Don't be like the fellow who said: "Whenever I feel like exercising, I lie down until the feeling passes." If you want to be an entrepreneur, you have to flex your muscles. You have to get out there and try.

Winston Churchill said, "Success is going from failure to failure with great enthusiasm." And Thomas Edison added, "Success is ninety percent perspiration and ten percent inspiration." Both Churchill and Edison knew that you had to get into the contest before you had any possibility of winning.

You may not win every race. In fact, you might go from failure to failure. But getting out and exercising will help you develop your talents—it will get you "in shape." Most people just do not try to accomplish anything, and never develop the entrepreneurial "muscle" it takes to succeed.

In my hometown are plenty of examples of the difference the right attitude can make. A friend, Peter Secchia, the son of Italian immigrants, was told by his extended Old World family that education was a waste of time and energy. Peter didn't listen.

Another friend, Paul Collins, heard from practically everybody that a young black man could be an athlete or a jazz musician but not a successful painter. Paul didn't listen.

A third close friend, Ed Prince, learned early that poor boys whose fathers die young could not succeed at business. Ed didn't listen, either.

Peter Secchia went on to become the United States Ambassador to Italy. Paul Collins's magnificent paintings hang in prestigious galleries and museums around the world. And Ed Prince is the chief executive officer of his own prosperous and admired corporation.

Each of these persons overcame the "brainwashing" of their inherited past—the negative thinking that could have crippled their entrepreneurial spirits. They fed on healthy, positive ideas and surrounded themselves with healthy, positive-minded people. They walked away from negative friends and acquaintances who would drag them down. And from their youth on, they exercised their entrepreneurial muscles. They dreamed dreams, took risks, and though at times they stumbled and failed along the way, they are winners today because their attitude was right!

Work hard to overcome the negative ideas about yourself that you have inherited. Feed on a healthy diet of positive, encouraging, hopeful thoughts. And start exercising your entrepreneurial muscles today. Have an idea? Try it! You will be surprised how successful you can be. I have a company of friends whose life stories prove it!

Bill and Hona Childers didn't grow up poor, exactly. "Just broke," Hona explains. Her father was a mechanic and operated his own garage. Bill's dad owned a small textile manufacturing plant. When Mr. Childers became ill, Bill dropped out of college to care for his father, and when he died, the plant had to be sold to pay the bills. There were no life savings, no insurance, no legacy. Several years later, Hona's father also died, leaving the Childerses with two teenage children, Billy and Beth, and two widowed mothers.

At that moment in their lives the Childerses could have felt sorry for themselves. They had more than their share of responsibility and not much income. After a stint in the army, Bill worked in Charlotte, North Carolina, in sales for a steel-strapping company, and Hona took part-time work as a Polaroid Girl, promoting cameras in shopping malls and hosting open houses in condominiums around Charlotte. They had no fancy degrees, no savings accounts, no rich uncles hidden in the woodwork. But they believed in themselves. Their attitude was right. They knew in their hearts that something would come along to give them financial stability, and when they saw the opportunity to own a business in 1973, they decided to take the risk whatever it cost them.

Today the Childerses live in a beautiful home with a mounted five-hundred-pound blue marlin on one wall of their trophy room and a thousand-pound elk that Bill shot in Colorado mounted on another. Best of all, their future and their children's financial future is guaranteed and both widowed mothers are cared for with love. Free from daily worries about paying the bills, Bill and Hona are also free to donate their time, money, and leadership skills to compassionate causes that they care about deeply. After Hurricane Andrew devastated Florida, the Childerses, along with Amway volunteers from across the country, appeared on the scene to bring hope and help to those in need. The Childerses began their business with big dreams, little resources, and a positive attitude. It was the positive attitude that made the difference.

This is a great period in history. We should be glad to be alive in it! Of course there are problems, but look at the past and at the problems we have already overcome. We are all tired of the prophets of doom and their shrill, pessimistic voices warning of our civilization's imminent destruction. "We're running out of resources!" "The banking system is near collapse!" "The coming great depression will destroy life as we know it!" "The end is at hand!"

Some of these doomsayers make good money from their false warnings. But instead of helping the situation, they cripple our spirits and lead us to despair. We must not listen to those who are constantly negative!

One of Dexter Yager's best positive attitude lines says it all. "I despise the guys who criticize and minimize the enterprise of other guys whose enterprise has made them rise above the guys who criticize."

When my son, Douglas, was just thirteen, he and I went boating on Lake Michigan. I remember the motor humming and the wind splashing us with spray as we flew across the water. "One day," I shouted to my son, "you'll have a boat that will go even faster than this one." "Afraid not," he answered. "The world will probably run out of gas before I get my chance."

I cut the engine. For a moment we drifted in silence. "I'm going to tell you something, Douglas," I said emphatically. "When you buy your boat, you won't need to worry about gas, because the boat will have a lifetime fuel supply built in." "You don't know that," he said skeptically. "You can't be sure."

"A few years ago, I didn't know that we would be flying from Washington, D.C., to Paris in just three hours, either," I told him, "or that we would be faxing mail back and forth across the country in seconds. But it happened. The insurmountable problems of yesterday look easy today. And we must go on believing that the insurmountable problems of today will look easy tomorrow."

I am an incurable optimist. I believe in the creative genius that God has placed within us to solve problems, like running out of gas or feeding the world's hungry. If we maintain our faith and our vision, we will continue to find solutions to the great problems of the world. Your attitude and mine will make all the difference in our success as human beings and as business entrepreneurs.

Six years ago, Dexter and Birdie Yager had succeeded in their business beyond their wildest dreams. Tens of thousands of people had been mobilized and trained through their vision and hard work. They were wealthy and powerful. Five different American presidents had invited the former beer salesman and his wife to be their guests in the White House. The Yagers were living on cloud nine. They had no idea that another huge test lay just ahead.

In October 1986, Dexter experienced a strange sensation in his right arm and leg. "I thought I had pinched a nerve," he recalls. "I didn't want to bother anybody with my problems, so I tried to ignore them until they went away. Only this time they didn't go away."

Three days later, Dexter couldn't walk. His right side was completely paralyzed. Paramedics rushed him to the intensive-care ward. Doctors were summoned. Tests were taken. His blood pressure had soared off the charts.

"The specialists warned me," Birdie recalls, shaking her head at the memory, "that if Dexter lived, he would never walk again. The family and I gathered around his hospital bed. We were afraid that this proud and energetic man might be forced to lie there paralyzed and helpless until his death. The best we could hope for, the doctors warned, was lifting Dexter in and out of a wheelchair for the rest of his life."

"It took some time," he recalls, "for it all to sink in. I had been rushing about the world for the past two decades caring for people that I loved. Now they would have to care for me. I was a cripple, the doctors claimed. I would never walk again."

How easy it would have been for Dexter to believe the doctors, to trust their diagnosis for his future, to let their predictions cloud and shape his dreams. But after a few days of lying there, he made his own decision about the future. Since that stormy day in the West End Brewery car, Dexter and Birdie had discovered one of God's greatest gifts, the power of a positive attitude. For the next six months they put that power to work as never before.

"Every day I struggled to bring my dead limbs back to life," he says quietly. "My right side was paralyzed, so I learned to use my left side instead. Birdie and the children lifted and turned, rubbed and nurtured me. Nurses and physical therapists stretched and pulled, rolled and pounded. Doctors prescribed and charted. Friends sent thousands of cards and flowers. The phone lines were jammed. People prayed. Inch by inch I dragged myself across those blue mats, looking down at my twisted arm and useless leg with growing hope. And through it all there was a voice in me saying, 'You can do it. You will walk again. Don't listen to the lie!' "

Late in 1986, a coliseum in North Carolina was filled with Dexter and Birdie's friends and distributors. The plan was simple. Birdie would wheel Dexter onto the stage. He would wave his good arm, share a few words of encouragement, and then be wheeled off the stage again. Dexter had a better idea.

The crowd waited in growing suspense. Their friend and mentor had been wounded. They thought they would be seeing what was left of him, and they wanted to remember better days. Then Dexter appeared. He wasn't in his chair. He was walking. It was more of a step, drag, step, but he was walking. People's eyes filled with tears, not of grief but of joy and gratitude. Dexter was walking.

It didn't matter that one hand hung limply at his side or that he had to drag his right leg. What mattered was this: with the help of God, his family, and friends, Dexter Yager had overcome. He was walking in spite of all those specialists and their dire predictions. Dexter believed in himself.

Whatever in your past has crippled you, whatever has made you feel like a loser, whatever fears you have about your personal or business dreams, listen to that voice within you that says, "You can do it. You will walk again. Don't listen to the lie!"

10

What Is a Mentor, and Why Do We Need One to Guide Us?

CREDO 10

We believe that before we can succeed as a compassionate capitalist, we must have an experienced mentor to guide us.

Therefore, we need to find someone whom we admire who has already achieved what we want to achieve and ask that person to help us reach our goals.

On November 9, 1950, United Nations military forces were on the verge of a full-fledged war with the Chinese communists in Korea. Without warning, two Chinese divisions poured across the Korean border. U.N. troops staggered backward in full retreat. Another five divisions, 300,000 combat-ready Chinese, were massed in Manchuria, about to cross the Yalu River. Stunned by the sudden turn of events, President Truman declared a state of emergency in the U.S. and urged all Americans to join the battle against "communist imperialism."

At a U.S. Army base near the 38th Parallel, Lieutenant Bill Britt, fresh from Officers' Candidate School, stood before his men. "All forces were on full alert," Bill remembers, "and at that stressful moment one of my new privates, freshly arrived in Korea, made a mistake. I can't even remember what he did, but I do remember that I chewed him out pretty badly while we were in ranks. He stood at attention before me and the rest of my men. I could see him blinking back tears of embarrassment." When he finished giving orders, the men double-timed to their assignments. He was rushing back toward his office when a weathered old sergeant moved gently into his way.

"Lieutenant, sir," he said respectfully, "could I talk to you a moment in your office?"

Bill entered his tent, walked to the desk, and turned to face him. "I had a very good relationship with my officers and my enlisted men. They respected me because I respected them, but this sergeant was unhappy with me and it wasn't hard to miss."

"Sir," he said, getting right to the point, "your power seat is right in that chair. Next time you have any trouble with a man in this outfit, you just tell me. I'll get hold of him and bring him here to you. Then I'll leave and you can chew him up one side and down the other."

Bill was surprised that he had been confronted. He was the lieutenant. But the sergeant soon proved to be not only older but wiser and more experienced as well.

"You have the right to do it either way," the sergeant concluded, "but this is what I would recommend to you, sir. Chew 'em out here, in private, not before the other men. They'll respect you for it."

It took courage for that man to confront a superior. But Bill knew the minute he started speaking that the sergeant was right and that he had been wrong.

"Sergeant," he said, moving around the desk to shake his hand, "you are exactly right. I should have known better. I appreciate your advice. I will not forget it."

They shook hands. The sergeant turned and rushed back to join his men. "During those rough days clearing mine fields and building bridges," Bill concludes, "I learned to depend on him for practical advice under fire. When I was transferred to another engineering division, I asked special permission for that sergeant to go with me. It's sad that I can't even remember his name, but in a very difficult time in my life, he was my mentor and my friend."

What Is a Mentor and Why Do We Need One to Succeed in Life as Well as in Business?

In the eighth century before Christ, the Greek writer Homer wrote an epic poem describing Odysseus's adventures during his ten-year voyage home after the Trojan War. While he was gone, he entrusted the care and education of his beloved son, Telemachus, to his faithful friend, Mentor. Almost three thousand years later that man's name has come to mean a wise and trusted counselor.

Over the years *mentor* has been used to describe a favorite teacher, a wise master, an insightful friend, an experienced educator, a seasoned guide. If we are fortunate, all through our lives, mentors appear to help us at our moment of need. For Lieutenant Bill Britt, newly arrived on the front lines of the Korean War, it was a sergeant who spoke with courage and with wisdom. Looking back over your life, what memories have you of mentors who have appeared, made their contribution to your life, become lifelong friends or simply disappeared?

When I was in high school, I met Jay Van Andel. I liked him from the moment we met. He was bright. He was steady. And he was always positive. We both dreamed of starting a business of our own. Ideas flowed out of me like water out of a Brooklyn fire hydrant in the midst of a summer heat wave. Jay knew how to regulate the flow, to ask questions, to make suggestions, to focus and direct our energy. We became partners and best friends. And though Jay would give me equal credit for our successes (and for our failures) for almost a half century, he has been a mentor to me—a wise and trusted counselor and friend—and I will always be glad and grateful for his friendship.

Mentors Are the Keepers of Important Traditions and Life-Shaping Stories. These stories are vital to our personal growth and to the accomplishment of our goals. Among her many gifts, Bill Britt's grandmother became just such a mentor for him when he was seven years old.

"My father was an alcoholic," Bill explains. "He was a good man when he was sober, but under the influence, everything changed. He kept our family in total chaos. We didn't know what would happen next. One Sunday morning my grandmother came to our house, wearing her hat and gloves. She took me by the hand and led me off to a Methodist Sunday school. 'I want you to meet the Lord,' she said, and that day I learned for the first time about my other Father, my Father in heaven who loved me and would be my mentor and friend forever."

Sometimes our parents turn out to be our most effective mentors. Other times they fail. When Leonard Bernstein's father was criticized for not having given his son more encouragement as a child, he answered, "How was I to know he would grow up to be Leonard Bernstein?" If Bill Britt's dad were alive today, he might say, "If only I had known." He failed as a mentor to his son. He passed on heartbreak and sorrow, a legacy Bill had to work to overcome. Fortunately, his grandmother stepped in and introduced her young grandson to the great stories of the Christian faith.

Mentors Pass On to Us Knowledge that Would Be Difficult for Us to Learn on Our Own. Without mentors we have to reinvent the wheel each new generation. Aristotle said, "What we have to learn to do, we learn by doing." It is true that we learn by doing, but a mentor can keep us from making the same mistakes she has made. A mentor speeds us ahead of the pack, gives us an edge, multiplies what we know by her own knowledge.

As a boy of eight, Francis Spellman, later a Roman Catholic cardinal, used to help out in his father's grocery store. One piece of advice he gave young Frank stuck forever in his mind. "Always associate with people smarter than yourself," he told his son. And then (one hopes he said this with a grin or a wink) he added, "And you will have no difficulty finding them."

"Dad was an auto-department manager for Montgomery Ward," Bill Britt remembers. "He worked hard and his bosses respected him, but every time my father lost his battle with the bottle, the company had to move him on to a different city, hoping to give him a fresh start. So, because we were always on the move, I was a very poor student in high school.

"My senior year we lived in Daytona Beach, Florida. To help pay the bills, I worked every night until eleven at a Sinclair service station on Main Street. At night, when he was drinking and a little crazy, my father would try to take the money out of the station cash register, so I had to guard the place every possible moment.

"All during those difficult high school years," Bill recalls with a grin, "my mother was a quiet, loving presence. She was always there for me when I felt discouraged or depressed. Then one unforgettable night when I had given up, I told my mother that I was dropping out of school. Instead of the understanding and sympathy I had expected, without a pause Mom looked me in the eye and said firmly, 'Over my dead body.' I suppose it was one of the shortest but most effective mentoring sessions of my youth.

"Needless to say," Bill adds, "I stayed in school. I had no time for sports or for all-school events like concerts or dances. I had no time for friends and, worse, I never learned to study. In fact, not once during those four years did I even take a book home. I just did enough to pass and somehow I escaped high school with a diploma.

"That's why I was so amazed in the Army when I was selected first for leadership training and then for Officers' Candidate School. I wanted to succeed, but I didn't even know how to read for a test, let alone how to write an academic paper. I flunked the first round of exams and thought for sure I would be dumped from the program. One afternoon I was called to the office of Captain Schwartz, a Jewish officer who had been wounded in Korea. At that time he was serving as an adviser to my O.C.S. class.

" 'Cadet Britt,' he said, and I knew by the sound of his voice that my dreams to become an officer in the U.S. Army had ended, 'you are definitely officer material.' I could not believe my ears. 'You are strong physically,' he said. 'You command the other men's respect. You are bright and quick to learn the drill. You'll make a fine officer in the U.S. Army. You have the IQ and the gifts of leadership, but you just don't know how to study.'

"I was so excited I could hear my own heart beat. This man was going to give me a second chance. He didn't see me for what I was as a student but for what I could become. He had taken time to recognize my strengths and was about to help me overcome a weakness that might have dragged me down into failure for the rest of my life.

" 'Sit down here, son,' he said, motioning to a chair beside his metal desk. 'Let me tell you a few little secrets about study habits. First, when the other guys go to bed, you make sure you stay up reading and underlining those books. Second, you find somebody in every class who knows the material, and you ask him to help you. Third, you make an outline for every subject. Every book you read, you fill in the outline a little more. Every lecture you hear, add more details. When a teacher quotes a book, find the book in the library and scan it. Add that material to your outline. . . .'

"Captain Schwartz took fifteen or twenty minutes and showed me how to study. In all my years in school, no teacher had looked at me closely enough to realize that I might have brains, I just didn't know how to use them. My grades shot up from 18 to 20 out of 100 to 90s and 95s. I graduated Officer Cadet School with honors because one man who knew more than I did about study habits took the time to pass on his insights to me. That officers' training class began with sixty-three soldiers. Thanks to Captain Schwartz, I was one of the twenty-three men who finished. When someone believes in you, it becomes the strongest motivating force on earth."

Mentors Teach Us What We Need to Know to Be Successful in Life.
Socrates, a classic mentor, described himself as "a midwife assisting the labor of the mind in bringing knowledge and wisdom to birth." Picture yourself pregnant with a dream. The mentor stands over you and helps you relax and breathe during the painful contractions while your dream is in labor. The mentor assists the dream down the birth canal and out into the light of day. The mentor holds your dream up by its heels and spanks it to life. Then the mentor places that newborn dream in your arms, smiles, and walks away to assist another dreamer in labor.

Four hundred years before Christ, Hippocrates, the Greek physician and father of medicine, described his work as a mentor for his young medical students. "Students are like the soil," he said. "And teachers are the planters of seed. It is the task of the teacher to plant at the proper season. Diligent students then cultivate the fields."

When the war in Korea ended, Bill Britt went home to North Carolina and enrolled for an engineering degree under the G.I. Bill at North Carolina State. He met Peggy Garner, fell in love, and got married. Bill's first job after graduation was assistant to the city manager of Raleigh, North Carolina.

"Bill Carper was my boss," Bill recalls. "He managed one of the great cities of the South, but almost every day he would call me into his office, sit back behind his big desk, look me in the eye, and ask loudly, 'Well, Bill, what did you learn today?' Before long I was asking myself that question: 'What am I learning from this board meeting or from that blueprint? What new information am I getting from this encounter with a colleague in the hallway or from that budget proposal?' Bill Carper wanted me to succeed as a city manager. He was my mentor and every day he took a few minutes of his busy schedule to push me to think, to analyze, to grow intellectually, and to develop the gifts that God had given me."

Mentors Teach Most Who Love Best. Augustine declared that teaching is the greatest act of love and that love is the best aid to learning. I don't know who added these words, but they've always been an inspiration to me: "Those who love most, teach best." Another version of this classic idea has become a favorite among a company of my friends. "They don't care how much you know," the saying goes, "until they know how much you care."

Think about the people in your life who have loved you best. Aren't they the very people who have taught you most? Peggy Britt's father was just such a mentor to Bill and Peggy during those early days of their marriage.

"My father filled our home with anxiety and deep concern about the future," Bill admits today, "but in Peggy's home I learned about father love. Her father, G. B. Garner, had a refrigeration-repair service in Raleigh. When you saw him walk down the streets in his baggy pants and work shirt, you wondered if he even had a suit or tie to wear. He didn't spend money on himself, always on his family. Everyone had a job to do in the Garner home, but there was a sense of love there that began with Mr. Garner's easy smile and trickled down to everyone who walked through their front door.

"His office was in his home, and day or night restaurateurs or grocers might call to report a refrigeration emergency. Mr. Garner was like a doctor who made twenty-four-hour house calls with his tools in his little truck. In the daytime Mr. Garner would rush off alone to repair a meat locker or an ice cream freezer. But when those emergency calls came at night, the whole family rushed to their assigned seats in Mr. Garner's truck and went with him."

"My father believed that the family should be together every possible evening," Peggy remembers. "We all thought it natural when the phone rang in the middle of our family time to jump into that old car he used as a truck with Dad, to hand him the tools and bring him cold drinks while he worked, and then to reward ourselves with a stop at the ice cream store when the work was done."

"You could feel Mr. Garner's love," Bill says. "He and his wife, Hattie Mae, were both great people, and they passed on their love to Peggy and me. Now we're trying to pass that same kind of love to thousands of our 'adopted children' in this business."

Mentors Have the Courage to Confront. Augustine was right when he said learning is facilitated by love, but sometimes insights also come from people who don't even like you. After all, sometimes confrontation is a kind of love. If people don't care about you at all, why should they go to the trouble to tell you where you're wrong and what you need do about it?

A young man in our company taught me that. Years ago, I was

standing before a large roomful of our most successful distributors at a conference in Rio. I was rather rambunctious in those days, pacing about the room, acting more like General Patton than General Schwarzkopf. When I finished my enthusiastic presentation and asked for questions, the crowd grew alarmingly quiet. Nobody spoke. They applauded politely and then just looked down or away.

"Are you sure there aren't any questions?" I asked, my eyes darting about the room, hoping someone would get a dynamic Q&A session started. Nobody spoke. Finally, after a long moment of awkward silence, a young man said softly, "I wouldn't dare ask you a question." He paused, swallowed hard, and then had the courage to go on. "I'm afraid that by the time I got through, you'd take my pants off and I'd end up standing in this room naked and exposed before everybody."

Without knowing or desiring it, I had been responding to people in a way that humiliated them. Instead of sharing information, I would blow them away. People were afraid to talk to me, but I had no sense of the power that I wielded over their lives. Without wanting to, I was driving them to the point where they didn't really care to be honest with me anymore.

That embarrassing confrontation happened some twenty years ago, but I still remember it every time someone asks me a question. The young man changed my life with one courageous confrontation. From that day I have tried to be sensitive to anyone who questions me. I try to feel where he is coming from. I try to wrap my answer in a spirit of understanding and love.

Mentors Make Themselves Available

When Greg Duncan, another of our successful distributors, was interviewed for this book, he told a story that moved me. I hope you understand the reason that I am about to share it. Greg's story gave me hope that I have improved.

"We were in a beach resort in Hawaii," Greg told Steven Zeoli, the director of our compassionate capitalism video series. "I had never been alone with Rich DeVos before. Lauri and I were fairly new in the business. I felt embarrassed to ask this busy man for an appointment. But I heard that every morning he walked alone on the beach. So the first morning in Hawaii, I got up at seven, ran down the hotel stairs, and jogged along the sand hoping to see Rich, but I missed him. The next morning I got up at six, but I missed him again. Finally I gave up, went into the hotel dining room, piled on the banana pancakes and coconut syrup from the breakfast buffet, and went to a table overlooking the water to eat alone. Suddenly Rich was there, fruit plate in hand, looking down at me.

" 'Good morning, Greg,' he said, remembering my name and looking me right in the eye. 'Mind if I join you?' I was twenty-eight years old. Lauri and I were fairly new in this business. There was no reason for Rich to remember me, but he did. I had so many questions about the business. I couldn't wait to hear Rich DeVos answer them. Instead he had me talking. We ate together for forty-five minutes and he hardly said a word. He'd just ask a little question, then another little question, and another and another until I had worked out my problems on my own. He taught me that leaders are listeners, that the most successful mentors know to ask questions and not to answer them.

"Before Rich left me that day," Greg remembers, "he gave me some advice I've never forgotten. 'The one bad thing about achieving what you have at such a young age,' he warned me, 'is that you might get complacent and end up staying where you are forever.' Then Rich put some dreams in my heart about affecting people for good that took a couple of years for me to believe that they were even real. 'When a dream comes true,' he advised me, 'always replace it with a bigger dream. And those big dreams will keep you alive and excited for the rest of your life.' "

After learning from his mentor in Korea, Britt has gone on to become one of the greatest mentors in the history of our company. The Britt network of distributors stretches from Britt Plaza in Durham, North Carolina, to every state in the nation and to dozens of countries around the world. He and Peggy Britt started with a product sample kit that cost just twenty-five dollars. Then, because they developed their mentoring gifts, they were able to mobilize hundreds, then thousands, then tens of thousands of people in the business.

Bill Britt labels his style of mentoring "father power." "In this business," he explains, "we could call it father and mother power. We up-line 'dads and moms' must learn to parent our down-line 'sons and daughters.' Like good parents we rejoice when our children grow up, when they become our peers, when they go on to do better even than we have done.

"We must remember," Bill adds, "like natural parents, our influence goes on for generation after generation. In the Old Testament book of Exodus, Moses reminds us that we aren't just showing love to our own children but to four generations that follow. When we love our 'sons and daughters,' when we mentor them with our loving example, they go on to love their 'sons and daughters.' And we sit back and watch with amazement as our 'grandchildren' and 'great-grandchildren' in this business go on to love as we have loved their 'parents' before them and to succeed in the business beyond our wildest dreams."

For most of us our parents are our first mentors. What they pass on to us, we pass on to our children and through them to our grandchildren and to generations yet unborn.

Stan Evans's father was a farmer. Stan credits his father's skill as a mentor for his success years later in this business. "Farmers traded equipment," he remembers. "Our neighbors would borrow Dad's planter when crops were going in, and we would borrow our neighbor's harvester at the close of the season. Sometimes Dad's equipment would come back rusty, broken, or out of fuel. But when Dad returned the machinery he had borrowed, it was always in better shape than when he had borrowed it.

" 'Don't just do what's right, son,' he said. 'Do what's generous. And your neighbor will never forget it.'

"If a piece of borrowed machinery came to Dad broken," Stan remembers, "Dad would fix it. If it needed tuning, Dad would give it an overhaul. If a belt was old, Dad replaced it. If a tire was flat, he would put on a new one. Of course, it cost him to be generous, but in the long run his generosity returned him rich dividends.

" 'When I offer to pay people for using their equipment,' my father explained, 'they always say *no*. So I figure fixing, fueling, and cleaning their gear before I give it back is a way of saying thanks. The average guy may grease it or hose off the mud,' he explained, 'but I want the man who risked his gear with me to remember that he got it back better than he lent it. Then, when I ask him for a loan again, he won't hesitate.'

"By his example," Stan remembers gratefully, "my father taught me to think about the other guy's feelings. To do for them what I would like them to do for me. I've tried to pass that rule on to my own family and to the people in this business. And the results have been profitable for us all."

Bernice Hansen has demonstrated "mother power" to Jay and me since 1950, when Walter Bass, Bernice's sponsor, and I drove to the

Hansen home in Cuyahoga Falls, Ohio, to talk to Bernice and her husband, Fred, about selling Nutrilite products. Harry Truman was president at the time, the minimum wage was just seventy-five cents an hour, and "Good Night, Irene" was America's most popular song when Bernice joined our company of friends.

After her husband's death, Bernice Hansen went on to establish one of our largest and most successful distributorships across America and in fifty-two countries around the world. Jay and I have always been just "the boys" to Bernice. Her contagious smile and strong, loving presence have been so important to us over the decades. Always embracing life with zest and enthusiasm, Bernice married Dr. Ralph Gilbert, a retired ophthalmologist in 1987. How many times over the past four decades, a word of council or advice from Bernice Hansen-Gilbert has helped give Jay and me new insight and direction. And we have done our best to pass on to thousands of others what Bernice and others like her have passed on to us.

Joe and Helyne Victor have also demonstrated parent power in their own family and to this entire business. Joe was a milkman in tiny Cuyahoga Falls, Ohio, when Fred and Bernice Hansen moved to town, bringing with them the dream that Jay and I had to build Amway through an independent network of distributors who owned their own businesses. Fred Hansen, a barber, got the dream from Walter Bass, who shared it while sitting in Fred's barber chair in Ada, Michigan. Fred passed on the dream to Joe and Helyne Victor in Cuyahoga Falls. And the Victors, in turn, passed it on to their sons and daughters-in-law, Jody and Kathy Victor and Ron and Debra Victor.

"I still remember that day when you delivered the first truckload of Frisk to our house in Cuyahoga Falls," Jody told me recently. "I was eleven years old. You hired me to paste labels on that first Amway product at a nickel a bottle. At night I lay in my bed, listening to you developing that first plan with my parents, the Hansens, and the Dutts. I was just a little kid," he added, "but already the dream was taking hold of me."

In the beginning our small manufacturing plant was in Ada, Michigan, and our original group of independent distributors was in Cuyahoga Falls, Ohio. As their business grew, Helyne Victor had the family's cherry dining room table sawed in half to make two desks for Joe and herself. Now the Victors have replaced that living-room-turned-office of thirty-two years ago with a complex of offices and meeting rooms. The senior Victors were in that small group of pioneers who signed our charter distribution plan and passed on the dream behind that plan to their children. Apparently, they taught their children well. Today, Jody and Kathy, Ron and Debra, have businesses that stretch across the country and around the world. Now Jody Victor has joined his father in the highest levels of leadership in our business.

"We lived in a very small frame house in Cuyahoga Falls," Jody remembers. "We had no living room, for it became my father's office. As a child, I watched hundreds of people from all walks of life come through our front door. It was so exciting. Before my young eyes, negative people became positive, non-producers became producers, the depressed and hopeless saw hope reborn.

"Why?" Jody adds, getting up suddenly from his chair and pacing the room enthusiastically. "Because my hero, my mentor, my father believed in those people. He displayed an enormous capacity of compassion for others. It was contagious. People changed overnight. And I was lucky enough to sit in the catbird seat and watch and learn and be changed myself. Thank you, Dad," he adds. And I would chime in my own thanks to the senior and junior Victors and to uncounted, unheralded people like them whose selfless service as mentors, in our business and in homes, schools and churches around the world has changed millions of lives for the good forever!

Brothers and sisters also have the power to pass on dreams and to inspire and inform the dreamers. Bill Britt saw his own brother enter the business and succeed. "Peg and I are so very proud of my brother, Bobby, and his wife, Mitzi," Bill told us recently. "You can't imagine how good it makes you feel to see those you love the most reach levels of achievement that they never dreamed."

After starting their own sales business, Greg and Lauri Duncan passed on the dream to Greg's brother, Brad. "And it wasn't just the business that Greg passed on to us," Brad recalls. "Greg and Lauri are models and mentors to my wife, Julie, and to me. They have the kind of marriage and family that we want to have. They represent the kinds of values in their church and in their community that we want to live out in our lives as well."

Brad and Julie Duncan are young in this business, but already they have achieved far more than people twice their age or experience. "And though we've worked hard," Brad admits, "we couldn't have done it without Greg and Lauri to inspire us and to show us the way."

Brad and Julie Duncan went on to sponsor Julie's parents, Bob and Louise Eckard, who have succeeded in building their own distribution company and Greg and Brad's father, David Duncan, another high achiever in our business and in other ventures of his own. "I have been a free enterpriser all my life," the senior Duncan admits. "I owned leasing companies and construction businesses, but it was my children that passed on this particular dream to me." David and his wife, Darlene, went on to sponsor their third son, Dru, in our company of friends. Now, the whole family has reached high levels of achievement in the Amway business.

Father power. Mother power. Brother or sister, son or daughter power. Each of us has the power to influence someone near us and through that single influence to help change the world. "When you get married and have kids," Bill Britt reminds us, "you aren't dealing with those kids only, but with their kids and their kid's kids. Whatever you teach—bad or good—is passed on from generation to generation. When you mentor your children you have a profound and lasting effect on your grandchildren, your great-grandchildren and on generations that follow. That's what Jesus did," Bill concludes with a grin. "He only sponsored twelve but he mentored well and now he has a billion and a half in his group."

Jesus As a Mentor

There are fifty-eight references in the New Testament to the word *teacher,* and more than half of these references are to Jesus. I looked up *teach* for its original Greek meaning and found it is a wonderful and far-reaching word that means "to instruct, to demonstrate, to apprise of, to prove, and to show." Jesus was regarded by his disciples and enemies alike as primarily a teacher skilled in all these tasks. He engaged in public and in one-on-one teaching, and his ultimate goal for the people that he taught was for them to pass on what they had learned.

Like Bill's sergeant in Korea, Jesus often changed people's lives forever in one brief encounter. Do you remember the New Testament story of the young woman caught "in the act of adultery"? A crowd of angry, deceitful men dumped her at Jesus' feet. They were not concerned about the woman's morality. They were out to trick the "teacher." The Old Testament law was clear. Adulterers caught in the act could be stoned to death. Jesus would have to choose between obedience to the old law and the life of that young woman.

Find a Mentor Who Listens. Surrounded by the noisy crowd come to trap him, Jesus didn't say anything at first. That's the first lesson to learn about mentors. Those who don't rush to give advice are usually the most trustworthy. Those who stop long enough to really listen will invariably give the best advice, if they give any at all.

Instead Jesus knelt down on the sand and wrote words with his finger. To this day, no one knows what words he wrote. In Cecil B. DeMille's classic motion picture, *King of Kings,* Jesus wrote the list of sins committed by those self-righteous men standing around him in the crowd. All we know for certain is that Jesus paused to listen, think, pray, let tempers cool, and get his own bearings before he even began.

Find a Mentor Who Asks Questions. After a long pause he looked up and saw the stones held tightly in their hands. The men had come prepared to execute the sentence of death. Ignoring their questions, Jesus asked one of his own. "Whichever man among you is without sin, you throw the first stone."

It was a question really. "The woman may be guilty," he implied, "but which of you is not guilty of the same sin?" Apparently the question stopped them in their tracks. That's another sign of a good mentor. The person who knows what to ask and when to ask it is much more helpful than the person who rushes in to answer.

One by one the stones dropped from their hands, and the men disappeared until the woman was alone with Jesus and his students. Once again Jesus asked a question, this time of the terrified young woman at his feet.

"Who condemns you?" he asked her quietly. Slowly she looked up from the ground where she was lying in a heap. She could not believe her eyes. Her tormentors were gone. She had a second chance. "No man, teacher," she replies. "Nor do I," he answers softly. Then, almost as an afterthought—and surely not in condemnation or in judgment—he added these hopeful words: "Go and sin no more."

Find a Mentor Who Gives Good Advice. In the end, the mentor had five short words of wisdom. What do you think Jesus was trying to say to that poor woman at his feet? Jesus had already said that he was not condemning her. He was advising her not to go on sinning, but don't you think the woman had come to that conclusion already on her own?

Lying there in the sand surrounded by her executioners, you can imagine her thinking, "God, if I get out of this one, I'll never take that risk again."

Jesus' words were words of hope. He knew how difficult she would find breaking away from the life she had been living. So when he said, "Go and sin no more," he was passing on to her the hope that she could and would succeed at what she had already resolved in her heart.

Find a Mentor Whose Advice Is Backed by Love. Jesus' words were the answer to the real question she was asking. "Can I change? Can this nightmare end? Is there any real hope for me?" "Yes," his answer implied, "you can do it." His words "Go and sin no more" may sound like condemnation on the first pass. But go back. Hear them once again as she must have heard them.

This is a wise and loving teacher whose reputation has spread across the land. He begins his reply with these words, "I don't condemn you either." And ends his advice with, "Go and sin no more." I am convinced she heard those words that day as words of hope and promise. She is forgiven. She will succeed. Now she can go and live her new life with his blessing. The love she felt from Jesus that day must have changed her life forever. Love is the ultimate test of a good mentor. As my friends in Amway often say, "Nobody cares how much you know until they know how much you care."

David Taylor began his own business when he was still the left offensive tackle for the Baltimore Colts. "Many people laughed and doubted that I could succeed in business for myself," Dave remembers. "My first attempts at presenting the plan to others were discouraging. There were many times I felt like giving up. Then I went to a group meeting where I met my mentors, Rex Renfrow and Bill Britt. They told me they loved me," Dave recalls. "They said they believed in me and were proud of me.

"I was shocked," he said. "For years I had been a football player. When Mean Joe Green knocked me down, he didn't help me up, brush me off, and say, 'Hey, man, I love you.' More likely he would spit on me and walk away. But my mentors in this business loved each other and passed on that love to me. Their advice was important, but it was their love that got me through those first difficult months."

Beware the Untrustworthy Mentor

Do you remember the name Jim Jones? In October 1978 a news bulletin from Jonestown, Guyana, shocked and saddened the world. For reasons we still find confusing, the "Reverend" Jim Jones and almost a thousand of his followers in the People's Temple took (or were pressured into taking) poisoned Kool-Aid in a sacrament of death. The first pictures of their bloated bodies lying in the jungle will remain forever in my mind. The story of Jim Jones and of his innocent disciples will always be a warning against unworthy mentors and a terrible example of the consequences for those who trust them.

A Worthy Mentor Will Not Abuse Your Time. Jim Jones kept his followers in a state of exhaustion. Before the People's Temple moved to Jonestown, the church had been located in the Tenderloin district of San Francisco. Jones and his followers worked night and day to help the poor, lonely, unemployed, drug addicts, ex-convicts, the old and the retarded. They served thousands of free meals a week to the hungry in their neighborhood.

The longer and the harder they worked, the more exhausted they became. No one knew it then, but exhaustion was one of Jones's goals for his people. When you're exhausted—even from doing good—you lose the ability to think, to make wise decisions, to protect yourself and those you love. If a mentor is pushing you beyond your limits, if you are feeling more and more exhausted, beware!

A worthy mentor encourages you to be physically and spiritually rested. She praises you for hard work, but warns you when you're pushing beyond your limits and helps you regain control of your life again.

A Worthy Mentor Will Not Abuse Your Money. Jones knew how little time busy people have to pay their bills or keep their finances in order. He knew how many people couldn't or didn't even balance their checkbooks. So he suggested that all their checking and savings accounts be held in the name of the church. For "their own good," he held their credit cards, mortgage papers, even stocks and savings bonds in his name. Inevitably he ended up controlling their money, and with it their lives. If a mentor wants to control your money, if you discover that he's cheating you or holding back even temporarily something that you are owed, beware!

A worthy mentor will help you gain control of your finances, but he will insist that you make your own final decisions about money. He will work for your financial independence and will never take advantage or misuse your money for his own good.

A Worthy Mentor Will Not Abuse Discipline. Too many people don't like to make decisions for themselves. They would rather have a strong person make decisions for them. Jones took advantage of this weakness. Not only did he tell them what was right and wrong, he instituted penalties for doing wrong that included verbal and physical abuse in private and in public. He yelled at them. He humiliated them. He spanked them and he had them spank one another. The spankings became beatings. The people lived in fear. If a mentor humiliates you in public, if she mistreats you verbally or physically in any way, beware!

A worthy mentor will never humiliate you, verbally or physically. If she makes a mistake and embarrasses you, an apology will follow quickly. Worthy mentors work to build you up, not tear you down. Their goal is your independence. They want you to depend on yourself, not on them.

A Worthy Mentor Will Not Abuse You Sexually. Jones was very subtle about his use of sexuality to mislead his people. He would sympathize with a wife whose husband had mistreated her. He would provide her the comfort and concern that she needed. As her trust in him grew stronger, the more sexual advantage he took of that trust. If a mentor is making sexual advances, using his power in your life to gain sexual favors, beware!

A worthy mentor will never misuse or abuse you sexually. He will act professionally, knowing that you are vulnerable and never taking advantage of your vulnerability.

A Worthy Mentor Will Not Abuse Intimacy. Jim Jones was a master manipulator. One by one he gained the confidence of his followers. He knew everyone by name. He spent time with every one of them alone. He loved to use gossip, half-truths, and lies to separate friends and to destroy relationships. He wanted the people to trust Jim Jones alone. And so he kept them isolated from their friends and families outside the People's Temple. Then he worked to isolate them from each other.

If a mentor is working to destroy your relationships, if he wants you to trust him and him alone, beware!

A worthy mentor values and promotes your relationships with your wife or husband, with your children and friends. She will constantly remind you that succeeding in those relationships is far more important than making a million bucks.

A Worthy Mentor Will Not Abuse Authority. From the beginning Jones worked to destroy his followers' confidence in any of the old authority figures in their lives. He showed them how untrustworthy their parents had been and encouraged them to quit calling or writing their families. He made fun of their former religious beliefs and of the important ideas that had guided them since childhood. He ridiculed books and libraries (unless they were books he recommended). He warned them against giving each other advice (unless they were quoting his sayings). And he refused to let them question his authority or to answer their questions honestly. If a mentor refuses to answer any question you ask, if he tries to cut you off from any outside source of information, beware!

A worthy mentor is open to any questions you have. He will not be threatened by your questions, but will do his best to answer them honestly, directly, completely. Mentors you can trust will respect you, your values, your spiritual beliefs, your traditions. They can share their experiences with you and you can decide how to respond, but they will never minimize or demean you or your beliefs.

A Worthy Mentor
Is Always Growing

In 1927, Charles Mayo wrote: "The safest thing for a patient is to be in the hands of a man engaged in teaching medicine. In order to be a teacher of medicine the doctor must always be a student." People who succeed in their lives and in their businesses never stop growing. They are great mentors because they look to others to teach them. With all their different gifts and experiences, they are united by the Golden Rule: "Love God and love your neighbor as yourself." Loving leads to growing. It is the secret of a successful mentor. It is the secret of compassionate capitalism wherever and whenever it is practiced. And it is the secret of personal fulfillment and of financial success.

Bill Britt may not have received that kind of love from his own alcoholic father, but the power of love to change someone was demonstrated to Bill by his grandfather when he was just a child. He still remembers the day when love held him in his arms, wiped away his tears, and gave him hope that someday, some way all would be well again.

"My grandfather's farm was just outside of Kinston, North Carolina," Bill remembers. "I can still see the small brick farmhouse with its wide front porch that went all the way around the house and Grampa's rocking chair sitting in its place of honor like a throne. From that chair Grandpa could look out over the vegetable garden and the smokehouse to the distant fields of tobacco and the green meadows where the cattle grazed along a quiet, running stream.

"My earliest memory of my grandfather, my very first male mentor, was when I was just three or four years old. In the evenings on that farm, I can remember my grandmother moving about the kitchen baking pies or ironing with one of the five or six irons always heating on the wood-burning stove and my grandfather sitting in his favorite chair, listening to the old Philco radio.

" 'Come here, Billy,' he would say with mock gruffness when the news had ended. And I would run to him in the evening as I had followed him about the farm all day. Suddenly he would lift me up in his arms and, holding me in the palm of one great, leathery hand, hoist me toward the rafters. In spite of Grandma's gentle protests, Grandpa would balance me high above the room in his hand and begin to sing his own country version of 'Turkey in the Straw.' Up and down I bounced, a little off balance, only slightly afraid, knowing at the same time that I was safe in the hollow of his strong hand.

"When I was six or seven, my father's alcoholic binges threatened to destroy our family. We all lived in fear of his temper tantrums. One afternoon my grandfather saw for himself how outrageous my dad had become. 'The boy will come home with me,' Grandpa said sternly at the close of one of his rare visits to our home. 'And he'll stay for a year, maybe more.' The next thing I knew, Mom and Dad had packed my clothes into a little suitcase and I was riding with my parents through the open fields to my grandfather's farm.

"After the long drive, we sat down to a late Sunday breakfast," Bill recalls. "I can still remember the taste of Grandma's buttermilk scratch biscuits dripping with home-churned butter and wild berry preserves. When the meal ended, Grandma hurried back into the kitchen and Grandpa went to sit in his rocker on the front porch. I was barely seven at the time. I stood on that porch listening to the silence, watching the white clouds in the dark blue summer sky. Suddenly I felt sad. Something inside me wanted to cry. I don't know why exactly, but the tears formed in my eyes and no matter how hard I tried, I just couldn't stop them.

"Suddenly I felt Grandpa's arms around me. Gently he lifted me up, carried me across the porch, and sat me down in his lap in that old rocking chair. I can still feel his rough, farmer's hand smoothing down my hair. I can still hear him whispering, 'It's gonna be fine, boy. You'll see. Everything's gonna be fine.'

"For a moment I lay there all stiff and bothered. I had never felt my father's arms around me. I had never leaned my head against his chest or let my tears fall against his face. Slowly my crying stopped. I lay back against my grandpa's woolen vest. And in that magic moment I heard a sound I had never heard before. Grandpa's heart was beating and I could hear it. It was a big old heart, filled with love, and at that moment I knew for the first time in my young life that I was loved and that with a love as big as my grandpa's love, everything would be fine again."

11

Why Are Goals So Important to Our Success, and How Do We Make and Keep Them?

CREDO 11

We believe that success comes only to those who establish goals and then work diligently to achieve them.

Therefore, with our mentor's help, we should begin immediately to determine our short-term and long-term goals, to write them down, to review our progress at every step, to celebrate the goals we accomplish, and to learn from those we don't.

Rex Renfrow started working for the federal government after serving four years in the military. He was proud of his GS-3 clerk-typist rating. That's about as low as you can get on the government's totem pole, but Rex didn't have a college education and was grateful for this entry-level position. He thought that if he really tried hard, he could work his way up to a national level in the Department of Agriculture. By then, he supposed, he would have enough laid aside to begin his own business. And he was willing to do whatever it took to get there.

"All those years working for the federal government," Rex remembers, "I thought I was free. I imagined that if I worked hard enough and long enough, if I improved my skills and followed orders faithfully, I would make enough money so that I could afford to start a little business of my own. Suddenly I was forty years old and standing in the very place where my dreams were supposed to come true. Instead they lay shattered at my feet."

For a while Betty Jo Renfrow worked to provide the couple their second income. When the Renfrows adopted Drew and later Melinda

Jo from the Children's Home in Greensboro, Betty Jo quit her job to stay home with the children.

"We decided that one of us would be at home full-time while the children were young," she remembers. "Maybe it was old-fashioned, but we wanted our home to be filled with the smell of cookies baking and the sound of children laughing and talking with a parent. We wanted one of us to be there when Drew or Melinda scraped a knee or lost a friend. We wanted our children to learn from us what it means to be loving, responsible human beings, not from baby-sitters or day-care teachers, no matter how wonderful they might be."

To help replace the second income, Rex took on extra night and weekend work as a service station attendant, pumping gas, changing oil, and cleaning windshields. The long hours and hard work didn't bother him. He had a dream to own a business and he would do almost anything to accomplish it. He moved his wife and two children wherever the government sent him, from North Carolina to New Mexico to South Dakota and finally to USDA headquarters in Washington, D.C., where Rex got up at five-thirty and often didn't return home until 6:30 P.M.

"Finally, after twenty-six and a half years working like a slave for a few bucks a week," Rex recalls, "I reached the rank of GS-14. All those years I thought that reaching that exalted rank would guarantee me the resources to take the next step and start a business of my own. That was my goal and every step up the ladder was supposed to be taking me nearer to it."

That morning as the sun rose over the nation's capital, Rex Renfrow didn't feel warmed or comforted by its light. He was sad and disappointed. He had worked his way up the bureaucratic ladder, but he was no more financially secure than when he had begun. Inflation had swallowed up every raise in pay. Betty Jo and Rex had no savings account. How could they? At the end of every month there was nothing left to save. And just the day before, when Rex asked his superiors when he could apply to advance again, they told him regretfully: "Rex, without a college education, this is as far as you can go."

"I had one dream," Rex remembers today, "to own my own business. But after spending half a lifetime trying, I began to think that dream could not come true. The crowning blow fell when my superiors told me that somebody like me without a college degree could advance no further no matter how hard I worked or how well I did my job."

To own your own business is a great dream. It must have been a terrible disappointment to Rex Renfrow to think that he could never make it. He had been dreaming that dream ever since he was a teenager working on his father's tobacco farm in North Carolina.

Do you have that same dream? Some people who follow that dream realize almost immediate success. For others, like Rex, it may be a long, hard journey. I've read some accounts of the Amway story that make it sound as though Jay Van Andel and I started our business one morning in Jay's basement and by evening we were millionaires. Although we look back with gratitude and amazement at the speed of our success, it also took us half a lifetime to see our dream come true. We, too, had our share of detours and even a disaster or two along the way.

During high school Jay and I began to dream of owning a business together. We used to meet after school to make our plans. During Jay's senior year, his father hired us for our first business venture. He owned a garage and a used-car lot. He needed to have two used pickup trucks delivered to a customer in Montana. We turned that first little truck delivery into an exciting four-thousand-mile, three-week journey west. We were in business. We were working for ourselves. And even when the tires went flat or the road grew rough, we loved every minute of the journey.

World War II brought on the first major delay along the road to owning our own business. We joined the Army Air Corps, and when we met back home on leave, Jay and I came up with our first real business venture, a flying school and air-charter service in Comstock Park, near our homes in Grand Rapids. But there were problems. To start with, neither one of us could fly. So after completing our military service, we pooled our savings, took out a loan, hired a pilot, bought a used Piper Cub, and put up a giant sign: "WOLVERINE AIR SERVICE." When the town's one runway turned out to be nothing but a streak of mud, we put pontoon floats on our little plane and used a nearby river for takeoffs and landings. Needless to say, our first business wasn't a smashing success.

With extra time on our hands, we drew up our second business plan, one of the world's first drive-in restaurants. We put up a little prefabricated building on the edge of the airstrip. On even days, I grilled burgers and Jay "hopped" cars. On odd days, we changed places. We didn't make much money, but we were following our dream. We had our own business and were working for ourselves.

In 1948, Jay and I bought *Elizabeth,* a thirty-eight-foot schooner. After closing down our other businesses, we planned to sail her on a year-long cruise down the Atlantic coast, through the Caribbean islands, and on to South America. It was a kind of vacation with a plan. We would learn about boats and sailing, about boat charters and the travel business. Of course, we had never sailed before. So, with a book on sailing in one hand and the tiller in the other, we began our journey. In a fog off New Jersey we got lost and ended up in the shallow marshes so far from the sea that even the Coast Guard was amazed when they found us and pulled us back into the Atlantic on a rope.

By the time we had learned to sail, poor *Elizabeth* had sprung a rather serious leak. One dark night in March 1949, as we sailed from Havana bound for Haiti, the crusty old schooner began to take on water. We bailed hard, but in spite of our desperate and rather hilarious efforts, our schooner sank in fifteen hundred feet of water, ten miles off the northern coast of Cuba. We were rescued by an American freighter and dropped back on land three days later in San Juan, Puerto Rico.

"Time to get a job and settle down," a friend advised us. But like Rex Renfrow and millions like him—maybe like you—we were still determined to run our own business, and though we didn't know exactly where that dream was leading, we followed it.

In August 1949, shortly after we arrived back home from our ill-fated voyage, Neil Maaskant, a Dutch immigrant and one of Jay's distant relatives, presented us with an opportunity to become independent distributors of Nutrilite Products, a line of food supplements. "How to Get Well and Stay Well" their little booklet read, and we signed on the dotted line. The development of a people-to-people marketing system would quickly become our third business venture.

In a few years we had recruited a wonderful team of other independent distributors for Nutrilite. With hard work and long hours, our business prospered. In 1957, Carl Rehnborg, the founder of Nutrilite, asked Jay to become president of the company. After careful consideration, Jay turned down the offer. Once again our dream held us together. Come hell or high water (or offers of a nice salary and a plush office), we would own *our own* business.

In 1958, we announced to our Nutrilite distributors that we would be adding new product lines, and in 1959 the Amway Corporation was born. Just thirty-four years later, more than two million independent Amway distributors in fifty-four different nations and territories grossed almost four billion dollars in sales.

Jay and I spent almost twenty years experimenting with various entrepreneurial plans before we founded Amway. And now, in looking back, we don't measure our success first in billions of dollars. We measure it in remaining true to our dream. All along we had wanted to own our own business.

What Is Your Dream? Maybe you don't want to own your own business. Maybe you like the idea of working for a great corporation or a wonderful small business in your hometown. Maybe you want to write a book, pastor a church, or run for political office. Perhaps you've chosen to make a career in the military, on a police force, or in a fire department. Whether you plan to start your own business, sell your athletic abilities or artistic skills, work for the government or in private enterprise, you have the chance to exercise your muscles as a compassionate capitalist, an entrepreneur, a person of value who is about to undertake the challenge of a lifetime. And whatever your dream, the rules are much the same.

First, you need to believe in yourself. That's why we talked earlier about the importance of having a positive attitude. Second, you need a mentor to guide you along the way. Then, with the right attitude and a little help from your friends you are ready. Now the process begins in earnest. Dream your own dream! Develop a plan to accomplish that dream and work hard to complete it! And whatever you do, don't give in to all the negative voices around you (or inside you) who are screaming out, "You'll never amount to anything" or "Even if you try, you'll never make it in this terrible moment of history!"

Follow Your Dream. Young Paul Collins sat on the edge of a chair in my office in Ada, Michigan. He had a dream. "I want to be a painter," he said. "This is a sample of my work." Paul's hand trembled slightly as he placed several paintings on my conference table. Vibrant, luminous faces stared up at me from the canvas in bright, bold colors. "Very nice," I said. "Thanks," Paul replied quietly. Then, trying to suppress his irrepressible grin, he added, "They are nice, aren't they!"

Paul Collins had the right attitude. Against all odds, he believed in himself. Paul is black. He grew up in a lower-middle-class home in Grand Rapids. He had no money. And though his teachers recognized Paul's gifts, they counseled him to get "a real job" and paint for a hobby. Paul refused to listen. If his teachers didn't believe in Paul Collins, he believed in himself. He had a dream and was willing to risk everything to follow it.

His teachers were not so confident. "You can't make enough money to support yourself by selling what you paint," they said. But once again Paul didn't listen and when he was just eighteen, he sold his first painting. After that little victory he became even more determined to use his gifts as an artist to make a living. That day in my office, as I looked down on those shining faces on the canvas and into the sparkling, determined eyes of their creator, it didn't take an art critic to see that one day Paul Collins's dream would come true.

Unlike Paul, Rex Renfrow didn't have a specific talent that he wanted to turn into a business. He just knew that he wanted a business of his own. That's okay, too. In fact, Rex had spent so much of his lifetime working to earn money to support his dream that he hadn't had time to flesh out that dream, to examine his own gifts, to study his options, let alone to make those important choices.

Then one night, about the time Rex thought that his dream to own a business was dead forever, he heard about our direct-sales program, began his own business, and went on to succeed in ways he had never dreamed. Amway is just one of millions of ideas for starting a business of your own, but for Rex Renfrow it was like sunrise at the end of a long, dark night.

You can dream of owning your own business, but somewhere along the line, your dream will have to get more specific. What kind of business do *you* want to own? How would you like to spend *your* life? What kind of work would *you* like to do? When I was a teenager, I wasn't blessed with an artistic gift like Paul Collins. (Nor did I work very hard to perfect what few gifts I had.) When people asked me that awful question—"What are you going to be when you grow up?"—I didn't have a clue. But my father had passed on to me a kind of dream about work that grew out of his personal nightmare. "Start your own business," he counseled. "Don't work for anybody but yourself."

For nineteen years my father worked for the General Electric Corporation. When I was in high school, G.E. offered my dad a promotion and a raise in pay if he would take a new position in Detroit. Dad loved Grand Rapids. His roots were there. He didn't want to force his family to move to a new city, to find new schools and a new church, or to make new friends.

So Dad turned down his one big chance to get ahead. For some reason or other, my father's boss in Grand Rapids turned against him, and the company, without a thought for his years of valued service, fired him. Just one year before retirement, my father lost his job, his benefits, and his pension. From that moment he was obsessed with one idea: "Work for yourself," he told me. "Start your own business." Eventually, my dad's dream for me became my own. But that dream was not enough. Jay and I had to make plans to support that dream. We had to get down to business, to ask ourselves, Where are we going with our dream and how are we going to get there?

Paul Collins had a dream to paint. Jay and I had a dream to start a flying service, then a drive-in restaurant, then a Nutrilite distributorship. Rex Renfrow just wanted a business of his own that he could be proud of, that would provide a lifetime source of income. What is your dream? Don't worry if you aren't sure what kind of business you would like to own. If you have a dream, even the broadest outline of one, follow it. Be faithful to it! If you don't have a dream yet or if you aren't sure it can be trusted, here are a few questions that may help you decide.

Is the Dream Really Your Dream? If you could choose any job, any vocation, any career in the world, what would it be? Forget for a moment what everybody else wants you to do. Your family, friends, or spouse all have their goals for you, but what do *you* want? Trust your feelings. Nurture that dream, or even the tiny fragment of a dream that excites you and gives you hope for the future.

The French philosopher Blaise Pascal said, "The heart has its reasons which reason knows nothing of." Do not listen to those voices inside you who want to limit your potential. Let your heart do the talking. Listen to the voices of those who dream great dreams for you. Then, dare to follow those dreams.

It wasn't enough for my father or for Rex's father to pass on their dreams. We had to be sure that their dreams were really our own. Even when our schooner was sinking, Jay and I knew we wanted to own our own business, to set our own schedule, to be free.

Is This Dream Appropriate to Your Gifts? A dream is one thing, but having the "right stuff" to realize it is something else. Helen Keller might have wanted to drive a car, but she would have been a menace on the freeways. Blindness eliminated some of her options. But she dreamed great dreams anyway. "We could never learn to be brave and patient," she wrote in 1890, "if there were only joy in the world."

Don't be afraid of your limits, but don't be foolish, either. If basic math stumps you, there might not be a future for you as a particle physicist. If you're five-five or sixty-five, there may not be a career for you in professional basketball. If you faint at the sight of blood, reconsider your dreams of becoming a great surgeon (or butcher, or professional boxer). But if one dream gets knocked out, dream another.

Think about what you are good at, what you like doing. "I'm not good at anything," you say. Nonsense! None of us has the gift of a pure genius like Mozart. Few of us will ever play the piano like André Watts. Chances are that you can't write best-selling novels like Stephen King. But we all have God-given gifts.

Most people who have succeeded don't consider themselves to be geniuses. But that does not mean that God has not given each of us rich gifts of ability, persistence, or the capacity for hard work. Remember what we said about heredity? Don't let anyone tell you that you don't have a gift. You do!

Sometimes people confuse genius with hard work. It is true that a few rare geniuses accomplish great things with an effortlessness that is amazing. If all musicians and composers measured themselves against Mozart, they would be very depressed people. But we sometimes don't appreciate the fact that great musicians, athletes, authors, artists, and yes, compassionate capitalists became great because they developed their "genius" through hard work. Vidal Sassoon said, "The only place where success comes before work is in a dictionary." Keep this in mind as you reflect upon your gifts.

Think about what you like to do, what comes easy for you (not because it doesn't take work, but because you enjoy it), what others say you do well. This will help you identify your gifts. If you put them to work in pursuit of your goals as an entrepreneur, the chances for success will amaze you.

Rex and Betty Jo Renfrow began to show our products and marketing plan to friends and neighbors in Washington, D.C. Rex continued working at the USDA, but in the evenings and on weekends he made phone calls, gathered people together for his presentation, and made follow-up calls. At last, after twenty-six years, he was building his own business. It was hard work. Don't believe the guys on late-night television. There is no quick or easy way to financial security or success. And even though it was slow and difficult at first, Rex and Betty Jo knew that just down the road, their work would result in lifelong dividends.

"It was an easy price to pay," Rex remembers. "Finally I was building something for me and for my family that would be ours forever. I had invested my life in other people's dreams. Now I was spending my time and energy seeing my own dream come true."

Do You Have (or Can You Find) the Resources to Support Your Dream? One of the reasons Rex Renfrow got so excited about our business was the low price of admission. "The start-up kit with its money-back guarantee cost me twenty-eight bucks," Rex remembers. "I figured I could scrape that up. I got excited. We said to ourselves, hey, what can we lose?"

Many businesses besides ours have low entry fees. Others cost more. Go to a franchise fair, for example. Check out the prices for buying into a hamburger or a pizza chain. See what the normal start-up costs are for renting and furnishing an office, a salesroom, or a studio. Add up the prices on office equipment, computer hardware and software. Even a telephone and a fax machine with stationery and five hundred business cards cost money. Is that kind of money available to you? Is it yours or is it somebody else's? If it isn't yours, how much of your future do you have to give away to get it?

"Getting into this business cost Betty Jo and me less than our anniversary dinner," Rex remembers. "And," Betty Jo adds with a grin, "that four-star restaurant offered us no money-back guarantee."

Whatever business you choose, be sure you have the resources to get you through the early start-up and low-income (if any) days. Remember the New Testament warning, before you undertake a project, be sure to count the cost.

Is This Dream Consistent with Your Values? Dreams are sometimes dangerous. They can collide head-on with what we believe to be right. They may even lead us down a path that destroys us. Think ahead. Decide at the beginning of the journey where the road is leading. If you reach your goal, if your dream comes true, will it bring joy or shame to you or someone you love?

In the major cities of this nation, young men are starting drug businesses of their own. Why would they want to sell hamburgers or newspaper subscriptions, automobiles, real estate or soap when the return on marijuana, cocaine, and heroin is so much greater? And yet one day those young men will look back to regret their choices—if they don't die first in a hail of bullets.

Rex and Betty Jo Renfrow had to ask themselves the same questions we all must ask:

Are the *products* good for the customers? Would I use them? Are they quality products sold at a reasonable price with a money-back guarantee?

Does the *presentation* have integrity? Is it clear? Can I trust it? Or is it packed with half-truths, exaggerations, and even lies?

Does the *plan* make sense? Is it fair? Is it generous? Is it liberating?

Are the *people* honest, fair, open? Will it be fun to spend my lifetime in their company? What will their influence be on me, on my spouse and on my children?

"Looking back," Rex remembers, "I realized that all along my dream had a human side. I wanted a business of my own, but even more I wanted a business that would let me help people. How glad we were to learn that this is a people-helping-people business," he adds. "Its values and my values go hand in hand."

Is This Dream Big Enough to Challenge You? Don't set goals that are too small or too safe. Dare to dream big dreams that are far beyond where you are. Anyone can set a goal safely to walk across the street. Take a giant step. See the world. Why settle for mediocre goals when you could achieve something really wonderful? Believe in yourself! Follow your dream! Those are the really big steps. Everything else will follow.

Most people who come into our business begin with small dreams. There's nothing wrong with that. They may sign up just to get a good discount on the more than three thousand products we carry. Or they may need four or five hundred dollars extra income a month to pay off their bills or to sock away a little savings for a rainy day.

Kaoru Nakajima told us an ancient Japanese legend to illustrate a point. An old Japanese farmer and his dog went walking in the forest. For ten years they wandered in those woods searching for a lost treasure. Suddenly the dog stopped at the base of a tree. For a moment he sniffed at the roots. Then he began to bark. The old man knew that the dog loved to bark, so he walked on, smiling to himself, expecting his dog to follow. But the dog just went on barking. The man stopped and called the dog's name. The dog refused to come. The man shouted and gestured angrily; finally he threw a stick at the dog, hoping that the stubborn animal would quit barking and obey. When the dog refused again, the old man returned to the tree, took a shovel from his pack, and began to dig. Within a half hour of digging, the old man discovered the priceless treasure.

"When someone tells me no," Mr. Nakajima explains, "I see it as the beginning, not the ending of our relationship. Like the dog, I go on pointing and barking. After waiting a week or two, I call back. My potential customer asks new questions. Each one gives me another opportunity to answer. Before long, if I don't give up, my customer begins to dig. The next thing I know, he's discovered the treasure. To most people, the answer no is final. For me, the answer no is the first step on the road to yes."

Develop a Plan and Work Hard at It! You have a dream. Now you need a plan. Plans outline where you want to go. They give you ways to measure progress. They give you a sense of clear direction and of purpose. Remember the bumper sticker: "Stand for something or you'll fall for anything."

Some people dream great dreams, but they never develop a plan complete with goals and tactics to realize their dreams. Without a plan you will end up going in circles and wasting your life away. Other people have plans, but they are inadequate. They don't understand how capitalism works, and so they fail.

Rex Renfrow thought his dream was to own a business. But that wasn't his dream at all. His real dream was to have the kind of steady income that would set him free.

"I was tired of the limits people placed on me," he admits today. "I was too creative and too energetic to have my abilities limited. I wanted to be free to make my own decisions about the future, and that meant money."

In the long haul, Rex wanted what we all want, a measure of financial security. To be really free requires money, not millions of dollars necessarily, but enough to pay the bills and to have a little extra saved for a rainy day.

We should never be ashamed of our desire for material welfare. We should be proud and grateful for every honest dollar we make. The money you earn will raise the quality of life for you and your family, and (if you are compassionate) it will also give you the power to help alleviate hunger, poverty, homelessness, and disease for those who suffer in your neighborhood and around the globe. Never forget that profit is the goal of a good business plan. What are your goals and how do you plan to meet them?

What Is a Goal? Define a goal any way you want: "the end result," "the ultimate intent," "the objective of your labor," "the target at which you're aiming," "the result or achievement toward which your labor is directed." Getting your goal clear in your mind is the first step in making a dream real, workable, possible. And for business, one primary goal is profit.

The long-term goal of financial security is reached by making and keeping a number of short-term goals. Rex Renfrow started in our business working evenings and on weekends hoping to supplement his income by $300 or $400 a month. Once that short-term goal was reached, Rex and Betty Jo set a larger goal of $1,000 a month in extra income. Then, while he was still working his new business part-time, they set a goal to match his USDA salary. When that short-term goal was reached, Rex quit his job at the Department. By then they owned a growing business. They had enough income to feel financially secure. Goal by goal, Rex and Betty Jo Renfrow saw their dream come true.

John and Barbara Sims got into this business because of their goal to spend more time together. "I got involved with the PTA," Barbara recalls. "Just running our children, Scott, Karen, and David, around town kept me busy. And John was so preoccupied with managing his garage and taking the wrecker out on emergency calls twenty-four hours a day that we seldom sat down together, let alone talked or planned or prayed." They reached their goal by starting a business that they could run together.

Jack Spencer was a high school teacher and a coach. He worked extra, late-night hours to get his master's degree. "I often worked seventeen hours a day because I was convinced that hard work and more education were the secrets to getting ahead," he recalls. However, when Jack completed his master's program, he was dismayed to find that the reward for all his effort was a mere twenty-five dollars per month take-home pay increase. Jack and Magee Spencer wanted to see a better return on the investment of their time and energy. They reached their goal by starting a business that had no income ceiling, no alleys or dead ends.

Dave and Marge Lewis wanted to build a successful business without leaving their village of Hersey, Michigan. "Success can't blossom in a small town," Dave says with a smile, "or so we were told. People informed us that we needed a mighty metropolis to make the financial and professional strides that elevate you to the top of your field." "But we liked Hersey," Marge adds, "and we wanted our children to grow up with all the benefits of a small, safe, tight-knit community." Dave and Marge reached their goal by starting a business that could prosper anywhere, small town or large.

Every successful business begins with a single goal. That goal soon becomes many short-term and long-term goals. They then must be backed by a series of actions or tactics that help you reach those goals.

What Are Tactics? These are the practical, day-by-day steps that we take to reach our goals. Remember the formula: MW = NR + HE × T? If MW (material welfare) is our long-term goal, then natural resources (NR), human energy (HE), and tools (T) are the tactics we have to reach that goal.

Natural resources. Most goods and even services involve the creative use of the earth's natural resources. Paul Collins's needs are fairly simple: paint and canvas. The business plans of those successful young entrepreneurs whom we discussed earlier used various combinations of natural resources to succeed: roses, carnations, and ferns (Roger Conner for his nursery); eggs, sugar, cream, and various natural flavors (Ben and Jerry); unassembled computer parts (Jobs and Wozniak); and even cow manure (the kids of KIDCO).

Our company and thousands of other businesses have transformed the earth's bountiful resources into thousands of wonderful products, and yet every day someone walks into our offices in Ada, Michigan, with some new product that raises the quality of life for those who use it. I dare you. Take up the challenge. Invent! Create! Transform! Dream! Brainstorm! Imagine! Risk! Try! The world is still rich with natural resources that could be reshaped by your creative mind. Go for it!

Human energy. Are you thinking to yourself, "Give me a break." Guys like Roger Conner or Ben and Jerry were just lucky. They happened to be at the right place at the right time. They had incredible luck and I'm just not that lucky.

Luck figures in. But in my experience, it is hard work, not luck, that brings success. Stephen Leacock said it this way: "I am a great believer in luck, and I find the harder I work, the more I have of it."

God has given you energy to use in transforming the earth and its resources. Like every other resource, your energy is limited. Don't waste it. Don't undervalue it. Develop a plan to make your own dreams come true, and use every ounce of strength and energy you have to succeed at it.

In our business, human energy is everything. Once natural resources have been transformed into the three thousand plus products we carry, all it takes is the energy of one man or woman to build a business so large and profitable as to stagger the imagination.

Tools. There are all kinds of tools available to help you make your work easier, more effective, more economical. Paul Collins uses various brushes, portable easels and aluminum frames to keep his canvas stretched. Jet planes, telephones, and fax machines also figure in his business plan.

Imagine the tools those successful entrepreneurs used to bring their plans to life. Roger Conner begged, borrowed, and bought old refrigerators to keep his flowers fresh. Ben and Jerry used aluminum vats and mixing machines to make their ice cream quickly and efficiently. Jobs and Wozniak needed simple tools and solder guns to assemble their first computers, and the kids of KIDCO needed shovels, wheelbarrows, and drying trays to get their fertilizer business started.

By the way, if your plan is to provide a service (instead of marketing a product), think about the tools you already have (or could borrow) to include in your plan that would make your life easier and your service more effective.

Entrepreneurs have to be particularly frugal and inventive. They use old cars to deliver pizza or medical prescriptions. They use their bikes for a newspaper route; their phones to conduct surveys; their pen, typewriter, or computer to write plays, music, poetry, or create handbills or other advertisements. Or they use their lawn mower to start a gardening business; their washer and dryer to take in laundry from a local campus, or an ironing board to press shirts.

All it takes to be a success in our business is a telephone, an order pad, a place to store products and materials, and a means of transportation to get you across town (or around the world). What business would you like to start? What are the tools already available to you? Impress yourself with your creativity.

Let's Review. Even if you believe in yourself and have a dream, you'll need a plan to succeed. Most of those plans include the creative use of natural resources, human energy, and tools. Now let's look more closely at how those plans are developed.

Paul Collins had a plan when he came to my office for the first time almost twenty years ago. "I want to paint portraits of the people of Africa," he said, and his enthusiasm was contagious. "And I was hoping that you would underwrite the trip." Already Paul believed in himself and in his dream, but in order to support himself as a painter, he needed to develop a business plan that made sense financially.

"I'll pay for the trip," I said, "but then I own fifty percent of the paintings." For a moment Paul stared at me glumly. "Fifty percent?" he said. "Fifty percent!" I answered. "But I'm doing all the work," he protested. "And I'm paying all the bills," I replied. Suddenly he smiled and held out his hand. "Partners?" he asked. "Partners!" I agreed.

Paul went to Africa and brought back a brilliant and moving collection of African portraits. His first major exhibition firmly established him as one of America's leading portrait artists. But he also proved his skills as a businessman. Paul's plan is simple. "I sell shares in myself," he says. "I use the money to travel, to set up my studio, to pay my family's expenses, and to paint. When the paintings are sold, I make a good living and my investors get their money back with a profit."

"Here's my business plan," Bill Swets said, handing me several typewritten pages. "It's everything I'm going to need to get started, including an itemized budget." Bill was a college freshman. A few weeks earlier he had asked me for advice on starting a business of his own. "Look in your own backyard," I told him. "There's a junkyard in my backyard," he answered. We both laughed. Then Bill's eyes began to sparkle. Days later he returned with a plan.

"My backyard is filled with treasure," he exclaimed. "Old chairs, tables, sofas, bed frames, mattresses, dressers, lamps, and rugs." He was grinning broadly. "Furniture is the most durable good in the marketplace," he continued. "It retains some value forever. But," he added, "people don't like to buy used furniture because the only place to find it is usually in a slum. I am going to sell used furniture in a clean, safe, upscale location. And here's a list of exactly what I need to get started."

I looked at Bill's business plan. Most plans answer these basic questions: who, where, what, why, how, when, and how much?

What do I want to do?
  Sell a product?
  Market a service?
  Promote my artistic or athletic skills?
How can I do it?
  What steps will lead me to my goal?
Who can help me get it done?
  Who are the people I will need to help me on my way?
What do I need to help me get it done?

What natural resources will I need?

What tools will I need?

Where can I do it best?

In a place already available to me?

In a space I need to develop?

How much will it cost to do it?

What monies will I need from start to finish?

Where will I get the money?

Do I have enough money of my own?

Do I need to borrow money?

Do I want partners to invest in my idea?

How long before I can earn the money back?

What will I charge?

How much income do I project?

Even in the best plan, you have to guess at some of the answers. Being an entrepreneur is risky. Do the best you can to draw up a complete and trustworthy plan. Set goals. Create a list of clear tactics describing exactly how you plan to meet these goals. Put a price tag beside each tactic and schedule the date you hope to have that tactic accomplished successfully. Then show your complete plan to your mentor to get her feedback. I paged quickly through Bill Swets's plan. There were four or five pages, typed single-space, answering all the questions that I listed above. Like most businessmen (especially bankers) I was interested in the bottom-line figure, what Bill thought his plan could cost.

"Fifty thousand dollars?" I whispered, looking up at him a bit surprised. "That's a lot of money."

"I know," he answered. "The two bankers I approached for a loan said the same thing—just before they laughed me out the door."

Later, Bill confessed that he was hoping that I would pick up the phone, call those same bankers, and guarantee his loan. Instead I began to ask him questions. "Why do you need carpet in your new store, Bill? Why not cement floors? What about all this drywall for partitions? Why can't you have an open display room? And do you really need three adding machines and two cash registers? Wouldn't one be enough to start?"

Before the meeting ended, Bill's start-up list was down to $5,000. Without a phone call from me, Bill's banker quickly agreed to share the risk. A few years later, Bill Swets has twenty new furniture-leasing showrooms in four different states. He had a simple plan and, after a few minor adjustments, it was a smashing success!

What's your dream? Do you have a plan for helping you see that dream come true? What are your goals and what steps (tactics) are you taking to reach them? Twenty years ago, Rex Renfrow heard about Amway's plan and bet his life on its success. Today, he and Betty Jo have a very successful distribution business that stretches across the country and around the world. They learned early on that compassion would lead to their success. "This business puts people first and profits second," Rex tells us. "From the beginning, our mentors showed us that we would get our needs met by helping other people get their needs met first."

"We have no guarantee that the people we help will be successful," Rex reminds us. "But in our experience compassion works almost every time. Helping others to get their lives together, helping them see their dreams come true, led to profits for our company and helped in the realization of our own long-term dreams."

On March 17, 1992, Rex and Betty Jo faced a terrible personal tragedy. Their adopted daughter, Melinda, died during an epileptic seizure. Within minutes, phones were ringing all across America. Flowers, cards, and letters by the hundreds began to arrive the very next day. Friends that Rex and Betty Jo had made in this business drove or flew to Fairfax, Virginia, to share the Renfrows' grief. More than one thousand friends overflowed their church for Melinda's memorial service.

"We had loved each of those people in the business," Rex remembers, "but we were still astounded by the love that flowed back to us in return.

"If a business is meant to give us profit," Rex adds thoughtfully, "then standing by my daughter's grave surrounded by the prayers and best wishes of so many friends, I became the richest man on earth."

12

What Attitudes, Behaviors, and Commitments Will Help Us to Succeed? (The ABC's of Success)

CREDO 12

We believe that there are certain attitudes, behaviors, and commitments (related directly and indirectly to our tasks) that will help us reach our goals.

Therefore, with our mentor's help, we should begin immediately to master those ABC's that will help us succeed.

One dormitory at the University of North Carolina was particularly noisy that night in 1971 when a handful of juniors decided to attend an Amway meeting in the home of Bill and Peggy Britt.

"Let's have a couple of beers before we go," Paul Miller shouted across the recreation room to his football cronies. Seconds later, tabs were pulled and beer was flowing.

It was no wonder they were celebrating. Nineteen seventy had been the most exciting season in the young life of Paul Miller and his Tar Heel teammates. Showing incredible grit, Paul had managed to fight his way back from serious back surgery into the starting lineup. "You'll never play football again," his doctors had told him. "You're wrong," Paul thought to himself, and just two days after leaving the hospital, still wearing a cumbersome back brace, he began walking his way to health.

That same year, he led his North Carolina teammates to the Atlantic Coast Championship and to the 1970 Peach Bowl. And Paul's senior year saw even greater victories. Again he led his team to the 1971 Gator Bowl and was selected to play in the Coaches All-American game in Lubbock, Texas, under coaches Bear Bryant and Bo Schembeckler.

"I thought the professional football scouts would be lining up to recruit me," Paul recalls, "but when the phone didn't ring and my mailbox came up empty, I knew the game was over and work had to begin. Unfortunately, like many of my classmates, I didn't have a life goal. I thought about business and law (and even went on to finish my law degree at Chapel Hill, pass the bar exam, and practice law for sixteen miserable months), but nothing really excited me until I thought about owning my own business. That's why I got curious about this company.

"I don't know how much we drank before we found our way to our first meeting," Paul remembers, "but I do know that I was blitzed upon arrival. We sat in the back row, elbowing each other and giggling like crazy," he recalls. "But I ended up buying the sample sales kit for twenty-seven dollars and went back to the dorm without a clue as to what I should do with it, let alone what I should do to have a successful business of my own."

To his credit, the very next day Paul took an order for a box of laundry soap from an unsuspecting stranger. Unfortunately, he didn't even realize that we were not a door-to-door sales operation. And though he made his first sale that way, he never bothered to call in the order or deliver the soap.

Years later, after Paul had met and married Debbie, he finally got serious about building a business. "I worked as Peggy Britt's stock boy," Paul remembers, "unloading and stacking cartons, taking and filling orders. I watched closely the Britts and other successful men and women in this business. Debbie and I attended meetings, listened to tapes, and read books until our brains went into overload. Finally, one day Debbie and I quit stalling and got down to doing the basics over and over until our business boomed and our dreams came true at last."

Now, less than twenty years later, the Millers have built one of the largest network of independent distributors in the history of our company. When they are asked how they did it, they answer without hesitation: "We just went on doing the basics."

When my son Dan was in his early teens, he asked me to teach him to play tennis. Anybody who has seen me on the courts knows that Wimbledon was never in my future, but I had learned the basics and was glad to pass them on. I knew in my head exactly how to toss the ball for a perfect serve, how to hold the racket, how to position for a return, and how to charge the net. I knew the basics in my head, but Dan went one step further. He practiced serving. He learned to be in position for his opponent's return. He developed speed and skill and stamina by doing the basics again and again and again, and one day, to my chagrin and surprise, my own young son beat me badly.

Whatever business you are building, the *basics* are pretty much the same. In the following ABC's of success, I've tried to summarize the basics as I've known and experienced them. On these next pages, I've listed twenty-six of those attitudes, behaviors, and commitments that Jay and I and a company of our friends have learned along the way. Just remember, knowing these basics is not enough. As you go on, remember these words of John Wesley: "Beware you be not swallowed up in books! For an ounce of love is worth a pound of knowledge." If there's anything I've learned, it is that when all our skills seem to fail us, hard work (doing the basics) and compassion will see us through.

Adversity Can Be Your Friend

When Lauri Duncan was just sixteen, she was thrown through a windshield in a head-on automobile accident. The broken glass cut deeply into Lauri's face. After barely surviving her ordeal, the young woman began years of reconstructive surgery. Imagine how difficult it must have been for a teenage girl to find her face deeply scarred.

"At first I wished the wreck had killed me," Lauri admits. "The long months in the hospital were miserable. Then, when I returned to school, my teachers and my classmates looked at me with pity in their eyes. Boys whom I found attractive didn't want to look at me. Each plastic surgery was a nightmare of pain and ugly new scars. No matter how hard I tried, I could not walk away from my tragedy. I had to face it in the mirror every morning and every night."

At one time or other, we all face adversity. Failure in a relationship or business, tragic illness, injury or death, the collapse of hopes or the destruction of dreams, brings suffering, distress, worry, and grief.

"Now I can look back at my tragedy," Lauri says gratefully, "and realize that it taught me two important lessons. First, I learned to accept the things I could not change, and second, I learned to do the things that would make a difference." Nine years later, Lauri married Greg

Duncan, and together they have built a wonderful family and a very successful business.

"Much of our success," Greg admits, "comes from celebrating the bad times as well as the good. Lauri taught me that," he says. "By seeing the bad times as our friend and teacher, they don't seem half so bad anymore."

Jeff Moore was an All-Army boxer, certain to get a berth on the Olympic team. Then came the long-awaited orders to report to Vietnam. In battle, Jeff's vehicle hit a land mine. His eardrums were blown out. He came home to discover that his war injuries had also ended his boxing career. After six months of futile surgery to correct his ear injuries, Jeff and Andrea Moore headed for Alaska to work on the pipeline. They bought a lodge and started a twenty-four-hour business of selling food and hunting and fishing supplies. Already burdened with a growing debt, the Moores' home and business burned to the ground.

About that time Jeff and Andrea began their own Amway business. They didn't give in to depression and fear. They learned important lessons about survival from the adversity they had faced. And though Jeff was afraid that a process server might stand up and interrupt him in the middle of a presentation, he pressed on. Today, Jeff and Andrea's bills are paid. They have a prospering business and the opportunity to show compassion in many ways to the people of their adopted state and across the country.

"No matter what came our way," Jeff says, "we never quit. In 1987 our newborn baby died. But life doesn't just stop because a tragedy jumps up in front of you. This business has taught me that in spite of the tragedies, in spite of the obstacles, you should stand up and go do what you're supposed to and quit whimpering about the circumstances."

If you have faced adversity, learn from those troubled times and begin again. If you don't have a college degree, or even a high school education, take what you do have and make the most of it. If you don't make a sale today, you will make one tomorrow. Ask yourself, what lesson can I learn from this tragedy? Let adversity be your friend and teacher.

Basics Are Forever.
Never Stop Doing Them!

A young man sat in a soundproof booth on the campus of Louisiana State University while a speech therapist evaluated his serious speech impediment. For Dan Williams, social and career situations could be traumatic. In the early days of Dan and Bunny Williams's now very large and successful distribution business, Dan's stutter threatened to undermine their dream. "If you call us and no one answers," Dan used to say with a grin, "don't hang up. That's me on the line."

The university speech therapist gave Dan a series of exercises that were supposed to help him overcome his stuttering problem. "But the real solution was in my hands," Dan recalls today. "I had to learn the basics of success on my own, and I had to spend my lifetime practicing those basics to achieve our goals."

From the beginning, humor was one of the basic techniques Dan discovered and used to control his stuttering. "Telling a good story relaxed me," Dan explains. "And it relaxed my audience."

"If Dan could become a success as a public speaker," Bunny admits today, "anyone can. In fact," she adds, tongue in cheek, "the reason our business grew so fast in those early days was that the people understood and learned the plan so well from Dan because with his stutter they heard it three or four times every single time he explained it."

At first Dan wrote down and carefully filed each humorous anecdote. Now, using spontaneous humor to accentuate points in his fast-moving seminars, Dan gains the attention and respect of audiences across the country.

"But humor was only one of the basics I had to learn and practice," Dan explains. "Getting my thoughts off myself and onto others was another basic technique that I learned in this business. In the early days," he said, looking me in the eye, "I watched you, Rich, pouring coffee, serving doughnuts and even cleaning up the occasional spill when you were president of the company and could have had someone else do it. Dexter Yager, a man who built his own huge independent business, rushed across an airport in Rio to help Bunny and me with our luggage when we were rushing to catch an international flight. Being alert to other people's pain, being sensitive to other people's needs is basic to success in this or any business. I learned that early on, and the more sensitive I got to other people's problems, the less a problem my stuttering became."

When Billy Zeoli invited Dan Williams to introduce forty of his top business associates to President Gerald Ford, Dan didn't stutter once. By learning and practicing the basics, Dan had escaped the prison of his handicap forever.

Bill and Sandy Hawkins are two of our top independent distributors in Minnesota. Their success had led them to the fulfillment of a dream that every compassionate capitalist has in one degree or the other. "After you get to a certain point," Bill says, "money becomes less and less important. Being able to give money away is something we really enjoy. We'll give more away this year than we ever made before," he added, "and that's just plain fun!"

The Hawkins family realized this wonderful goal by doing the basics over and over again. "You can do a lot wrong in this business," Sandy says. "We sure did. But if you're out sharing the opportunity enough, a lot of right things will happen."

What are the basics of your business? Have you even tried to draw up a list of the actions you have to perform regularly to succeed? If you repeat the basics faithfully, your business will prosper. If you get lazy and let one day go by and then another and another, you will fail.

Kaoru Nakajima points out, "A guard dog who only barks once will never awaken his owner or scare away a thief. The successful guard dog will not stop barking until his job is done!" You want to succeed in business? Just keep barking! Do those basics faithfully every day and you will succeed.

Count Your Pennies and Your Dollars Will Never Be a Problem

Remember G. B. Garner, Peggy Britt's father, the man with the refrigeration-repair business? He was a young man when the stock market crashed in 1929, and he passed on to his daughter this priceless lesson.

"My father taught me responsibility with money," she tells us. "He said it this way: 'If you have any money to spend, you have just that much money to put away for tomorrow.' "

During these days of mounting deficit spending by individuals and by nations, there's an old French proverb that we need to remember: Out of debt, out of danger! Brian Herosian, a former football player with the Baltimore Colts, said it this way: "I walked around life carrying a bag of money with a hole in it until one day I realized I had to plug the hole myself."

We have spent wildly far too long, imagining the money would never run out. Now it's gone. Isn't this an appropriate time to ask ourselves this question on a regular basis: Do I really need this or can it wait? Isn't it time we took our credit cards out of our purses and wallets and put our savings-account book in their place? How much have I saved today? this month? this year? We must learn to measure our success by the money we have put away, not by the money we have spent.

Greg Duncan asks this question: "If you were offered a retainer of ten thousand dollars a month or a penny the first month, two pennies the second month, four pennies the third, eight pennies the fourth, and so on for thirty months, which would you take?" I've not figured it out, but Greg will urge you to take the pennies. He swears that if you double what you have every month, you will end up with $10,737,418.24 on the thirtieth month.

Save your pennies. Put off immediate gratifications. Work for your long-term goals. You may have to do without in the beginning, but in the long haul you will prosper.

Decide What Is Important to You and Do It, Whatever the Cost!

Our good friend Bill Nicholson, who has helped lead our company into a period of unbelievable growth, tells this moving story about his father. When Bill was still a young man, he and his dad went fishing. They both led busy lives. They had not spent all that much time together. There was so much catching up to do, so much life to be lived ahead. Suddenly, in the boat that day, Bill's father clutched his chest at the beginning of a fatal heart attack. The last words Bill heard his father say were, "Not now. Not now!"

Mark Twain once said, "Don't do today what you can put off until tomorrow." It isn't true. We set important long-range goals. Then every day something important, something urgent, something critical, comes up to delay us. If it is important to you, find a way to start on it today! We don't know what Bill's dad was thinking that moment he died. We just know what he said, "Not now! Not now!" Every time I hear the story I determine again to spend what time I have left doing what is important to me.

Every Person You Meet Has More Potential Than You Dare Dream!

In a speech before an arena full of cheering people, Chris Cherest once said, "If those two Dutch boys from Grand Rapids, Michigan, can go from being bankrupt and shipwrecked to owning a business whose worth is in the billions with an NBA team to boot, then anybody can do it." I have to agree.

Brian Hays was approached by a truck driver with the opportunity to start a business of his own. "I thought he was a poor little guy, making a few extra bucks," Brian remembers. "I almost wrote him off. Thank God I listened to his presentation of the Amway plan." Today, thanks to a truck driver without fancy clothes or pedigrees, Brian, the youngest vice-president in Motorola history, and his wife, Marguerite, have a very successful distribution business, and that has given them the financial freedom to work for the compassionate causes they support, including the Christian Children's Fund and the Salvation Army.

When Dan and Jeanette Robinson met Richard, they were not impressed. "Richard was a shoe shine inspector," Jeanette recalls with a grin. "He couldn't even look you in the eye. His hair was shoulder length. His beard was tangled and unkempt. He rode an old dirt bike and mumbled when he talked. But we made our presentation anyway, and Richard and his wife decided on the spot to start their own business."

"We really underestimated old Richard," Dan admits. "Within a few weeks he had shaved off his beard and bought his first suit and tie. With every contact his self-esteem grew right before our eyes. Today he and his wife own a prospering business and a new lease on life as well."

How difficult it is to judge a book by its cover, the old saying goes. Always remember that the person you think most likely to succeed may drop out or fail, and the person you think most likely to fail just might knock the ball right out of the park. Take a risk on "losers." You'll be surprised how often they turn into winners and pass on to you the prize.

Failure Leads to Success. Risk Failures. Learn from Them!

In our business, as in yours, the stories about those who failed at first but then went on to triumph are legend (and often very funny). Joe Foglio is just one example. One night in San Diego, Joe was showing our sales plan to a group of couples around a large dining room table in a neighbor's home. As he spoke, the neighbor's huge Rottweiler dog got excited, ducked under the table, and had his doggie movement right at Joe's feet. Shortly afterward, he visited a psychiatrist's home and was invited to make his presentation in a large Jacuzzi where his hosts and their friends were waiting, naked. A third ill-fated presentation happened in a dark and isolated neighborhood. In the darkness Joe could hardly find the house, and when he entered and switched on the lights, he discovered his hosts living in a condemned building with a yellow police tape warning all not to enter. At a fourth presentation in a downtown warehouse turned studio, Joe excused himself before the presentation began, walked into the rest room, switched on the lights, and found a two-foot-long lizard leering up at him from the bathtub.

Chris Cherest made the sales presentation one hundred fifty times without one success. Jerry Boggus remembers his first months in the business as a "string of failures." "We did everything wrong at least twice," he remembers, "just to be sure that it was wrong." But Joe, Chris, and Jerry didn't quit. They made mistakes. The failures piled up. But with each one, a valuable new lesson was learned. They examined the reasons for their failures, and they went on to build very successful businesses.

Frank Morales has a cute little formula that got him through his own failures. "SW-SW-SW," he says. "Some will. Some won't. So what?" In Frank and Barbara's experience, one-third of the people contacted will be interested. One-third of those will get involved. And just one-third of those will go on to achieve success in the business. Whatever the averages are for you—in your business or in ours—don't worry about failure. Every person who says no brings you closer to that person whose yes will change your world and his.

Huw Wheldon, a British broadcaster and TV executive, said to a group of would-be producers, "The crime is not a failure. The crime is not to give triumph a chance."

Goals First.
Everything Else Will Follow!

Margaret Hardy was born in the West Indies and came to New York when she was fifteen years old. Her husband, Terral, is from Spartanburg, South Carolina. Both had been told from childhood that black men and women could never reach the heights that whites attain. They joined us because we judge all people by one standard. If you produce, you will be rewarded whatever your race or creed.

Still, the Hardys had been damaged by a lifetime of limitations. They still remember when their teenage son, Quentin, already in love with the business, suddenly threw down our magazine, the *Amagram*, and mumbled tearfully, "We'll never be Diamonds. Will we?"

"Suddenly," Terral explains, "Margaret and I realized that our son was right. We would never make the Diamond level because we had not set that goal for ourselves. We had set goals, but they were too low. That night, together as a family, we wrote down a long-term goal that changed our lives. We will reach the Amway Diamond level in the next twelve months." Margaret and Terral made that level and beyond. Their son, Quentin, now a college graduate, has his own growing business, and it all began when they finally decided to set a goal and reach it, whatever it cost them.

David Humphrey was still a practicing physician when he began a distribution business. A nurse introduced Dave to our plan and invited him to attend a company seminar. There, Dr. Humphrey became so excited about owning his own business that he stood up before the whole crowd and announced that he would reach the Diamond level, a difficult achievement, in a very short period of time.

Coming off the stage in a state of excitement and confusion, he turned to the first person he met and asked sheepishly, "What did I just do?" Smiling, that person replied, "I don't know, but it's going to be a heck of a year."

If you are serious about meeting your goals, telling the world in clear and certain terms will help you meet them. At least you should confide your goals to somebody who will encourage and confront you along the way. The Humphreys not only met their goals, they went on to even higher levels of achievement in this business.

Most of the limits we face are ones we set for ourselves. We don't have clear long-term goals. So why are we surprised when we don't reach them? What are your goals for this year? for this decade? Have you written them down? Have you charted your progress and changed your course appropriately? If you don't have goals to guide you, you may be getting nowhere. If so, you have no one to blame but yourself.

Hard Work Before Success. Sacrifices Will Be Necessary!

Kenny Stewart continued his daytime construction job and worked late every evening and all weekend to get his business off the ground. While still playing for the Baltimore Colts, Brian Herosian spent two nights a week at a university getting his accounting degree and built his business on the side. Ron and Toby Hale took all the money they had to buy twenty-five "Selling America" records to give them to their friends. Al Hamilton was so afraid to make his first presentations that he literally shook before they began. This former tool and die maker for Ford was shy, inexperienced, and terrified of public speaking, but he did it anyway.

In Hiroshima City, Japan, Shuji and Tomoko Hanamoto wanted "to be free to fly over the big, blue sky" from the "small, luxurious cage" where their jobs in industry kept them. They had to give up all the perks—the regular salary, the company scuba diving trips in Okinawa, the benefits and bonuses—to begin their own business. Even worse, when Shuji's father learned that he had joined in our business, he used an old Japanese expression of anger and disappointment. "Don't come through my gate," he told his son. There is no greater sacrifice than to go against a parent's wishes; but Shuji Hanamoto had a dream and he was willing to pay that price.

These folks worked hard and sacrificed much, and their businesses skyrocketed to success. Today, they are financially secure, free to work less and to enjoy life more. One last note: Shuji Hanamoto invited his father to a rally in Hiroshima City where two thousand people stood and cheered as Shuji and Tomoko were awarded their achievement pins. On the front row that night, Shuji's father beamed up at his son and joined in the applause.

If You Care for Others, Others Will Care for You!

Stan Evans made a mistake. A distributor ordered five gallons of car wash that was not shipped on schedule. When he called to complain, Stan replied without a moment's hesitation, "You're right. I made a mistake. I'm on my way." That distributor was two hundred miles away, but Stan Evans personally drove the product the four-hundred-mile round-trip to keep his word. That distributor will never forget it.

"My word is gold," Stan says. "When I promise something, I deliver it. People want to know that they can trust you. Once they do, they will be loyal forever. If I owe someone a bonus of a dollar-fifty, I will send it on time no matter how small. Because I know that distributor will treat me with the same courtesy and respect."

Two of Bill and Peggy Florence's distributors were having trouble with their marriage. Bill and Peggy opened their homes to the young couple. "We spent, over the next few months, more than a dozen evenings counseling them," Peggy remembers. "We believe in the old biblical principle that leaders are really servants. Our job is not just to get more business, but to help people to go where they want to go with their lives."

"In this business," Bill adds, "we've seen dozens of marriages saved and families healed because people, not product, come first. When the bleeding stops and the wounds heal over, the people go back to work with new commitment. Their business thrives. By helping them get what they want, we in turn see our own dreams come true."

Just Do It. If You Don't Act, You Will Never Know.

A Nike billboard hangs above Times Square, eight stories high. "JUST DO IT." How often we vacillate back and forth, pro and conning things to death. Aesop wrote, "I will have nothing to do with a man who can blow hot and cold with the same breath." In the last New Testament book, John writes, "You are neither hot nor cold, so I will spew thee out of my mouth."

Dan Robinson was a wholesale paper salesman when he and his wife, Jeanette, began their business in 1979. "Inflation was wiping us out," Dan remembers. "We had built the home of our dreams, but we lost it when we couldn't keep up with the taxes. Something had to be done and done quickly." Dan and Jeanette took the plunge, and since that exciting day they have moved up a level in our business every year.

Tim Bryan was teaching fifth grade and his wife, Sherri, was working as a legal secretary when they first saw our plan. "I wanted to stay home with our children," Sherri remembers. "I didn't want to miss those early, growing-up years. It was scary to begin a whole new business, but we did it and we've never looked back or been sorry for a moment."

Is there an unpleasant task waiting to be done? Just do it. Is there a risky step that needs to be taken? Just do it. Is there an adventure you're excited about but afraid to begin? Just do it. You want to start a business of your own? You want to ask the boss for a raise or your supervisor for a new position on the line or your co-worker to turn down his stereo or, or, or . . . Just do it! If you don't act, you will never know. If you don't act now, you may never act at all.

Kids Should Be Included!

Greg and Lauri Duncan, like most of our successful distributors, have involved their children in the business from day one. "When Devin was just eight and Whitney, our daughter, was six," Greg explains, "they learned to answer the telephone and take important messages. They went to meetings with us. They heard the success stories and were excited by them. They asked to start their own business selling Active-8 [one of our fruit juice products] on our front lawn."

The Duncans set a goal to reach a new level in their business in a very short time. "We included our children in making that goal," Lauri explains, "and when we failed, we felt embarrassed at first, as if we had failed them. In fact, we hadn't failed them at all. Looking back, we realized how important it was for our children to see us fail as well as succeed; for one day they, too, will fail and by watching us re-load, re-cock, re-aim, and re-fire, they will learn how to pick up the pieces of their own failures and start again."

Bill and Peggy Florence, two of our most successful distributors, live in Athens, Georgia, with their three children. I am proud to say that Bill and Peggy named their two fine sons Rich and Jay; and their daughter, most appropriately, they named Hope. All three children have been involved in the business from their earliest childhood. Hope, now sixteen, earned enough money working with her family to pay for her own new car.

"We learned from leaders in this business," Peggy declares, "that we don't give our children everything they want. Instead we help them learn and practice the principles of success. We let them go through the struggles—our struggles and theirs—so that they, too, will understand what it takes to get ahead."

"We haven't been too rough on them," Bill adds quickly. "The kids are well rewarded for their work." In fact, Rich, Jay, and Hope Florence have traveled with their parents to company events in Australia, Hawaii, Europe, and across the United States. Whatever your business, let your kids play a part. Let them learn about real life while you are still there to cheer their victories and hold them through their failures.

Chuck and Jean Strehli are another example of parents who involved their children in this business and its benefits. "Ten years ago," Jean recalls, "when Tamara was just fourteen and her brother, Scott, was thirteen, we were already sharing with them our professional goals. Why should children be left in the dark and never really know what their parents are doing?" she asks wisely.

"We're their primary examples," Chuck adds. "What they are going to know about life, they will learn from us. From the beginning we tried to teach them the importance of making commitments and following through on them."

In 1980 the entire Strehli family spent seven months in Germany to establish their European business. Together as a family they learned the language and customs of that country. Now, although the children are adults, they still return to Europe occasionally for business, travel, and skiing in the Alps.

When I'm talking about children, how could I not include at least a mention of our own? From the beginning of their lives, we have seen our kids as real people with opinions worth considering. Early on they amazed us with their valuable ideas and communication skills.

When our daughter, Cheri, was just a junior in high school, she complained to me that I had set the family curfew too early. But she didn't just ask me to change it. She had surveyed all the families in our neighborhood. She had her facts in a row. I can still see her in the living room, her survey results spread out on the coffee table, pacing up and down, making her presentation. She was calm, determined, and reasonable. And she went away with a victory.

Today, all eight of the Van Andel and DeVos offspring are hard at work making this company better. Together with Jay and myself, our children make up the family council policy board. We meet monthly for brainstorming and long-range planning. Our children have become our peers in helping us guide this company, and each of them holds a special role in shaping Amway's future.

Nan Van Andel is our Vice President of Communications and Public Relations. Steve Van Andel is Vice President and Chairman of the Executive Committee. David Van Andel is our Vice President of Manufacturing and Operations and a member of the Executive Committee. And Barbara Van Andel is the General Manager of our Amway Properties, including the Amway Grand Plaza Hotel in Grand Rapids, Michigan, and the Peter Island resort complex in the British Virgin Islands.

Helen and my children are also deeply committed to the Amway Corporation and its two million independent distributors worldwide. My eldest son, Dick, has recently succeeded me as President of the Amway Corporation and is a member of the Executive Committee. Dan DeVos is Vice President and a member of the Executive Committee. Doug DeVos is our Vice President for North American sales. And Cheri (DeVos) Vanderweide, until opting to spend more time as wife and mother, used her skills in fashion and color to improve and update our entire Artistry Cosmetic line.

Who would ever dream that our children—yours and mine—would

ever grow into such responsible, creative, and committed adults? Including them in your business from the beginning is so important to their growth and understanding. Leave them out now, and they may never have the interest or the ability to join you, let alone to find their own way in the world of business.

Loving Others Is the Key to Success!

Tom Michmershuizen, Ken Morris, Gary Smit, Larry Miller, Jack Wright, Larry Shear, and the brothers Bob and Jim Rooker have been with Amway for thirty or more years. Their generous and sacrificial acts of love toward Jay and me, their fellow employees, our independent distributors, and our customers have taught us much about loving others.

Dave Taylor reminds us all that behind success is one unbreakable rule. "It is: love people and use money," he says, "not love money and use people." Treat them all with love: customers, suppliers, contractors, co-workers, bosses, or employees, and the love you give will return to you, as the Bible says, "pressed down, shaken together, and running over."

"Where do you go to get your marriage built up?" Dave asks. "Where do you go to get your self-confidence restored and renewed? Where do you go to hear people tell you that you are a winner and that you can do something with your life? These things are not taught us in schools," he notes. "Too often they aren't even taught us in our homes or churches. We have to do it for each other and when we do, our people become more loyal and hardworking and our businesses succeed."

Mentors Know What You Don't Know. Listen to Them!

When Renate Backhaus decided to start her own business in Germany, she was already a practicing physician with a specialty in sports medicine. "My husband, Wolfgang, and I were both excited about the freedom a successful business would bring us," she explains. "We went to the meetings. We tried and liked the products. We learned the networking sales plan. We rushed right in and failed," she admits.

"Looking back now, we can see quite clearly why we did not succeed at first. I had just finished a seven-year graduate school degree. We had both been in universities so long, we thought we knew everything. We didn't listen to our mentor. We thought we were smarter than he was. When we finally stopped to listen, our business grew rapidly."

Along with Peter and Eva Mueller-Merekatz, Wolfgang and Renate Backhaus have entered into the eastern half of unified Germany and have built large businesses. "Without our mentor's advice," Mrs. Backhaus admits, "we would have failed. With his advice, we succeeded beyond our dreams."

In Chekhov's *The Cherry Orchard,* a wealthy woman asks a young man, "Are you *still* a student?" His answer is one I've adopted for my own. "I expect I shall be a student to the end of my days." Jay and I have taught tens of thousands of successful businessmen and -women. But even as we taught them from our experiences, they go on teaching us from theirs.

Never Look Back. Keep Going Forward One Step at a Time!

Lew Riggan was a full captain with American Airlines. His wife, Darlene, was a fashion stylist and coordinator. Both Riggans were well established in their respective fields and well paid for their efforts. It was quite a shock when Lew stood before the distributors in his Amway organization and announced his resignation as a pilot to work full-time in this business.

"There were a thousand young pilots standing in line to take my place," he remembers. "The moment I quit, the airline replaced me. They had no choice. I couldn't hesitate. I couldn't look back. But we had a dream and we couldn't accomplish that dream part-time."

"And we've never been sorry," adds Darlene. "There were times of insecurity and wonder, but we kept moving toward our goal of financial independence. We were tired of seeing each other on an 'appointment only' basis. We wanted to be free to work together and to have enough financial security that we could support the causes that we love."

Today their dreams have come true partially because they burned their bridges and never looked back. I love the advice Dave Severn once gave to his group of distributors: "Don't be like the high-rise window washer," he warned, "who stepped back to admire his work."

There isn't much time in this business (or in any other, for that matter) to step back to admire your work or to wonder if you're headed in the right direction. Of course we should be thoughtful, we should learn from our mistakes and from our failures, but there is no time to brood. When you succeed, pat yourself on the back, take a five-minute break to celebrate, then get back to work. When you fail, have a good cry and then wipe your tears away. There is work to be done. There are frontiers to be explored. There are new limits to test and incredible victories to be won.

Opportunity Is on Its Way. Be Ready for It!

Jack Daughery shared this saying with us: "When the student is ready, the teacher will appear." I've thought a lot about the wisdom in those words. Opportunity is all around us, but only when we're ready will we be able to grab the chance and never be sorry for what might have been.

What does it mean to get ready for the opportunities ahead? It isn't a college degree that prepares you, though a college degree may help. And though money is important, it isn't cash in the bank that will pave the way. Friends in high places? An influential network? A resumé to die for? Recommendations by the pile?

No, what makes you ready to recognize and to reach out for the golden ring when it suddenly appears is something mysterious, something powerful inside your heart and head that says, "I can do it and I will." That's a gift we give each other. Sometimes it's a gift we have to give ourselves. These may be difficult financial times, but there are as many opportunities to make a success of your life now as there have ever been, maybe more. Get ready. Find a friend or a company of friends who believe in you, and one day soon you will believe in yourself. On that day opportunity will come, the teacher will appear, and you will be ready.

Angelo Nardone was completing his master's program in special education at American University when opportunity knocked. A fellow student told him about our marketing and distribution plan. He rushed home to share the idea with his wife, Claudia, a secretary in the Department of Defense. Immediately they took the plunge and in a very short time they owned a successful business. "Take control of your life," Angelo advises. "Control the circumstances, never allow circumstances to control you."

People Come Before Product. First Things First.

In every business where long-range success is important, people come before product, and yet how many hours we can spend rearranging the dust on our shelves while just outside people are waiting to be listened to, to be loved, to be mobilized and trained. Let the dust rearrange itself. Take time with people, and you will see success in your business before you know it.

Craig and Carole Holiday, two friends in this business from San Juan Capistrano, California, summarize the principle perfectly. "It's your dream that gets you to people's front door," Craig says. "But it's their dream that matters after that. When we enter another person's home or business, we leave our dreams on the threshold so that we can focus on the dreams and the dreamers inside."

Carole says it this way: "You say to yourself, 'Gee, I want to be successful; so I'm going to drive all those miles to all those people's homes. But once I get there I'm going to ask myself, 'What's their dream? What is it they want out of life and how can I help them accomplish it?' "

In recent months I have watched my daughter, Cheri Vanderweide, make a difficult decision about her life's goals. Cheri has special gifts in fashion and design. After watching her help transform our cosmetic line, I have no doubt that she could be on the fast track for a career in any one of many related fields. But when her first child was born, she decided that her profession would have to be limited to part-time work to enable her to reach her deeply felt goals as wife and mother.

What are your goals? Do you have them listed in their order of importance to you? Today, for example, what is at the top of your list to accomplish and who are the people who can help you get it done? Helping people to help themselves is the key to lasting success. Are you convinced? Are you doing it? How quickly that which seems urgent squeezes out that which is truly important in our lives. "And meanwhile," writes Virgil, "time is flying, irretrievable time is flying."

Quitting Means You Didn't Really Try. Stay with It Until It Happens!

When Jay and I were just beginning this business, I traveled to Phoenix to present the Amway marketing and distribution plan. Only one man, Frank Delisle, Sr., attended the meeting. He had come by bus from another distant city and en route cashed a check at a Lucky store to pay his expenses. Frank knew there was no money in the bank to cover his check until his return on Monday, but he arrived at the meeting and sat alone in the hotel meeting room we had rented.

I could have cancelled that meeting, apologized to Frank, and jumped on the next airplane home. Instead I gave Frank the entire presentation. He nodded, shook my hand enthusiastically, and we parted. I thought the entire trip had been a failure. It was a perfect time to quit. But Frank went home, shared his enthusiasm with his wife, Rita, and together they built one of the biggest organizations in our company's history. He also covered the check in time, and for years later, I called him Lucky to remind us both of that fateful day we met.

When you begin a new endeavor, there will always be times when you wonder if you've made a terrible mistake. Another successful entrepreneur in my company of friends calls this time the "faith period." He remembers his early days in the business with his wife "when we worked and we felt like we were not going anywhere, that we were not making any progress." Those are difficult times, to be sure, but they will pass. "You just stay at it," my friend advises. "Keep doing the right thing and good things will happen."

After less than one semester in college, I quit and never went back. I've always felt bad about quitting. In my head I know that a college degree is not necessary to succeed in business (and now I have dozens of honorary doctorates from prestigious schools across the nation). Nevertheless, I wish I hadn't quit.

When Helen and I had children, we were both determined that they would get their college degrees. Our son Dan was the first to fulfill that dream. When he graduated from Northwood University with excellent training in business administration, I felt so proud. I invited our friends, our neighbors and even people off the street to celebrate Dan's achievement with us.

Now, all four of our children hold college degrees, but I still remember Dan walking across the stage to get that first DeVos diploma. My son had stayed the course. He had proven his intellect and his determination. He had succeeded where I had quit, and I almost burst with pride.

Those who quit too soon, always wonder what might have been. But those who go on working faithfully, day after day, putting in the hours, doing the basics, refusing to give up, one day soon join millions of others in the winner's circle.

The urge to quit is the last obstacle between you and your dreams: the new home, new car, cash in the bank, the vacation in Europe or Tahiti. Hang in. Everybody wants to quit now and then. Just don't do it.

Risk Everything to See Your Goals Accomplished!

"Who dares, wins!" Every success story in our business affirms these words. I don't know one person who hasn't risked something before he could get ahead.

For some it is money. Angelo and Claudia Nardone both had secure government jobs in Washington, D.C., but they were tired of their limited incomes. So they risked their jobs, began a distribution business and today, besides the financial success they have realized, they raised millions in our drive for the Easter Seal Society.

For some it is family reputation. Midori Ito grew up surrounded by wealth and gentility. Her family tree included a former prime minister and the governor of Tokyo. It was a great loss of face for Midori to start her own network sales business. She risked it all and won!

For some it is fame. E. H. Erick was the host of a popular television show in Japan when he saw the opportunity. He risked his celebrity to begin a business of his own and won!

For some it is security. For thirty years Frank Morales was an executive with Diamond International. His wife, Barbara, was a co-founder and the chief operations officer of the National Bank of Southern California. They risked it all to begin their own business and won!

What is your vocational dream? What would you risk to pursue your dream? "Nothing ventured, nothing gained," the old proverb goes. We might add, "Risk much and you will gain much."

Sow Enough Seed and You Will Reap a Great Harvest!

Almost three thousand years ago, King Solomon wrote, "Cast your bread upon the water and it will not return unto you void." In ancient Egypt after the winter floods along the Nile River began to recede, the farmers knew exactly when to throw their seed onto the thin layer of silt that remained. Some farmers waited until a more convenient time. Others cast a little here and little there and were satisfied. But those who cast enough seed at the right time and in the right place guaranteed themselves a rich harvest.

Remember Chris Cherest, who made his presentation one hundred fifty times and everyone said no. "It took two and a half hours in those days," Chris remembers. "I went out for almost eight months, night after night, house after house and no one said yes.

"But I had a dream for our future," Chris explains. "And my dream was so big I had no place else to take it. Finally I learned that my dream wasn't enough. I had to listen first to other people's dreams and once I understood that it was trying to fulfill my dream that got me to the door, but it was trying to fulfill their dreams that made them say yes, the whole thing changed. When I tried the one hundred fifty-first time, the young couple said yes and the rest is history."

In Canada, Andre and Francoise Blanchard have a lot to teach us about sowing seed. Andre was a supervisor for a grocery-store chain in his home province of Quebec. With only a seventh-grade education and limited skills in English, Andre had reached the limits of his profession at ninety-seven dollars a week in 1967. Francoise was making more money as a legal secretary, but even when combined, their salaries did not pay the bills. They could not see the day when they would realize even some of their dreams.

"For thirteen years," Andre remembers, "we spent every free moment planting seeds. We presented the sales and marketing plan to hundreds of people. We made thousands of phone calls and traveled hundreds of thousands of miles. There were times we doubted. There were times we grew weary and ready to quit. But we have never stopped sowing seed, and the harvest has been plentiful beyond our wildest dreams."

Today, Andre and Francoise live in a mountaintop home with an indoor pool. But more important than the financial security they have achieved, the Blanchards are free to spend time with their children and to invest their lives in compassionate service for the children of Quebec. "Sow enough seed," wrote the ancient prophet, "and you shall reap a great harvest." Quit sowing seed, he should have added, and nothing at all will grow.

Tithe Your Income to Those in Need, and Great Things Will Happen!

The independent distributors in our company include all the colors of the rainbow. Every race and creed are represented in cities and countries around the globe. There are no rules about giving, no standard set in place. But over the years we've learned, one by one, that the more generous we are in helping those in need, the more we have to be generous.

Don and Ruth Storms had explored many different vocations before beginning their own successful direct marketing business. Don had been a gospel singer, a minister, and then a home builder before Dexter Yager put him to work.

"Running a successful business is a lot like being a minister," Don reminds us. "From the beginning Dex told Ruth and me that learning to serve is the key to success. 'The purpose of living,' Dex told us over and over again, 'is giving.' Once we discovered the truth of that little saying, our lives changed and our business prospered."

In the sixteenth century, Francis Bacon said, "In charity there is no excess." Helen and I say, "You can't outgive God." When Helen decided that we would write a check representing ten percent of gross income to our church and to charities every month, she set us in a wise and fruitful direction. Try it. Find a need and meet it. See what it does for you, for your family, and for your business to help others whose needs are greater than your own.

Understanding the Basics Before You Begin!

Invariably you will find that those who succeed in business don't begin until they've asked and answered a lot of important questions. You remember them: who? what? where? how? when? why? and how much? When you sit down with someone pushing our products, our sales plan or anything else for that matter, don't be satisfied until you have collected all the frank, honest, well-supported answers that you need.

Linda Harteis remembers her lack of confidence in her ability to handle her share of the business that she and her husband, Fred, had begun. "I learned that we really aren't asked to handle things until we are ready," Linda says. "In the beginning I could not have done what I can do now. Responsibility comes a little at a time, and if you take the time and energy to learn how to accomplish each task along the way, before long you are doing what you never dreamed that you could do. We both just kept looking toward the things we wanted for our children, and in the evenings, while Tonya, Freddie, and Angela slept, we built a future for our family."

There is a legend about a French saint who is said to have carried his own head for six miles after his execution. Upon hearing the story, a noblewoman answered, "The distance doesn't matter; it is only the first step that is difficult." Take the first step carefully. Be sure you understand what must be done. Then be confident that you can and want to do it. Once you know, put the old questions aside and launch out on your adventure. There will be plenty of time for new questions along the way.

Value Friendship Above All Else!

In the book of Proverbs is advice from Solomon: "Forsake not your friend, for there is a time of calamity at hand and you'll need a house to flee to." When I look back over my years in this business, I remember especially the moments shared with Jay Van Andel, my lifelong partner and oldest friend. Whether we were facing failure or success, Jay and I faced it together. Sure, we argued. Sure, there were bad times among the good. But how bleak it all would have been without Jay to share those times together.

One of the secrets to our friendship has been our agreement from the beginning never to say, "I told you so." There were difficult times along the way when we disagreed on a decision that had to be made. When the verdict was in and I realized that I had made the wrong decision, Jay never once made me feel stupid or guilty. In all these years I've never heard him say, "I told you so." And trust me, there were times he had every right to say it.

Dallas and Betty Beaird have built an entire business on friendship. "We don't go out recruiting," Dallas explains. "We just develop friendships and start our friends in the Amway business. We've never advertised to find people. We've always just reached out to people with friendship and found that they, too, want success."

When something good happens, we want to share it with our friends. But at the same time, we must not pressure or con our friends into anything they don't really want for themselves. We dare not risk our friendships or use them to get ahead. If we start seeing our friends only as business opportunities, we will lose those friends forever. Share your dream but understand, the next step is in the hands of your friend. In the meantime, value the friendship above all else or you will end up alone and friendless.

Looking back on her marriage to Charles Lindbergh and the kidnaping and murder of their child, Anne Morrow Lindbergh describes perfectly the role of a friend during hard times. "Both of us are groping and a little lost," she confessed, "but we are together."

Over the years I've made thousands of friends in and out of this business. How much more important that has been than all the money we have made or will make together. How sad I feel at the news of every new death in the ranks of those I call friend. Helen Keller said, "With the death of every friend I love, a part of me has been buried, but their contribution to my being of happiness, strength, and understanding remains to sustain me in an altered world."

Do you have a friend in your business? What are you doing to sustain that friendship? Have you called your friend recently to see how she is doing? Have you had lunch or dinner together? Have you sent flowers or a surprise card just to say "Hello, friend. I'm thinking about you"? I'm beginning to believe that having at least one good friend may be the most important task we have. Friends comfort or confront us when we need it. Friends help up keep our goals. Friends can be trusted to tell us the truth.

Winners Heeded! Whiners Ignored!

Most of us like winners. Our company events are built around recognizing the achievement of those who perform. We cheer and holler and jump up and down like a bunch of crazy kids to show appreciation to our friends in this business who have set goals and met them.

They are winners. They believe in themselves. And the more you hang around winners, the more you'll find yourself believing that you can be a winner, too.

The flip side is often tragic. In *Henry IV,* Part 1, the young prince with his life in shambles cries out, "Company, villainous company, hath been the spoil of me." Hang around with whiners, faultfinders, crybabies, prophets of doom, naysayers, complainers, racists, those who judge and those who hate, and you'll end up just like them. Hang around with winners and one day you'll find people cheering you!

Compassion can be taught us by circumstances which are tragic. We learn to find hope, gain patience from slow progress, and avoid self-pity from the plight of others. Helen and I attended the wedding of Tom and Kathy Eggleston, whom we have known for over a decade. She is a pediatrician and he is Chief Operating Officer for Amway, responsible for ten thousand employees and over two million distributors operating in sixty countries and territories.

We were prayerful when their first child, James Warren, was rushed to surgery after birth to close an opening in his diaphragm, which had allowed his internal organs to compress his lungs. Despite major operations, Jimmy was unable to eat solid food by mouth for three and a half years. Imagine his anxious parents wondering if their son would ever be able to enjoy a hot dog. It was only after his younger brother Jack began to eat that Jimmy overcame the dread of bloating from a high-calorie liquid tubed into his tummy every four hours.

When Jimmy was thirteen months old and forming words, he had a respiratory arrest; his father discovered him a bright shade of purple one morning in his crib. His mother saved his life with her knowledge of CPR, but Jimmy required a tracheostomy—an opening in his neck to allow oxygen to be administered continuously—for many months. He learned to cover the plastic opening to create sounds as if he were speaking.

All of these complications made his dislocated hips, absence of cruciate ligaments in his left knee, and only a stump for his right leg less a crisis, since they were not life-threatening. One night as their father was reading to Jimmy, Jack, and Tommy, Jimmy asked, "Why do they have two legs and I have one?" His father answered, "When God made you He loved you so much He wanted to keep a part of you for Himself."

Today, Jimmy is six years old, walks with a prothesis using either a walker or crutches. He loves all sports, has skied, eats popcorn and hot dogs (and anything else), and sings songs. Because of a severe curvature of his spine, he wears a body cast at night for correction. The first night he was to wear it he said he was scared. His father told him, "Jimmy, you are a prince. This is your armor to protect you from anything." Jimmy told him, "Great, now I need a horse."

Like his parents, Jimmy faces problems head-on. He doesn't whine or pout or feel sorry for himself. Naturally there are sad, disappointing, and fearful times. But the Eggleston family knows with God's help, they will prevail. The same holds true for you.

Xcuses Aren't Helpful. Forgive! Forget! Move On!

Don and Nancy Wilson recall having these three excuses for their failure in starting their own business:

"Number one," Don remembers, "we didn't have enough time. Nancy was nursing ten hours a day and I was coaching sixty to eighty hours a week. Number two, we didn't see ourselves as salesmen. Nancy was so shy she couldn't even lead a group in silent prayer, and I felt embarrassed when I tried to pitch a product and not a baseball. And number three, we didn't have any confidence that we could succeed."

"Don was a jock," Nancy adds, "and I was tall, thin, and gangly, a kind of academic nerd. We didn't believe in ourselves, so we sat around believing our excuses.

"Then Dexter Yager appeared," Nancy says gratefully. "He loved us. He told us we could do it. He brought us books to read and tapes to hear. We asked questions and learned how the business works. When I told him I could never stand up to speak before a crowd, Dexter laughed and said, 'Just picture them all sitting there in their underwear.' The next time I got up in front of a crowd, my fear was gone and I almost broke out laughing."

"We made a few phone calls," Don remembers. "We succeeded at one presentation and then another. With each victory we got a little more confident, and Dexter was always there believing in us, loving us, teaching us, pushing us toward our goals." Today, Don and Nancy Wilson own a prosperous Amway business. When they quit making excuses, their lives began.

John Crowe is a man who has plenty of reasons to feel sorry for himself, but, like the Wilsons, he doesn't believe in excuses. On June 15, 1981, his wife, Jennie Belle, was spending the weekend with her parents with their new son, John Crowe III, who had been born with a life-threatening birth defect. John returned to his home around midnight after showing our sales plan in a nearby town. Four or five men high on PCP ambushed him in his own driveway. They forced him into his house and threatened to kill him if he didn't give them exactly what they wanted.

"I knew in my heart that they were going to kill me," John told us. "So I went for the nearest gun. In the ensuing scuffle I managed to shoot one of the robbers three times, but I was also shot in my head and my left hand at point-blank range with a .357 Magnum. When the police arrived, I was near death. Somehow, a shock-trauma unit revived me and I was helicoptered to a nearby hospital. Within twenty-four hours our network of friends had donated two thousand pints of blood. Many of them stood in line for hours waiting for a chance to give their blood to save my life. Over the next six months, five thousand more pints were donated on my behalf."

Because John could have identified the criminals, the police warned him that his life was once again in jeopardy. Friends in this business not only guarded him in the hospital day and night, they fed, comforted, and protected his wife and family. "Before the shooting, I was a gymnast," John explained. "Afterward, I found myself paralyzed and fighting for my life."

In the hospital John felt deserted by God. Just six months before the shooting, his son had been born with a serious birth defect. Now John was paralyzed. He went through a time of asking God, "Why should I love you, when you let this all happen to me?"

All during those difficult, lonely hours, John remembered that first night in intensive care when his mentor Bill Britt, who had flown to the hospital and picked up John's wife and son en route, whispered in his ear these ancient words from the New Testament: "All things work together for good to them who love God and work together for His purpose."

John Crowe saw how God worked through his family and friends to comfort and encourage him. It didn't take long for John to realize that God was there in the midst of his suffering through the people that he loved.

"I had a simple choice," John remembers. "I could have felt sorry for myself and quit the business. Or I could be grateful for life, pick up the pieces, and move on. With the help of our friends, I moved on. Helen Keller has a saying that I printed and tacked up on my office wall. 'If you keep your face to the sunshine, you never see the shadows.' So every day, when the shadows threaten to plunge my world into darkness, I just turn my face to the sunshine, and once again my life is filled with light."

In spite of his paralysis, John Crowe, with the loving help of his wife, Jennie Belle, has built a distribution business that is a model to my company of friends. "We didn't do it for big homes or cars," John admits. "When the life of your newborn son is threatened by an esophagus that is just a half inch too short, you don't care about Cadillacs or mansions. But thanks to our financial security, we can provide our son the lifelong care he may need and even more important, we are free and at home when he needs us to give the kind of love that keeps him strong."

Carpe diem, wrote the Roman poet Horace. "Seize the day!" Excuses are like an open wound. They bleed away our strength until we die. And the clock goes on ticking the minutes and the hours away.

What "reasons" do you use to keep yourself from trying? Whom do you blame for your failures? "Seize the day!" If excuses are standing in your way, label them for what they are. Reach out to someone to teach you. Believe in yourself and "seize the day!"

You Can Do It! Never Quit Believing in Yourself!

Brian Herosian had everything he ever wanted: a contract to play football for the Baltimore Colts, a beautiful wife, Jane, and his first child, Ben, about to be born.

"Almost overnight, my perfect world fell apart," Brian remembers. "The Colts dumped me. I found myself out of work and not really prepared to find a good job, especially one that paid what I'd been getting. To make matters worse, my son was born without feet and missing one hand. 'Möebius' syndrome,' the doctor told us sadly. 'Very rare. Only three cases in all of Canada.'

"Then in 1979, my wife lost control of our car and hit a semitrailer truck head-on at sixty-five miles per hour. Pinned in the wreckage beside her, I could see that Jane was dead. In the intensive-care ward, doctors told me that my neck was broken and that I would be lucky to ever walk again."

If you ever find it difficult to believe in your future, remember Brian Herosian. He rose like a phoenix from the wreckage of his life's dreams. "It wasn't easy," Brian remembers. "Without God's help and the help of friends in this business, I might have gone down under all my doubts and disappointments."

But Brian did not go down. We asked him how he had managed to hold on during those dark, lonely days. "I had to start all over," he told us. "I was smart about football. I could block and tackle and run, but I was dumb about free enterprise. So I got hungry for knowledge. I read a book a week and listened to a new tape every day. I found mentors, people who were in life where I wanted to be, doing what I wanted to do. I wasn't afraid to ask them questions. I was open, teachable. I trusted God to get me through each day, and I never stopped believing in myself."

Today, Brian Herosian has a successful business, a beautiful new wife, Deidre, and a growing family. Brian's fifteen-year-old son, Ben, has also triumphed over his handicap. Today he is a successful student and an aspiring writer.

What kept Brian believing in himself? It's a mystery. But it is the key to your future as it was to Brian's. If you believe in yourself, you will succeed. If you don't, follow Brian's advice. Read the stories of other people who have triumphed over tragedy. Listen to stories on tape that inspire and inform you. Find a group of people who are positive and who believe in you. Trust God and believe in yourself. And like Brian, you will rise from the ashes and see your new dreams come true.

Zero in God's Hands Is the Beginning of a Whole New World!

When Jay and I began our business, we had nothing. Our other business schemes, the flying service, the drive-in restaurant, and the old schooner had left us with a zero balance. But we went on believing in ourselves and trusting God. I don't know who or what you believe in, but for Jay and me it was never enough to believe in ourselves. We also believed in a loving Creator whose dreams for us were far greater than any dreams we could have on our own. Now look at what we—God and all of us—have done together.

I wish I had more ways to thank the millions of people who have made our company a success, but all of us would be ashamed to take credit for what God has done. All the natural resources that we use in this business are God's creation, not ours. All of the human energy spent, from research and development to customer service and delivery, is God's gift to every one of us. And the tools of capitalism and the goods and services that have been produced are a direct result of God's invitation to each of us to subdue the earth and to use the products of our hands and hearts to honor our Creator.

In 1981, at the opening of Amway's Grand Plaza Hotel in Grand Rapids, I stood on a great sweeping stairway with my partner, Jay Van Andel, on one side and former President Gerald Ford on the other. It was time for me to cut the ribbon and to officially open the hotel for business. A large crowd of our company of friends and business associates had gathered for the spectacular occasion. Television cameras and photographers all waited for me to speak. I hadn't planned my words for the occasion, but suddenly, from deep inside my soul, the words came: "To God be the glory. Great things He has done!"

Often at the bottom of a new composition, Bach would scribble these words: *Deo Gloria.* "To God be the glory!" If I had a flow pen big enough, I would write those words across the face of our factories, warehouses, and our offices everywhere. "To God be the glory. Great things He has done."

If you have a zero balance in your financial, spiritual, or psychological bank, don't be afraid. Trust what you have into the hands of God and watch with amazement what will happen. In 1939, with the Axis powers under Adolf Hitler threatening all the world with tyranny, King George VI read this story in his Christmas radio address to the people of England.

"And I said to the man who stood at the gate of the year: 'Give me a light that I may tread safely into the unknown.' And he replied, 'Go out into the darkness and put your hand into the hand of God. That shall be to you better than light and safer than a known way.' "

In Conclusion

An elderly woman stood at the doorway, dishtowel in hand, shielding her eyes from the sun and staring off into the distance.

"Here comes that 'guru' again," she said with a kind of motherly growl.

Don Wilson rushed to the open door of his rundown little farmhouse clinging to a brush-covered hill in Maine. A long white car had just turned off the country road in their direction.

"In one way," Don remembers, "my mother was right. Dexter Yager was my guru in those early years. Along with a few other important mentors including Rich DeVos and Jay Van Andel, Dexter taught me almost everything I know about the basics of this business."

For years, Don's wife, Nancy, had been a registered nurse working in open-heart surgery in a large medical clinic in New Hampshire. Don was a high school teacher and basketball coach who ran the town's peewee athletic programs on the side. The Wilsons were both educated and experienced at their jobs but their combined salaries could barely pay the bills.

"One more child," Don recalls with disbelief, "and we would have qualified for food stamps. So we signed on with Amway, hoping that owning a business would provide us the kind of steady, trustworthy income that we needed."

"We were flops at first," Nancy admits. "Don used to say we were ninety-day wonders. After ninety days in the business we wondered what we were doing there. After twenty-nine months we still weren't making a living at it. Then Dexter Yager found us and showed us the way."

"He believed in us," Don says gratefully. "He had faith that if we could just learn the basics, we could make it to the top." Dexter Yager knew that there is no shortcut to seeing dreams come true. Before you will ever succeed in our business or in any other, there are certain skills and disciplines that you need to learn and practice. Dexter passed on his skills and disciplines to the Wilsons, and they went on to build a successful business of their own.

One evening, Don and Nancy were eating dinner with Don's parents. The "rustic" cabin in Maine was history. The old brown sports car with 177,000 miles on it had been junked. The pile of bills had been paid. With Dexter Yager as their mentor, Don and Nancy had prospered.

"I was afraid he was just another guru who wanted something out of you," Grandma Wilson said, remembering those first visits with a sheepish grin. "He was our guru, Mom," Don replied. "He taught us how to have a successful business of our own."

"And he did want something out of us," Nancy added quietly, "our very best."

Mrs. Wilson cocked her head like a puppy and just grinned in reply. "I recognized that look," Don recalls. "Mom grinned like that when her dime-store hearing aid acted up or was on the blink. 'Mom needs a new hearing aid, Dad,' I said without thinking. 'Well, I can't afford one,' he answered defensively." The Wilsons were on Social Security. Their fixed income didn't allow for any major extras. Don and Nancy were just beginning to feel successful, to know the joy of having a little extra cash.

"How much is a good hearing aid?" Don inquired of his father. "Five hundred bucks," his dad replied. Don didn't think. He just reached into his pocket, pulled out his wallet, removed five one-hundred-dollar bills, and pushed them across the table.

Don's father was offended. "We don't need your money," he said, pushing the money back. "Take it anyway," Don argued, shoving the bills across the table once again. For a moment there was a standoff. Then Don said, "Dad, wouldn't it be nice if Mom could hear you better?" Suddenly his father just melted. Taking money from his son wasn't easy, but how wonderful it would be for his wife to hear better again. Tears filled his eyes as he reached for the money. "Thank you, son," he said. Mrs. Wilson put her hand on her husband's hand. She, too, began to cry. By the time the waitress returned with their dinners, everyone around the table was crying.

"Before that moment," Don recalls, "I never realized what joy it would give me to reach into my pocket and hand my parents five one-hundred-dollar bills. Having a business of our own made it possible to feel secure and to help those we love to feel secure as well. Now we've given them a new car and flown them on vacations to Hawaii, Great Britain, and Europe."

And it all began for Don and Nancy Wilson, for Paul and Debbie Miller, and for millions like them when they decided to take free enterprise seriously. They learned the basics and they did them faithfully. And the rest is, as they say, history. You, too, can succeed. Seize the day! Find a mentor. Learn the ABC's of success and put them to work for your own future. Give it a try. What can you lose but the opportunity to see your dreams come true and to help others see their dreams come true as well?

During those college years when Paul Miller was enjoying his championship season with the North Carolina Tar Heels, the team's locker-room attendant was Morris Mason, a wise and loving black man who served the players for forty long years.

"He spent his life helping athletes and their coaches," Paul remembers. "I was just a teenager when I came to Chapel Hill, feeling inferior, terrified I would never make the team, but every time Morris Mason looked me in the eye and called me Mr. Miller, I stood tall and hopeful once again. He did so much more than hand out towels or massage tired bodies. His kind words and gentle smiles in the midst of so much stress and tension healed our souls as well."

In 1982, when Paul and Debbie Miller heard that Morris Mason was about to retire, they decided to honor him by endowing a scholarship in his name. University officials planned a banquet to honor Mason for his years of service. Athletes and coaches from across the South came back to Chapel Hill for the occasion.

"I'll never forget that night," Debbie says. "Paul and I sat at the head table with Mr. Mason and his wife. When the Morris Mason Memorial Scholarship was announced, the audience stood and cheered. Mr. Mason sat looking on in stunned silence. He was smiling, but tears ran down his cheeks and dampened his plain gray suit. 'Thank you,' he finally said. 'Thank you very much!' "

"We've made a lot of money in this business," Paul says. "Thanks to capitalism, we've bought our share of fancy cars and beautiful houses. But that night in a little banquet room near the university campus, I saw what compassionate capitalism can do. I will forget the fancy cars and the beautiful houses, but I will always remember the look in Mr. Mason's tear-stained eyes. 'My, my, my!' he said. 'All those children studying in this great place, remembering my name. How can it be? How can it be?' "

PART IV

Reaching the Goal:
Helping Ourselves
and Helping Others

13

Why Should We Help Others to Help Themselves?

CREDO 13

We believe in helping others to help themselves. When we share our time and money to help guide, teach, or encourage someone else, we are only giving back a part of what has already been given to us.

Therefore, be a mentor. Whom could you help to reach his goals, to see his dreams come true?

Willie Bass was not a handsome man. He was only fifty years old, but he looked weary and worn. Time had been tough on Willie. His face bore the scars of countless brawls. "Didn't get 'em makin' love," he'd say, grinning mischievously. Willie was a country boy born into poverty on a farm in North Carolina.

A welder all of his life, Willie spent his days bent over hot steel, squinting through a mask, wielding his torch. Over the years vaporized metal from countless welding rods had found their way into Willie's lungs. As a result of breathing in the poisoned vapors, his lung capacity had been reduced by fifty percent.

What Willie lacked in appearance and in lung capacity, though, he made up in character. He was committed heart and soul to his wife, Naomi, and to their only daughter. Willie knew that his family was dependent on him, and when the doctors told him that he was much too ill to continue his work as a welder, he refused to quit. He'd shuffle step by step to the bus stop, gasping and heaving for air. Day after miserable day, Willie would put on his welder's mask, pick up his torch, and breathe in death so that those he cared for could live. He would not fail the ones he loved. He would rather die trying.

Willie's modest house had an equally modest mortgage payment of $112 a month, but if Willie quit, his disability check would only amount to $186. The family couldn't survive on such a small amount.

So he found himself trapped without a ray of hope behind walls of disability and need. Every morning he stumbled off to work again, and every evening he staggered back up the steps of his little home nearly dead with fatigue.

What should be done for Willie Bass?

We could pretend we didn't notice Willie. We could walk around him and go our way, hoping that some good Samaritan would see Willie in time, bind up his wounds before he bled to death, load him on his donkey, carry him to an inn, and pay the innkeeper in advance for his services.

We could make Willie an object of our charity. When we see him sitting by the freeway off-ramp holding up his little hand-painted sign "Unemployed welder will work to eat" we could roll down our window, hand him a dollar or a five, and hope that some government welfare program will rescue Willie, give him food stamps and transient housing for his family.

Or *we could help Willie to help himself.* Ron Hale did just that more than twenty-four years ago. That's how we know about the story. Willie Bass and Ron Hale were neighbors. From time to time Ron noticed Willie slowly making his way to and from the bus stop. There was something about Willie's grit, as well as his gait, that made Ron remember him. When the Hales found themselves strapped financially, they had started their own distribution business. The more they learned about Willie, the more they realized how badly he needed a way to escape his cycle of despair. Eventually the Hales decided that they would do what they could to help Willie help himself. If he would let them, the Hales would be his mentor.

Jim Floor was a successful lobbyist for the Southern California Gas Company. He was the liaison officer for his company with the City Council of Los Angeles, the mayor's office, and the L.A. County Board of Supervisors. Unlike Willie, Jim and Margee Floor were leading the good life. They had a large home in a beautiful Los Angeles suburb, and Jim had an impressive salary, a travel allowance, and a generous expense account.

On the surface, no one would compare Jim Floor to Willie Bass. But just beneath the surface, Jim, too, was dissatisfied. He had dreams for himself and his family that he just wasn't meeting. Fred Bagdanov, one of Jim's friends and co-workers, began to take a special interest in him. Fred had just started to reap the rewards of owning his own business, and he put Jim Floor at the top of his list of people whom he would like to teach.

Now, a decade and a half later, amazing things have happened in the very different lives of Willie Bass and Jim Floor. And I am hoping that what happened to them will inform your own decision to become a mentor and inspire you to join the exciting ranks of people helping people to help themselves.

Step 1. A Mentor Believes in a Person's Potential to Succeed. "When we looked at Willie," Ron remembers, "we didn't see a defeated and disabled old man. We saw a person with great possibilities who had taken some wrong turns and needed to be helped back on the right road again."

"When we saw Jim and Margee Floor," Fred recalls, "we saw two people like ourselves, successful and ambitious by anyone's standards, but dreaming bigger dreams and unsure how to make those dreams work."

People who help people help themselves must first try to see others as God sees them. That's why I began this book talking about our Creator's dreams for every one of us. Whatever mess we've made of life (or whatever mess we've inherited), God still believes in us. Whatever level of success we've achieved in life, God sees us as capable and worthy of so much more. This is the good news (and this is where the people-helping-people process begins). If God goes on believing in us, we are free to go on believing in each other.

Until Ron came along, almost no one believed in Willie's potential, not even Willie. But Ron saw past his limits. Any man who worked that hard to keep his commitment to his family had something special. He believed in Willie and in Willie's future. And he was willing to act on that belief.

It was a lot easier for Fred to believe in Jim Floor. Jim was already a success. There were no apparent reasons that he couldn't move on from success to success. But it would not be easy for Jim to be convinced that he could or should move on. He was getting by fine, thank you. Why go to all the extra trouble of starting a business, taking new risks, climbing out of the fur-lined rut and moving on with his life? Jim had all kinds of defenses in place, and Fred somehow had to get past them if he was to succeed as Jim's friend and mentor.

Although Willie and Jim were obviously different, they were the same in one respect. They each had someone who believed in his potential to succeed, and for Willie and for Jim, as for so many millions of others, a brand-new, life-giving process began when someone finally believed in them.

Step 2. A Mentor Has the Courage to Tell That Person That She Has Potential. It was one thing to imagine Willie's possibilities, but another still to convince Willie. No matter how much you believe in someone, until you've reached out to tell him, to help him believe in himself, it's just so much wishful thinking.

Over a period of several weeks Ron spoke to Willie about owning his own business and the hope and freedom that came with the territory. Willie just smiled and shook his head. He wasn't stupid. He knew how high the odds were stacked against him. To begin a business at his age and in his physical condition seemed a dream far beyond his reach. The Hales talked. Willie listened and little by little hope was conceived and began to grow in his heart.

"When Fred Bagdanov, a co-worker at Southern California Gas, first invited me to talk about starting my own business," Jim remembers, "I promised him I would come and then I skipped the meeting. Old Fred was determined to mentor me, so he made an offer I couldn't refuse. He came to our house and presented the plan. He risked embarrassment and rejection to reach out to us."

For the entire two hours and thirty minutes of his presentation, Fred seemed understandably nervous but sincerely interested in Jim's future. Jim respected and appreciated Fred for his concern and Jim could see how the numbers worked, but he just didn't feel the need to start a business, or so he told Fred.

"Actually, I felt plenty of need for financial security," Jim admits today, "and for the personal freedom it would guarantee. I just couldn't admit that I had a need, not to him. We were co-workers and friends. I was too proud to be honest."

Almost fourteen years later, Jim and Margee Floor are very successful in our business, and they've become experienced and successful mentors themselves. "When he decided to mentor me," Jim admits, "Fred experienced the two main problems a mentor has to overcome."

First, people do not like to admit that they are not where they would like to be in their lives. In the face of that resistance, a mentor has to be honest and patient. Mentors should tell their own story. They should share their own doubts, admit their own weaknesses. Give the person time. Don't push. Once they really trust you, they'll probably admit their needs, too.

The mentor's second problem is in getting people to open their minds to anything that is new or different. The British novelist Rosamond Lehman said it this way: "One can present people with opportunities. One cannot make them equal to them." Again, don't rush. Make your point clearly. And then give them all the time they need. Listen carefully to their questions. Answer honestly and to the point. Use your own story to illustrate and little by little closed minds will open.

Willie Bass and Jim Floor were two men on the opposite sides of the tracks, but their would-be mentors had much to overcome for both. Lovingly, patiently Ron and Fred had to wait out Willie's and Jim's doubts, their questions, and their fears. Only then could they really begin the adventure of people helping people to help themselves.

Step 3. A Mentor Presents a Practical Plan and Helps Put That Plan into Action. "It took me three months just to convince him that he could do it," Ron Hale admits. "For about eight or nine months," Ron remembers, "we helped Willie call people and gather them. We did the speaking for Willie at his meetings—at all hours of the day and night—and we followed up on those who had questions about or interest in the products or the distribution plan."

While Ron guided Willie, Fred Bagdanov had his hands full with Jim Floor. Fred was just a beginner himself. But he was smart. When he didn't know the answer to one of Jim or Margee Floor's tough questions, he called on others with more experience to answer them. Fred gave the Floors audio tapes, books, and pamphlets for business insights and for personal inspiration. And he invited them to functions where experienced speakers gave talks and personal testimonials on running a successful business.

For the mentor, these start-up months demand long hours and hard work. This is the time-consuming, patience-testing stage in helping people to help themselves. After all, people who have never really believed in themselves before, like Willie Bass, are like newborn children. They need to be fed before they can feed themselves. They need to be carried for a while before they can walk. And above all, they need to be held and loved a lot. And people like the Floors, who believed in themselves but who knew nothing about the business, had to be loved and nurtured just as carefully.

"It's very difficult for anybody to become successful on his own in this very competitive dog-eat-dog world," Jim Floor reminds us. "We need each other not just during these difficult start-up times but forever. It's hard to help people realize how much more power we have working together, how much more we can do collectively than if we try to work alone. That's the genius of this business," Jim adds. "Mentors soon find themselves being mentored. Those being mentored soon find themselves teaching the teachers. Soon everybody benefits equally. People helping people to help themselves goes both ways forever."

Eventually, Willie worked up the courage to make presentations himself. His first presentation was a "wild story," Ron recalls. With his impaired lungs, Willie spoke in a strong but halting voice. He had never taken a speech class. He was no slick salesman. And having none of the usual social graces, his presentation was memorably straightforward. But Willie spoke the unvarnished truth. His language was very "colorful." And he didn't hesitate to use adjectives—with great enthusiasm—that most people would *never* think to apply to products like soap or auto polish.

Willie's first presentation was a success, not because he was slick, but because he was sincere. People could sense the hope in his message. But where did Willie get that hope? He got it from the Hales and others. That's the most important gift you receive from people who believe in helping people to help themselves. They believe in you and eventually you begin to believe in yourself. They have hope for your future, and little by little that hope dawns in your heart.

For Jim and Margee Floor, the presentations were easier. Jim was experienced as a public speaker and though Margee wasn't a skilled communicator, she quickly developed public-speaking skills as she participated in training sessions. Soon, their business began to grow. "We entered to make four or five hundred dollars extra a month," Jim recalls. "Soon we had tripled that, and we began to realize that having our own business meant there were no limits but those we imposed on ourselves."

About that time Jim Floor was promoted and moved to an even more responsible position with Southern California Gas in Sacramento. His income soared. The Floors moved into a rambling, expensive new home in a prestigious suburb of the city. Now they were wheeling and dealing with the most important leaders in their state from the governor's office to members of the state legislature.

"For a moment," Jim remembers, "I was dazzled and preoccupied by our new life in the state capital. I lost the vision of having my own business. I quit expanding my customer base, and my presentations to other people dwindled down to nothing. But good old Fred, my original mentor, kept after me. Cliff Minter, my new friend, became my second mentor, calling and writing me, keeping me honest about my dream and its pursuit. When he called to see how I was doing, I lied. 'I'm doing fine,' I said, pretending that I was still on target when I was missing by a mile.

"Then I went to a function three hours away in Redding. I heard Dave Severn speak about those who begin a task and never bother to complete it. At the end of his talk Dave stopped and spoke as though to me. 'There is someone in this room,' he said, 'who has a God-given gift that he's wasting, and it makes me sick to think about what could have happened if he had only stayed true to his vision.' The speaker didn't know me," Jim says, "but his words struck my heart like a hammer. I went back to Sacramento, made up a list of everybody I knew or had even met in that town, and began to contact them one by one."

Step 4. Mentors, Those Being Guided, and the Rest of Us All Share in the Benefits. Helping people to help themselves may be difficult, especially at first, but in the long run there are amazing benefits. Those benefits are shared not just by the mentor and by those he is mentoring, but in ripples of influence that spread across the face of the earth.

Those being guided share in the benefits. Since making more money is a primary goal, let's look at financial benefits first. Fortunate folk like Willie and Jim, who have mentors to help them discover their potential, who then dare to act on their potential, and who succeed even in small ways will realize amazing financial gains.

Look what happened to Willie Bass. Thirteen months after he had started his own business, he became a direct distributor with our company. His income doubled and then tripled. He quit his job as a welder. He had the money to find medical help for himself and to create a better quality of life for himself and for his family. For the first time in their lives, after the bills were paid, Willie could begin to accumulate money in his bank account to provide for his family's security after he died.

Like Willie Bass, Jim and Margee Floor saw amazing results when they began to work seriously on their business once again. "Our business grew in leaps and bounds," Jim remembers. "For the first time in our lives, our income continued even when we weren't working. By owning our own business, by sharing in the long-range profits, our investment of time and energy just kept on producing year after year. After three years, I gave my termination notice to Southern California Gas. I would never have to work for someone else again. And Margee and I saw our dream of financial security come true."

But helping people to help themselves concerns far more than money. Imagine what happened to Willie's sense of self-worth when he triumphed over the cycle of despair that had imprisoned him for most of his adult life. Imagine the new hope in his heart when he thought of putting his welder's torch away forever. Imagine the new freedom he experienced when he didn't have to struggle down to the bus stop every day, gasping for air, and the joy he realized when he could spend the years he had left with his wife and family. Making money is only part of what happened to Willie Bass. Making money gave him new hope, new freedom, and new joy. What could be better than that?

Jim and Margee Floor also discovered that the benefits went far beyond money. "We were free," Jim remembers. "We could be together as a family. We could plan our own schedule. We had quality time together at last. Of course, our new business made demands on us, especially during those first two or three start-up years, but we were still free to come and go, to travel or stay home as we saw fit.

"And one of the best benefits of all," Jim remembers, "is the new network of friends we made. Their reasons for starting their businesses were much like our own. They wanted to regain control of their lives financially so that they could regain control of their lives in every other way as well. We were drawn together by the dreams and the values that we shared.

"It is very difficult to describe the people-helping-people atmosphere that is created by coming together with those who share your values," Jim adds. "Rich and Jay, our master mentors, passed on to us the principles that once guided this entire nation: belief in human potential, getting bills paid and finances in order, setting goals, writing them down and keeping them, delaying gratification to reach those goals, working hard, being honest, staying accountable to a group of people who have our best interest in mind and who do not judge us for our shortcomings, people helping people to help themselves. . . .

"Too many of our schools don't teach these principles anymore," Jim says. "Even the homes and churches of this nation often fail to pass them on to our children. To find a circle of like-minded friends, friends we will cherish forever was the greatest benefit of all."

Mentors also share in the benefits. Willie and Jim might have started their own businesses, but their mentors, Ron Hale and Fred Bogdanov, shared in the financial and personal profits. In network or multilevel marketing, mentors reap a great harvest when those whom they teach find success.

Did the Hales just get money for their labor? Helping Willie Bass wasn't quick and it wasn't easy. The Hales invested years of love and attention in Willie and his family. They believed in him, nurtured him, and stood by him. And the Bogdanovs? What did they gain from reaching out to mentor Jim and Margee Floor? And why did Fred stay at it even after the Floors moved to Sacramento and quit working on their dream? Did Fred do it for the money or was there more?

What I'm about to say may not seem believable to you. That's okay. I understand. I don't think I would have believed it either, in the beginning. But the Hales, the Bagdanovs, and now the Floors and couples like them who have become successful at this business put the joy of helping people before the joy of making money. Believe it or not, they have discovered that seeing another person's dreams come true is far more rewarding to their own sense of self-worth and to their own personal fulfillment than the money they may make in the process.

I could get really defensive here. I am tempted to shout and carry on in defense of the millions of people who have successful network or multilevel marketing businesses. But I won't. I'll let the cases of Willie Bass and Jim Floor stand on their own merits. What do you think Willie would say to those charges? How do you think he felt about the Hales and their contribution to his life?

"Thirteen years later," Ron says, "when Willie Bass died, I stood at his grave and remembered. How many times he had taken my hand in his. How many times he had looked me directly in the eye, searching for a way to express his love and his gratitude. How many times he had said to me, 'Thank you, Ron.' And then not able to communicate all that was welling up in his heart, he would just stand there gripping my hand and smiling at me through his tears."

The Hales and couples like them around the world make a lot of money helping people to help themselves. If those they helped are grateful for their assistance, what right has anyone looking on to doubt their motives? The Hales worked hard to see their dreams come true. In helping Willie Bass they accomplished that and so much more.

The whole world benefits when people help people to help themselves. How did the world change for the better when Willie's life got turned around? It isn't enough to talk in terms of increased productivity, greater spending power, a source of new tax dollars for the government, or tithed dollars to the church. What happened to Willie and to every other man or woman who learns to stand alone affects us all. Like ripples spreading across a pond, one person's renewal helps give hope and healing to the entire world.

Consider Willie's family, for example. Imagine the new hope they had once Willie had hope reborn in his heart. Their lives were changed, too, and their influence spread to every person they touched. What about Willie's neighbors? How were they affected by seeing Willie standing tall in his new suit or driving up in his new car after all the years of watching him struggle to the bus stop gasping and wheezing? What about Willie's co-workers, his job foreman, and his boss? Can't you hear them spreading the word: "What happened to old Willie?" and "If it can happen to him, it can happen to me!"

The Hales have a favorite saying: "When you help people, *you* become the hero, but when you help people help themselves, *they* become the hero." What if the Hales had been content to help Willie by giving him money, or driving him to work, or referring him to some assistance program? They would have been rightly commended for doing good. But what about Willie? Would people have commended him? In all probability, he would have ended up the same proud but tired and hopeless man that he had been. And worse, through the Hales' act of charity, he might have felt even more hopeless, dependent, and even demeaned.

What the Hales gave Willie was a gift of immensely greater value. They gave him the ability to help himself. And with that gift came other rich gifts: recognition, reward, freedom, and hope. Rather than making Willie a slave to dependency, they taught him how to be free. They gave him the gift of self-reliance.

To Stand Alone, We Need Each Other

Self-reliance is an ancient and coveted value. To stand strong and alone is a common theme in our culture, but how we get to that enviable place where we can do so is not a story often told. We aren't just born with courage, integrity, or hope. We don't just decide one day to be strong and independent. Something happens to each of us along the way that gives us the strength and the know-how to be self-reliant. How does it happen?

The answer is simple, but it is not easy. We give the gift of self-reliance to each other. Over the years my friend Fred Meijer has given that gift to thousands of his employees. Fred's father, Hendrik Meijer, is a legend in our town. Hendrik came to Holland, Michigan, from his native Netherlands in 1907. He was a twenty-three-year-old factory worker with a strong dislike for capitalism. Nevertheless, this young rebel in wooden shoes opened a grocery store during the Great Depression and parlayed that store into Meijer, a hugely successful chain of supermarkets–discount department stores that his son now owns and operates.

Fred has many marketing and management skills, but one story in particular illustrates his special gift at passing on to people the gift of self-reliance. From the mid-fifties to the mid-sixties, our nation was torn by racial unrest. In Montgomery, Alabama, when Rosa Parks was arrested and jailed for not moving to the back of a bus, a black boycott of the businesses of that city began. A Southern Baptist preacher, Martin Luther King, Jr., organized and expanded that boycott into a civil rights movement that swept across the nation.

About that time Fred Meijer needed a receptionist in his busy main office in Grand Rapids. Three women applied, one of whom was black. When his personnel manager assured him that all three women were equally qualified, Meijer said simply "Then hire Mrs. Pettibone." "But she's the Negro woman," the young man answered. "She will be the first person everyone sees." "I know," Fred answered. "Hire her." "But why?" the young man asked again. "Because the other two white women can find a job somewhere else. Mrs. Pettibone can't."

Think back in your own life. Try to remember courageous and

thoughtful men and women who have reached out to give you a chance to prove yourself. Be grateful for them. Each impressive story of the great men and women who have ever lived is really made up of dozens of little stories of other men and women who helped to make them great.

Helen Keller became blind and deaf as a young child, cut off from the world, angry and afraid. Today her name is held in reverence by schoolchildren across the nation. But Helen Keller didn't fight her way out of the darkness or the silence alone. Her parents first begged Alexander Graham Bell to help them. Through his contribution, Helen got a teacher, Anne Sullivan, partially blind herself. Anne dreamed great dreams for her wild young student. She was Helen's faithful, fearless mentor for all those childhood years. In 1904, Helen Keller graduated cum laude from Radcliffe College.

Today her words of wisdom are quoted around the globe, but it was her mentor, Anne Sullivan, and other mentors at the Horace Mann School for the Deaf in Boston and at the Wright-Humanson Oral School in New York City, that shepherded Helen toward greatness. She was not a self-made woman. Without her mentors Helen Keller would have died in a dark and silent world.

Each of us can trace our self-reliance to someone in our past. Don't ever think we got here on our own. Not only is it arrogant, it's dangerous and misleading to believe even for a moment that we don't need each other. Think back. Try to remember. Who helped shape that quality in you that led to your success? John Donne wrote the famous words, "No man is an Island, entire of itself; every man is a piece of the Continent, a part of the main."

The saying "The gods help them that help themselves" does not come—as many mistakenly believe—from the Bible, but from *Aesop's Fables,* written in the sixth century, B.C. In fact, the sentiment is totally opposite to our Judaeo-Christian tradition. Do you think Aesop knew how hard it is for a person to help himself without someone else to show the way? Do you think he realized how dependent we are upon each other to learn how we can be self-reliant? Do you think he knew the joy of *helping people to help themselves?*

It's the way the world turns, one generation helping the next to stand on its own. Parents teaching children how to be self-reliant. Children passing those same truths on to their children and grandchildren. And through the centuries, people helping people to help themselves.

When Jesus said, "Love one another," he gave us the foundation upon which we build our entire case. Helping people to help themselves is the finest and most effective way to "love one another."

I'm always amazed when I hear someone say, "Why doesn't so-and-so get his act together?" My response is, Why don't you *show* so-and-so how to do it? People aren't born with the knowledge of how to become self-reliant. They don't always know how to help themselves. At the very center of compassionate capitalism is the desire to teach people the way to success, the same way the Hales taught Willie.

Our business is rooted in the belief that if we can show people how to help themselves, they will. My speeches around the world are based on two simple themes: "You can do it!" and "Here's how!" It seems like such a well-proven and trustworthy idea. Yet governments and many private institutions (knowingly or unknowingly) put all their efforts into making people dependent and incapable of helping themselves. I believe that most attempts to help people that do not eventually make them self-sufficient are doomed to failure.

Charity Alone Is Not Compassion. A nineteenth-century British churchman got into hot water when he said, "No people do so much harm as those who go about doing good." I believe in charity. Compassion is the theme of this book. I know that there are people in this world who cannot help themselves and who may never be able to help themselves. These people, too, deserve our love and practical, sacrificial concern. I'm going to spend the next chapter sharing that vision and the exciting stories of compassionate capitalists who have been captured by it.

But in the meantime, remember that handouts may send people down a road of diminished self-worth. Charity, no matter how well meaning, can be devastating to self-esteem. Charity often succeeds only in leaving people without the ability or incentive to solve their own problems.

This is not compassion. The government has been particularly slow in learning this lesson. It has been throwing money at social problems for decades with little to show for it. The government has confused the creation of social-service bureaucracies with compassion. These institutions, in spite of their good motives, often demean and crush every bit of self-esteem people possess. They start out to be vehicles of compassion, but they end up in failure.

Genuine Compassion Helps People Help Themselves. Any other kind of compassion is fake. Genuine compassion does more than provide short-term relief. Handouts are a temporary solution at best. They do nothing to change important issues that make people needy in the first place. And these short-term solutions come at a high cost. Some people think that social benefits come free. They don't. They are expensive. They raise the price of goods and services for everyone and make dependent people ever more dependent.

Compassion often begins with charity to meet emergency needs, but real compassion is more than charity. Helping people in the short run is not enough. Real compassion is helping people help themselves—for the long haul.

What would you do if you walked out of your front door one morning and found the paperboy bleeding on your lawn? You would rush to help him, wouldn't you? That's charity. Without thought you would do everything in your power to save the boy's life. When we are confronted with desperate, life-threatening need, we try to meet that need. We ask nothing in return.

But when the life-threatening emergency is over, another kind of compassion is called for. Long-term compassion—*people helping people to help themselves.* How did the paperboy get hurt? Whose fault was it? If a hit-and-run driver mangled the boy's bicycle and nearly took his life, witnesses would need to be sought, the license plate traced, and the guilty party brought to justice. The reckless, irresponsible driver would need to be punished.

But if the paperboy himself had been careless, if he had not looked when crossing the street, or if he was carrying too large a load for his small bike to handle, the next level of compassion would be to show that boy what he had done to cause the accident and help him understand how he must change to prevent a reoccurrence.

We must do our best to stop the bleeding wherever people suffer, whether it is in the former Soviet Union or in our own desperate, decaying neighborhoods. Compassionate capitalism requires no less of us. But we must also have the courage to go the second mile, to help people help themselves so that they never have to go through such suffering again.

In a Truly Compassionate System, All Effort Is Directed Toward Making People Independent and Capable of Standing on Their Own Two Feet. Compassion builds new jobs in which people can maintain their own ego satisfaction and sense of self-worth. True compassion gives people the opportunity to work and then rewards them for a job well done. We *must* reward people who work. This is active compassion. Passive compassion—the kind that demands nothing—does not make sense. True compassion gives people the genuine opportunity to win in life.

People don't mind working hard if they think they have a chance to succeed. And conversely, if there is no penalty for refusing to work, some people won't even try. Without either, you have two reasons not to do the right thing! In the final analysis, people *must* work and begin to help themselves.

When sociologist Christopher Jencks, a professor at Northwestern University, was interviewed in *Fortune* magazine, he said this in response to a question about reforming the welfare system in the United States: "The first thing we must do is to build programs that reward behavior the society believes in. Society has every right to insist that recipients of public support work and be law-abiding. . . . A proper anti-poverty agenda would reward work effort instead of penalizing it. . . . Our current policies pull the rug out from under those who would try to be self-reliant."

When we help others to help themselves, we reward them for working. We teach them how to become self-reliant. Dan Minchen, a Xerox employee, is one person who helps others become self-reliant. The subject of a feature in the *Los Angeles Times,* Dan used to be a reporter for a Buffalo, New York, radio station. He was assigned in 1971 to cover the Attica State Prison riot. The images that he saw on that assignment stuck with him a long time. The men inside Attica's walls were quite literally imprisoned in their despair and hopelessness. Even when they were paroled, those walls remained.

After all, what is someone who has been in prison supposed to do when he gets out? Who will teach him how to get a job, tackle his personal problems, make a life for himself outside of crime? Who will be his mentor? Well, Dan Minchen, for one. He, among others, is a participant in a community-service program supported by his company. Xerox and a few others, like IBM, have programs that allow employees to take a leave of absence and work full-time for community organizations. What a great idea!

In the case of Dan Minchen, Xerox paid him his regular salary to work for Cephas Attica, Inc., a religious service organization that helps prepare former inmates for life outside the walls. Cephas operates halfway houses, provides job training, and gives counseling to those wanting to make the transition to regular society. In the *Times* article

Minchen said, "When you sit next to someone who is doing thirty years to life and you look at him and see he looks so much like you . . . it doesn't turn you into a person who wants to abandon prisons. . . . It's very important to be connected to people who are different." When we help people to help themselves, we make a connection that enriches the lives of both the helper and the one helped.

Our company is built on the principle of helping people help themselves. Our distributors succeed only when everyone below them succeeds as well. Successful distributors know this. Rex Renfrow knows this particularly well. At the root of his success is his gift for helping others.

"You have to make time for others," Rex says. "There are many times I've gone to help others make presentations when I didn't feel like it. I knew I had another job to go to in the morning, but I would make myself drive an hour or maybe even two hours sometimes. I went to help people whom most others wouldn't give the time of day to. Helping people is so important. When you take interest in a person and look them square in the eye and say, 'I'll help you,' it's powerful. Sometimes you are able to help people in very special ways and meet needs in areas of their lives you could never anticipate.

"You earn for yourself by first giving. We constantly reach out and touch other people. We give of ourselves. And when we do, when we help people like this, they learn to know that you care. So the basis of their business becomes the same. They learn to help others help themselves too."

Tens of thousands of American businesses, large and small, believe in the same principle of helping others to help themselves. Real compassion begins when you become a mentor and teach others how to succeed. As the old expression suggests, "Give a hand, not a handout." Most people who are on the streets, broke and hungry, want a way to support themselves, not just short-term charity.

Xerox and IBM help people out by lending their employees, and their employees' expertise, to help other institutions. Giving money to nonprofit organizations is necessary and helpful, but giving them the expertise of your best employees leaves a lasting legacy. People can pass on skills. Since 1971 Xerox has lent the skills of more than four hundred of its employees to worthy organizations. IBM, with its twenty-one-year-old program, has put more than a thousand of its most experienced people out in the community.

We will succeed directly in proportion to the way we help other people succeed. When we reach out to help other people grow, we grow ourselves. And if the others don't grow, we know we tried. Sometimes you put time into people who won't go very far. It's sad to see someone with potential who refuses to move forward. But it is even sadder to see those who have potential try their hardest and fail. It happens, but for every one who fails, there will be many others who will succeed.

In Mexico recently, Amway sponsored concerts by the Mexican State Symphony, a wonderful orchestra with a talented conductor who asked me during a post-concert reception why we would use company funds to support such charitable and cultural events. "Because we believe in giving back to the community where we operate," I replied. "But you aren't even making money in Mexico yet," he exclaimed. "You've just begun operations here." "And we won't make money in Mexico," I answered, "not until thousands of Mexicans are making money from their own businesses will we see any profit, but in the meantime we give on faith that one day here, too, we will realize profit. Until that time," I added, "it's good business to be generous."

"Most Mexican companies need to learn about that," the conductor said, "but who will teach them?" "You will!" I said. "Me?" he answered, looking surprised and somewhat afraid. "Yes, you!" I said. After a long pause he added, "Will you help me? Will you come down and meet with wealthy people and share your dream?"

Late in 1991, I returned to Mexico. My new friend and I met with business and banking leaders. I didn't do much. I just cheered silently while the Mexican conductor made impassioned pleas for support. Those wealthy business people were moved by his presentation and responded generously. It was the beginning of something wonderful. Giving money to that orchestra was only the first step. Then that orchestra and its conductor had to learn to help themselves.

I am thankful for every opportunity I have to help people help themselves, because other people have certainly helped Jay and me. The successes of Willie Bass and Jim Floor were part of a long chain of successes, linked first to the Hales and the Bogdanovs, and then back to their mentors and so on.

Success is never achieved in isolation. I don't know of any successful person who wasn't guided along the way. I don't understand when successful people lack the urge to help others. When they refuse, they break the cycle of loving care that enables each new generation to succeed. A lack of compassion in one generation always has an effect on those that follow. Helping others to help themselves breaks down the paternalism and degrading dependency that has characterized so many attempts to end poverty.

Success couldn't buy Willie a new pair of lungs. But it did buy him thirteen years of inner peace and security. The Hales gave Willie the gift of helping himself, and he in turn gave the gift of hope to the rest of us.

Jim Floor told us a moving story to prove this point. Two and a half years ago, a couple with their own new distribution business was driving home to Sacramento from a function in Los Angeles. The father was tired and asked his sixteen-year-old daughter to drive while he took a nap. Confused by her father's sudden directions, the young girl tried to make a quick turn and swerved into the path of a truck. Both parents were killed. The sixteen-year-old and her eight-year-old brother survived, but both were left with emotional scars from the accident and a terrible sense of loss.

"But those children lived in the people-helping-people atmosphere I described," Jim tells us. "Immediately they were literally adopted into the homes of their parents' up-line mentors, a young couple who had no children of their own. From the moment their natural parents died, those two young people had new parents to love, cherish, and mentor them."

The story doesn't end there. The counselor-psychologist who helped the teenager and her brother during the early stages of their grief was so impressed with the people helping people she met, that she found a mentor and started her own business just to be a part of that great, loving family.

Be a mentor. Help others help themselves. The benefits will surprise you and they go on forever. On the other hand, if we don't reach out, the consequences will be grave. The world has great needs, but we can only solve them one person at a time. In the Talmud you can read these words, "The house that is not open for charity will be opened to the physician." Be a mentor. Help heal yourself as you help to heal the world.

= 14 =

Why Should We Help Others Who *Cannot* Help Themselves?

CREDO 14

We believe in helping others who cannot help themselves. When we share our time and money with those in need, we increase our own sense of dignity and self-worth, and we set in motion positive forces that bring hope and healing to the world.

Therefore, be a giver. What are you doing to help end human suffering in your neighborhood or around the world?

At midnight, the long white hospital corridors were still packed with anxious parents. Fathers with cups of cold, stale coffee in their hands paced helplessly in shadowy halls and crowded waiting rooms. Frightened mothers cradled crying babies in their arms. Nurses rushed from room to room giving shots and words of comfort where they could. Doctors, still clothed in green surgical caps and gowns, surrounded by anxious clusters of family and friends, tried to explain illnesses with names nobody can spell that threaten the lives of innocent children.

"Spina bifida?" Jim Dornan said quietly, and his wide, unblinking eyes told the story of another parent whose newborn child had entered the world under the threat of lifelong suffering if not premature death. "Nancy and I listened to the doctor with growing fear," Jim recalls. "We didn't have any insurance for maternity. We had saved up just enough money for Nancy to stay in the hospital for three days. We were only admitted after we had presented our little box filled with cash to prepay the hospital expense."

Eric Dornan had eight hours of surgery before he was twenty-four hours old. Almost immediately the infant developed hydrocephalus and was rushed into brain surgery to install a life-giving shunt into his brain. Time and again the shunt failed. Finally, Eric was transferred to Children's Hospital in Los Angeles. During the first nine months he had nine brain operations. "Our son hardly came home from the hospital during his first twelve months of life," Nancy Dornan remembers. "So we just camped there in his room beside him."

During the first few years of Eric's life, the Dornans' medical bills passed the $100,000 mark with no end in sight. Now Jim and Nancy Dornan have become another entrepreneurial success story, but when Eric was born, they had just started their little business. The Dornans were barely paying the mortgage each month when they were confronted by this tremendous new financial need.

"Almost immediately we found ourselves deep in debt," Jim remembers. "We didn't care about mink coats or Rolls-Royces. Big houses or expensive vacations didn't matter to us. All we wanted was enough money to save our son's life, to give him what he needed without having to worry about each new expense and to give us the freedom to be with him during his times of suffering."

Most capitalists are like Jim and Nancy Dornan, really. They work to meet their needs and raise the quality of life of those they love. Sylvia Pankhurst, a well-known British socialist, said, "I am going to fight capitalism even if it kills me. It is wrong that people like you should be comfortable and well fed while all around you people are starving."

Sylvia Pankhurst was wrong about capitalism. During the last two centuries it has been the compassionate capitalists among us who have done more to meet the needs of the starving, homeless, sick, and dying than all the opponents of capitalism put together. There have been, and I suppose there will always be, greedy capitalists who refuse to help those in need, but don't let their ugly memory overshadow the generations of compassionate capitalists whose generosity has brought hope and healing to millions of people who could not help themselves.

Today the need for compassion continues. With runaway population growth that leads to poverty, hunger, homelessness, and disease, complicated by regional and ethnic conflicts, the epidemic of AIDS, and natural disasters, the world is facing unimaginable human need. And compassionate capitalism is the best if not the only way that we can bring hope and healing to the world.

Massive problems do exist. It is for our own good that we solve these problems now while we still have the chance. We must not get cynical or pessimistic. We don't have to do everything ourselves and we don't have to do it all today. All compassion requires from us is that we take that first small step.

Helping the men and women who have recently put an end to communist tyranny is already proving to be one major test of the power of compassionate capitalism to heal and change the world. We cannot afford to gloat over the failure of the ideas of Karl Marx. Communism has had tragic consequences for millions of people—who were deprived of a decent living, robbed of dignity, cast into despair, and even murdered. Our response to them must be loving and compassionate.

But what does it mean to be compassionate to our former "enemies"? That is not an easy question. Of course we cannot let our friends starve during their first cold, barren winters of freedom. And we must do everything we can to help them make the difficult and dangerous transition from totalitarianism to democracy, from communism to free enterprise.

You don't have to fly across the Atlantic, though, to find plenty of innocent, desperately needy people who are struggling to survive these difficult times. In the last few decades the hopes of millions of our own people have fallen through the cracks. Now many of our inner cities look like war zones. Crime, drugs, and gangs plague our streets and make victims of young and old alike. Parents are unemployed or underemployed. Children go without a decent education or adequate medical care. Whole families are hungry and on the streets.

The old saying "Charity begins at home" should be taken seriously. If we don't take care of our own, how long can we go on taking care of others? There are innocent people at home and abroad in desperate, life-threatening need. We must all give money, time, and energy to help meet those needs.

When Helen and I were newlyweds, she insisted that we tithe our gross income to our local church. "Here's the tithing envelope," she told me that first Sunday morning. "Ten percent of what we make goes into it!" With Helen, tithing wasn't optional. And once the money was inside the tithing envelope, no one dared borrow from the fund. We were making $100 a week, and giving $10 was no small matter. Now we make a lot more. The little tithing envelope has become a foundation. But Helen still checks the books to be sure that I am giving our proper share to the church and to the charities that we support at home and around the world.

Like most American corporations, we, too, believe in supporting charitable causes. In Malaysia I sat at a banquet with a royal princess. She had granted us a special audience because of our company's work with street children. Like hundreds of international corporations who give volunteer aid around the world, we sponsor day-care centers and nursing homes in Malaysia and hundreds of other similar projects in countries where we do business. It is the least we can do. When I explained that to the princess, her reply surprised me. "I can't tell you how unique this is," she said, "to see a company using part of its profits to help the children."

In fact, it is not unique for individuals and corporations blessed by free enterprise to share their income with those in need. Every year billions of dollars are given to churches and synagogues, to charitable and cultural causes, by generous individuals and corporations in North America, Europe, and now in Japan. Charity is necessary, and for the past two hundred years capitalists have been the source of an unprecedented outpouring of charity around the world.

Much of what I know about compassion I have learned from my family and my friends in Grand Rapids. These women and men from my hometown may not be as well known as those historic examples whose stories I told earlier, but they are even better known to me and to my community for their exemplary service to the needy among us.

Gretchen Bouma, a volunteer leader of the Gleaners of West Michigan, collects food from restaurants and businesses and provides it to the poor and hungry.

Billie Alexander, one of the founders of Project Rehab, has committed her life to people in our area who are struggling with alcohol, drug abuse, and addiction.

Betsy Zylestra, now a full-time social entrepreneur at the Grand Rapids Center for Ecumenism, was a longtime volunteer for the Grand Rapids chapter of Habitat for Humanity, an organization committed to building homes for our city's homeless.

And my wife, Helen, the first truly compassionate capitalist in my life, didn't just talk about giving. Every Sunday, whether we had money in the bank or not, she wrote a check to our local church for ten percent of our income.

"Can't we wait to tithe, or at least give a little less until we're on our feet financially?" I asked quietly one of those first Sunday mornings. Helen just smiled sweetly and placed the envelope in the plate. I wish I could name all the women and men in my life who have taught me to be a more compassionate capitalist. I'm not there yet, but thanks to them, I am on my way.

From the beginning of our partnership, Jay Van Andel and his wife, Betty, have been important examples to me and to this community of compassionate capitalism at work. They weren't satisfied with just giving financial support to their favorite causes. They volunteered time and valuable ideas in their leadership of dozens of local and national organizations ranging from the 4-H Foundation to the Gerald Ford Library, from the American Chamber of Commerce to the National Endowment for Democracy. Recently, Jay was honored for chairing the capital-funds campaign for Grand Rapids's spectacular new riverfront Public Museum, just one of his countless gifts of time, money, and creativity to help transform and renew our city.

But Jay's most impressive acts of compassion are seldom seen or recognized. He believes strongly in the biblical advice about charitable giving that we "not let our right hand know what our left hand is doing." Often Jay acts spontaneously from his heart, even if it goes against what his head may be telling him.

Tom Michmershuizen holds two company records, one for his thirty-plus years of loyal, loving service and the second for having the longest name in payroll history. Tom has countless memories of Jay's spontaneous, generous acts of compassion during those early, hungry days of Amway's history.

"During our first or second year of operation," Tom recalls with a grin, "I was driving our secondhand bus filled with top distributors and company officials when the engine made a terrible noise and stopped us along a country road. Jay was the first one out on the pavement. After looking under the hood for several long minutes, he groaned, asked for the toolbox, and began to remove and repair the rotor while the rest of us watched in awe.

"In the midst of all the chaos, Jay noticed that I had gotten grease on my suitcoat. 'Sorry your coat got dirty,' Jay said. 'Get it cleaned tomorrow and send me the bill.' Then, two weeks later, completely out of the blue, Jay sent me a handwritten note. 'Sorry about your suit,' he wrote. 'Go down to the George Bulliss Men's Store on Wealthy Street and pick out a new one.' When I appeared, rather sheepishly, at the finest men's store in town, the clerks had been alerted. Following Jay's instructions, they outfitted me with a complete wardrobe: suit, shirts, ties, belts, shoes, and even a topcoat worthy of a corporation president."

We all have memories of Jay's thoughtfulness. I especially remember the day when he discovered that one of our independent distributors had two sons who were dying from a fatal inherited disease. Just to bring a little joy into their lives, Jay took the boys on a company plane ride out over Lake Michigan. The two children had so much fun, Jay decided then and there to fly them and their family to Disney World in Orlando so that they could visit the Magic Kingdom before they died. Jay paid for the trip, and after receiving the children's thanks, he told me the story with tears in his eyes. Both boys died shortly thereafter, and Jay still remembers the joy their excitement and gratitude brought him.

So many of our friends in Grand Rapids have demonstrated compassionate capitalism at work. Even when Paul Collins was still a struggling young artist, he used his talents compassionately. Now Paul auctions paintings, creates posters and advertisements, and even holds art exhibitions to raise money and to raise public consciousness on behalf of the causes close to his heart.

My dear friend, Ed Prince, founder and chairman of the board of the Prince Corporation, is one of the most compassionate capitalists I have ever known. Ed's father died when he was just twelve years old. He worked his way through the University of Michigan and vowed early in his life that if he ever made money, he would share it.

Ed and Elsa Prince tithe not only their personal income but that of their corporation as well. Besides the hundreds of important causes they have supported with money and time over the years, they founded the Evergreen Commons, one of the most effective senior centers in the United States with a corps of over a thousand volunteers. The dream of Evergreen Commons began so simply. It is a fascinating example of how business entrepreneurs can be social entrepreneurs at the same time.

One Sunday afternoon, Ed and Elsa took a stranger on a ride in their boat through the channel in Holland, Michigan. "Thank you," the gracious old woman said when they returned to shore. "I've never ridden on the lake before."

Ed and Elsa were surprised to discover that hundreds of senior citizens who had spent their lives in Holland had never had a chance to ride on the lake. So they bought a pontoon boat and offered free rides to the elderly of our community. Their daughters, Emily and Eileen, picked up the seniors in the family van, drove them to the boathouse, took them on an hour ride around the lake, and, because there was no toilet on their boat, waited until the last fifteen minutes of the ride to serve lemonade and cookies to their elderly guests.

As they sailed more than five hundred elderly people on their pontoon boat, Ed and his family were learning about the needs of Holland's senior citizens. Finally, Ed and Elsa sat down with Marge Hoeksma, an organizer for senior citizens, to talk about what they could do to help fill those needs more substantially. The Evergreen Commons, now serving more than thirty-five hundred senior citizens every month, was born because two compassionate capitalists and at least a thousand volunteers cared enough to act.

Another close friend, Pete Cook, founder and chairman of the board of the Mazda Great Lakes corporation, has exemplified compassionate capitalism in Grand Rapids for many years. Pete grew up in humble circumstances. He worked his way through local Davenport College as a janitor. After graduation, Pete went on to build one of the great Michigan corporations. Out of gratitude for the blessings he had received from God and from the free-enterprise system, he donated a large, beautiful building to his alma mater, where young people learn the art of compassionate capitalism. The building is called the Peter C. Cook Entrepreneurial Center. It is just one of Pete's many lasting gifts to our community and to the world. The lives of countless needy people have been touched by the millions of dollars and thousands of hours that Pete and Pat Cook have given to this community.

Marvin DeWitt, a compassionate capitalist friend from Zeeland, Michigan, has two buildings named in his honor by Northwestern College in Orange City, Iowa, just one of the many religious and educational institutions that look to Marv and Jerene DeWitt for counsel and support. Marv and his brother, Bill, are turkey farmers. They began the Bil Mar Corporation in 1938 with seventeen turkeys. "Fourteen hens and three toms," Marv recalls with a grin. "And to close the deal, I had to borrow thirty dollars from my sister that she had saved from doing housework at four dollars a week."

The DeWitt family saw their turkey business through blizzards and heat waves, turkey diseases, economic doldrums, and a devastating fire that destroyed ninety percent of their production facilities and put more than a thousand of their employees out of work. Looking back over the years, Marv says, "God was good to us." And when asked what led to his success in business he adds, "We worked hard and we didn't spend more money than we made."

Recently, Marv and his brother sold Bil Mar and their entire Mr.

Turkey operation to the Sara Lee Corporation for a hundred and sixty million dollars. In a gesture of goodwill and generosity virtually unheard of in corporate America, the DeWitts set aside five million dollars from the sale to be apportioned to employees, based on their salary and years of service. Already, during the months following the sale to Sara Lee, Marv and Jerene DeWitt have donated millions of dollars to the individuals and institutions they support.

Another of my friends who has taught me about compassion is John Bouma, a successful building contractor and developer in Grand Rapids. John's father was the janitor of the Grandville Christian Reformed Church. "My life revolved around that church," John remembers. "There were times I wondered if I would ever travel more than a few blocks away from it in any direction."

John's skills as a builder and manager led to his success in business and to his travels around the globe, but it was not financial success or the opportunity to see the world that motivated him to begin his building career. Responsible for many of our community's finest structures, John gave me the ultimate definition of compassionate capitalism. "One of the main reasons I started my business," he said, "was to help people." John's generosity has extended his positive influence far beyond Grand Rapids. John and Sharon Bouma took advantage of the opportunities provided them by the free-enterprise system. Through hard work and careful planning they have raised their standard of living and at the same time have reached out to help those who suffer around the world.

Like them, Jim and Nancy Dornan began their business to help somebody else. In this case it was their son, Eric, born with an imperfect spinal cord. While still a child, he had multiple seizures and then a stroke. For a while his right hand didn't work. Then his legs failed. Just as he was regaining his strength, the shunt in his brain would block again and he would be rushed to the hospital for another major operation. At seventeen years of age, Eric weighed just fifty-five pounds and already he had survived thirty life-threatening operations on his brain. For the past eighteen years, the Dornans' medical bills have included such high-ticket items as $3,000 braces, $7,000 wheelchairs, $500 a week for physical therapy, a spinal fusion with rods inserted in his back from neck to waist, and hundreds of thousands of dollars in other surgical and hospital costs.

"We have a health-insurance policy now," Jim explains, "but our deductible is in the tens of thousands of dollars. Without our own business, we could not have paid the bills. In fact," he adds sadly, "we learned that up to seventy percent of the fathers whose children are born permanently handicapped end up leaving their families because they just can't stand the grief, the guilt, and the financial failure that all too often goes with the territory. But with our own business," Jim says gratefully, "we not only continue to take care of Eric's expenses, we can reach out to help others who are not as fortunate as we have been."

For the past few years the Dornans and their friends and co-workers have helped support the Olive Crest Treatment Center, a program for abused children who have been taken by the courts from their violent parents. "The children range in age from toddlers to teens," Nancy explains. "Don and Lois Velour, the founder of the Olive Crest Treatment Center, have purchased twenty-five homes in safe, comfortable neighborhoods. The state pays a set fee for the care of each child. All the additional monies must be raised by volunteers."

These abused children have been supported and cared for in part by Jim and Nancy Dornan and their friends. Most social entrepreneurs, like the Velours and their Olive Crest Treatment Center, work full-time meeting human and environmental needs. What would they do without the support of compassionate capitalists like John and Sharon Bouma, Ed and Elsa Prince, Pete and Pat Cook, Jim and Nancy Dornan, and millions like them across America and around the world?

These men and women who work full-time in the private or public sector, in athletics or the arts, may not seem as heroic or as committed as the full-time social entrepreneurs, but I know the time and money, the ideas and the energy they volunteer. To me, these compassionate capitalists are the unsung heroes on the front lines in the war against suffering.

If you are already a compassionate capitalist, giving time and money to help those who cannot help themselves, I salute you. If you aren't, won't you join us? I know it sounds expensive and time-consuming to take on a cause like abused children or people living with AIDS or the emotionally or physically handicapped (differently abled), but whatever the cause, in the long haul it will be the best time and money that you have ever spent.

Becoming a compassionate capitalist. To become a compassionate capitalist requires at least the following six steps. It really isn't important how they happen or in what order, but all six stages are required before we can ever really make a difference.

1. We must quit making excuses.
2. We must believe in ourselves.
3. We must get the facts about human need.
4. We must find our own cause.
5. We must decide on a plan.
6. We must work hard to complete it.

We Must Quit Making Excuses

Unfortunately, too many people expect someone else to solve the problems that we face. They are hoping that other individuals or other institutions will mobilize to meet the needs. They sit around and wait, pointing their fingers and building their walls, when in fact there is no more time for waiting, nobody else to blame, and no walls high enough to protect us from the consequences of our inaction. We cannot go on using these familiar excuses to keep us from helping those who cannot help themselves.

What Problems? I Don't See Any Problems. We like to pretend that the problems will go away if we ignore them long enough. Some people even manage to avoid the problems so long that they actually convince themselves that the problems do not exist.

In Florida, after Hurricane Andrew's terrible devastation, I saw a woman wearing a brightly colored T-shirt that read: *"I Am Queen of Denial."* There are times that not seeing the long-range problems helps to get us through our short-term stress. But more often than not, denial is a major stumbling block to putting the power of compassion to work.

It's Their Fault, Not Ours. "They made the problem," people shout at political rallies and across backyard fences, "let them solve it." How easy it is to blame! "The poor don't want to work," I've heard it said. "The rich don't pay enough taxes" comes the quick defense. We don't get anywhere by blaming anybody, rich or poor. After blaming we move to correct the inequity with a law, a new tax or limit. "We must force the poor to work," some say. "We must limit what the rich can make," others reply. And so it goes: blaming leads to desperate, unhelpful acts, and the problems go on being unsolved and the needs go on being unmet.

Imagine what would happen if the players on my Orlando Magic NBA basketball team came to me complaining about the speed and skills of Michael Jordan of the Chicago Bulls, blaming him for a loss. "He jumps too high," they might say, or "He runs too fast. It isn't fair. Make him wear weights on his feet. Blow the whistle when he runs more than fifteen miles an hour. Penalize him if he jumps more than five feet off the court."

That would be crazy. When Michael Jordan soars through the air, our whole team (and the millions of fans who watch) dream of soaring as well. God gave Michael wonderful gifts, but he went on to develop and discipline those gifts. Now he is setting a higher standard of play for all of us. By his example, Michael Jordan urges us to recognize *our* gifts and to develop and discipline them. Don't limit Michael Jordan. Let him inspire us with his achievements. And in the process we will all be inspired to reach new standards of excellence for ourselves.

It's the Government's Problem, Not Ours. Too many people still believe that the solutions lie in Washington, D.C., or in the state capital or in city hall. Agencies are formed. Appointments made. Bureaucracies grow. Taxes are raised. Billions are spent. But nothing seems to change. The problems go on getting worse and worse while less and less seems to be done about them. The government seems better at creating problems than at solving them. In fact, in many areas, the government *is* the problem.

We're Doing Enough Just Keeping Our Business Going. Jim Janz, one of our most successful Canadian distributors, gave this warning: "When you're working in our kind of business, there is a danger that we get so busy helping others to build their businesses (because that in turn helps us build our own) that we forget the needy all around us. It is not enough to serve those who will in turn serve us."

We'll Do It Later. Most people want to help those who cannot help themselves, but we are prone to procrastinate. So many of us want to give generously of our time and money, but we wait until we're bigger or richer or freer. We wait and wait and wait until suddenly it's too late. "If we aren't compassionate when our business is small," Jim Janz warns, "it is not likely that we will ever be compassionate at all."

There are endless excuses to keep us from ever acting compassionately. Here are a few more examples of the excuses we all have known: *"I'd like to help, but I'm just too busy right now ..."* *"I'm a little behind on my bills ..."* *"I just don't know where to begin ..."*

When Jim and Nancy Dornan heard about the one hundred and sixty abused children at Olive Crest, they could have made endless excuses. They had their own son Eric to care for. Wasn't that enough? Their surgical and hospital bills consumed hundreds of thousands of dollars. How could they give more to help others? During one life-threatening period in Eric's life, Jim Dornan slept beside his little son in the hospital room for three straight months. Where could he find extra time to help care for abused children?

The Dornans had reasons not to give time or money to the children, but they refused to let those reasons become excuses, and so they reached out and what a difference it has made to them and to the children. That leads us to the second step on the road to helping people who cannot help themselves.

Believe in Yourself

Becoming a compassionate capitalist begins with the decision that you can make a difference. We don't have to solve the world's problems by ourselves. But we must believe in ourselves enough to be convinced that we can do something.

"We had no idea of the money or the volunteer hours that could be raised," Jim remembers, "before we gave it a try. We didn't think we could do much, but looking into the faces of those children made us want to do something. The next thing we knew, we had mobilized hundreds of thousands of dollars for the cause, and what a great feeling it was for all of us."

Do you believe in yourself? Are you convinced that you could make a difference? Are you willing at least to try? If so, you are ready to move on to stage three.

We Must Get the Facts About Human Need

We can get so bogged down worrying about the world's needs that we may become paralyzed, unable to help solve any one of them. Or we could try so hard to help every cause that our resources would dribble away and we'd end up exhausted, a part of the problem and not the cure. The person who aims all over the place never hits anything.

Stan Evans watched his father serve their rural community. "He worked hard to make a living and to pay the family bills," Stan recalls, "but when the workday was over, he was a volunteer. He served our county on the soil-conservation district board, the school board, and the fire district board. One at a time he took on the problems in our town, and one at a time he helped to solve them. My father taught me that if you get involved with too many causes, you dilute your gifts, you hurt your family, and you eventually wear down yourself."

You can see by the boards he chose to serve on that Stan Evans's father was interested in the productivity of the earth, in the education of children, and in the safety of his community. And one by one, he did something practical to solve those problems in his hometown. What problems are you especially interested in? What needs do you get excited about meeting? Do you understand those problems? Have you researched those needs?

We must understand a problem before we can contribute to its solution. The problems we face are complicated, and it's easy to make mistakes in judgment. We are responsible for getting the facts for ourselves. If we don't, we run the risk of doing more harm than good. Compassionate capitalists are informed.

Our friend, Kaoru Nakajima saw a Seeing Eye dog leading his master through an airport in Japan. "It was the first guide dog I remember seeing," Mr. Nakajima explains. "I was moved by just watching that dog work. So when I returned from my journey, I looked up the Guide Dog Association in Japan. I visited their offices and saw the dogs in training. I read through their annual reports and discovered how dependent that organization was on donations to survive. When I concluded my little investigation, I donated one million yen to their cause. The other day I saw a young blind woman walking rapidly and without fear behind her guide dog through the streets of Osaka. I had a rush of good feeling in my heart knowing that in some small way I had helped that woman who could not have helped herself."

The solutions to the world's problems are not out there—in some government bureaucracy—they're right here in our own neighborhoods. When we go out to get the facts about the problems, we are taking the first concrete step toward solving them.

There are many pressing problems that need our attention urgently, problems relating to people and the planet. We need a healthy environment to live in, but we want a just society too. Our goal is not just a healthy earth, but healthy people to inhabit it. Let's look at just some of the facts.

We Must Find Our Own Cause

Causes come to us in many ways. Sometimes we are moved to action by someone we meet by chance along the way. Without ever planning it, our interest in that person and his need begins to grow in us. The next thing we know, that person becomes a cause that brings us joy and costs us time and money.

Poverty. In 1991 an estimated 36 million Americans—or about 14.7 percent of our total population—lived in poverty. "The poor are our brothers and sisters," writes Mother Teresa. "They are people who need love, who need care, who have to be wanted." *What are the facts about poverty? What can we do to help close the gap between the rich and the poor? Who are the poor in our town who cannot help themselves and what can we do to help them?*

Infant Mortality. We have the highest infant-mortality rate of any country in the industrialized world. *What are the facts about infant mortality? Why do our infant children die? And what can we do to save them?*

Inadequate Health Insurance. We have a health-care system that leaves 37 million people without any health insurance. Many of the solutions being offered are dangerous and misleading, but something has to be done. *What are the facts about health care? Who are the people and what are the volunteer organizations reaching out to help? How can we join in?*

Illiteracy. We have an educational system that is inadequate and deteriorating rapidly. High school students graduate without being able to read or write. Experts claim that twenty to thirty million Americans are functionally illiterate. *What are the facts about education? What needs to be done in our schools? Could I volunteer as a teacher's assistant, a coach, a tutor, a class parent, a friend of our neighborhood school or library? What can we do to help?*

Crime and Drugs. Our drug-related crime and murder rates are among the highest in the world. *What are the facts about crime and drugs in our town? What needs to be done to help the children and other victims where we live? What churches, organizations, individuals, are out there on the streets taking real risks to help those in need? How can we help?*

Homelessness. There are estimates that as many as three million Americans are homeless, that the average age of a homeless person is just thirty-two years old, and that whole families make up twenty-five percent of our homeless population. *What are the facts about homelessness in this country? Who are the homeless in our town? What can we do to help them find suitable housing and to begin productive lives again?*

Compassionate capitalists are desperately needed to help solve all these human problems. Everywhere are people who need emergency help before they can find their way to self-reliance. The government has made some feeble attempts, but on the whole governmental bureaucracies have failed miserably. Creating opportunities and incentives for our poor neighbors to enjoy the benefits of the free-enterprise system is a challenge waiting for a solution. Where government has failed, compassionate capitalists must step in and fill the gap with new ideas and effective action.

Discrimination. Racial, religious, sexual, and age discrimination are all serious problems in need of compassionate solutions. We owe it to ourselves—and to our country—to become informed on these issues. Do not settle for simplistic explanations or one-sided views. Let your compassion be informed and critical.

What are the facts? What needs to be done about discrimination in our school, church, or neighborhood? Is this a potential place of service for me?

Management–Labor Relations. Compassionate capitalism includes both those who labor and those who manage. Each has a responsibility to the other. A truly compassionate capitalism could have a revolutionary effect on the marketplace—a revolution that Marxism could never produce.

What are the facts? What needs to be done in healing the relationships in your family, between teachers and students, between your boss and his employees?

Liability. Everybody suing everybody else is the fruit of a society that never takes responsibility for its own actions. The liability problem costs our nation billions of dollars. It makes consumer products more expensive. It prevents new innovations and inventions from coming to market. It hikes medical costs exorbitantly. It raises auto insurance rates. The compassionate capitalist says, How can we find a way to stop this awful situation? What fair and equitable means can we devise to settle disputes and give just awards? How can we stop rewarding greed?

What are the facts behind all this suing one another? What should we do when we have been wronged? Can we take responsibility for our own mistakes and stop expecting others to pay for them?

The National Debt. We are a nation addicted to short-term pleasure. We want it all now. We don't like to wait. So we buy things on credit—before we've really earned the money. Compared to other industrialized nations, Americans save practically nothing. Why save when we can borrow? That's our national mentality. Is it any wonder that our politicians do the same? The compassionate capitalist wants to leave a legacy for future generations, that of a balanced national budget and abundant natural resources.

What are the facts about this nation's debt? What can we do about it? Are we working to stay out of debt ourselves?

Before Jim and Nancy Dornan got involved with the children of Olive Crest, they read about the growing problem of child abuse in America. They learned that one of four children in this country will be seriously injured by a parent before her fifth birthday. The statistics were bad enough, but those numbers came to jarring life when the Dornans visited one of the homes for abused toddlers and saw with their own eyes the bruised faces and broken limbs, the burns and terrible scars.

When we see the problems firsthand, when we meet the people in need and talk honestly to the people already on the scene trying to help them, something changes in us. Our focus becomes clearer. Our goals narrow down. When we personalize problems, we are in a position to make a difference. When we depersonalize problems, then it's somebody else's mess to clean up. Do you see the difference? We—you and I, each of us—have something to contribute. We can make a difference, but first we need to get the facts.

I've listed above some of the problems that concern me the most and a few choice facts or statistics that help me understand those problems. But this is just a warm-up list. What is the need in your neighborhood (or out there in the world) that you want to help meet? Deciding on your own cause is the third step on the exciting journey to helping people who cannot help themselves.

Sometimes Causes Come to Us in Person. Remember my friend Dan Williams, the controlled stutterer who went on to become one of our most successful distributors in California? During a visit to President Ford's home in Vale, Colorado, he met a family whose little daughter, Maggie, had a serious stuttering problem.

"She was a beautiful little girl," Dan remembers. "But her stuttering caused her so much embarrassment. During lunch that day I told Maggie about my lifelong struggle to control my own stuttering. She was fascinated. Before long we became friends. Over the past few years I've worked with Maggie and her parents. Helping that little child overcome her stuttering problem and counseling her parents along the way became a real cause for me."

Other Times, Emergency Need Is Thrust upon Us. Without warning we may have to decide if we will help victims. Through a neighbor Max and Marianne Schwarz discovered a little girl in their hometown in Germany who needed an immediate bone-marrow transplant. Without that serious and expensive operation, the girl would die.

Friends and neighbors had been collecting money, but the emergency fund was forty thousand deutsche marks ($27,000) short of the goal. Max and Marianne had to decide. Would that little girl become one of their many causes? Already they were helping to support an orphanage near their hometown and a cancer hospital for children in East Germany. "We wrote the check," Marianne remembers. "We were grateful that our business had been profitable that year and glad to share those profits with a child in need."

When Hurricane Andrew howled destructively across Florida and Louisiana, the Amway Corporation rushed a million and a half dollars worth of food and cleaning supplies into the devastated area. Volunteer distributors from across the country, who gathered at their own expense to distribute the emergency supplies, brought money, tools, and other aid to assist.

Bill Childers spoke for all our distributors when he said, "We're just a small part of the puzzle. So many other good people chipped in to help. We worked side by side with the Red Cross, the Salvation Army, International Aid, dozens of corporations large and small, and individual volunteers from across the nation who saw a terrible need and reached out to meet it. I'm proud of our Amway folks," he added. "They proved that they mean it when they say, 'If you need help, just call and we'll be there.' "

Sometimes Causes Come to Us Because We've Seen Similar Suffering in Our Own Lives. Peter and Eva Mueller-Meerkatz had a child who was mentally disabled. Their deeply felt personal experiences led them to adopt a handicapped community right in their own village.

"We support that little community," Peter says with a smile, "because they need us. That's all. Once, the patients were intelligent, productive human beings with academic degrees and businesses of their own. Each of these dear folk went through some kind of trauma that led to their mental or emotional undoing. They could no longer take care of themselves. So we stepped in."

The Mueller-Meerkatz family underwrites the Rocco Corporation to help employ these men and women through jobs they can still perform. "They fold and stuff mailings," Eva says proudly. "They make cookies. They put calendars together. We are constantly looking for jobs they can do to help support themselves and at the same time help renew their own sense of dignity and self-worth."

Jim and Nancy Dornan chose their work with abused children for one simple reason. "We love children," Nancy explains, "and we hate to see them suffer. Besides," she adds with a grin, "we only had two sons, Eric and David, and one daughter, Heather, of our own. Why not take on a hundred and sixty more?"

After my heart-bypass surgery I got to thinking about what I had learned from my own brush with death. First, I discovered how important hospitals are when we face days and nights of suffering. But hospitals and their staffs also need help from us in return. New lifesaving technology is expensive and often not accessible to people on low incomes. To show our gratitude to Butterworth Hospital and its skilled and dedicated personnel, Helen and I donated a new wing to the Butterworth Hospital complex. In honor of my wife's service to this community, the trustees named our gift the Helen DeVos Women and Children's Medical Center.

Second, I learned again that contributions in time and energy are often just as important as money. All of us, employers and employees alike, live busy, stressful lives. Most of us wake up running in the morning and slip into bed exhausted at night. And yet the time that we donate as volunteers to the charitable and religious organizations we believe in—whether to stuff envelopes or to guide financial campaigns—is so important to the health and well-being of our communities. Currently, trying in some small way to practice what I preach—again out of gratitude to the hospital and its staff—I chair the board of directors of the Butterworth Health Corporation.

Third, during my bout with heart illness, I learned that too many of us, including myself, don't know enough about preventive medicine. As a result, we don't know how to care for our bodies. When something does break down, it is too late. For that reason I invited Steve and Patricia Walters Zifferblatt to join our company of friends in Grand Rapids.

I met Dr. Zifferblatt when he was director of the Pritikin Health Institute in Santa Monica, California, and Pat was its program director. This husband–wife health team helped save my life. Although I looked fit enough, Steve and Pat insisted that I take an extensive physical while visiting their Pritikin Center. During a treadmill test they noticed signs of heart irregularity. Shortly after that, I was admitted to Butterworth for my six-way-bypass heart surgery.

Steve and Pat love to remind us all of the old proverb "Your life is in your hands." They carefully considered my invitation and then moved to Grand Rapids and headquartered their Better Life Institute in our Amway Grand Plaza Hotel. The Zifferblatts represent a third kind of gift, the gift of ideas and their power to change (and to save) lives. This year Steve and Pat Zifferblatt have traveled across the nation and around the world on behalf of Amway and their Better Life Institute, teaching proper exercise techniques, stress reduction, weight control, lifesaving behavior change, and healthy cuisine to our company of friends. Their seven-day residential program in the Amway Grand Plaza Hotel has benefited and probably helped save thousands of lives already.

I am discussing these three gifts of physical health that Helen and I have given for one reason only, to show from our own experience how often we give—money, time, and ideas—to organizations and individuals who first reached out to touch our lives when we were in need.

As Albert Schweitzer said, "The purpose of human life is to serve and to show compassion and the will to help others." His cause led him to an isolated village in Africa. What cause is getting hold of your heart? Where will it take you? Deciding on a cause, any cause, might be for you as for these others the beginning of the most exciting and rewarding journey of your lifetime.

We Must Develop Our Own Plan

Once our cause is clear to us, we must develop a serious plan to guide our actions. We need to write down specific goals and when and how we plan to reach them. We need to chart our progress, recruit folks to help us, change course when need be, and celebrate when we accomplish our task.

Sometimes We Start from Scratch. Dexter and Birdie Yager were determined to start a summer camp to help children understand and participate in the free-enterprise system. They had never built or managed a camp. But with their family's help they developed a plan. "We knew we would make mistakes," Dexter admits, "but we are giving the idea a try, and every day we grow a little more in the direction of our goal."

Other Times We Participate in Other People's Plans. Al and Fran Hamilton got interested in the United Negro College Fund. "Their motto—'A mind is a terrible thing to waste'—really got to us," Al remembers. "So we decided to help end that waste. For the past seven or eight years we've been working with Lou Rawls in his telethon for the United Negro College Fund. We open our homes to a large dinner dance party every year to present the need to our neighbors and friends and to motivate them to give. I guess we have contributed pretty close to fifty thousand dollars over the last few years. And every time I see another young black man or woman graduating from the great black colleges and universities, I feel good for the tiny bit we've contributed to their success."

After experiencing the death of his first wife and the suffering of his son, Ben, Brian Herosian went to work to help end similar suffering. For five years Brian and Deidre Herosian were national fund-raisers for the Cystic Fibrosis Foundation. Today they are working with the hearing impaired.

"When my family was suffering," Brian remembers, "people often said to me, 'Something good will come of this.' Their words didn't help much then," he admits. "In fact, there were times I felt like screaming at them! What good could come from my wife's death or my son's terrible suffering? All the good in the world would not be enough. I still don't think that kind of sympathy is worth much in the midst of our personal crises, but looking back, I find that what they were saying was true. One good thing that happens to us when we suffer is the growth of our sensitivity to other people's suffering."

Since 1984 Amway and its independent distributors have raised $9,600,000 for Easter Seals. Those millions came from thousands of smaller gifts given or raised by our distributors through benefit dinners, auctions, sidewalk sales, raffles, bowl-athons, and individual contributions. All over this nation Amway's compassionate independent distributors have organized and implemented the drive and then given their time and money to reach the goal. As a result of their compassion, our corporation has become one of only five corporate sponsors who make up the National Easter Seal Society Telethon's "Million Dollar Club."

Once Jim and Nancy Dornan made their commitment to those abused children, they began making plans to keep it. "They needed more homes for the children," Jim recalls, "so we planned a bowl-athon and asked volunteer bowlers to get sponsors to donate dollars for every pin they knocked down in competition."

"That first Christmas," Nancy remembers, "we wanted to be sure that every child had a significant gift under his or her Christmas tree. So we asked the children to fill out their own wish list, and we passed out those lists to other concerned friends and neighbors."

"We planned and we plotted," Jim says, "and then we went to work!"

We Must Work Hard to Complete It

Taking on a cause can be a dangerous thing. I suppose that's why letting someone else do it is easier. Getting involved in the lives of those who suffer requires all the extra time, money, and energy that we have. To see dreams for other people come true requires the same kind of hard work and commitment that we give to realizing our own dreams.

Jan Severn volunteers her extra hours as a teaching assistant. "If our children are going to get the kind of education they need, we all need to make ourselves available to help out wherever we can."

Dr. Stuart Menn began his business to give him time to volunteer research work on behalf of people who struggle with sleep disorders. "A practicing physician has to work hard just to keep up with his patient load," he explains. "Normally there is no extra time for research and no extra money to buy lab equipment or hire research assistants. That's why I started my business," he explains. "Since medical school I've been taken with the idea of finding help for those who cannot sleep. So I spend every extra minute in the lab working, researching, writing, reading, experimenting, testing, and reviewing to that end."

"I'm not happy unless I'm helping people," explains Frank Morales. He and his wife, Barbara, have built their successful business with one primary goal, to use the extra time and money to help the people in their community. In 1963 they moved to Diamond Bar, California. Since then Frank has served as president of the homeowners' association, founded a YMCA, been appointed honorary mayor, and served as chairman of the Walnut Valley Unified School District board for thirteen years. He has given away thousands of volunteer hours, and the calls for help never stop coming in.

"It's hard word," Frank admits, "but there are little perks along the way. I got to hand my own kids their diplomas when they graduated from the eighth and twelfth grades," he remembers. "Those are the kinds of exciting extras that sometimes come when you try to help in your own hometown. I'm not trying to be a hero," he adds, grinning. "I volunteer because it's fun for me. And when you see the good that is accomplished, it makes you feel that your life has counted for something."

The sign hanging above the bowling alley read, *"Bowl-athon To-night."* Inside, every lane was filled with excited volunteers come on behalf of the abused children. The noise of balls rolling down alleys and hitting wooden pins was accompanied by noisy cheering, loud laughter, and stamping feet.

Toward the middle of the evening, Jim and Nancy Dornan pushed Eric's wheelchair through the happy, boisterous crowd. Eric was a teenager now, but he weighed just seventy pounds. The shunt inside his skull drained toxic fluids from his brain, but he still suffered seizures regularly. Stainless steel rods were fused to his spine from his neck to his waist. A stroke had seriously limited the use of his muscles in his arms and legs. But Eric was there to bowl for the abused children, and he was determined to do his part.

Jim and Nancy put on their bowling shoes and pushed Eric's chair out onto the alley. For a brief second the noisy crowd that packed the bowling alley grew silent. Jim picked out a bowling ball and knelt beside his son. Eric's weak and trembling arm reached out to touch the ball.

"Ready, son?" Jim asked quietly.

"Ready," Eric whispered, looking down the long lane at the ten white wooden pins in the distance.

Nancy pushed Eric's chair into place. Jim guided his son's hand. Eric aimed carefully and the bowling ball bounced slightly on the smooth wooden floor and began to roll. There wasn't one person in the crowd that night who didn't pray for a miracle as the ball moved slowly in a great arcing motion toward the pins. Jim held his breath. Nancy blinked back her tears. Eric held his breath and waited.

"Strike!" the crowd yelled in unison, and both parents leaned down simultaneously to hug their son.

"For the children," Eric said, looking up at his father and grinning like a champion.

The crowd erupted in applause. People laughed and cried and reached down into their pockets as Eric said, "For the children."

"We raised $190,000 that night," Jim remembers, "to put down payments on two new homes for abused children. One home was for children two to four years old," he says. "Children who had been taken from their parents forever to help end their suffering and save their lives. One donor brought a check for $40,000 from McDonnell Douglas," Jim added, "but there was no gift that night that even compared to the gift that Eric gave us all."

Like Jim, Nancy, and their son Eric, you and I can make a difference, if only we believe it. And when we do, lives will be changed—our lives especially—and the hungry will be fed, the naked will be clothed, and the sick and the dying will be comforted.

15

Why Should We Help to Preserve and Protect Our Planet?

CREDO 15

We believe in helping save the planet, our island home. When we share our time and money to help preserve the planet, we are really helping to protect ourselves.

Therefore, be a friend of the earth. What could you do today to help preserve the planet?

Matthew Ipeelie sat on a short, sturdy stool in the bright Arctic sunlight carefully examining a small ivory bear. His dark leathery skin bore testimony to many seasons of harsh polar sun and cold, dry winds. Deep squint lines framed his intense dark eyes. Matthew's stool was next to the steps leading up to his house. Though less elegant than his ancestors, it was well suited to the far north.

In defense against the permafrost, Matthew's house was perched atop stout wooden piers, a four-square monument to Inuit ingenuity and modern materials. The piers were short enough that a man could wiggle underneath on his belly, but a bear couldn't—a prudent design feature. Sheathed in plywood paneling and with a tin roof, the house was heavily insulated against the cold and heated with a wood-burning stove.

Sitting outside was a privilege reserved mostly for summer. In winter the temperature was bitter cold, and Matthew, bundled up in many layers of clothing, couldn't work on anything as small and delicate as the ivory bear. A black and gray malamute dog slept next to him, half under the house and half in the sun. These were the dog days of summer, Alaska style. As Matthew examined the bear, he mumbled to himself. The dog's ears pricked up. In the wilderness, people and animals pay close attention to one another.

Having studied the bear for a full five minutes, Matthew drew out a knife. It had a small hooked blade and a thick wooden handle. He carefully made an incision, and the faint suggestion of a mouth appeared on the bear's snout. Matthew stopped, held the bear at arm's length, and contemplated what he had done. It pleased him. Changing his grip, he drew the blade over the incision several more times, deepening it until the mouth looked just right. Then he set it down. It was finished.

In a way, the bear seemed like a simple piece of work: small, spare, and lacking intricate details. But in fact, it was not simple. It possessed a quality that was very powerful but hard to define. Like a prehistoric cave painting, Matthew's work seemed to portray the essence of the animal.

"I saw a book of Audubon bird illustrations once," Matthew said. "I liked them, but something seemed wrong. The drawings were good. They had detail drawn with great skill. But no soul." He paused for a moment thoughtfully. Then he added, "The spirit of the bird didn't show. I want to show an animal's spirit.

"Up here," Matthew continued, "people believe that animals have souls too, not just people. We believe the earth and all its creatures are living things, and if we harm them needlessly, we injure the spirit of the Great One." Matthew pushed himself up from the little stool. At seventy-one, he moved with an economy of motion that comes from a lifetime of surmounting difficult, roadless terrain. He walked around to the windward side of his little house and pointed north. "We call our land Nanatsiaq, which means 'the beautiful land.' "

The view from this side of the house was breathtaking. To the north and west was the cold, rugged Brooks Range, holding fast between the barren tundra of the North Slope and the stunted forests of central Alaska. To the east were rivers and streams beyond number, many of them emptying into the mighty Yukon.

"You see that haze in the distance?" Matthew asked. Visibility was spectacular, maybe fifty miles or so. But as the eye pans up from the horizon the color gradually changes. The air has a slight amber tint, unmistakable at the horizon, that gradually fades to a deep blue the farther up you look. "It is what you call smog," Matthew explains. "Pollution. I don't know where it comes from, but it wasn't there when I was a boy." It is hard not be shocked by the thought of it. Smog? Here?

Matthew Ipeelie, Inuit artist and wilderness resident, illustrated a very important fact. Even in the most remote areas of the world, even in those places we consider the last sanctuaries from the grit and pollution of our major cities, evidence of the need for responsible environmental stewardship is apparent.

The life-style of Matthew, attuned to the earth and respectful of its creatures, offers lessons for all of us. No, we can't all live as he does—I'm not advocating a return to the wilderness—but we can adopt some of his values. We can learn from Matthew that "every creature is God's creature, and the earth a gift from the Great One."

There is no sense in talking about the possibilities for success, or the opportunities that free enterprise creates, without an awareness that success and opportunity for future generations depend on our ability to sustain the earth for future entrepreneurs. No resources, no wealth! The pollution visible from Matthew Ipeelie's cabin is a reminder that what we do sometimes has global consequences.

I don't know about you, but I am pretty overwhelmed when I think about how complex—and sometimes how controversial—the issues are that surround the problem of environmental stewardship. I don't have a specific solution for you. But I can tell you what our company is doing, and maybe our experiences will be helpful to you.

Our Corporate Commitment to This Planet

The success of Amway is based, in part, on the conviction that what we sell is environmentally responsible. We don't want to sell products that pollute our hometowns or damage our global atmosphere—or tint the horizon amber in Matthew Ipeelie's Alaska.

To make sure we don't ever forget our responsibilities, we have written the following environmental-mission statement.

The Amway Corporation believes that the proper use and management of the world's limited resources and the environment are the responsibility of industry and individuals alike. As a leading manufacturer of consumer goods with a direct sales network of more than a million independent distributors worldwide, Amway recognizes its responsibility and role in fostering and promoting sound environmental stewardship.

This simple statement is Amway's credo about our responsibility to the earth. We believe this is the right thing to do. But belief isn't enough. Just as the Christian tradition says that faith without works is dead, a credo doesn't really mean much without action. But where do we start? How do we keep from getting overwhelmed by the headlines, the doom and gloom?

If you start thinking about all the problems of the world, they are really local problems. If you start off worrying about smoke-belching factories in Eastern Europe, you'll only get depressed. There's not much you can do about that. But what we can do is solve problems in our own hometowns. Sometimes a solution to a local problem ends up being part of a global solution. Matthew Ipeelie's "environmental policy" begins with himself, with an inner commitment to do what's right and preserve those things that enrich his life.

My environmental concern began with a personal commitment too. The first product marketed by our company was a liquid organic soap. From the beginning, L.O.C., as we call it, was biodegradable, free of phosphates, solvents, or any other ingredients that pollute the earth. This product was way ahead of its time. But what made us want to develop and market such a product? Did we have outside pressure from environmental groups? No. Did we have to comply with some detailed mission statement? No. Was there a government mandate? No. The stimulus was simpler and more personal than that.

Jay and I have had a lifelong commitment to our hometown, Grand Rapids, Michigan. Our city is bisected by the Grand River, from which the city takes its name. Other lakes, rivers, and streams bring the landscape to life around our world headquarters in nearby Ada and across central Michigan. We grew up fishing, swimming, and playing in those lakes and streams. But in the period between youth and adulthood we noticed some changes, and these worried us.

Some of the streams and rivers started accumulating sudsy residues along their banks. They harmed the fish and plant life, and looked and smelled terrible. We didn't want any product that we made to contribute to the problem. After all, it was our community. So we developed a product that wouldn't hurt the water or fish and plant life—or leave a lot of suds on the riverbanks. We want our grandchildren and their grandchildren to have the same opportunity to play in beautiful, unpolluted, natural waters as we did.

Environmentalism—the real thing—begins with the individual who decides to take action in her own hometown. It starts with the smallest acts. What we really have to do is begin by picking up the papers on our own streets. The little things matter. We can't talk about the big issues until we clean up our own acts. We cannot clean up the world until we clean up our own neighborhoods. Cleaning up the earth begins by doing what we can do right now, in our own hometowns.

But cleaning them up doesn't mean that we don't support greater environmental causes. We do. We must weigh the decisions we make every day. If we buy environmentally friendly products, we are making positive contributions to the environment. We avoid the kind of consumption that creates more problems. We act responsibly. Compassionate capitalists must be compassionate consumers as well.

We have tried to do a lot more than make biodegradable soap. Most of our products are biodegradable. We concentrate our products so consumers use less of them. Our containers are disposable, so if you put them in a fire they turn into ash. They don't stay around forever as a hardened plastic. We don't test our products on animals. We don't use ozone-damaging propellants in our aerosols. We recycle our office waste. We've created a biodegradable packing material from soya products in order to end the mountain of Styrofoam pellets that used to fill our shipping cartons.

At our company, we weren't trying to start a "green revolution." We just did what seemed right to us. But as we got big, the impact of our environmental decisions grew too. In 1989, the United Nations gave Amway the U.N. Environmental Programme Achievement Award. U.N. secretary general Javier Perez de Cuellar gave the award to Jay and me at the U.N. Headquarters on World Environment Day. To tell you the truth, I was surprised. We were the second corporation ever to receive the award.

But I was surprised, too, because what we were doing didn't seem all that extraordinary. It just seemed right. The key to most environmental issues is simple: people should do the compassionate thing. It didn't seem to take any special effort, just a little conviction. The simple act of caring for our community grew in its impact as other people in our company were set free to do compassionate acts as well. Compassionate capitalists enable people to help the environment.

In 1990, Amway was the principal sponsor of an Earth Day observance hosted at the United Nations by the U.N. Environmental Programme. The U.N. is serving a useful purpose as an information gatherer and surveyor of global conditions. This event reminded me that in my own lifetime, solid progress has been made in solving many environmental problems.

But compared to the first Earth Day, this was a pretty dignified event. The first celebration happened on April 22, 1970, in New York and Chicago, and in cities and towns all over the country. More than twenty million people came together. I must confess, I wasn't too sure about what I saw on television.

Do you remember the scene? They came in bell-bottom jeans with T-shirts, long hair, and beards, in miniskirts and crop-tops: men, women, children, and dogs with bandannas—a veritable menagerie of people, pets, and political persuasions. It was quite a sight.

That first Earth Day brought together many different people and viewpoints. Compassionate care for the earth was discussed. A movement was launched. But, sad to say, there wasn't enough commitment to bring about the changes that are still needed. Real environmental progress won't come from huge rallies, endless, ineffective legislation, or constant finger-pointing and sloganeering. Real progress will come from the action of compassionate individuals.

Considering the Problems of Our Planet

So where do we apply this commitment? The United Nations has identified these critical issues related to the global environment. I'm concerned about each of them, but I don't have the solutions to any one of them. Our company is sponsoring a variety of research projects around the world in the hope of developing more answers. In the meantime, it's important for all of us to know what the problems are. The future of the environment and the future of capitalism are one and the same.

Deforestation. Forests are the third most valuable commodity in the world, after oil and natural gas. But of even more importance is the role forests play in the maintenance of life on our planet. They provide a habitat for millions of species of animals, protect soils from erosion, and help regulate the earth's weather. But our forests are disappearing at a ferocious rate—everywhere, including the United States.

When Columbus discovered America, we had forests covering 1,235,000 square miles. Now we have about 85,000. In the area surrounding my hometown, in the last century one hundred thousand or more trees were logged every year with no attempt to replant. We're doing better at that now, at least around Grand Rapids. But the problem remains, and it is a serious one.

Degradation of Farmlands. New, scientifically developed strains of rice and other grains have increased worldwide production of food by over 140 percent. That's the right idea, but the consequences have been mixed.

Those new plants have turned out to be greedy little things. They want lots of water, fertilizer, and pesticides. Whereas crop yields went up fifty percent, the amount of fertilizer needed to feed them sometimes went up as much as 4,500 percent!

It's the old good news–bad news dilemma. Before long all of these fertilizers, pesticides, and water also took their toll on the land. Ground water became polluted with chemicals. All the heavy watering left salts in the soil.

Animal Extinction. My grandchildren are very concerned about pandas, but how does the possible extinction of the panda bear make any real difference in our lives? If some obscure little bug dies out, what's the big deal? As I tell the kids, the issue is *biodiversity,* which refers to the variety of life. Biodiversity is extremely important—it is the foundation on which a variety of ecological "services" are built.

Biodiversity provides us with the essential "services" of cleaning our air, maintaining the earth's temperature, recycling wastes, producing soil nutrients, and controlling disease. And, to be blunt, biodiversity is worth a lot of money too.

Soil Erosion. This occurs when you lose topsoil to wind, rain, or some other cause. Obviously, topsoil is essential for agriculture. We need topsoil most critically for the production of food. In the U.S. we lose about four billion tons of topsoil every year—that's enough to fill a train of freight cars that would encircle the globe twenty-four times.

Acid Rain. This is one of the most controversial and difficult issues we face. Acid rain is the result of industrial pollution that rises in the air and mixes with rainwater. In some places, particularly Eastern Europe, researchers say that acid rain is having terrible consequences. In Poland, they claim, the rain is so acidic that it eats into iron railroad tracks. In Ontario, Canada, some say that three hundred lakes have become so acidic fish can't live in them anymore. In Athens, Greece, ancient monuments are purported to be dissolving away like melting ice cubes every time it rains. I'm still not sure how serious the problem is. But I'm open and searching for the facts. That's all we can ask from one another. Once we are convinced by the accumulation of real facts, then, whatever it costs us, we have to act.

Ozone Depletion. Scientists are still gathering and analyzing the facts, but it appears that a lot of damage to the ozone layer has been done. In 1988 an authoritative study conducted by an international task force of one hundred scientists concluded that the ozone layer had been depleted by as much as three percent in just twenty years. That's a lot.

Some big companies, in an act of ethical courage, decided to phase out production of chemicals called CFC's in an effort to stop the destruction of our ozone layer. Our company had made the decision more than ten years earlier to phase out CFC's in our products.

The Greenhouse Effect. The earth has it own natural air-conditioning system. At the moment the thermostat is set at about 55° F. That's the average temperature for the globe, compared to, for instance, Venus, where it's a bit warmer—about 858° F. We don't have to worry about warming up to Venus's temperature, but evidence does indicate that the earth is heating up slowly. Nobody really knows how fast or what the consequences are, but estimates range from 2.7° to 8.7° F. over the next fifty years.

The cause of the rise in temperature is the so-called "greenhouse effect." This is due to the accumulation of gases in the atmosphere, which holds in the sun's heat. Carbon dioxide is the main culprit. This gas is produced by cars, factories, all kinds of machines that burn fossil fuel. Since 1800 the amount of carbon dioxide in the atmosphere has increased by more than 25 percent. Before 1800 the level had remained constant for thousands of years.

The Spread of Deserts. This is also called desertification. It's the process of perfectly good, fertile land turning into bone-dry deserts. Desertification is the final process of land degradation mentioned earlier. In fact, it's related to several of the problems discussed above:

deforestation, salinization, and erosion. The United Nations estimated in 1980 that 26 billion dollars were being lost annually in agriculture to desertification.

Water Contamination. First the good news. There is exactly the same amount of water on the earth today as there was before humans started using it. None of it has been lost. Now the bad news. A lot of it is contaminated (with salts or industrial pollutants), inaccessible (locked in glacial ice or underground reservoirs), or hard to recover (almost two-thirds of the world's river runoff is lost in floods).

Of all the water on earth, only about 3 percent is fresh. Protecting its purity is an important job. The Environmental Protection Agency has identified more than 700 chemicals in our country's drinking water, and 129 of these are toxic. Thirty-five states have identified poisonous industrial wastes in their groundwater.

Our water is one of our most precious resources. In fact, we at Amway are so concerned about it that our company sponsored a pavilion at the Genoa Expo '92 world's fair. My partner, Jay Van Andel, was appointed the official American ambassador to this important event. This pavilion focused on the importance of water in the development of the U.S. and the need to protect this valuable resource.

The U.N. lists these problems as catastrophic. But are they? How real are the doomsday scenarios? The decision to become a compassionate capitalist involves the responsibility to learn about the world we live in. We must understand a problem before we can contribute to its solution. The problems we face are complicated, and it's easy to make mistakes in judgment.

Getting the Facts About This Planet

We are responsible for getting the facts for ourselves. Compassionate capitalists are informed. They read widely and wisely. They have critical minds. Being critical in the true sense does not mean nitpicking. A critical mind wants to know the objective facts, to ask the hard questions and make well-reasoned judgments.

Compassionate capitalists are also open-minded. They listen to opposing positions. Their loyalty is not to some party line but to the truth. We have minds of our own. We need to use them.

Learning to develop a healthy skepticism is a good start, especially about numbers. "You know what statistics support?" asked a college student. "Statisticians!" he added quickly. There is a dangerous truth lurking just under the surface of his little joke. Our newspapers and magazines, television reporters and commentators, are all skilled at throwing around statistics. We can use numbers to prove or disprove anything. But be wary. You know what else they say about statistics: they're like a bikini—what they reveal is interesting, but what they conceal is vital. Have an inquiring mind. Look behind the numbers. It has been said that facts speak louder than statistics.

When you're seeking the facts, don't be afraid to press people. If they don't know something they purport to have the facts about, get them to say so. Conversely, if you don't know much about some issue, temper your comments until you do. This promotes honesty in yourself and others. We often don't hold people accountable for what they advocate.

Once you have committed yourself to getting the facts, there are plenty to dig out. Compassionate capitalists can't afford to be ignorant. Ignorance is dangerous. Ignorance ignores problems. We can't afford to be like a person Dorothy Parker once described: "His ignorance was like the Empire State Building—you had to admire it for its size."

There are many problems crying out for solution by compassionate capitalists. We need to be concerned about them. After all, our future depends on their solution. But how do we even begin to solve all these environmental problems, let alone meet the human needs around us? As I said before, we must begin with a personal commitment to our own community.

With all its problems, the world is a wonderful place. God has equipped it with resources we still have not discovered. We human beings may have our weaknesses, but over the centuries we have demonstrated our strengths and resilience as well. Don't give in to despair. Don't let the doomsayers frighten you. There is still plenty of hope, plenty of possibilities, and plenty of reasons to be optimistic about the future.

Deciding on Your Plan of Action

Now that we know a little more about the world's human and environmental needs, it is time to develop our own individual plans to help meet them. Here is a simple outline of the steps we might take to develop our plans for compassionate action!

1. Narrow down the possibilities to one human or environmental need that causes you to feel compassion in your town (or even in your neighborhood).

   For example, not world hunger, but *one hungry family* you might know. Not world illiteracy, but *one student* you could tutor. Not depleting fossil fuels, but *recycling in your home.* Not water shortage, but conserving the water *you use in your house.*

2. Decide exactly what you want to do to meet that environmental or human need.

   One hungry family: Provide temporary emergency food. Provide access to other food banks, emergency supplies. Help find temporary or permanent employment. Check on medical, educational, transportation needs.

   One student you could tutor: Check to see if a school near you has a volunteer tutor program. Decide how much time you can give. Once you have a student to tutor, keep your commitment.

   Recycling in your home: Find a brochure or article that explains recycling. Share information with your family to build a team. Discover all you can about your town's recycling program. Equip your garage with recycling bins. Get yourself on line with a pickup service or work out regular deliveries to a recycling center.

   Conserving the water you use in your house: Get copies of your last water bill. Determine how much water you have been using. Bring your family in on your plan to preserve water. Equip all water-related appliances with water-saver devices. Help your family set goals for new water use, such as amount of time/ new ways of bathing; cutting water use in hosing sidewalks, driveways; amount of time/new ways of washing dishes, cleaning; watch next bill/celebrate water savings.

3. Write out the steps you are going to take. (See example above.)
4. Put a time and a place by every step.
5. Check off each step when the action is taken.
6. Celebrate your successes (including those who helped you).
7. Learn from your failures (to do it better next time).
8. Pick a new environmental or human need and begin again.

Compassion Begins at Home. If the examples above seem rather basic, forgive me. I know how much more each of us could do to help end the suffering and the waste in the world, but for me, world solutions begin at home. Once we have begun to meet the human and environmental needs in our town, then we can expand our goals to meet those needs around the world.

Compassion Begins One Small Step at a Time. I know, too, that you are capable of achieving far bigger things in your own community than just feeding a hungry family or tutoring a failing student, preserving water or recycling your family's paper, glass, and metal waste. But if you haven't begun meeting the world's needs in these small ways, are you really going to do something greater?

And there are so many greater things to be done. We must practice compassionate capitalism on a broader scale as well. Poverty is a principal cause of many environmental problems. Poor and ineffective government regulation is another. Free markets and environmentalism are not incompatible!

An article in *BusinessWeek* recently reported something I have been advocating for many years: "Want to clean the air, rescue the rain forests, and cut government red tape—all at once? A fresh way to do these things is to enlist market forces. First, by finding and selling goods that make saving endangered areas more valuable than exploiting them. Second, by writing laws that use incentives, not regulations, to rein in polluters."

Whenever possible, we must find incentives for people to become self-sufficient. The U.N. World Commission on Environment & Development said in 1987 that poverty is as destructive of nature as industrialization. Where people are prosperous, they have more options. Not just the exploiters but the poor, too, are clearing the Amazon forests, to grow food or cattle and feed their children. Although the results are destructive, the motivation can be understood by all of us. It's hard to think about the long term when you're hungry.

Compassionate capitalism offers real hope for more people to become self-sufficient. The possibilities for increasing self-sufficiency in the United States, and abroad, are limited only by our imagination and resolve. We must find every way possible to encourage entrepreneurship and local solutions to environmental problems.

For example, Cultural Survival Enterprises is an organization dedicated to helping natives form cooperatives to harvest and sell rainforest products. It sells fruits, nuts, and oils from rain-forest plants and trees, and puts the money back in the hands of the natives. In its first year it sold nearly a half million dollars worth of these products. In its second year it sold several million dollars worth. CSE makes *sustainable* rain-forest crops, like Brazil nuts, more valuable than timber.

Local solutions like rain-forest co-ops are far more effective than massive government programs. Local solutions get to the root of the problem. Instead of a big, unwieldy bureaucracy imposing environmental rules on poor, hungry people, the people themselves are empowered to make their own solution—and make a living at the same time.

I have found in my own business experience that incentive is one of the most powerful forces in nature. If we can provide incentives (rewards), on a broad scale, to do the right thing, people will come through. I don't believe that many folks really want to harm the earth and its creatures. I know there are some greedy ones out there, and some plain stupid ones too. But for the most part, if given the opportunity and incentive, people will act responsibly.

Financial incentive is very powerful, but it's not the only kind of incentive. Recognition can be potent, and idealism is often its own reward. The satisfaction of doing something for our neighbors and our planet can be one of the most powerful incentives there is. Altruism often leads to social entrepreneurship.

Sometimes the incentive can be altruism mixed with a little competitive spirit. Take Collin Meyers of Osage, Iowa, for example. In 1979 several teachers at the local high school started a contest to see who could bring in the lowest utility bill. Meyers managed to reduce his bill by sixty percent in a single year. He bought a new, energy-efficient refrigerator, re-insulated parts of his house, caulked the windows, installed an insulated front door, replaced his old, inefficient furnace with a new one, put in a high-efficiency water heater, and bought a gas range to replace his old electric one. A small incentive went a long way for Mr. Meyers!

Love of the land in combination with the practical need for cooking fuel can be an incentive. In 1985 a Kenyan women's development network, Maendeleo Ya Wanawake, disturbed by the deforestation of their country for firewood, began a campaign to encourage the building of wood-saving, improved cook stoves among their one hundred thousand members. Their efforts succeeded in saving thousands of trees, and the wildlife and vegetation dependent on them.

Rewarding these kinds of efforts is important. In fact, our company has set up a fund to reward grass-roots environmental activists. Take, for example, Fred White, the Chicago Park District's recycling program director. White had read about "timber" made from recycled plastic. "Why not use this material to help rebuild our aging playgrounds?" he wondered. His interest in plastic timber led him to establish a citywide program called "Plastics on Parks."

The program, nicknamed "POP," collects discarded plastic containers and turns them into timber. Chicago residents can take their plastic trash to 263 different collection sites around the Chicago area, and since 1989 they have been bringing it in by the ton. More than two million pounds have been collected and converted into building materials for more than half of the city's 663 playgrounds. That's a lot of "trash" diverted from valuable landfill space. The plastic timber is used to build playground walls and seating areas. "Initially," White says, "it's more expensive, but it saves money in the long run because it lasts thirty to forty times longer." A bonus is that it requires much less maintenance and resists graffiti.

David Kidd, an avid outdoorsman, was canoeing not long ago and was struck by the natural beauty of the woods that lined both sides of the river. It occurred to him that all that natural beauty was also serving an important purpose. "Trees are like vacuum cleaners of the environment," says Kidd. "Every single leaf is sucking in dirty air and breathing out cleaner air." Right then and there, Kidd decided that he would organize the planting of millions of trees.

He discovered that you could buy two-year-old seedlings for about ten cents apiece. But millions of seedlings would require more money than Kidd had. So he solicited the help of local Rotary Clubs and other groups to buy seedlings in bulk and gave them away to anyone who would promise to plant them. Today, Kidd's American Free Tree Program, based in Stark County, Ohio, is that state's largest private volunteer project. Volunteers have planted more than 826,000 trees. In October 1990, Kidd received the Teddy Roosevelt Conservation Award from President Bush. Kidd said proudly, "We need to send a message across the country that it *is* possible to change the direction of things in our world, because the environment is not simply an issue—it's where we live."

Dr. Max Shauk, a math professor at Baylor University, started thinking about alternative fuel sources after the oil shortages of the 1970s. He came to the conclusion that a viable alternative to fossil fuel was ethanol, a type of alcohol made from agricultural products. "You can make ethanol from sugar beets, corn—almost anything that contains starch or sugar," says Shauk. "It's also inexpensive, renewable, and emits fewer pollutants."

In 1980 Shauk started test-flying experimental aircraft using ethanol fuel. Nine years later, Shauk and his wife, Grazia Zanin, flew six thousand miles from Waco, Texas, to Paris, France, in a Velocity homebuilt aircraft. The flight earned him the highest award in aviation, the Harmon Trophy—an award also given to Charles Lindbergh, Amelia Earhart, and Chuck Yeager. Shauk is now Director of Aviation Services at Baylor, where he continues to demonstrate the viability of ethanol fuel. "Petroleum is a finite resource," says Shauk, "but almost every country in the world has the means to make ethanol."

Jim Alderman, a biology and oceanography teacher at Cape Henlopen High School in Lewes, Delaware, has been helping students get hands-on experience at conservation. The students live adjacent to the Atlantic Ocean and Inland Bays, a sensitive environmental area. Over the years, students have planted more than three miles of dune grass to stabilize the eroding beaches and have worked to make the Inland Bays more friendly to rapidly disappearing shorebirds.

Thanks to the students' efforts, the outlook is looking better for Delaware's endangered population of shorebirds. The students have adopted a stream that they monitor for signs of pollution, built a boardwalk through a sensitive area of Prime Hook National Wildlife Refuge, and analyzed bacteria samples in lagoons. Alderman says proudly, "These projects really help them understand that we live in a very fragile environment."

The stories of these people make me feel proud and hopeful. But I don't want to imply that making good choices is always easy. My own company has struggled with some of the choices we have made. Sometimes being a good citizen is expensive. The U.N. environmental award we received caused us to do some soul searching.

What products were we selling that still had the potential to do harm to the environment? Not many, we discovered. But a few products, like a caustic drain cleaner in our product line, seemed to have the potential for harm. We dropped it. That one decision alone cost us several million dollars. But it was the right decision. We also decided to change some of our packaging to reduce waste and encourage recycling.

I want to be honest with you. Sometimes making a decision for the planet is costly. The only short-term reward may be a clear conscience, and for a while it may mean money out of your pocket. But in the long run, it's the right decision no matter how you look at it. In the long run, resources are preserved, wealth is increased, future generations' opportunities are enhanced, and a legacy is maintained.

In 1989, at the main gallery of the United Nations General Assembly in New York, the Amway Environmental Foundation sponsored an exhibit of contemporary Inuit masterworks from the Amway collection. We called the show Masters of the Arctic.

We dedicated the show to Inuit artists like Matthew Ipeelie, whose people inhabit the far north of Alaska, Canada, and Russia. That exhibit has proven to be enormously popular. It is full of beautiful and strong imagery—representations of bears, seals, whales, caribou, owls, walruses, all kinds of creatures. Many of these animals are hunted by the Inuit people, but with great reverence and a concern to take only what they need. To them, animals are more like neighbors than animals, to be treated with respect, even awe. It's easy to see this in their work, and I think this is why the exhibit has been so well received.

The show has traveled since 1989, and in June 1992 I flew to Rio de Janeiro, Brazil, to open the exhibit in honor of the Earth Summit. I came early to preview it, as I have done many times before. The exhibit had not yet been officially opened—that was my job—and as I walked around the hall I found myself alone. On a small pedestal I saw a little white bear. It reminded me of Matthew Ipeelie. This bear was not made of walrus ivory, like Matthew's, but white and gray marble. It was the work of Kaka Ashoona, an Inuit artist from Cape Dorset, Canada.

But like Matthew's bear, it was full of life, and standing on all fours, its head tilted to one side, it seemed to say, "Hey, you, look at me!" Its mouth was carefully incised, just like the mouth Matthew had carved on his bear. Simple but unbelievably expressive. This carving had been made with a lot of love and a thorough understanding of bears. Kaka Ashoona, just like Matthew Ipeelie, really knew his neighborhood—and the creatures that lived in it.

I thought about the dedication that appeared in the first program of

Masters of the Arctic. It read, "Through their art and the example of their history, the Inuit demonstrate to a world increasingly concerned about the effects of environmental damage that it is possible, indeed necessary, to exist in harmony with the natural order. This exemplary coexistence with nature is particularly meaningful in that it has continued for thousands of years in one of the harshest and most demanding environments on earth, in which the Inuit have not just survived but produced the rich heritage of art which this exhibition presents."

My dream for my own community—and for the nation and the world—is that they, too, will survive for thousands of years, like the Inuit. But for that to happen, we must come to know our neighborhoods in the same way that Matthew Ipeelie knows his. We must know them inside out. And then we must take care of them. Each one of us as individuals can only do so much. But each of us must start at home.

And each of us must also do all in our power to provide incentives and opportunities for people to do the right thing. We cannot expect our government or some organization to do our work for us. Each of us must take personal responsibility. Perhaps if all of us do that, Matthew Ipeelie's grandchildren will see nothing but blue sky again. And perhaps we will all learn to see what so many can no longer perceive: the earth and its creatures are a living, sacred gift from God.

16

What Happens When We Reach Out to Help Others?

CREDO 16

We believe that when we share our time, money, and experience to help others, we complete the circle of love that leads to our own personal fulfillment and prosperity.

Therefore, whenever you grow weary of well doing, remember the Law of Compensation. In the long haul, every gift of time, money, or energy that you give will return to benefit you.

Teddy Stollard, the story goes, was a ten-year-old "lemon." His face was never washed, his hair was never combed, and his clothes were always wrinkled. When he wasn't looking—and sometimes when he was—the other kids called Teddy "Stinky." He was the most unsightly child in Miss Thompson's fifth-grade homeroom class. When she called on him, he slumped over in his desk, mumbled an answer, or stared belligerently into space.

Miss Thompson tried hard to treat all the boys and girls equally. But Teddy was hard to like, and in little ways it showed. Miss Thompson hated to call on Teddy, and when she graded his papers, her red marks were a little bolder and a little larger than for any other student. "I should have known better," she admits today. "I should have paid more attention to Teddy's file."

First grade: "Teddy shows promise. Some kind of conflict going on at home, and Teddy seems deeply affected by it."

Second grade: "Teddy seems able but distracted. Apparently, his mother is seriously ill. He receives little help at home from either parent."

Third grade: "Teddy's mother died this year. The boy is intelligent enough, but he seems unable to concentrate. Father doesn't return our calls."

Fourth grade: "Teddy is slow but well behaved. He cried occasionally for his mother. His father shows no interest."

The Christmas celebration in Miss Thompson's fifth-grade class included a tree decorated by the children and colorfully wrapped gifts piled high on the teacher's desk. The day before vacation, the entire class crowded around Miss Thompson to watch her unwrap her presents. At the bottom of the pile, the teacher was surprised to find a gift from Teddy Stollard. While the other gifts were wrapped in gold foil and shiny, bright ribbons, Teddy's gift came in plain brown paper held unevenly in place by Scotch tape and string.

"To Miss Thompson," the crayon letters read in a child's awkward scrawl, "From Teddy."

When she opened the present, out fell a gaudy rhinestone bracelet and a bottle of cheap perfume. The bracelet had half its stones missing, and the perfume bottle was nearly empty. The girls laughed. The boys snickered. But in the spirit of Christmas, Miss Thompson raised her hand for silence. While the children watched, she put the bracelet on her arm and dabbed a bit of perfume on her wrist.

"Doesn't it smell lovely?" she asked the children. Taking their cue from Miss Thompson, they agreed with an appropriate chorus of oohs and ahs. At the end of the day, when their parents had taken the other children away, Miss Thompson noticed Teddy still sitting in his desk looking up at her. He was smiling.

"Teddy?" she asked, knowing that he had a long walk home and wondering why he hadn't started.

Slowly, Teddy got up from his desk and moved toward his teacher.

"You look pretty in my mother's bracelet," he said, his voice barely rising above a whisper. "And you smell almost like her now with that perfume on your arm."

Suddenly Miss Thompson realized that those two "dime-store" gifts had been the boy's most prized possessions. She struggled to blink back her tears.

"Teddy," she said, leaning down toward the child, "thank you for your presents. I liked them very much."

"That's okay," Teddy answered. For a moment the child just stood there smiling up at his teacher. Then without saying another word, he took his jacket from its peg and hurried from the room.

The Teddy Stollard story ends years later. At the close of this last chapter, I'll tell you what Miss Thompson began for them both with her one small act of compassion. In the meantime we need to ask ourselves: Why should Miss Thompson or anybody else for that matter be compassionate? Why didn't she giggle with her students when those two rummage-sale gifts fell out of that plain brown paper package? Why did she place that ugly bracelet on her arm and dab that "used" perfume on her wrist? Why did she raise her hand to stop the children's giggling and clue them all to admire Teddy's gifts?

Fortunately, Miss Thompson realized at that moment that Teddy had a terrible, aching need. She had just seconds to decide between her two possible responses. One would give her student life. The other would condemn him. But not just Teddy's future was at stake during that second in time. Miss Thompson's decision had long-term consequences for them both.

What might have happened to Teddy (or to Miss Thompson) if she had laughed at him, or more likely, if she had just buried Teddy's gifts on the bottom of that pile of presents? What did happen to Teddy (and to his teacher) when she honored his gift above the others and singled him out for praise? Although I've changed the names, the story is true. The teacher's act of compassion changed Teddy's life and Miss Thompson's life forever.

At this moment you and I find ourselves in a similar situation. Forgive me for repeating the obvious, but we are living in dangerous, troubled times. Like Teddy, our neighbors at home and around the world are in terrible need. Some need help to help themselves. Others just need help. How will we respond? Whatever choice we make will have consequences not just for those in need, but for each of us as well.

Practicing capitalism that has no heart or conscience will lead to terrible, long-term suffering for all of us, rich and poor alike. But compassionate capitalism—seeing a need and reaching out to meet it—will positively affect the lives of both those who give and those who receive. We all know how good it feels to be on the receiving end, but sometimes we forget the other half of that universal promise. Those who work hard and give generously of their time, money, and experience will receive back many times what they have given for their deeds.

Almost two thousand years ago, Jesus explained it this way: "Give, and gifts will be given you: good measure, pressed down, shaken together, and running over, will be poured into your lap; for whatever measure you deal out to others will be dealt to you in return." These were farm people. They bartered fish or fruits of their fields for grain.

In exchange, the grain merchant poured into their "lap" (actually a leather shopping bag worn by peasant farmers) from a bushel basket that he had filled, then pressed down, then filled again, then shaken, then filled again until the grain was spilling over the side. "Give," Jesus commanded them, "and your reward will be like that, pressed down, shaken together, and running over."

In Amway, we call that little promise or paradigm the Law of Compensation. Another way Jesus explained it was this: "Sow enough seed and you'll reap a great harvest." It's an old maxim implanted in the hearts and minds of every new generation. And it isn't just a Christian ideal. It is held in honor by every major religious faith. Buddhist, Hindu, Muslim, Jewish, and Christian traditions all support the idea that "God loves and honors a cheerful giver." Ancient legends, fairy tales, modern movies, and even a television series or two illustrate the fact: "Those who give will receive." Even pop culture makes the claim: "What goes around, comes around."

Every day in a hundred different ways we are given the same two choices that Teddy Stollard presented Miss Thompson. And the choice we make has serious consequences both for the person in need and for the rest of us. Jesus told his famous parable of "the talents" to help us understand this point.

A rich man about to take a journey gives five pieces of gold into the care of one servant, two pieces of gold into the care of a second servant, and one piece of gold to a third. The first servant doubled the five pieces by trading wisely. The second invested his two pieces of gold and doubled their worth as well. But the third servant, afraid to risk, to trust himself or others with what he had been given, hid the single gold piece in the ground and waited for his master's return.

When the rich man got back from his journey, he rewarded the first two servants for their wise stewardship of his gifts. "Well done, thou good and faithful servants," he told them, "thou hast been faithful over a few things, I will make thee ruler over many: enter thou into the joy of thy lord." When the third servant appeared trembling before his master with that single gold piece still clutched safely in his hand, he said, "I was afraid and I hid thy gold piece in the ground and here it is." The rich man was angry. This servant had not been faithful. "Take the gold piece from him," said the master, "and give it to those who risked."

The point of this harsh little parable has troubled folks for centuries. Whatever we have in life, Jesus says, is not ours. All of life is a gift to us. For a few short years we have been appointed the stewards (or lease holders) of what we are given. We are expected to invest them wisely, and multiply them. Whether they are little or great, we are called to be good stewards of our talents. And, Jesus warns, we are held accountable to that end. It is the same with making profit or with giving gifts. When we plant enough seed, we reap a great harvest. Not planting leads to want, hunger, and death.

By now you know that I believe that capitalism is the one great economic hope for the world. But I believe as well that heeding this Law of Compensation, practicing *compassionate* capitalism, is the only way we will ever see that hope realized. And I am not alone in this belief. In a recent statement, an encyclical entitled the "One Hundredth Year," Pope John Paul II specifically endorsed what he called a "business economy," while at the same time taking past capitalists to task for not being compassionate stewards of our wealth and freedom.

Even the loudest defenders of the capitalist system have praised this encyclical for going beyond the questions of economics to those of morality and values. Many conservatives who are accustomed to advocating capitalism's strengths rather than focusing on its weaknesses agree on the need to address important moral issues within the free-enterprise system.

Our company has shared these concerns for some time. We, too, recognize the need to avoid blind loyalty to the free-enterprise system. Capitalism is not perfect. We must not worship the false gods of wealth by any means or competition at any cost. Competition fairly waged and wealth responsibly acquired are beneficial to society. But these benefits of capitalism, and many others, can be abused if we forget the Law of Compensation. When we are compassionate, we will be treated with compassion in return. When we are not compassionate, we all will suffer.

Free enterprise is not a perfect or finished system set in concrete two centuries ago by Adam Smith. Capitalism must change, grow, and improve. Free enterprise is a living system. Like the roses in my wife's garden, old, dead branches must be pruned away so that new, green limbs may grow and fragrant, colorful buds may bloom to life.

Capitalism is springing up around the globe in many new varieties. The capitalists in Japan or the Philippines act differently from the new capitalists in the Soviet Union, Poland, or Hungary. The capitalists struggling in the enterprise zones in China don't do the same things that their counterparts do in the mountains of Chile or Peru. Even the capitalists in Mexico, Canada, and the United States, though neighbors, practice varieties of capitalism that are different from one another.

Nevertheless, whatever kind we practice, I am convinced that there is just one principle that we can trust to guide us every step of the way. That principle is compassion. It doesn't matter where you live, or how the free-enterprise system works in your country. If we are to save the world from economic chaos and despair, we must all discover (or re-discover) compassionate capitalism for ourselves.

We must be compassionate with the world's natural and human resources. We must be compassionate with the air above and the ground below, the seas, forests, deserts, and all that live within them. We must be compassionate with the products we choose to develop and market, and with the facilities we build or lease. Employers must be more compassionate with their employees, and employees must be more compassionate with their employers. Compassion must be considered when we plan our packaging, our pricing, even our advertising campaigns. And we all must let compassion guide us as we use our profits, our wages and bonuses, our time and our talents.

Saint Paul gave us guidelines for the journey toward a more compassionate capitalism. These apply to men and women of any faith or ideological belief. Paul first wrote these words in his ancient letter to the people of Galatia, a Roman province in Central Asia Minor, now Turkey. The little dog Snoopy quotes them two centuries later to his master, Charlie Brown, when he trudges faithfully through the snow to deliver the dog his dinner. "Let us not grow weary in well doing," Snoopy says, "for in due season you shall reap if you faint not."

The apostle Paul and the dog Snoopy are both getting at the same idea. Once again, it is the Law of Compensation: Do good! Work hard at it! And you shall be rewarded!

Do Good. For the past few centuries, we who have benefited from the free-enterprise system have proven to be more generous with our time and with our money than any other people in history. In this country, for example, last year alone eighty million of us volunteered to do good. And the average volunteer donated 4.7 hours a week, for a total of 19.5 billion volunteer hours.

Although the ranks of volunteers are greatly strengthened by the presence of millions of experienced and energetic retired people, the average volunteer is somewhere between the age of thirty-five and forty-nine. And not only Americans with comfortable incomes volunteer. More than twenty-five percent of all volunteers come from households with incomes of $20,000 or less.

Compassionate capitalists have also proven to be generous with their money. In 1987 people in this country gave $76.8 billion to do good. Those figures may represent just two percent of the individual donor's gross income given to charity, but it is a start. Seventy-five percent of all American families donate an average of $790 a year. According to the *Economist* magazine, "The poor give a bigger proportion of their incomes than the rich, and surprisingly, both poor and rich are more generous than the people in the middle."

In my company of friends, I am proud and grateful for those compassionate capitalists who lead the way in giving time and money, energy and ideas to do good. For the past fifteen chapters I've been telling their stories. And I've barely scratched the surface. There are so many more whose names I would like to mention.

Al and Fran Hamilton do good when they help raise funds for Easter Seals. Frank Morales does good when he serves on the school board or starts a YMCA in his community. Dan Williams does good when he helps a little child to overcome her stuttering. Jody and Kathy Victor do good when they help support a medical team in Africa, and Toshi and Bea Taba do good when they give time and money to their local church in Mililani, Hawaii.

I'm not going to define for you what it means for you to do good inside or outside your business. Doing good is something you want to define for yourself. Sir Francis Bacon said, "In doing good, there is no excess." Life calls us to reach out and use our lives lavishly for doing good. In the past chapters I break that goal into two different questions: What are we doing to help people help themselves? And what are we doing to help people who cannot help themselves?

One troubling statistic we found concerned the role of corporate giving. In 1989 philanthropy from American businesses accounted for just five percent of all giving in this nation. Apparently, company contributions, which rose sharply during the 1980s, have flattened. Again, quoting the *Economist,* "Even when profits were rising, donations did not."

I know the economy is struggling slowly to recover. I know profits are down and costs are up. I know it isn't easy to be generous right now when there are dark clouds over our economic future. But there are companies out there who are leading the way, and whether we agree or disagree with the causes they support, we need to be caught up in their generous, caring spirit. Their examples illustrate again the Law of Compensation. Generous giving is good for business.

Vermont entrepreneurs Ben Cohen and Jerry Greenfield are two fascinating examples. These two high school friends, you'll recall, turned a $12,000 investment (and a $5 mail-order course in ice cream making) into the multimillion-dollar ice cream company Ben & Jerry's. Of course, much of their company's success is due to their delicious and innovative products. If you've tasted their rich, creamy ice cream with large chunks of nuts, dried fruit, and chocolate and whimsical names like Chunky Monkey and Cherry Garcia you will agree, but when surveyed, the public also support Ben & Jerry's for their "commitment to helping meet the needs of the people in our world."

Rain Forest Crunch uses nuts from the South American rain forest, paying harvesters directly. Chocolate Fudge Brownie features brownies baked by a Yonkers, New York, group whose profits go toward housing the homeless and teaching them trades. "We will do $750,000 of business with them this year alone," says Greenfield. A new flavor, Georgia Peach Light, will rely on peaches grown at family-owned southern farms.

The Ben and Jerry Foundation is funded with 7.5 percent of the company's pre-tax profits and uses its resources to provide community-oriented activities with loans and grants. And, in a move not greatly admired by many of their fellow business entrepreneurs, Ben and Jerry's has instituted a company-wide five-to-one salary ratio, mandating that no Ben and Jerry's employee, including corporate officers, can earn more than five times the amount of the lowest-paid employees.

Needless to say, Ben and Jerry's has set a controversial standard, and they are taking flack for it. *Fortune* magazine editors critique their style "along a spectrum ranging from touchy-feely-cuddly to furiously militant." *Restaurant Business* magazine quotes analysts who say "the company grew despite the wishes and dreams of its owners, who have strived to keep things *weird* and who clearly prefer what they see as social responsibility to corporate success." Whatever you think about the causes they espouse, you have to admit that they have taken seriously the Law of Compensation, and in a very competitive market their profits and reputation are growing.

We business entrepreneurs—whatever our politics—have an incredible opportunity. All those social entrepreneurs out there on the front lines of suffering, giving their lives to do good, need us to support them. And every generous person I know, corporate executive or individual giver, who has reached out to help has received in return the same measure, only "pressed down, shaken together, and running over."

That's why remembering the Law of Compensation at this very moment becomes so important. Do you believe that if you sow enough seed you will reap a great harvest? Then start sowing now. Find a cause you believe in and sacrifice to support it. Find a productive, trustworthy social entrepreneur or service organization and adopt it as your own. Whatever you do, do it thoughtfully and generously, and in the long haul you will benefit most!

Work Hard at It. How do we measure up to the "hard work" standards being set by the average compassionate capitalist in this country? If the typical volunteer spends an average of 4.7 hours a week doing good for others, how much do we spend? If the average family gives two percent of their gross income to charity, what percentage do we give? What goals do we have for giving time and money? Are they written down? How many hours a week would we like to volunteer? How much money do we want to give away? No one can set those goals or follow through on them but us.

Nobody can tell you how much time or how much money you should give before you can consider yourself a generous and trustworthy steward. But my company of friends have strong opinions. How easy it is to make excuses at the end of every month to use all or part of our tithe to help build the business or pay the bills. How quickly we could find ourselves not giving anything except an occasional token gift in the offering or a token check to a local charity. But as Helen has taught me, when you work hard at tithing, when you make and keep that commitment whatever the price, you will be surprised and pleased by your returns.

Dave Severn, a successful entrepreneur and a committed compassionate capitalist, says it this way: "God had made it perfectly clear. Those who have been given the ability to produce are obligated to take care of those who can't." When it comes to giving ten percent of his gross income away, Dave is determined. "Ten percent of the money I make isn't even mine," he says. "It belongs to God and I would rather live on ninety percent of my income that is blessed than steal from Him and live on one hundred percent that is cursed."

I respect Dave for his strong opinion. He doesn't spend much time talking about the "cursed" part, but Dave sets a tough example and he makes me think. Most of my friends who have proven their commitment to compassionate capitalism, including Dave and Jan Severn, don't really donate time or money out of fear. They do it because it is fun, because it makes them feel good about themselves, and because over the long haul it pays amazing dividends. When we are working hard to see dreams come true for ourselves and for our neighbors, it doesn't seem like hard work at all.

Nevertheless, nothing can or will be accomplished in your life or in mine without a great deal of effort. I'm always surprised when I talk to people who believe in themselves, who dream big dreams and even make plans for accomplishing their dreams, yet somehow think that it will all be accomplished without hard work.

Hard work means long hours. You must count on working long hours if you want to be a successful compassionate capitalist. Even while you are in school, you can have time and money to donate to do good, if you manage your time well. Successful people value time and use it carefully. They don't spend their evenings watching television and their mornings sleeping in. They are more productive because they set aside more time to produce. You don't have to get up early and work late, but you don't have to succeed either.

If I work forty hours a week, and you work eighty hours a week, why should I be surprised that you make more money or have more money to give away than I do? That's one of the incentives of compassionate capitalism. We have the opportunity to make more by working more. And in working more, I can save more and end up with money—capital—that I can invest to grow my business or to use on behalf of those in need.

Long hours and accomplishing our plans go together. The Nobel Prize-winning economist Milton Friedman popularized the old saying, "There's no such thing as a free lunch." That's another way of saying there are no shortcuts. Success is not free, we have to work for it. Long hours are part of the price.

Hard work means persistence. To be persistent is to "continue steadily in some course of action." It has been said that there is no such thing as great talent without great willpower. Becoming an NBA star means that you have stood on a basketball court somewhere practicing free throws or jump shots since you were big enough to hold a basketball in your hands. Being a concert pianist means you practiced chords and runs for hours every day since you were big enough to crawl up on the piano bench. One of the keys to becoming a successful compassionate capitalist is to have the willpower to keep on going.

Almost without exception, successful people have had many failures. Jay and I certainly have. But we didn't give up and you can't give up either. Perhaps we were just stubborn. Stubbornness and persistence are closely related. Persistence in a good cause is called "perseverance" and in a bad cause "obstinacy."

Obstinacy is a trait associated with mules. Perseverance is a quality attributed to saints. It's best not to get the two mixed up. Let our "stubbornness" be persistence, the kind that never lets go of a worthy goal. We must not let it degenerate into stupidity. But we must be steady in our pursuit of success. It seldom comes overnight. Persistence will eventually bring us through to our goal.

Hard work means discipline. A sixteenth-century writer once said, "I am indeed a king because I know how to rule myself." Self-discipline is a very important quality for aspiring compassionate capitalists. To have self-discipline is to be in control of our own lives.

I'll admit that any advice that has the word *discipline* in it is not likely to have broad appeal. But it should. I'm not talking about discipline that others impose on us. I'm talking about discipline that we impose on ourselves. That's quite different.

The more self-discipline we have, the less subject we become to the discipline of others. In a perfectly self-disciplined society, we wouldn't need laws. But most people are not very self-disciplined and so we need them.

A self-disciplined entrepreneur sets his own rules. A disciplined lifestyle means we can advance toward those goals we've been talking about. Through self-discipline we find freedom. If we don't have discipline, someone else will end up in charge of our lives. We have to choose.

Hard work means keeping your perspective. In "The Ballad of John Henry," John's wife and child look on helplessly as John swings his sledgehammer in a life-and-death battle with a newfangled steam hammer. John wins the race, but he dies in the attempt.

Hard work does not mean blindly working ourselves to death. We must resist spending our lives as a slave to a dream that cannot or should not happen. We must stay alert. Maintain perspective. And sometimes our dreams have to change along the way.

Keeping our perspective, knowing when we are succeeding, knowing when we are failing and knowing when it's time to give up one dream and move on to another, requires asking and answering some frank and painful questions: Do I like what I'm doing? Am I doing it well? Do I have a plan and am I working hard to accomplish it? What are the chances that I will succeed? Am I keeping up with the information in my field? Am I improving my skills? Am I generous to the others working with me?

San Francisco Giant pitcher Dave Dravecky dreamed of a great comeback after he had fifty percent of the major pitching muscle removed from his arm during cancer surgery. After months of painful therapy, he threw eight strong innings to defeat the Cincinnati Reds, 4–3. The whole world cheered when Dave's dream appeared to be coming true.

Then, five days after his triumph, tragedy struck. During a sixth-inning pitch in Montreal, Dave's arm snapped. The young athlete doubled with pain and disappointment. He would not realize his great comeback dream. He would never pitch again. Worse, after months of radiation and painful infections, doctors had to amputate his arm.

But when one dream died, another dream was born in him. In spite of his disappointments, Dave had the courage and the perspective to put aside the old dreams and to begin the new. What is your dream? Where is compassionate capitalism leading you? Do good! Work hard at it! And you shall be rewarded!

Compassionate Capitalism Helps Guarantee Our Own Welfare! In many ways, compassion is a guarantor of our freedom and our future. How? It's simple. If I treat you with compassion, it is far more likely that you will treat me in the same way. If I am greedy and do all that I can to acquire wealth by hoarding power and exercising special privileges—in other words, if I restrict your freedoms—can I then expect you to respect mine? Without compassion, my behavior only encourages greed.

But what if I am compassionate to you and promote your liberty? What if I guarantee you the same rights and privileges that I have? Or, what if I do more than that? What if I actually promote your rights and privileges? In that case, my compassionate concern for your welfare serves to insure not only your potential for success but mine too.

Compassion has benefits for both the giver and the receiver. The Golden Rule—"Do unto others as you would have them do to you"—

is another way of stating the Law of Compensation. It is both a profound religious statement and a very practical piece of advice. Compassion yields spiritual benefits, and it also happens to be in your own best interest.

John Hendrickson, formerly a high school teacher from Wisconsin, and his wife, Pat, have built a very successful business. Being generous with their time and money has been a major ingredient in the Hendricksons' success.

"Sometimes," Pat says, "it isn't wise to be generous. For example, when John was a high school teacher and band director in Minnesota, the kids loved him. Thanks to John's leadership, his band won recognition in competitions across the region. However, John soon realized that no matter how well he performed, the taxpayers would never let him earn as much as they did. When he finally turned down his contract," Pat adds, "even the principal congratulated him. John could have stayed there forever. That would have been generous for the district but fatal for our financial future. Owning our own business, we are free at last to be generous in the ways we want to be and to the people and causes we believe in."

"We made a trip to England recently," John explains, "to do some meetings for some of our friends who are just starting out. The trip cost us thousands of dollars, but we did it, not just to be generous, but in the hope that one day that trip will pay dividends for us as well. Every benevolent giver has a motive," John adds. "I don't think giving time or money is as idealistic as some people pretend. We give to help those in need, of course. But we also give to satisfy our own needs, and for Pat and me it has always proven true that the more time and money we give away, the more we receive in return."

Compassionate Capitalism Helps Relieve a Troubled Conscience. Do you remember how in your childhood, your conscience seemed so alive and ever present? If you did something wrong you were consumed by guilt. Kids are terrible at hiding it, for their consciences are powerful. As we get older we lose a sense of the immediacy of our conscience.

But they do not go away. Some adults manage to banish theirs to a distant place—they are the most frightening of people. But for most of us the banishment is only partial. We still hear a voice. A long time ago, Shakespeare spoke for all of us who are afflicted with a tormented conscience when he wrote (paraphrased with apologies):

> My conscience has a thousand tongues
> And every tongue tells a tale
> And every tale condemns me for a villain
>
> *(RICHARD III,* V:3)

Maybe your conscience is not troubled by another person's suffering. I suppose there is nothing we can do about that. Acts of compassion are born and take shape in the privacy of your own conscience. No one can shape it for you.

But if I were untroubled by my conscience and I could look at the suffering all around me and still feel nothing, that alone would trouble me. Pangs of conscience are a good sign. It pays to heed them. At least when we are troubled, we are alive. A troubled conscience is like a compass on a ship. In the dark and stormy night, it leads us home.

The price of an unsettled conscience is an absence of inner peace—a thousand inner voices condemning us. A compassionate heart and a peaceful conscience are of immeasurable value. The pursuit of compassionate capitalism is the pursuit of inner peace.

Compassionate Capitalism Helps Center Our Lives. Let's put it another way: one of the rewards of compassion is the peace of knowing that we are doing the right thing. Religious people might say they are cooperating with God's will and experiencing the reward of inner peace. Others might say they are rewarded when they are in harmony with the cosmos—in congruence with the forces of nature. But for atheists, too, the practical benefits of compassion should be compelling. You have some focus or center for your life.

Compassionate Capitalism Begins with Our Hearts. If we try to do the "right thing" without an inner commitment, it will not work. It will just be duty and drudgery. It won't be compassion. We'll be burned out in a week or soon hate ourselves. Do the internal work first. Take a day off from work. Walk the streets of your town or city. See your neighbors in need. See sadness and suffering in the eyes of your children and the world's children. Let their needs grow in you until your passion begins to grow as well. Get sad. Get angry. Get going. Then you will come to love what you do. Your heart will kick in and, succeed or fail, your conscience will be at peace.

Don't worry! Compassion is not about gushy emotions. Neil Kinnock, the British Labour Party leader, said, "Compassion is not a sloppy, sentimental feeling for people who are underprivileged or sick

. . . it is an absolutely practical belief." Compassionate capitalists are passionate about issues, problems, and most especially about people. They see a world that is alive, a world for which they have strong feelings.

These spring from a mature and informed conscience—one that knows there are real-world consequences that result from a lack of compassion. Compassion is intelligent. But it does involve the emotions. You cannot be passionate without feeling something in your gut.

Compassionate Capitalism Always Results in Action! Compassion is more than an emotional commitment. It requires a second step. You must put your inner commitment to work. It's the *action* part of compassion that we mentioned earlier. Compassion isn't just a warm feeling, it gets things done.

Action validates our inner commitment. The word *validate* is related to the word *valor.* They both come from a root that means "strong." We use the word valor to describe war heroes. When we take action, we not only validate our compassion, we also make it strong. Without action we are just phonies, moral dilettantes.

Compassionate Capitalism Helps Us Make a Difference. When you take action against suffering of any kind, your life begins to count for something. Through action you make your mark in the world. As the old proverb says, "Footprints in the sands of time are not made by sitting down." If we are afraid to get a little sand in our shoes, it is unlikely that we will make a mark.

But if you take action and forge ahead, you will make a difference. Your path may not be straight. In fact, most people take a lot of detours, get lost from time to time, double back occasionally, and yes, sit down once in a while. But by taking action, you leave a trail of good deeds that can be looked back on with pride. You can say with satisfaction, "I've done something that counts."

Compassionate Capitalism Leaves No One Out! I have strong political beliefs, but Amway is a business. People of all political persuasions are welcomed and needed in our corporation and (I hope) in yours. Everyone who comes, regardless of political loyalties or commitments, has the right to be respected and embraced. There will always be those who support enthusiastically one party, candidate, or solution over all the rest. Good business provides open forums for free expression. Compassionate capitalism insists that everyone has the right to her political belief and that unpopular views and those who hold them have an equal right to be heard.

The same is true of religion. When we celebrate our free-enterprise system and the heritage that makes it possible, both in the U.S. and in Canada, we are at the same time celebrating a history of fierce religious independence and freedom. These countries were founded primarily by people who came here in search of religious freedom. You cannot embrace compassionate capitalism without also embracing and defending the religious freedom of all people. Amway is well established in at least fifty-four different countries. There is no religious belief (or lack of belief) that is not respected in our ranks. I feel strongly about my own religious faith, but I will fight hard to see your right to believe or not believe protected. That is a basic tenet of compassionate capitalism, and we must never forget it.

Compassion Now Will Help to Save Us in the Future. There is a selfish side to helping those who cannot help themselves. Such service may also prove to be very much in our self-interest. If we go on allowing others to suffer without reaching out to help, our comfortable worlds may be overturned.

I don't for a moment sanction the rioting and looting we've seen in our inner cities these past years, but we have to acknowledge the troubling fact that too many of our brothers and sisters in this great nation are beginning to believe that they have no way to help themselves. They are hungry, homeless, and out of work. They have inferior educational opportunities and inadequate health care for their children. They feel disenfranchised, cut off from even the possibility of ever gaining earning power and privilege. Their lives are miserable and they have nothing to pass on to their children but this legacy of suffering.

Who among us won't understand if they turn to a tyrant to lead them? Who can't figure out why they feel angry and seek vengeance? Who can blame them if one day they strike back with violence or bloodshed? It is past time for those of us with resources to share what we have generously with those who have nothing.

During Hitler's Third Reich, a thoughtful and courageous German pastor, Martin Niemöller, wrote these words about the average German citizen:

First they came for the socialists,
And I did not speak out—because I was not a socialist.

Then they came for the trade unionists,
And I did not speak out—because I was not a trade unionist.
Then they came for the Jews,
And I did not speak out—because I was not a Jew.
And then they came for me,
And there was no one left to speak for me.

Compassionate capitalism is a lifelong adventure. No one can tell you where or how you should begin. Just remember that one small act of caring is a beginning. And in that small act—whatever it is—you will be rewarded, and that reward will inspire you to go on to do bigger and better things. Compassion is contagious. Once you have begun, your life will be changed forever.

What one small act of compassion would give you joy? What cause has been pulling at your heart? What person out there is doing something that inspires you and what could you do to help?

That Christmas in Miss Thompson's fifth-grade class, a bond was created between Teddy Stollard and his teacher. With Teddy's junk bracelet still on her arm and his cheap perfume still reeking from her wrist, Miss Thompson decided to do her best to help that little boy turn his life around. Suddenly she saw in him possibilities she had never seen before. She got a vision in her heart for what he might become and went to work to see it happen.

At the end of almost every day, Teddy and Miss Thompson went to work. She guided his trembling hand until he could write in clean, clear sentences. She drilled him on his spelling and math. She read to Teddy and had him read to her. They learned songs, poems, and even short stories by heart and quoted them to each other. Miss Thompson put her harsh red pen away and decorated Teddy's papers with stars and exclamation points. On every appropriate occasion she praised him alone and in front of the class.

By the end of that school year, Teddy Stollard showed dramatic improvement. He had caught up with most of the students in Miss Thompson's class, and his grades were advancing on the leaders. One afternoon as they were saying good-bye, she took his hand in hers and said, "You did it, Teddy, and I'm proud." She was amazed when the child corrected her softly. "I didn't do it, Miss Thompson. We did it together."

During the summer, when Teddy's father lost his job and moved away, Miss Thompson rushed to add a long positive note to Teddy's permanent file.

Fifth grade: "Teddy is an exceptional child. He was damaged by his mother's death and his father's disinterest, but he is well on his way to recovery. Whatever extra time you have to invest in Teddy will bring you real reward."

Now we will see in the lives of Teddy Stollard and his teacher if the Law of Compensation really works. When we invest our time, money, and effort in someone else, what do *we* gain? When we are compassionate, does it really bring *us* lasting dividends?

Miss Thompson didn't hear from Teddy for seven long years. Every Christmas season when the children in her fifth-grade class gathered around the teacher's desk to watch her open their presents, Miss Thompson told them the story of Teddy Stollard and his mother's old bracelet and half-used perfume. And every year she wondered if her efforts on his behalf had been wasted.

Then one day she received a short note from a distant city in the handwriting she still recognized as little Teddy's: "Dear Miss Thompson, I wanted you to be the first to know. I will be graduating second in my high school class. Thanks, teacher. We did it! Love, Teddy Stollard."

Four years later, another note came: "Dear Miss Thompson, they just told me I'll be graduating valedictorian of my class this year. I wanted you to be the first to know. The university has not been easy, but we did it. Love, Teddy Stollard."

And four years later the last note came: "Dear Miss Thompson, as of today, I am Theodore Stollard, M.D. How about that? I wanted you to be the first to know. We did it. I am getting married next month, the twenty-seventh to be exact. I want you to come and sit where my mother would have sat if she were alive today. My dad died last year. You are the only family I have now. Love, Teddy Stollard."

Do you find it strange to conclude a book about compassionate capitalism with the story of Miss Thompson and Teddy Stollard? Actually, when I first read the story, originally told by my friend Chuck Swindoll, I saw it as a parable that makes our calling as compassionate capitalists both simple and clear. Every day we must decide. Will we rush past the needs of people and our planet on the road to profit, or will we pause long enough to help along the way?

Miss Thompson almost rushed past her opportunity to aid Teddy. She was busy just getting through the average day. Teddy looked like such a loser. Spending extra time and energy on his behalf seemed such a waste. But Miss Thompson did it anyway. And for her compassion she was rewarded with the ultimate prize: the discovery that her act of compassion helped someone else to help himself. You want to be a successful capitalist? You want to see real, lasting, genuine profit? Let compassion lead you every step of your lifelong journey.

A CREDO
for
Compassionate Capitalism

CREDO 1

We believe that every man, woman, and child is created in God's image, and because of that each has worth, dignity, and unique potential.

Therefore, we can dream great dreams for ourselves and for others!

CREDO 2

We believe that most people feel that they are not living up to their potential and are grateful for any practical, realistic help they can get to change for the better.

Therefore, we all need to take an honest look at where we are, where we want to be, and what we may need to change to get there.

CREDO 3

We believe that change for the better begins when we order our lives around those individuals and institutions that we value most, for example: God, country, family, friendship, school, and work.

Therefore, we need to decide what we want to be and do, and we need to arrange our goals accordingly.

CREDO 4

We believe that getting our finances in order—paying off our debts, learning to share with others, setting financial limits and faithfully living within them—is the beginning of getting our lives free to move forward.

Therefore, we need to get our bills paid and our financial priorities in order.

CREDO 5

We believe that work is good only if it leads the worker to freedom, reward, recognition, and hope.

Therefore, if our work is not satisfying (financially, spiritually, psychologically), we need to end that work as quickly as we can and begin work that is.

CREDO 6

We believe in capitalism (another name for free enterprise) because it provides us and our world our one great hope for economic recovery.

Therefore, if we don't know what capitalism is or how it works, we must find out now. Our financial future depends on it!

CREDO 7

We believe that practicing compassionate capitalism is the secret to real financial success.

Therefore, we need to ask ourselves daily: "How compassionate am I in caring for my co-workers, my supervisor, my employer or my employees, my suppliers, my customers, and even my competitors and what difference does it make?"

CREDO 8

We believe that owning our own business (to supplement or replace our current income) is the best way to guarantee our personal freedom and our family's financial future.

Therefore, we should seriously consider starting our own business or becoming more entrepreneurial in our current business or profession.

CREDO 9

We believe that developing a positive, hopeful attitude is necessary to reach our goals.

Therefore, with our mentor's help, we should design a program (using books, tapes, special meetings and events, associations with friends and co-workers, recreation, and worship) that will help us develop a positive, hopeful, productive attitude about our life and its potential.

CREDO 10

We believe that before we can succeed as a compassionate capitalist, we must have an experienced mentor to guide us.

Therefore, we need to find someone whom we admire who has already achieved what we want to achieve and ask that person to help us reach our goals.

CREDO 11

We believe that success comes only to those who establish goals and then work diligently to achieve them.

Therefore, with our mentor's help, we should begin immediately to determine our short-term and long-term goals, to write them down, to review our progress at every step, to celebrate the goals we accomplish, and to learn from those we don't.

CREDO 12

We believe that there are certain attitudes, behaviors, and commitments (related directly and indirectly to our tasks) that will help us reach our goals.

Therefore, with our mentor's help, we should begin immediately to master those ABC's that will help us to succeed.

CREDO 13

We believe in helping others to help themselves. When we share our time and money to help guide, teach, or encourage someone else, we are only giving back a part of what has already been given to us.

Therefore, *be* a mentor. Whom could you help to reach his goals, to see his dreams come true?

CREDO 14

We believe in helping others who cannot help themselves. When we share our time and money with those in need, we increase our own sense of dignity and self-worth, and we set in motion positive forces that bring hope and healing to the world.

Therefore, be a giver. What are you doing to help end human suffering in your town and around the world?

CREDO 15

We believe in helping save the planet, our island home. When we share our time and money to help preserve the planet, we are really helping to protect ourselves.

Therefore, be a friend of the earth. What could you do today to help preserve the planet?

CREDO 16

We believe that when we share our time, money, and experience to help others, we complete the circle of love that leads to our own personal fulfillment and prosperity.

Therefore, whenever you grow weary of well doing, remember the Law of Compensation. In the long haul, every gift of time, money, or energy that you give will return to benefit you.